BUTTER AND GUNS

America's Cold War Economic Diplomacy

DIANE B. KUNZ

THE FREE PRESS

New York   London   Toronto   Sydney   Singapore

THE FREE PRESS
A Division of Simon & Schuster Inc.
1230 Avenue of the Americas
New York, NY 10020

Manufactured in the United States of America

10   9   8   7   6   5   4   3   2   1

Library of Congress Cataloging-in-Publication Data

Kunz, Diane B.

   Butter and guns: America's Cold War economic diplomacy / Diane B. Kunz.
      p.   cm.
   Includes index.
   ISBN 0–684–82795–6
   1. United States—Foreign economic relations—History—20th century.   2. United
States—Foreign relations—1945–1989.
   I. Title.
   HF 1455.K855   1997
   337.73—dc20   96–20409
                                                                        CIP

ISBN 0–684–82795–6

For Gaddis

Contents

Tables and Figures

Acknowledgments

This book marks my third volume on economic diplomacy, a subject that first attracted me during my seven years of practicing corporate law on Wall Street. Throughout this period I have accumulated numerous intellectual debts.

I have been most fortunate to have had the assistance of talented and dedicated archivists. In particular, I would like to thank Henry Gillet, archivist of the Bank of England, David Humphrey of the Lyndon Baines Johnson Library, and Karen Holzhausen of the Gerald R. Ford Library. The Lyndon Baines Johnson Foundation and the Gerald R. Ford Foundation provided welcome support.

Various men who participated in the events I have chronicled gave generously of their time. In Britain, I was fortunate to be able to speak with the Honorable Raymond Bonham Carter, Lord Bridges, Sir Alec Cairncross, Lord Franks, Sir Nicholas Henderson, Lord Jay, Lord Jenkins, Sir Jeremy Morse, Lord Roll, Lord Sherfield, and Sir Denis Wright. In the United States I benefited from the recollections of Francis M. Bator, Lucius Battle, McGeorge Bundy, C. Douglas Dillon, John Kenneth Galbraith, George C. McGhee, Robert V. Roosa, Walt W. Rostow, James Tobin, Cyrus Vance, Adam Watson, and Walter Wriston.

Harold James, Fumiko Nishizaki, Maarten Pereboom, and Robert Schulzinger each read my manuscript—their help was invaluable. Michael Schaller rendered important guidance on Japanese-American relations. Andrea Ashworth and Shawn Smallman provided wonderful research assistance. My colleagues in the Yale History Department have shown me the real meaning of collegiality; in particular, I would

like to thank Cynthia Russett for her substantive assistance and continued friendship going far beyond any expectation.

During the early stages of this book I derived great benefit from frequent discussions with William C. McNeil. His untimely death in April
1993 left a void in the field of economic diplomacy.

Bruce Nichols at The Free Press was my editor. His efforts convinced
me that Maxwell Perkins still lives.

On the most profound level, I could not have written this book
without the support of my family. When I began this project, my sons
Charles and James were in nursery school. They are now in fifth and
sixth grade, respectively, well able to sort documents for payment of $1
per hour. William and Edward make up the junior ranks, providing welcome distraction. My husband, Tom, continues to bear with good cheer
and exemplary grace the burdens of having a working wife who is also a
mother.

This book is dedicated to Gaddis Smith. First as dissertation director,
then as colleague and friend, he has taught me how to be an historian:
"Teach him what has been said in the past; then he will set a good
example to the children. . . ."

Diane Kunz
New Haven
December 1996

1

Introduction

[The American people] must assume the leadership
of the world, [accepting] wholeheartedly our duty
and responsibility as the most powerful and vital
nation in the world.

Henry Luce, *Life*, February 17, 1941

In 1947 Walter Lippmann, the preeminent columnist and commentator, coined the phrase "Cold War" to describe the erupting hostility between the United States and the Soviet Union. For forty-five years the clash between the two superpowers and their allies defined geopolitics. But the Cold War was more than a military confrontation. It was a total conflict between the West—the American-led capitalist democracies—and the East—the Soviet Communist bloc. For the first time in its history, the United States stayed on a permanent war footing. The unprecedented national security state won the Cold War. And it allowed the United States to develop the premier consumer-driven economy. The American experience during the Cold War proved you could have it all. The United States recorded unprecedented domestic prosperity while building a permanent military establishment at home and abroad that triumphed over the Communist challenge. Rather than being mutually exclusive, domestic economic policy and Cold War security strategy, combined with a third factor, the American-centered international economic framework, produced maximum prosperity for Americans and for the capitalist world. Economic diplomacy

1

provided the engine that drove the economic and security train of the "free world." At the same time it melded the United States and other capitalist nations into a long-standing economic and military alliance. Previous histories of the Cold War have stressed open conflict and diplomacy. It is high time for a new history stressing economics.

The importance of economic factors to national survival and success are consistently underrated. Moreover, without a sound economic base, a country's foreign policy is built on sand. In the aftermath of World War II, the British Empire foundered on the shoals of its bankrupt exchequer. Mikhail Gorbachev could not save the Soviet empire because its economy had ground to a halt. The United States built its Cold War hegemony on the base created by the World War II production miracle. Washington then converted the bipolar geopolitical confrontation into fuel that powered its domestic economy. This synergy proved crucial. In an era of mass warfare, the electorate must be persuaded of the wisdom of its leaders' policies. What won the support of the American people for the Cold War battles of the last half-century was the combination of a perceived threat from the Soviet Union and the continued provision to most Americans of the good life. This relationship proved especially important in the American context. We worship at the altar of rampant individualism. As a society we lack an ideological basis for government intervention in the domestic economy. The budget battles of the mid-1990s illustrated the way in which this ideological black hole hamstrings the public sector in peacetime. The Cold War solved the uniquely American problem by providing the best possible justification for government expansion—national security demanded it.

When President Dwight Eisenhower denounced the emergent military-industrial complex as a threat to democracy and the American way of life in his Farewell Address, he won the hearts and minds of liberals for the first time in his presidency.[1] But Ike was wrong. The ongoing funding by the federal government of a significant defense industry, the burgeoning bases throughout the nation, the hundreds of thousands of American troops stationed abroad . . . they had made the affluent America of the Cold War era possible. The national security state fathered economic growth at home while underpinning American economic diplomacy abroad.

The American half of the bipolar world rested on two sets of alliances. The economic system, known as the Bretton Woods order, determined the economic course of the capitalist world. Created and run by the United States, it allowed Western nations to share in the affluence that the United States had established amid the carnage of World War II. American leaders designed the international economic system to suit American needs. When relative American economic dominance declined, President Richard Nixon dictated a revision of the system that increased American perquisites. Western nations had no choice but to hide behind and also economically stand behind the United States. Throughout the Cold War our allies benefited from their ongoing economic and security relationship with the United States. American economic diplomacy played a crucial role in preserving U.S. hegemony abroad and American prosperity at home. From the intricacies of Bretton Woods revisions to the oil shocks to the Third World debt crisis, the United States called the economic tune to which the rest of the world danced.

Allied acquiescence in American desires grew out of the imperatives of the continued Cold War conflict. Throughout the period a consensus existed among the Western allies that the Cold War needed to be fought. The military part of the European alliance rested on the NATO pact between the United States and its allies; diplomats hammered into place comparable relationships between the United States and its partners in other geographic areas. Economic diplomacy continually bolstered military planning, as well as on occasion substituting for it. The Marshall Plan, the Alliance for Progress, and the economic and security relationship among NATO allies—each of these illustrated the importance of economic diplomacy during the Cold War.

But economic imperatives rarely trump pressing political or nationalist needs. Winston Churchill knowingly led his nation to economic ruin to defeat the Nazis. Yugoslavia, Czechoslovakia, and the Soviet Union each split apart, although the economics of the situation in every case dictated continued unity. During our own Civil War, the South sacrificed its patrimony in its bid for independence. As we shall see, the failure of economic sanctions to affect various parties during the Suez crisis of 1956 and the Gulf War illustrate the truth of this proposition, as does the failure of the oil boycott to affect American policy toward Israel in any meaningful fashion. But the seeming advantages of economic diplomacy over military tactics lead politicians to keep searching for an economic magic bullet.

Other nations have possessed the economic and military dominance that the United States enjoyed during the post–World War II era. Indeed, at the height of its power the British Empire not only boasted the world's strongest navy but also possessed in the City of London a global financial center. But the price for this naval hegemony and international financial power was paid domestically. British bankers eschewed their home markets and sought higher rates of return abroad. The vast majority of British men and women eked out a miserable life. Similarly the Soviet Union during the Cold War matched the United States missile for missile. It also controlled the East bloc's foreign financial policy. But the Soviet system could not deliver consumer goods to home markets. In a time of growing globalization, when radio, television, telephones, films, tape cassettes, and faxes spread news instantly, the yawning consumption gap between East and West could not be concealed. Ultimately the East bloc imploded.

The military confrontation between the United States and the Soviet Union took center stage during the Cold War. But the Soviet Union presented another challenge. Its leaders damned the capitalist society of Western nations as immoral, inefficient, and doomed to extinction. More important, Moscow devised and ran a competing command economy for itself and other Communist countries featuring state control purportedly following socialist principles. During the 1960s the Soviet Union claimed it would soon match then surpass American production. Marxist doctrine, with its promise "from each according to his means, to each according to his needs," had great appeal, particularly in the developing world. The Western challenge was to prove that this formula in practice produced far less consumption rewards than the state socialist model. The 1959 Moscow "kitchen debate" exemplified this systemic competition. The two superpowers had agreed to exchange displays of scientific, technological, and cultural innovation. Vice-President Richard Nixon and Soviet Premier Nikita Khrushchev faced off in an up-to-the-minute model American kitchen at an exhibition held outside Moscow. Nixon proclaimed that "we hope to show our diversity and our right to choose. We do not want our decisions made at the top by one government official that all houses should be the same. . . . We have many different manufacturers and many different kinds of washing machines, so that the housewives may have a choice."[2] The historian David Potter had predicted in his 1954 study, *People of Plenty*, that "it was not our ideal of democracy but our export of goods and gadgets, of cheap machine produced grain and magic-working medicines, which opened new vistas to the human mind and thus made us 'the terrible instigators of social change and revolution.'"[3] Thirty-five years later, his observation proved accurate.

Economic diplomacy served as America's first line of offense in the Cold War. From the Marshall Plan to the use of economic sanctions against Saddam Hussein, economic diplomacy permitted the United States to wage the Cold War generally without significant sacrifice. Economic diplomacy also served as the bridge between American security policy and the U.S. domestic economy. As relative American strength declined, America's allies paid for a growing share of NATO's defense burden. In exchange for their agreement to stand behind the United States, Washington permitted its allies to hide under its nuclear and conventional umbrella. The United States supported NATO because containing communism was central to American foreign policy. But its ability to pass off a portion of the costs to its allies made the decision far less painful.

Throughout the Cold War era virtually all American leaders supported a multilateral economic order. Yet the success of the American Cold War synergy was as much inadvertent as planned. Despite the assertions of conspiracy theorists, few officials or business leaders in fact sought the Cold War to manufacture domestic prosperity. Instead, Americans waged the Cold War for geopolitical and ideological reasons. While the divergence in economic systems provided one of the philosophical bases for the bipolar confrontation, the Cold War was not fought over the split. But it turned out that the national security state also provided the perfect basis for American domestic prosperity and the raison d'être for a Western alliance that functioned in both the security and economic spheres.

This history will repeatedly demonstrate that guns and butter are not mutually exclusive. On this point economics textbooks, and common sense, have it wrong. Consider the background to the Cold War. By 1943 civilian reconversion had moved steadily to the top of the American agenda. U.S. officials increasingly debated what kind of foreign economic policy would best ensure domestic prosperity after the war. During the New Deal years the Roosevelt administration enacted legislation establishing an edifice of state control over the marketplace. Entities such as the Securities and Exchange Commission, the National Labor Relations Act, and the Agricultural Adjustment Act curbed traditionally unfettered American capitalism. In the balance lay the nature of the federal government's postwar economic role. One school of thought advocated traditional American business independence, rejecting any place for Washington in American international finance or commerce.

On the other side stood, first, the so-called "national-collectivists," who wanted Washington to continue where Herbert Hoover left off and launch a high-powered sales campaign for American businesses abroad. But the third school, the so-called multilateralists, envisioned a very different role for the United States. Percy Wells Bidwell, the Yale economist and research director of the Council on Foreign Relations, a cardinal advocate of this philosophy, sought universal tariff reductions and an international trade organization. Modeled on the Federal Trade Commission, this body would have the power to stop unfair trade practices, including monopolistic actions. To Bidwell and the other "Wise Men" such as Elihu Root, Henry Stimson, Dean Acheson, John J. McCloy, and James Forrestal, the notion of the United States serving as a passive "city on the hill" role model would no longer suffice. These men, having made their nest eggs, crowded Washington during the war. Bidwell-style multilateralism easily won the battle. It succeeded by combining America's economic, military, and diplomatic interests into a coherent package.[4]

Understanding that a return to high unemployment would bring intractable pressure to keep out imports, Bidwell linked the success of his blueprint to domestic legislation nurturing full employment. Roosevelt administration officials generally supported such legislation. Haunted by two depressions—the great one of the thirties and the post–World War I slump—the National Resources Planning Board drafted a citizen's economic and social bill of rights. Summing up its position, the board maintained that the administration should formalize a policy to "promote and maintain a high level of national production and consumption by appropriate measures" as well as "underwrite full employment for all employables" and provide education, nutrition, and housing.[5]

Across the Atlantic this notion of cradle-to-grave security had been embodied in the Beveridge Report, a 1942 British study that quickly became a best-seller. Conservative and Labour politicians, then serving together in a wartime coalition, acknowledged that British postwar society would demand and must receive protection from want and provision of basic requirements. In the United States, however, the power of New Deal liberalism had waned in the face of resurgent business confidence and conservative triumphalism. While Roosevelt backed a full-employment bill that Congress took up in early 1945, his support was not enough to prevent the legislation's evisceration.[6] Thwarted in their attempt to obtain congressional approval for domestic initiatives, administration officials increasingly turned to foreign economic policy to solve domestic economic dilemmas. Will Clayton, a founder of the world's largest cotton-exporting company, became the high priest of this strategy. Expanding international trade would benefit both the United States and the world at large, require little in the way of socialist planning, and cost the taxpayers nothing. Clayton, of course, never emphasized that while an open trading system would help American consumers, it might badly affect certain American producers.[7]

Before any trading system could be established, two problems needed to be addressed. The first was the lack of an international financial system. The Depression had destroyed the private bank/independent central bank structure that had flourished during the 1920s. Private bankers, especially in the United States, slunk behind the woodwork, while Washington, London, and Paris (and Berlin, for that matter) took over their central banks. The 1935 amendments to the Federal Reserve Act emasculated the Federal Reserve Bank of New York (FRBNY), transferring much of its power over international transactions to the Federal Reserve Board in Washington. Either a new international financial structure would have to be created or the old one resurrected. At the same time, a new supply of international credit needed to be found for devastated European and Asian economies.

The massive wartime destruction had a double-edged effect: generating the need for substantial rebuilding while ensuring that the ravaged nations could not develop domestic sources of capital.

In 1943 British and American officials separately prepared international financial blueprints. The British plan, orchestrated by the economist and statesman Lord Keynes, called for the United States to use its gold reserves and currency stocks to provide most of the capital for a multibillion dollar reconstruction and currency stabilization fund. The provisions automatically transferring resources from countries with balance of payments surpluses (creditor nations) to countries running deficits (debtor nations) were aimed at the United States, the only country with a surplus. Since Keynes believed that a successful international order required rich and poor nations to cooperate, his plan placed obligations on both debtor and creditor countries.

Treasury Secretary Henry Morgenthau and his adviser Harry Dexter White considered themselves paid-up members of the multilateralist camp. They embodied the evolution that had occurred in official Washington—the acceptance of American responsibility for a major role in the stabilizing of the world monetary system. Yet they rejected the expensive and open-ended financial obligations that Keynes had suggested. White's plan called for an institution with far less capital, a much more measured and finite American contribution, and obligations only for debtor nations. At the same time Morgenthau had a second item on his agenda. Suspicious of bankers, he wanted to move the locus of international financial power from London and Wall Street to the U.S. Treasury Department.[8]

The 1943 preparations led to a full-scale international conference in July 1944. Held in the New Hampshire resort of Bretton Woods, these negotiations created institutions featuring a limited U.S. government financial contribution and retained a strong private-sector role. More like a club than a bank, the International Monetary Fund (IMF) would serve as the regulator of the international financial system. The IMF Articles of Agreement required its member countries to pay an annual subscription and agree to abide by certain economic rules of good conduct. The IMF would supervise each member country's currency, in the process providing foreign exchange to help with balance of payments problems, promoting currency stability, and ending the destructive devaluations that crippled the interwar financial order.

Each member nation agreed to establish a par value for its currency and to keep its exchange rate within 1 percent on either side of the par value, which "shall be expressed in terms of gold as a common denominator or in terms of the United States dollar of the weight and fineness in effect on July 1, 1944."[9] Members, by right, could vary exchange rates by up to 10 percent; the IMF could object to any larger change. Applicant nations would have to prove that devaluations were required to "correct a fundamental disequilibrium." Every member pledged to subscribe its "quota" share of the IMF's capital: 25 percent in gold and the remainder in the member's own currency.[10] The IMF's initial capital was set at $8.8 billion, of which $3.2 billion would come from the United States.

The Articles of Agreement allowed each member nation to borrow automatically 25 percent of its quota. Anything more (in IMF parlance, "further tranches") needed to be approved by the IMF's executive directors. Debtor nations requested and received significant protection from possibly destructive free market forces, although the extent of war-caused devastation was not yet known. If a particular currency was in too much demand, a scarce-currency clause allowed members to impose exchange controls on transactions with creditor nations. As well, the IMF could take measures to protect its holdings of the sought-after currency, selling gold for the currency or borrowing it from creditor nations. The IMF Articles further provided for a transitional period; for the initial five years of the fund's existence, member nations could automatically retain exchange controls. Thereafter they would have to confer first with IMF officials.[11]

At the center of the newly minted international financial system lay the American commitment to make gold available to foreign governments at $35 per ounce, the price set by the U.S. government when it fixed the value of the dollar in 1934. In this fashion the United States agreed to provide the guarantee for an international gold exchange standard: countries that stabilized their currencies could either directly link them to gold or link them to the dollar. The IMF recognized the centrality of the dollar's role by permitting par values to be expressed in terms of the dollar as well as in gold. Because the United States had pledged to continue the dollar's link to gold, foreign currencies backed by dollar reserves would have an indirect gold backing. Apparently no one considered what would happen should the United States devalue the dollar.[12] Voting share was largely determined by quota size. Each nation received 250 votes plus one additional vote for every $100,000 of quota.

The Roosevelt administration believed that Soviet representation at Bretton Woods augured well. In the opinion of Secretary of State Cordell Hull, Soviet participation in the IMF was as important as Soviet membership in the United Nations. For those who shared Hull's ideology, a trading world was synonymous with a peaceful world. In keeping with the trend of American wartime diplomacy, the United States treated Soviet officials more gently than British allies. American suspicion of British economic chicanery died hard, while Roosevelt's optimistic reading of Josef Stalin's intentions and the sentimentalized picture of a kindly Uncle Joe nurtured by American propaganda allowed American officials to retain faith in the notion of postwar Soviet cooperation. Washington still glossed over the contradictions between the nature of the Soviet system and the design of Bretton Woods. The Soviet Union boasted a command economy with an artificially fixed ruble value. As citizens could not own significant property and could not engage in overseas transactions, exchange rates were meaningless. Moreover, the IMF and World Bank disclosure requirements were anathema to Soviet leaders. Information is power. No matter how desperate, Stalin would not admit the truth about the Soviet economy—that it functioned on the basis of labor camps, the decimation of whole classes of people, and the suppression of any dissent.

Morgenthau and his team, having won their battles with Keynes and other British negotiators, left Bretton Woods well pleased with their success.[13] The simultaneous creation of a World Bank (formally the International Bank for Reconstruction and Development) gave hope that ravaged European nations could find a ready source of capital to rebuild their economies and infrastructure.[14] Yet even before the negotiations had been completed, New York bankers and conservative politicians launched a campaign against the agreements. Wall Streeters such as George Whitney, the president of J.P. Morgan and Co., and

Randolph Burgess, a former high-ranking official of the FRBNY, now head of the American Bankers Association, wanted a far smaller American commitment abroad, while Winthrop Aldrich, the head of the Chase National Bank and John D. Rockefeller Jr.'s in-law, sought to scuttle the agreements completely. The United States and Britain should instead work to "shun totalitarian tactics in international trade and to adopt economic liberalism."[15]

Many congressmen also viewed the agreements skeptically, if not with hostility. During 1945 suspicion of Europe reemerged in Congress. Senate Minority Leader Robert A. Taft, the son of a former President, with his own White House ambitions, declared that joining the IMF was like "pouring money down a rat-hole."[16] Congressman Mill (R. Nebr.), for example, returned from a trip to England to forecast that the British would use the lend-lease program to cheat the United States out of millions of dollars.[17] The British diplomat Sir Roger Makins in January 1945 detected a prevalent sentiment in the United States that "Britain and Russia were pursuing their own selfish interests in Europe."[18] Congress's prohibition of lend-lease money for reconstruction and Truman's abrupt cutoff of lend-lease funds for all operations in Europe on May 11, as well as the administration's tough battle over the extension of the Reciprocal Trade Agreements Act (RTAA), all reflected these suspicions. Morgenthau and company counterattacked effectively. Thomas Dewey, Roosevelt's 1944 challenger, endorsed both Bretton Woods agreements while well-connected administration officials such as Dean Acheson, who in 1933 had resigned from the Roosevelt administration because of its foreign economic policy, testified in favor of the legislation. The President's team worked two sides of the street simultaneously. On the one hand, they reached out to the New York group, accepting various changes to the Bretton Woods agreements that further dampened American criticism. On the other hand, they exploited the fears of Wall Street, which lay deeply embedded in the hearts of Southern and Western bankers. In the end the Bretton Woods legislation passed the House by a vote of 345 to 18 on June 7, 1945, and received Senate approval a month latter by a tally of 61 to 16.[19]

Concurrently, the White House persuaded Congress to renew the Reciprocal Trade Agreements Act. Secretary of State Cordell Hull had

been the driving force behind the Roosevelt administration's decision
to seek legislative approval to negotiate bilateral tariff-cutting agreements with American trading partners. Hull's religion was simple: free
trade made for a peaceful world. Congressional assent in 1934 to the
first RTAA led to a slow expansion of American trade during the
Depression decade; Roosevelt officials hoped the war's end would
ignite rapid growth. The debates, which ran parallel with hearings on
the Bretton Woods agreements, revealed both a majority in favor of
increasing American economic ties abroad but also a strong suspicion
of foreigners. Typically, Taft, as the head of the isolationists, conjured
up the specter of British businessmen allowing Americans to pour their
blood and money into the Pacific war while the competition stole
American markets.[20] After tough lobbying the administration got its
renewal and extension. The bilateral RTAA framework strayed far
from the multilateral goals now cherished by the State Department,
but renewing RTAA was necessary before any further progress could be
made. Paradoxically, it was precisely RTAA's nationalistic profile—it
did not subject the United States to multilateral rules but preserved a
framework that gave maximum influence to domestic interest groups—
that allowed the administration to obtain a hefty congressional majority supporting the renewal legislation.[21]

The Bretton Woods agreements went into effect on January 1, 1946.
Both New York and London bankers swallowed their disappointment
as officials moved into Washington offices. American negotiators had
won the major battles over the design of these institutions. This result
derived as much from the other golden rule (he who has the gold rules)
as from the universal acceptance of American ideas. British diplomats
in particular disliked the configuration of the IMF. Lord Beaverbrook
expressed the prevalent sentiments when he informed the British War
Cabinet that "this is the Gold Standard all over again. And at a
moment when the United States has all the gold and Great Britain has
none of it."[22] But the overwhelming economic strength of the United
States allowed it to determine the shape of the international organizations then on the drawing board. American goals became international
reality; multilateralism often became unilateralism in disguise.

Thus the stage was set for an unprecedented era of multilateral economic cooperation. In 1933 Roosevelt, then in his most isolationist

phase, had rejected American international financial cooperation. Eleven years later the United States commissioned the construction of unheard-of institutions. Diplomats understood that an internationalist foreign policy was a prerequisite not only for a peaceful world but for a prosperous one. But having created the necessary framework for a multilateral world, administration officials assumed they had completed their task. After the United States had allocated $8 billion each month on wartime expenditures as well as expending $125 billion in lend-lease appropriations for its allies during the war, legislators as well as the general public were reluctant to designate significant amounts for reconstruction.[23] As it stood Washington had founded an international economic order with the potential to succeed. But insufficient funds paralyzed the new system. Congress had never appropriated foreign aid during peacetime. Just as the German and Japanese war machines had unfrozen Washington monies during the early 1940s, another war would have to begin before the American people and their elected representatives would consent to backing an active foreign policy with the appropriate economic resources.[24]

2

The Forties

On May 8, 1945, V-E Day, Harry S Truman had been President for less than a month. Truman's virtues loom large today, but in 1945 many doubted his ability to carry out the legacy of his predecessor, Franklin D. Roosevelt. He also lacked the charisma that Roosevelt had displayed throughout his twelve years in office. Truman had come to public attention in 1941 as head of the Senate Special Committee to Investigate the National Defense Program. Truman, the driving force behind this oversight group, intended to keep watch over the exploding national defense budget. His good showing as committee chair made him a prominent figure; for the first time he escaped his earlier reputation as a failure. He and his wife, Bess, still made their Independence home with her mother, who never tired of pointing out to her daughter that she could have married better. Truman had only become senator with the assistance of the Missouri political boss Tom Pendergast; Truman's decision to stick by his patron when Pendergast faced federal criminal charges almost lost him his Senate seat but exemplified his loyalty, which was constant although sometimes misguided.

When an ailing Roosevelt learned in the summer of 1944 that Vice-

President Henry Wallace was too liberal for the Democratic convention to accept again, he selected Truman as his running mate. The nominee's best qualifications were his relative anonymity and team-player reputation. Roosevelt spoke to Truman only twice after the inauguration. No wonder that when Truman, on finding out about FDR's death, asked Eleanor Roosevelt if he could do anything for her, she replied, "Is there anything *we* can do for *you?* For you are the one in trouble now." Although obviously hardworking and straightforward, Truman, as he would have readily admitted, had little knowledge of foreign affairs in general or American policy in particular. Instead, as *Time* magazine Washington correspondent Frank McNaughton reported, Truman relied on "very definite ideas, settled convictions, [and] deep determinations." He would need these traits for at the new president's side stood Roosevelt's advisers. In keeping with the latter's style, they offered counsel from every vantage point.[1]

Victory in the Pacific was assured by May 8. Two questions now replaced war issues on the public's mind: what was America's place in the world and what was the U.S. government's role in the international and domestic economy? (Worries about the Soviet Union would emerge only later.) The American role in the postwar world needed to be clarified. Isolationists and internationalist-interventionists had fought a bitter contest in 1940–41; many wondered whether this schism would reappear now that the war's end approached. Media tycoons such as Henry Luce, whose *Time* and *Life* magazines reflected and channeled American impulses more effectively than any other publications at midcentury, best expressed the exultant internationalist view. In 1941 Luce had proclaimed this the American century; now *Life* lectured the American people that "the nature of power is that it must be wielded. . . . if it is left to kick around in the market place it will be wielded by someone else."[2]

The American people were not yet convinced. Much hope resided in the United Nations Organization. The United States had not only attended but hosted the first meeting of the new world body in San Francisco during the spring of 1945. This demonstrated to many that the United States would not repeat its post–World War I refusal to join the League of Nations. The San Francisco conclave also revealed that the tensions among the three members of the Grand Alliance—the

United States, Great Britain, and the Soviet Union—while serious, were not yet fatal. As a result many Americans continued to believe that the United Nations would keep the peace, sparing the United States major expense or responsibility.

Congressional debates reflected these sentiments. Quite a number of lawmakers had not recanted their opposition to American entry into the war in Europe. After the war's end Senator Robert Taft of Ohio predicted that "the time is coming when I can . . . show that we would be much better off if we never had entered the war."[3] Economic concerns strengthened negative attitudes. As U.S. armed forces advanced, apprehension about America's economic future steadily increased. Ironically, the unprecedented wartime economic prosperity fed these fears. Americans remained haunted by the Great Depression, and the winding down of war production combined with the imminent return of millions of servicemen and women raised fears of a new economic downturn. Willow Run, the huge Ford war production plant, closed. This predictable event seemed terrifying. Some businessmen welcomed the statement by the War Production Board Chief of Operations George Batcheller that "after V-J day business will be on its own," but most Americans worried.[4]

Accepting the need to keep postwar American employment high, the Roosevelt administration in January 1945 introduced a bill making it the federal government's responsibility to ensure "sufficient employment responsibilities," estimated by former Vice-President and current Secretary of Commerce Henry Wallace to mean sixty million jobs.[5] Businessmen saw this measure as disguised socialism. Opponents eviscerated it. As finally passed, the most important provisions of the Employment and Production Act of 1946 (notice the omission of the word "full") were those that created the Council of Economic Advisors (CEA). Liberals attempted to convince themselves that having the CEA at the President's beck and call would ensure liberal, Keynesian policies. But not only could the President consult any economist he wished whether liberal or conservative, he was also free to ignore that advice once given. In contrast to Britain, whose Parliament enacted the ideas put forth in the Beveridge Report, the 1946 legislation neither guaranteed a right to work nor "freedom from want."[6] Rather, it signaled the increased prestige of private enterprise and big business.

Wartime fiscal policy further raised the temperature of the debate. During the war the middle and upper classes, always the vocal groups, had not seen their income rise at the same rate as had poorer members of society. They blamed the income tax and wartime inflation. The Revenue Act of 1942 lowered the amount of income exempt from income taxation. During the following year Congress passed the "pay as you go" plan, which deducted income tax from employee pay checks and packets. Numbers told the story: Seven million Americans filed income tax returns in 1941 while forty-two million did so three years later.[7] The ever-widening income tax withdrew some purchasing power from the economy, making inflation far less corrosive than could have been the case; nevertheless, by the end of the war the cost of living had increased significantly. As a result taxpayers felt threatened by Washington, fearful that government foreign aid and domestic programs would hit them hard. The war-driven deficit, unparalleled in American experience, multiplied fears of higher taxes; these anxieties were nurtured by the revelations in the summer of 1945 that of the total expenditures of $422 billion for the period 1940–46, the government raised $179 billion from taxes, while needing $243 billion in loans.[8] Letters to congressmen urging tax cuts began streaming into congressional offices just as the Truman administration attempted to launch ambitious economic diplomacy and assistance programs.

The Roosevelt administration bequeathed a two-pronged approach to international economic questions: U.S.-sponsored multilateral institutions and American funding of multilateral aid organizations. Initially Truman and his officials followed the plans that the Roosevelt team had begun. The Bretton Woods discussions of July 1944 had produced the blueprints for institutions designed to handle the international economic problems that conferees knew would emerge concurrently with the war's end. By V-E Day the International Monetary Fund (IMF) and the International Bank for Reconstruction and Development (IBRD, or World Bank) were almost a reality, while the concept of the International Trade Organization (ITO) became the subject of serious discussion in Washington and elsewhere.

The structure created by the Bretton Woods agreements might aid recovery in the future; it did nothing for the famine and hunger then gripping Europe. The Roosevelt administration had intended the

United Nations Relief and Rehabilitation Administration (UNRRA) to become the vehicle for relief aid to Europe. Designed by the State Department and launched at a White House conference on November 29, 1943, this unprecedented governmental aid effort ($530 million spent through September 30, 1945) fed millions of people. North Americans had actually increased their daily food consumption during the war; UNRRA with its 3,200 employees (1,900 in the field and 1,300 in Washington and London) provided a way for the fourteen billion tons of food the United States sent abroad in 1945 to reach its destination. Yet UNRRA faced heavy opposition in Congress, in large part because legislators disapproved of the fact that while it supplied 72 percent of the funds, the United States did not control aid distribution. Reports from the field about bureaucratic snafus and inefficient management fed earlier doubts; senior staff members dismissed over a thousand of UNRRA's initial employees by December 1945 for "incompetence, inefficiency, lack of adaptability and misconduct." As antagonism toward UNRRA grew, *Life* called for scrapping it.[9]

More generally, rumblings of dissension among the Big Three allies cast a pall over hopes for the United Nations. Indications of public indifference in the United States to foreign affairs steadily multiplied in the autumn of 1945, while continuous chafing over occupation policy in Germany and Soviet actions in Eastern Europe alarmed Truman and his officials. After Germany's surrender American diplomats expected free elections to determine the nature of Eastern European governments. But Soviet officials, emboldened by the presence of their troops on the ground, began setting up puppet governments in Romania and Bulgaria.[10] The United Nations seemed powerless to stop this confrontation. Nor did it seem at all capable of ameliorating the disastrous conditions prevalent in Europe and Asia because of the war.

Washington's first unilateral steps involved money, specifically, loans. Great Britain emerged from World War II totally broke. Having relied on loans from the Empire and Commonwealth for much of the wherewithal to fund wartime expenditures, it now owed these countries in excess of $13 billion.[11] Labour's election victory in July 1945 ensured that socialist measures, notably the nationalization of basic industries and the creation of a National Health Service, would be high on the British government's agenda.[12] Simultaneously the new government led by Prime Minister Clement Attlee fully intended to maintain the Empire as well as defense responsibilities to the Commonwealth and in such strategic areas as the Mediterranean and the Middle East. The Labour government also bore the military and financial responsibility for the British-occupied zone of Germany. How to meet these obligations presented the cabinet with its main challenge. Complicating this task was the fact that any British discussions with the United States would be conducted on a difficult tightrope: London officials had to convince their Washington counterparts to regard Britain as an equal of the United States while at the same time extracting billions of dollars in aid. If they failed at the former task they faced a total eclipse by the United States and the Soviet Union. If they failed at the latter responsibility, the nation and the Empire would disintegrate.

In short, Britain's new position in the world was a pale shadow of its former role. Once two-fifths of the globe was under British rule and "the sun never set on the British Empire." Now, only the United States could have it all. Britain would learn these facts only slowly. The noted economist and sometime adviser to the British government Lord Keynes returned to the United States in August 1945 to begin negotiations with the new American team that had replaced the Bretton Woods orchestrators Henry Morgenthau and Harry Dexter White. Heading the Treasury Department was Fred Vinson, who would soon depart for the Supreme Court. His colleague Will Clayton, by contrast, proved to be a mainstay of Truman administration foreign economic policy. A Southerner who stood six feet, six inches and towered over his British counterparts, Clayton had turned his cotton finishing and brokerage firm—Anderson, Clayton and Co.—into a behemoth; by 1940 it controlled 15 percent of world cotton production. Unlike many of his competitors, Clayton had taken New Deal acreage restrictions as a signal to expand overseas. His experience earned him the reputation as the White House expert on international trade issues, as well as giving him a personal stake in foreign trade expansion. In his positions as assistant and then undersecretary of state, Clayton dominated discussions of a loan to Britain.[13]

British leaders, aware of their nation's physical and financial exhaustion, had deluded themselves into believing that Roosevelt's oft-repeated principle of "equality of sacrifice" would garner them an outright American grant or, failing that, an interest-free loan. (The British politician Lord Jay later explained British delusions by observing that Keynes was too optimistic because it was an optimistic period. Britain's victory over the Germans inspired a sense that nothing was impossible.) When Clayton made it clear that the best he could do was an interest-bearing loan accompanied by rigorous conditions, the Treasury and Bank of England had "hysterics."[14] But the State Department believed that a quid pro quo for American financial assistance was appropriate; Clayton at one point suggested tying the loan to an agreement on airplane landing rights. In the event, the loan, signed on December 6, 1945, contained two major conditions, both connected to the American government's embrace of free trade. The British government agreed to make the pound sterling convertible into other currencies not later than one year after the loan went into effect. British importers would thereafter be able to obtain dollars with which to purchase American goods, while American exporters would be able to receive dollars for their sales. Both countries also agreed not to use import restrictions to discriminate against each other's trade. In this way Washington intended to unravel the "imperial preference" system (under which goods from Britain, the Commonwealth, and the Empire were exempt from tariffs and trading restrictions placed by Britain and other Commonwealth countries on goods from other countries, notably the United States), and increase American sales to Britain, its Empire, and the Commonwealth. American objections to imperial preference had already led to clauses aimed against it in the Atlantic Charter and the Lend-Lease Consideration Agreement; now London's dire straits allowed Washington to cut the heart from Britain's preferential trade system.[15] The forced dismantling of the "sterling area," the group of nations that used the pound as their main currency, was a terrible blow to Britain. The economic dependence of the Empire and Commonwealth on London had brought the British government a significant discount on its bill for war-related costs. The sterling area also made British goods more attractive to other nations in the currency bloc that were short of dollars and maintained the prestige of the City of London as the premier center for international finance, trading, and insurance. At a time when tangible indicia of British strength were fast disintegrating, British leaders unrealistically exalted this money-center role. Yet Whitehall had no choice but to accept American conditions.

In exchange for these painful promises, the American government agreed to lend Britain $3.75 billion at 2 percent interest, with repayments to begin in 1951 and to stretch out over fifty years. This interest rate, effectively 1.62 percent, was sufficiently below market rate to require a $300 million Treasury subsidy.[16] The United States also agreed to lend Britain a further $650 million at the same terms; London would then return this sum to Washington, which would accept it in full settlement of Britain's $25 billion bill for American wartime lend-lease shipments. Temporarily, at least, London's dollar gap, a shortage of dollars needed to buy American goods, had been solved. Britain now had the seed money to reconvert its industry to a peacetime basis.

The loan had a stormy reception from legislators on both sides of the Atlantic. The *Economist* reflected prevalent British sentiment when it protested that "in moral terms we are the creditors; and for that we shall pay a hundred and forty million dollars a year for the rest of the twentieth century. It may be unavoidable but it is not right." Robert Boothby, a close friend of Churchill, labeled the loan an "economic Munich." Boothby believed that just as the British government had appeased Adolf Hitler in 1938, it was appeasing the United States now. But Parliament, persuaded by two interlocking arguments, approved the loan. As Keynes pointed out, an alternative trading block policy based on Britain's trading only with countries that would accept sterling rather than dollars would consist of "countries to which we already owe more than we can pay, on the basis of their agreeing to lend us money they have not got and buy only from us and one another goods we are unable to supply." Churchill, for his part, understood that: "the long term advantage to Britain and the Commonwealth is to have our affairs so interwoven with those of the United States in external and strategic matters, that any idea of war between the two countries is utterly impossible, and that in fact, however the matter may be worded, we stand or fall together. It does not seem likely that we should have to fall." While Churchill spoke specifically about occupation policy, his words applied equally well to the Anglo-American loan. This philosophy, fully shared by the Labour government, would underpin British foreign policy in the postwar world.[17]

Members of Congress proved hardly more enthusiastic. Truman sent his message to Congress urging passage of the loan agreement legislation on January 30, 1946. Ironically it was the administration's success in achieving its foreign economic policy that now caused the President difficulties. In the past year Congress had already authorized international economic commitments in excess of $13 billion. Not surprisingly, congressmen became nervous at the idea of another $4.4 billion pledge, particularly since this loan would be by far the largest single appropriation and would represent an abandonment of the multilateral framework embodied by the Bretton Woods agreements.[18] Britain's domestic and foreign policies also pushed domestic political buttons that had been turned off by the war. Representative Emanuel Celler (D., N.Y.), charged that the money would pay for "too damned much socialism at home and imperialism abroad," while Representative Dewey Short (R., Mo.) said he would vote against it "as long I know they've got the crown jewels."[19] Irish-Americans who remained bitter about British treatment of Ireland and Jews who deeply resented the Labour cabinet's record in the Middle East encouraged these sentiments. In response the administration lobbied hard. Senate passage was never really in doubt but the House was a different matter. Senator J. William Fulbright wrote the former ambassador to Moscow W. Averell Harriman that he feared the House would kill the loan.[20] The loan became law only thanks to sudden fears of the Soviet Union's global intentions. In short a common enemy meant the United States needed stronger allies and would be willing to transfer billions of dollars to achieve this goal.[21]

In one of the most celebrated speeches of the twentieth century, the former and future prime minister of Britain, Winston Churchill, proclaimed on March 5, 1946, that "from Stettin in the Baltic to Trieste in the Adriatic, an iron curtain has descended across the Continent."[22] While the speech did not have the official blessing of the administration, it reflected a shared suspicion of Soviet intentions that had been steadily increasing over the last eighteen months. Ironically, during the war relations between the United States and the Soviet Union had often been smoother than those between the United States and

Britain.[23] The Big Three conferences at Teheran and Yalta had sketched out the pattern of the postwar settlement, laying the basis for the division of Germany and permitting the Soviet Union free reign in Eastern Europe.

The tenor of Soviet-American relations changed after Roosevelt's death. One of the great unanswered questions is whether they would have remained amicable had Roosevelt lived. The Potsdam conference, the last of the Grand Alliance summit conferences, commenced amid the wreckage of a Berlin suburb in July 1945. Germany's future dominated the discussions. The State Department had decided that carving up Germany had been a mistake. Truman also now objected to moving Poland's borders westward to the Oder-Neisse line and refused to approve a fixed sum for German reparations to the Soviet Union, although at Yalta American diplomats had reluctantly accepted the figure of $20 billion for reparations-in-kind as a "basis for negotiations." Soviet forces, pledged to depart from wartime positions in Iran within six months of the war's end, showed every sign of making their sojourn permanent. With Soviet threats to Turkey intensifying as well, the Truman administration's reassessment of Soviet policy accelerated.

The so-called long telegram sent by the American diplomat George Kennan played a major role in this process. Invoking his extensive experience in the Soviet Union and Eastern Europe, Kennan painted a picture of a paranoid, suspicious Communist government that drew malevolent strength from the confluence of international Marxism and Russian nationalism: "World Communism is like a malignant parasite which feeds only on diseased tissue." Stalin's government was "a political force committed fanatically to the belief that with [the] US there can be no permanent *modus vivendi*, that it is desirable and necessary that our traditional way of life be destroyed, the international authority of our state be destroyed, if Soviet power is to be secure." Kennan concluded that "many foreign peoples, in Europe at least, are tired and frightened by experiences of past, [sic] and are less interested in abstract freedom than in security." That this security was economic as well as political was obvious.[24]

Concurrently in February 1946 Stalin made an election speech for membership in the Supreme Soviet. Although Western observers were well aware that the campaign was a farce, the content of the speech signaled the failure of American economic diplomacy toward the Soviet Union. Stalin announced a new Five-Year Plan that would restore conditions in the Soviet Union to their 1941 level, and pledged the Communist party "to organize a powerful new upsurge of the national economy which would enable us for instance to raise the level of our industry three fold, as compared with the pre-war level."[25] This feat would be accomplished neither with Western help nor with Western trade but purely by Soviet Communist efforts. U.S. officials had once hoped that American economic power could buy Soviet acquiescence in a liberal economic world order. Now Stalin publicly indicated the futility of positive economic diplomacy. The decisive break occurred in September 1946 when Truman forced Henry Wallace, the most left-wing member of the cabinet, to resign because the conciliatory tone of his September 12 speech deviated too far from the hardening administration position. As had happened before, the major clashes with Moscow centered on Germany.

The future of Germany had been on the table since 1943. Concurrent with ongoing discussions over a zonal division of Germany, Secretary of the Treasury Henry Morgenthau devised a plan calling for the pastoralization of Germany, removing its heavy industry and substituting an agricultural economy for Europe's industrial heart. Only in this manner, believed Morgenthau, could the allies ensure that a Fourth Reich would never emerge. Although during the Quebec conference Churchill had acquiesced in the blueprint, the British government never embraced the Morgenthau Plan. By the end of 1944 high-level American officials openly lobbied against the scheme; Roosevelt's death ended any possibility of its implementation. Much of Morgenthau's influence was personal—he had been Roosevelt's Dutchess County neighbor. Also of importance was the process that transforms the dissent of the past into the orthodoxy of the present. The reparations fiasco succeeding World War I and the belief (whether or not factually founded) that the insistence on large payments by Germany to the Allies had been immoral as well as uneconomic had achieved general acceptance in government circles.[26] Economic factors militated against the Morgenthau Plan as well. While dismantling Germany's war-making capacity remained important, the more dependent Germany became, the more expensive the role of occupier. The denouement of the Potsdam conference ensured that policies within each zone would increasingly diverge and German zonal divisions would begin to calcify.

The split in the former Grand Alliance publicly widened in the summer of 1946 during the Paris Conference of the Council of Foreign Ministers. The future of Germany became the breaking point. The zonal divisions mandated by the wartime conferences left the Soviet Union with a heavily agricultural area that produced the bulk of Germany's food, while the Western zones, administered by Britain, the United States, and France, contained the industrial heartland. With Soviet-promised food shipments lagging, the U.S. military governor, General Lucius D. Clay, unilaterally halted further reparations for the Soviet Union on May 23. Tensions flared higher when Secretary of State James F. Byrnes, supported by British Foreign Secretary Ernest Bevin, proposed an immediate German peace treaty. Unknown to the Soviets, the American and British governments had already agreed on July 30 to merge their two zones into a "Bizone." This step eased the financial strain on Britain and improved the administration of the occupied territory. It was also another brick in the wall between West and East.[27]

During a break in the conference Byrnes went to Germany and remarked that the United States might be called on to retain troops in Germany indefinitely. Clay acclaimed this remark as the first public indication of an American intention to remain in Europe. Byrnes's speech did not escape the notice of Soviet officials either.[28] As the Truman administration moved closer to a final decision on its Soviet policy, American voters gave their verdict on Democratic government, returning Republican majorities in both houses of Congress for the first time since 1930.

Economic anxiety sparked the Republican victory. Lingering fears of a depression coalesced with anger over mounting inflation. Wartime shortages and accumulated savings had generated unprecedented pent-up purchasing power. Simultaneously, public pressure and congressional action had eviscerated the Office of Price Administration, the federal government's price control agency. Prices skyrocketed; as the New York Daily News put it: "PRICES SOAR, BUYERS SORE, STEERS JUMP OVER THE MOON."[29] A wave of strikes hit the

United States, upsetting friends as well as foes of organized labor, notably the President, who at one point tried unsuccessfully to draft striking railroad workers. With a housing shortage frustrating newly burgeoning families, not surprisingly many Republican candidates trounced their opponents on Election Day.

For the first time in sixteen years the Republican party would control committee chairmanships. Exuding a euphoria like that of Newt Gingrich and his fellow Republicans in January 1995, many Old Guard legislators hoped to repeal the New Deal. Given the seniority system, important committee chairmanships would go to the long-serving Republicans from the Middle West. The Republican domestic agenda featured legislation curbing the power of organized labor, which had grown dramatically since the passage of the 1936 Wagner Act, known as "Labor's Bill of Rights." The Taft-Hartley Act, passed in 1947 over Truman's veto, banned the closed shop and secondary boycotts. But despite Republican legislative control Truman won from the Eightieth Congress rent control legislation, the creation of an atomic energy authority, federal aid for housing and slum clearance acts, and an increase in the minimum wage to 75 cents an hour.[30]

The Democratic loss of control over Congress had an even more limited effect on Truman's foreign policy. But initially the White House ran scared. As a State Department memorandum had pointed out in October 1946, Midwestern Republicans, now riding high, almost uniformly voted against every foreign policy bill from 1940 through 1946.[31] The cooperation of Arthur H. Vandenberg, senator from Michigan and newly anointed president pro tempore of the Senate and chairman of the Foreign Relations Committee, largely saved the administration. Throughout the war Roosevelt attempted to create bipartisan support for his foreign policy. Republicans like Henry Stimson and Frank Knox joined Roosevelt's cabinet and the Dulles brothers, John Foster and Allen, became regular members of American delegations. Yet, unlike Vandenberg, these men, pillars of the internationalist wing of the Republican party, had little standing with the powerful isolationist segment of the deeply divided party. Vandenberg had started his career as an ardent isolationist; his about-face came only after Pearl Harbor. A friend of Truman's from their Senate days, this former newspaper reporter explained his conversion to a companion as they suffered through an attack of German robot bombs: "How can there be immunity or isolation when men can devise weapons like that?" Now in January 1947 he proclaimed that "partisan politics, for most of us, stops at the water's edge."[32] Because Vandenberg's conservative credentials were above reproach, his embrace of Democratic policies gave them a legitimacy in Republican circles they otherwise would have lacked. Furthermore, his unimpeachable standing in the Senate proved of great practical value to the Truman administration.

Events in Europe during the winter of 1946–47 tested Vandenberg's skill. On the surface 1946 seemed a year of recovery for the Continent. The Anglo-American loan, available in July, had helped British exports to surpass prewar levels, while in May 1946 the administration had granted a $720 million credit to France.[33] In early 1947, however, the Western European recovery abruptly halted. The worst winter in decades hit Britain and the Continent. Record cold and snow paralyzed industry and transport, dashing hopes of quick recovery. Chancellor of the Exchequer Hugh Dalton informed the British cabinet that "we were racing through our United States dollar credit at a reckless, and ever accelerating speed." France faced a bread and wheat shortage, and conditions in Italy and the German Bizone were no better. UNRRA had gone out of business in December 1946. Clayton, touring Europe during the spring, reported, "It is now obvious that we grossly underestimated the destruction to the European economy by the war. . . . One political crisis after another merely denotes the existence of grave economic distress. . . . Without further prompt and substantial aid from the United States, economic, social and political disintegration will overwhelm Europe."[34]

Clayton's statement reflected the evolution in Washington's world view over the preceding two years. When World War II ended, ardent internationalists believed that the political and economic structures midwifed by the United States—the Bretton Woods institutions on the one hand and the United Nations on the other—would be sufficient to ensure American hegemony and global peace and prosperity. But economic and diplomatic events had rendered these assumptions obsolete. By early 1947 it became obvious that Western Europe could not even make it to the beginning of the road to recovery without significant American economic assistance. As the dollar shortage eroded European orders for U.S. products, many Americans also began to understand that American prosperity increasingly depended on European economic improvement.

Moreover, European economic difficulties had broader geopolitical ramifications. U.S. diplomats concluded that penury-produced pessimism might well lead to a search for a new political order. What if dissatisfied Western Europeans converted the already significant domestic support for Communist governments into a landslide in favor of them? The growing hostility between the Soviet Union and the United States meant that Communist governments in Western Europe might threaten American peace as well as U.S. domestic prosperity.

3

The Marshall Plan

... our thesis has been that political problems can be
solved in spite of their apparent difficulties provided
that economic problems are solved.

Sir Roger Makins, May 1945

Peace had come to Europe but peacetime conditions were far away.
The years of fighting and German occupation had devastated
almost every country in Europe. Britain had bankrupted itself waging
its struggle against Hitler. In France a quarter of all buildings had been
destroyed, while less than half of the nation's railroad tracks remained
serviceable. Conditions only worsened the farther east one traveled.
Nazi brutality had spiraled out of control in Eastern Europe. Little of
value remained in the Soviet Union, Poland, or the Baltic states. During 1945 food production in most liberated countries fell below
wartime levels.[1] Europe's traditional network of trading connections,
industrial links and financial ties now lay in tatters. Political conditions
proved problematic as well. The Grand Alliance among the United
States, Great Britain, and the Soviet Union had frayed during the war;
once peace came it rapidly disintegrated.

To American diplomats the connection between Europe's economic
crisis and communism was clear: chaotic conditions made "European
society vulnerable to exploitation by any and all totalitarian movements."[2] In response Washington launched the Marshall Plan. This

quintessential example of positive economic diplomacy accomplished three goals. It raised Western Europe from its knees, launched the American challenge to the Soviet Union, and bolstered the American economy. This last point runs counter to current wisdom—how could massive government expenditures be a net plus to the domestic economy? Yet the Marshall Plan proves it possible. Investing to protect prosperity at home generated peace and prosperity abroad. Once the vital interests of the United States seemed to be at issue, spending unprecedented amounts of American dollars for foreign aid was amply justified.

The Cold War came early to Greece. Royalist and Communist factions fought for control of that strategic nation. Britain mainly bankrolled the monarchist forces, while Communists drew on Yugoslavia for sustenance. The United States, although taking a backseat to Britain, had already contributed $200 million to support the monarchy via the United Nations Relief and Rehabilitation Administration (UNRRA) and the Export-Import Bank, and through a surplus property credit. In December 1946 Washington had also directed the aircraft carrier *Randolph*, together with a cruiser and two destroyers, to call at Athens on their way back from Turkey.[3] But on February 21, 1947, British ambassador to the United States Lord Inverchapel delivered an official communication from his government to Undersecretary of State Dean Acheson informing the United States that His Majesty's Government would no longer provide either civilian or military aid to the government of Greece. The admission that Britain could no longer afford to play in the same league with the United States, painful as it was, reflected the harsh reality of London's finances. British officials had prepared the ground for this note, allowing the Truman administration time to consider what its response should be.

The British announcement gave Truman and Acheson an opportunity to adopt a far-flung activism against the Soviet Union and the spread of communism. They deliberately chose not to take a low-key approach, partly because of advice from Senator Arthur Vandenberg. A report drafted in September 1946 by special counsel to the President Clark Clifford and his assistant George Elsey bolstered Truman's resolve. This policy paper on Soviet-American relations supported and extended Kennan's thesis and jibed with the hard-line position taken by the increasingly influential Acheson.[4] American officials decided that neighboring Turkey should receive aid as well: as Secretary of the Navy James Forrestal explained, it would be "an impossible military situation" if Turkey fell under Soviet control.[5]

As a result, on March 12, 1947, before a joint session of Congress, Truman proclaimed that "it must be the policy of the United States to support free peoples who are resisting attempted subjugation by armed minorities or by outside pressures." Vandenberg had advised Truman to pull out all the stops; the President did as directed.[6] He sought $250 million for Greece and $150 million for Turkey. Truman did not point out that "our side" consisted of what *Time* magazine called a "stupid and reactionary" Greek government.[7] Neither did he mention that Stalin had kept his wartime promise and stayed out of the conflict. In fact the President never alluded to the Soviet Union at all in his speech. No matter—it was obvious that Moscow was the target.[8]

The stalemated Council of Foreign Ministers' meetings held in Moscow in March and April 1947 reflected the growing hostility between British and American officials and Soviet diplomats. At the beginning the newly appointed secretary of state, George Marshall, "was not inclined to be hopeless or anti-Soviet."[9] But Marshall's trip to Moscow convinced him that the United States could not negotiate with the Soviet Union. On his return the secretary's radio broadcast to the American people radiated foreboding.[10] Few in the Truman administration still harbored any faith that the chasm between Washington and Moscow could be traversed.

The European economic crisis peaked in the spring of 1947. Both General Lucius Clay, the U.S. military commander in occupied Germany, and British officials concluded that the position of Germany was "truly appalling." The British diplomat Sir Roger Makins came back to Britain after postings abroad and tried to buy a farm to raise food for his family. Former President Herbert Hoover returned from an official inspection of European food supplies to reinforce these points and emphasize the other side of the coin—the alarming escalation of American occupation costs. Any plan would have to address both aspects of the problem.[11]

Truman now weighed in: Marshall's pessimistic precis had convinced him "that there was no time to lose in finding a method for the revival of Europe."[12] George Kennan, head of the State Department's newly created Policy Planning Staff, took charge of drafting a plan to provide massive assistance to Europe. He delivered his first report to Acheson on May 21. Concurrently Undersecretary of State Will Clayton recommended a multibillion dollar program, to be paid out of increased federal taxes rather than government borrowing. Of equal importance to Clayton was his conviction that the time for multilateral programs had passed, especially as the United States would pay the bill: "*The United States must run this show.*"[13]

At the Harvard commencement on June 5 Marshall unveiled his eponymous plan.[14] The speech, based on Kennan's report but also showing the hands of the diplomat Charles Bohlen and Marshall himself, exhibited the best traits of American diplomacy. After discussing the plight of Europe, Marshall bluntly stated that Europe "must have substantial additional help, or face economic, social and political deterioration of a very grave character." American assistance was necessary, for without "the return of normal economic health in the world . . . there can be no political stability and no assured peace." Then came the truly stirring words: "our policy is directed not against any country or doctrine but against hunger, poverty, desperation and chaos." For only a healthy economy could "permit the emergence of political and social conditions in which free institutions can exist." Marshall dismissed piecemeal assistance, instead calling for aid that would be "a cure not a palliative." Finally he declared that "it would neither be fitting nor efficacious" for the United States to draw up a plan. Rather the initiative must come from Europe.[15]

Truman administration officials recognized that the United States had previously underestimated the depth of the European crisis. They assumed that relief and recovery were intertwined and both needed to be addressed. The realization that Europe had been caught in a vicious cycle—without dollars it could not purchase the raw materials to produce needed goods but without the goods it could not generate dollars—constituted another key principle. As Table 3–1 indicates, the huge jump in imports from the dollar area over prewar levels accounted for much of the gap.[16]

The United States would temporarily make up the deficit but, as Clayton had urged, only in a unilateral fashion. Marshall's statement

TABLE 3–1
DOLLAR AREA IMPORTS[a]

Country	1937 Dollar Area Imports (%)	1946 Dollar Area Imports (%)
Belgium	9	18
France	10	36
Great Britain	11	18
Italy	11	58
The Netherlands	8	25
Poland	14	44

[a]New York Times, May 18, 1947.

that any initiative must come from Europe had been inserted "in order to blunt the edge of accusations by Communist parties in individual European countries to the effect that their Governments were allowing themselves to become the tools of American imperialists."[17] Washington never seriously intended to relinquish control over any aspect of the Marshall Plan. As with the Bretton Woods agreements, the Marshall Plan would represent unilateralism in the clothing of multilateralism.

It is indisputable that charitable considerations played a large role in the Marshall Plan. However, they were inseparable from concerns of realpolitik. Officials worried about the socialist influence on many European governments and the heavy inroads Communist parties had made in France and Italy. No one in Washington in May 1947 feared the imminent arrival of Soviet tanks in Paris or Rome. But as Kennan's Policy Planning Staff paper pointed out, "economic maladjustment . . . makes European society vulnerable to exploitation by any and all totalitarian movements."[18] In other words, a hungry, suffering electorate might vote Communist governments into power.[19] The Marshall Plan, wrote Kennan in December 1947, was a form of containment.[20]

American officials also recognized the connection between economic diplomacy and international influence. They maintained their earlier conviction that economic aid could buy diplomatic success even though the promise of economic assistance had failed to change the behavior of the Soviet Union. These dollars would blunt Moscow's threat and, at least some in Washington thought, could be used to nur-

ture a United States of Europe. The concept of an integrated Europe
had been debated on both sides of the Atlantic during the interwar
years; after 1945 American support for a united Europe intensified.
John Foster Dulles advocated "the reconstruction of Europe along federal lines and for the connection to it of a decentralized German con-
federation."[21] Dulles's speech highlighted a central advantage of
European integration: it would provide a permanent basis for German
recovery while simultaneously assuaging French fears of a German
resurgence. Economic factors bolstered this strategy. Integration, first
economic and then political, could cut the costs of recovery to the
United States while at the same time creating ties that belligerent leaders would find difficult to sever.[22] The question of Germany was indeed
central to the formulation of the Marshall Plan. A multinational
approach to Europe would clothe actions that could never be accomplished on a bilateral basis, in particular the reintegration of the Ruhr,
Germany's industrial heartland, into Germany. Benjamin Cohen, a
counselor to the State Department, explained in a speech given on
June 12 that "Europe needs German products and German markets. . . .
Europe's recovery is as important to the economic health of a peaceful
world as Germany's economic recovery is to the economic health of
Europe."[23]

The Truman administration's grand design also explained the decisions not to criticize the Soviet Union and to extend the invitation to
all European nations. This last point had been the subject of much
debate. The State Department knew that Congress would never
approve aid for the Soviets. American officials no longer harbored any
illusion that economic aid would affect Soviet diplomacy, nor did they
wish to turn the Marshall Plan discussions into a Council of Foreign
Ministers–style stalemate. As Bohlen explained, "we gambled that the
Soviets could not come in and therefore we could gain prestige by
including all Europeans and let the Soviet Union bear the onus for
withdrawing."[24] Fortunately for the administration, Stalin never called
its bluff.

The "plan" aspects of the American proposal differentiated it from
previous aid programs. This innovation became both substantively and
procedurally important. Truman officials now could claim that the
administration had developed an aid program to end all aid programs.

Rather than simply dispensing relief, the Marshall Plan would provide Western Europe assistance to construct an industrial plant sufficient to make a recovery to prosperity possible, obviating the need for further American assistance. This vision tapped into a version of capitalism nurtured by government intervention first made popular in the United States by New Deal creations such as the Tennessee Valley Authority and the Rural Electrification Administration and then carried into the war through the Defense Plant Corporation that helped finance the wartime production miracles.

Domestic considerations played their part too. In the beginning of 1947 indications pointed to a slight business recession. Then came news of Europe's mounting troubles. State Department economic offi- cers Ben Moore and Harold van Buren Cleveland concluded that the result "could be serious if a drop in European purchases happened to coincide with the recession." Clayton put it bluntly: "let us admit right off that our objective has as its background the needs and interests of the people of the United States. We need markets—big markets—in which to buy and sell."[25] With commodity prices falling, Clayton's view seemed indisputable.

To make the formal request for aid, British Foreign Secretary Ernest Bevin and his French counterpart, Georges Bidault, agreed to meet in Paris on June 27. For appearances' sake the Soviet Union was invited as well. Surprisingly, Foreign Minister Vyacheslav Molotov almost imme- diately agreed to join the tripartite conclave.[26] Bevin had already met with Clayton, who had come to London to supervise British delibera- tions. At this stage the Marshall Plan was less a blueprint than a series of vague proposals. (In fact during this period the American initiative did not yet have a definite name, although "Marshall Plan" was achiev- ing general usage.[27]) During a conference held on June 24, shocked British representatives discovered that the American government envisioned that Britain would subsume its needs within a general Euro- pean plan rather than stand together with the United States on the other side from the Continent. The American conception represented a serious demotion for Britain, which, having endured so much as one of the Big Three, intended to remain a world power rather than be rel- egated to the ranks of the European poor. Neither Britain's financial plight nor its surrender to the United States of financial and political responsibility in the Mediterranean and the Middle East had altered London's world view. Washington, by contrast, had taken these developments as proof that in the postwar world only two superpowers existed: the United States and the Soviet Union. At the same time U.S. diplomats realized that a multilateral approach would also allow the inclusion of Germany as well as Italy in the Marshall Plan.[28]

An article published in *Pravda*, the Soviet Communist party newspaper, on June 25 concerning the upcoming tripartite meetings signaled Moscow's stance in Paris. The article depicted the American initiative as a desperate attempt to avoid a forthcoming American depression. By contrast Kennan and Bohlen proved equally skeptical of Soviet intentions; they told the British diplomat Jock Balfour on June 24 that the Soviets had only one aim: to see what they could extract from the United States. The two Americans also reiterated that the United States "would never participate" in a program on the UNRRA model, which they described as one "where all countries shared in the administration of available supplies and only a few countries made a physical contribution."[29]

The Paris discussions confirmed American predictions. Molotov opened the first session by putting the Soviet plan on the table: the three governments should simply ask the United States how much it was willing to give and demand reassurances that such an amount would be appropriated by Congress. During the course of five meetings Molotov attacked the Anglo-French idea of a joint plan. Any such collective action, maintained the Soviet foreign minister, would constitute interference with the sovereignty of individual countries and would particularly infringe on the economic independence of smaller states. The last meeting occurred on July 3; Molotov rejected the French proposal to issue invitations to other European states and warned Bevin and Bidault that this course of action would lead not to a united Europe but to something very different.[30]

Molotov then departed from Paris, refusing to join in the Anglo-French invitation to other European nations for a further conference. His exit played right into the State Department's hands. Averell Harriman, now secretary of commerce, gave the British foreign secretary the credit for orchestrating the conference: "Bevin had the courage to invite Molotov and the bluntness to get rid of him."[31] Not only was the administration spared the impossible task of asking Congress to provide aid to the Soviet Union but the Soviet walkout had rendered it impossible to work within the Economic Commission for Europe (ECE) or any other existing multilateral framework. Bevin, who had characterized the Molotov departure as a "clean break" with "no doors left open," and Bidault now immediately sent cables inviting all European nations except Spain to "collaborate of their own free will" to help construct a European response to Marshall's offer.[32] With the invited diplomats gathering in Paris, the administration could concentrate on the more difficult part of its task: marketing the Marshall Plan to Congress and the American people.

Although Harry Truman successfully hung the "Do-Nothing" label on the 80th Congress, its achievements were indeed impressive. During the spring of 1947 Congress debated not only the Truman Doctrine legislation but also a $350 million general foreign relief package. Vandenberg played a crucial role in achieving passage of both bills, especially in beating back a House attempt to slash the latter.[33] But he also publicly stated that these bills "for the present" completed the current aid program.[34] As of May 31 the U.S. government's total appropriation of postwar aid and structural economic support had approached $20 billion. Now the President wanted far more money. Administration officials needed to sell the positive aspects of the Marshall Plan and assuage fears about any potential negative effects on the United States. Key to their strategy was the red flag of the Communist threat.

The public relations campaign aimed to mobilize the elite, ordinary citizens, and the press in order to convince Congress, the ultimate arbiter. Truman announced on June 22 the formation of three committees to study different aspects of the Marshall Plan: Julius A. Krug, secretary of the interior, chaired a committee charged with inventorying American national resources, while Edwin G. Nourse, chairman of the Council of Economic Advisors, headed a group that would investigate the impact of foreign aid on the American economy. Finally, Harriman led a nonpartisan committee detailed to determine the quantity and quality of American resources available for foreign economic assistance and advise the President on the limits within which foreign aid might "safely and wisely be extended."[35]

The Harriman Committee was most important. Harriman, a suc-

cessful diplomat as well as the former chairman of the Business Council, was the perfect link to the corporate world. Described by British
diplomat Lord Franks as "a loner . . . whose intellect served his will,"
Harriman assiduously nurtured the support of his business colleagues,
who represented the most important domestic interest group. The reputation of corporate America, devastated during the Depression,
soared to recovery on the back of the World War II production successes. Businessmen had influential connections with the media and
Congress. If they were convinced of the Marshall Plan's merits, the
administration's battle would be partially won. That most businessmen
were Republicans further increased the value of winning them over.
Not only did the Truman administration recognize the importance of
this constituency but the White House's center of gravity had moved
steadily rightward during the preceding eighteen months. A sign of the
times: Harriman, an investment banker and robber baron scion, had
replaced the most left-wing of Roosevelt's appointees, Henry Wallace,
as secretary of commerce.[36]

These committees also constituted a response to former President
Hoover and the noted financier Bernard Baruch, who had both warned
that increased foreign aid could jeopardize the American economy.
Hoover put it dramatically: " 'The greatest danger to all civilization' lies
in the possibility that the United States will impair its economy 'by
drains which cripple our productivity.' " For his part Vandenberg had
urged on June 13 the creation of a special bipartisan high-level advisory
council to coordinate planning and advise Congress and the White
House. Truman had taken the hint. Positive committee reports would
provide the administration factual ballast while allowing Vandenberg
to defuse Republican opposition to the Democratic initiative.[37]

The first press reports heartened the administration. The New York
Times titled its initial editorial on the Marshall Plan "Our Duty in
Europe's Crisis." But many papers queried the relationship between the
Truman Doctrine and the Marshall Plan. Were they supplementary,
complementary, or contradictory? Overall, the idealism of the Marshall
Plan captured the support of those who thought the Truman Doctrine
too belligerent. The planning aspect also appealed—editors frequently
lauded the concerted scheme over the piecemeal aspect of previous aid
bills. So far, what the British embassy had labeled the "State Depart-

ment's campaign to impress the public and to elicit support for costly proposals" appeared right on target.[38] The solidification of Communist control in Hungary, coupled with apparent Communist gains in Austria, France, and Italy, added impetus to the Marshall Plan campaign, both at home and abroad. Ambassador Jefferson Caffrey in Paris reported that events in Hungary "'hysterically frightened' leading French officials." In Italy the formation of a Christian Democratic cabinet without Communist participation sparked a summer of political turmoil.

The connection between communism and compassion was clear on Capitol Hill. As the influential New York Republican Congressman James Wadsworth told a member of the British diplomatic service, "most of his colleagues on Capitol Hill viewed the Marshall Plan from the strategic rather than the economic standpoint and would only be disposed to favour [sic] proposals along the lines which it had foreshadowed in so far as they might serve to prevent the extension of Soviet power in the direction of the Atlantic Seaboard."[39] *Life*, with its hand on the heart of American opinion, summed up the growing consensus: "at some point the break had to come. There had to come a break in the postwar roll of Russia across Europe. There had to come a break in the process of awful disintegration of the European economy. . . . for Americans it is now vital that we resolve our remaining doubts and fears and go ahead and capitalize on the Marshall gamble."[40]

Yet by mid-July support for the Marshall Plan had lost some of its momentum. The influential Alsop brothers, Joseph and Stewart, speculated that the administration's poor politicking would bring about an overwhelming congressional rejection of Marshall Plan legislation if the administration submitted it for a vote now.[41] To change the tide, Marshall on July 11 spent two and a half hours before a secret session of Vandenberg's Foreign Relations Committee. His high-level briefing about the growing Communist menace left senators "tight-lipped and obviously jolted."[42] The rejection of the invitation on the previous day by Polish and Czechoslovak officials, who had earlier indicated their acceptance of the Bevin/Bidault summons to Paris, added fuel to the Cold War's fire.[43]

Throughout the summer the Marshall Plan and the Communist threat commanded top-level attention. Private and official statements

illustrated the connection between American planning and the growing acceptance of the notion of an implacable Communist menace.
Using the "X" pseudonym, Kennan now published "The Sources of
Soviet Conduct" in the July 1947 issue of *Foreign Affairs*. This article
elaborated and expanded Kennan's argument first introduced in the
"long telegram" of a year earlier. At the heart of Kennan's policy of
"containment" (the word was his addition to the Cold War lexicon) lay
the conviction that the United States must counter the Soviet threat
by the "adroit and vigilant application of counter-force at a series of
constantly shifting geographical and political points, corresponding to
the shifts and maneuvers of Soviet policy."[44]

Few Americans seemed immune from the sense of peril. Harold
Stassen, a putative Republican presidential candidate in 1948, called
the confrontation between the United States and the Soviet Union
"the greatest competition of systems in all history."[45] Yet for all their
anti-Communist rhetoric, not one member of the Republican congressional leadership had committed to support the Marshall Plan. The
House had established its own committee, named for its leading member, Christian Herter (R., Mass.). Its members set sail for Europe to
investigate conditions for themselves.[46] A special House committee on
Post-War Economic Policy and Planning also embarked, as did Krug,
Nourse, and Harriman committee members. The State Department
encouraged these trips and urged other congressmen to take the tour
(one new congressman who did so was Richard Nixon). The "locals"
knew how important these visitors were and reacted accordingly. As
one Bank of England man put it: they are "coming to find out what is
wrong with us, and the London Committee on the Marshall Plan takes
the view that they will be very important people to convince that
Europe means business about the Plan. It has therefore been decided to
take a lot of trouble with them when they are over here."[47] Rapidly
deteriorating conditions greeted the visitors; as the State Department
summed it up on August 7: "without additional US assistance this year,
the situation in the UK, France and Italy may so deteriorate economically, politically and socially that our objectives in Western Europe and
elsewhere may be unobtainable."[48]

On July 15, as required by the terms of the Anglo-American loan agreement, Britain resumed financial convertibility, allowing nonresidents to exchange pounds for other currencies. The result was a disastrous hemorrhage of dollars as individuals and other countries traded in their unwanted pounds for scarce and valuable dollars. The prime minister's announcement on August 6 that Britain would immediately reduce purchases of foodstuffs from hard currency areas (particularly the United States) by £12 million ($48.4 million) each month probably breached the Anglo-American agreement provisions on trade discrimination but did nothing to stem the dollar flow. On August 15 the British government, in clear violation of the agreement, immediately suspended sterling convertibility. The Attlee cabinet had no choice— by current estimates continued convertibility would have exhausted the loan within two weeks.[49]

France continued to face economic trials amid political tribulations. Strikes, a disastrous harvest, severe budgetary crises and political disagreements made the summer in Paris a difficult one.[50] In the meantime Paris remained the venue for the sixteen-nation discussions. The working group now had a name, the Committee on European Economic Cooperation (CEEC), and a chairman, the capable Sir Oliver Franks of Great Britain, who also led the British delegation. Clayton arrived in Paris to mold the CEEC report into acceptable shape. Throughout August indications mounted that the present discussions "did not meet the essential standards of (a) establishing a self-sufficient European economy, (b) utilizing maximum opportunities for self-help or (c) concentrating aid at points where it will have immediate recovery effects."[51] On August 26, Kennan, at the height of his influence, "moving between vision and gloom in the usual way," suddenly joined Clayton in Paris. The CEEC then reduced its estimates of Western Europe's dollar deficit for the next four years from $29.2 billion to $22.6 billion. Yet the State Department still thought that the CEEC draft report looked too much like a wish list and too little like a cooperative self-help plan. American ambassadors accredited to the sixteen participating countries advised their host governments to scrap the deadline of September 15 and revise the report. The British government continued to balk at the American emphasis on joint planning. Franks's instructions directed him to ensure that any negotiations after the CEEC conference adjourned be bilateral, not multilateral. Bevin worried that any revisions in the CEEC report would not only be confusing but "would so impair national sovereignty that many of the countries would rebel."[52]

In short, conditions in Europe were terrible. Britain was unwilling to accept its de facto international demotion and domestic American support for the Marshall Plan was imperiled. The administration then upped the ante. Acting Secretary of State Robert Lovett at his September 3 press conference "publicly asserted the gravity with which the government was viewing the growing international financial crisis." Marshall told a press conference the next week that without emergency aid Europe faced "intolerable hunger and cold."[53] Now Congress would have to be sold not on a single aid package but rather would need to pass both an interim assistance bill and a long-term program.

As reports of the increasingly perilous European situation flooded in, the State Department urged Truman to call a special session of Congress.[54] Diplomats warned the President that if France descended into chaos, so would Germany. French politicians, in particular, milked their ongoing economic and political woes to obtain the maximum amount of American aid. Reports from high French officials predicting "that unless France receives clearer indications that interim aid will be forthcoming in the near future, the Ramadier government will fall shortly after the Assembly reconvenes and that it will be next to impossible to exclude the Communists from a new government" provided an effective spur to Washington.[55]

Truman initially responded by conferring with congressional leaders and asking the chairmen of the Senate and House Foreign Affairs and Appropriations Committees to call their groups together. For a start, the various committees could consider the CEEC's official report, delivered to the State Department on September 22. Since this document had been approved by the State Department, it did not stray far from American expectations. It estimated Western Europe's dollar deficit (excluding World Bank loans) over the next four years at $19.33 billion, requested year long chunks of aid that would diminish over four years, stressed cooperative principles, and warned that disaster would strike without such aid.[56] The report set forth four basic precepts to govern the recovery program: a strong productive effort by each of the participating countries, the creation of internal financial stability, maximum cooperation among participating countries, and a solution to the problem of the participating countries' balance of trade deficit with the American continent, with emphasis on export growth.[57] The timing of the report proved perfect. In spelling out these basic principles, the CEEC report had given Marshall Plan advocates something definite to discuss without tying the administration too closely to anything specific.

During this period, the public relations campaign continued at full steam. Although Gallup polls consistently reported that less than half of those questioned had heard of the Marshall Plan and only about one in seven could articulate its goals, media opinion continued favorable.[58] Newspapers covered the CEEC report in depth, with many columnists pressing the Communist connection. As a British observer wrote, "a typical headline is 'Red Chaos Threatens Europe in Six Months.'" To convince legislators who had returned from the grand tour (many remained abroad), the White House on September 29 held a briefing session featuring Truman, Marshall, and Lovett.[59]

The White House campaign, which some observers had seen as flagging, received a boost at the beginning of October when the Soviet Union together with foreign Communist parties issued a manifesto reviving the Comintern (renamed the Cominform), the Communist international organization pledged to converting the world to communism. The alarm was general—Undersecretary of State Lovett predicted that without American aid the nations of Western Europe "would go to the Soviet [Union]."[60] On October 23 Truman called a special session of Congress, to convene on November 17. He promised to ask legislators to address two problems: the threat of inflation at home and the crisis in Western Europe. While Truman had been reluctant to convene an extra meeting with the Eightieth Congress, once congressional leaders informed him they would not countenance a diversion of existing appropriations, he had no other choice.[61]

Attempting to fuel an unstoppable steamroller, the White House orchestrated a conference on October 27 that included leaders from all sectors of society. Truman warned his audience of the need for American funding for European reconstruction since "the fate of this country and the whole world will depend upon the wisdom and promptness with which we respond to the challenge of European reconstruction."[62] With the administration's blessing and assistance, the Eastern establishment formed a Citizens' Committee for the Marshall Plan to Aid Europe (the official name later became "Committee for the Marshall Plan to Aid European Recovery"). At its organizational meeting on October 30, Henry Stimson agreed to serve as national chairman; its Executive Committee included Robert Patterson, a former secretary of war, Winthrop Aldrich, a Rockefeller in-law and the chairman of the board of the Chase Bank, John Winant, a former American ambassador to Britain, and Alger Hiss, the head of the Carnegie Endowment for International Peace. Working hand in glove with the State Department, the CMP began by collecting a million signatures on a pro–Marshall Plan petition. Acheson, having resigned his post as undersecretary of state on June 30, 1947, and resumed his partnership with the prominent Washington law firm of Covington and Burling, became a leading force behind the committee. He crisscrossed the United States, talking to any group that would listen, emphasizing whatever he had been told would play best: economics, humanitarianism, the importance of the United Nations, or anticommunism, all in an attempt to prove that the Marshall Plan was not "Operation Rathole."[63]

Allen Dulles, in 1947 the president of the Council on Foreign Relations, also worked tirelessly on behalf of the Marshall Plan, while his brother John Foster kept in frequent contact with Vandenberg. The administration encouraged Foster's interest, sending him State Department briefings and appointing him to various delegations.[64] While the *Wall Street Journal* sniped at the Marshall Plan, the American Bar Association strongly endorsed it, urging its members to adopt a completely bipartisan attitude toward foreign policy.[65] Americans for Democratic Action (ADA), a liberal group trying to distinguish itself from the apparently radical ideas of Henry Wallace, also lobbied energetically. Its secretary wrote Acheson that the ADA endorsement "differentiates us from all the phony liberals who talk about aid to Europe but back away the minute Russia makes clear its opposition to such action."[66] Many ADA chapters boasted of university faculty support; academics warmly endorsed the plan.[67] The program drew backing from farmers' organizations; the expectation of higher profits over an extended period of time neutralized the predicted opposition of the farm lobbies.[68] Opponents of the Marshall Plan also organized but their efforts lagged behind those in favor of the legislation. The "antis" included the National Economic Council, the American Labor Party, and the Illinois Manufacturers Association. As Harry Price of the Governmental Affairs Institute reported, "As more people became familiar with the Plan, resistance slackened."[69]

The endorsement by the Krug, Nourse, and Harriman committees lent further support to the administration's efforts. Although not surprising, their blessings strengthened Truman's case before Congress.[70] CEEC members, having transferred their base of operations to Washington, also spent much of their time lobbying congressmen.[71] Still the White House worried about a lack of groundswell. Fortunately, in the autumn of 1947 the administration was able to capitalize on the fact that congressional thinking had "reached, unmistakably, a point where the question was not whether to provide rehabilitation assistance, but how much and in what form." Taking advantage of this situation, Truman, with the cooperation of the Republican leadership, decided on an ambitious program for the special session. He would request $2.6 billion in interim aid to be divided up as follows: $597 million in interim aid to France, Italy, and Austria; $500 million for the American army of occupation including Germany and Korea; $1.5 billion for the last quarter of fiscal 1948 (March through June) aid on the long-range Marshall Plan; $60 million for China.[72]

Progress, unfortunately, moved in fits and starts. Taft announced that he was "absolutely opposed" to the interim aid package, while the Herter Committee's report was wishy-washy. Luckily, Vandenberg, a man who had never been beaten in his committee, repeatedly saved the day.[73] Vandenberg led his Senate Foreign Relations Committee to endorse the interim aid bill unanimously, then goaded Congress into passing an interim aid package that provided $522 million for France, Italy, and Austria as well as $18 million for China. Since the State Department believed that the interim aid bill passed only because many members were "holding their fire for the long range recovery program," this victory brought little cheer.[74]

The administration continued its battle after Congress took its Christmas break. Vandenberg scheduled hearings before his committee, to begin on January 7, while Taft attempted to form a Committee Against the Marshall Plan.[75] The senator from Ohio did not waste a lot of sympathy on Europe; he wrote to a correspondent on January 9 that

"I have always been astonished at how little war and other calamities ordinarily affect the life of the people." Taft also considered challenging the constitutionality of the Marshall Plan proposal on the grounds that the Constitution did not allow peacetime foreign aid. Fully aware of Majority Leader Taft's standing in the Senate and mindful of the fact that 1948 was a presidential election year, the administration now stressed bipartisanship. Allen Dulles, for one, concurred, lamenting to State Department official Frank Wisner on January 8 the misfortune of having to fight for the Marshall Plan "when politics is at its height."[76]

The congressional hearings began on schedule. Marshall had been virtually commanded by Committee Chairman Charles Eaton to open the House Foreign Affairs sessions. The secretary's job was to defend the request for a $17 billion program to be spread over four and one quarter years. Both the amount and the fact that it would be a multi-year authorization were unprecedented. The State Department had selected this amount, a 25 percent cut from the CEEC report, because it was the upper limit of the Harriman Committee's recommended appropriation. A parade of notables followed: Bernard Baruch, Allen Dulles, John Foster Dulles, James O'Neill, National Commander of the American Legion, (if O'Neill was National Commander) H.J. Heinz II, Walter Reuther, president of the United Auto Workers, and Hamilton Fish, an anti–New Deal, isolationist congressman, all urged enactment of the Marshall Plan. Henry Wallace stood out as one of the few dissenters, assailing the program as a step toward war.[77] Congressional hearings concluded at the end of February. On March 1 Vandenberg opened the Senate debate. He spoke against a background of lessening inflation at home and worsening tensions in Europe.[78] The December Council of Foreign Ministers' conclave had concluded with nothing to show for the weeks spent in meetings. More important, during February a Communist government took control in Czechoslovakia. This denouement, coming one decade after the Western sellout of Czechoslovakia to the Nazis, gave the event a special resonance. As Marshall informed the cabinet on March 5: "The strategic and political situation in Europe makes it imperative that the ERP [the European Recovery Program had become the official name of the Marshall Plan] legislation be enacted without crippling amendments."[79] Marshall had warned the President that while the ERP legislation was on track in the Senate, the lack of progress in the House was troubling. Truman on March 17 rallied his forces with a strident speech urging immediate passage of the Marshall Plan legislation; he advocated a draft and universal military training as well. The combination of a request for military training with an exhortation to Congress to pass the Marshall Plan evidenced Truman's belief that military and economic weapons were, in the President's famous phrase, "two halves of the same walnut." The Czech crisis made American action unavoidable; the Marshall Plan, based on the premise that the expenditure of money would prevent the need to sacrifice American lives, seemed the "cheapest" option of the programs. Military containment would come; economic containment was here. Although editorial reaction split over the military aspects of the President's speech, virtually every paper supported the Marshall Plan.[80]

Two weeks later the congressional campaign neared its end. A bill calling for the appropriation of $5.3 billion in its first year, and thereafter until June 30, 1952, such sums as might be necessary, passed the Senate by a vote of 69 to 17 on March 13 and reached the House floor. It differed most importantly from the administration's blueprint by calling for an autonomous agency to administer the Marshall Plan. The four-year cumulative aid figure disappeared and the initial authorization shrank from $6.8 billion by shaving the period covered from fifteen months to one year.[81] The rising Communist aggression convinced holdouts such as Taft to drop their opposition to the Marshall Plan; the senator from Ohio, while not actually voting for the bill, was paired in favor. On April 2, one day after the administration's target day, the House leadership informed its flock that this night the European Recovery Bill would be passed, no matter what. On a day when the New York Times headline read "U.S. Flies Food into Berlin as Russians Block Traffic," the House passed the final version 318 to 75. The next day, a proud President signed the legislation into law.[82] On June 28 Congress authorized the actual appropriations. The Marshall Plan was underway.

The Marshall Plan legislation called for the creation of an Economic Cooperation Administration (ECA). For this critical job Truman tapped Paul Hoffman, the president of the Studebaker [car] Company. Vandenberg's rating of Hoffman as one of the best American administrators showed the wisdom of the appointment.[83] Harriman became the

ECA's ambassador to Europe, making himself at home in an elegant office in Paris on the Place de la Concorde, where he held court under a bust of Benjamin Franklin.[84] A veritable army served under these officers. In 1948 Congress created the powerful Office of Special Relationship (OSR) to coordinate ECA's efforts. By 1953, at the end of the Marshall Plan, OSR employed 630 Americans and more than 800 Europeans.[85]

American aid came in several varieties: dollar grants, grants-in-kind, and loans. To coordinate the European end the CEEC transformed itself into the Organization of European Economic Cooperation (OEEC) in March 1948. The amount of aid given under the Marshall Plan from April 3, 1948, until June 30, 1951 (when remaining aid was folded into the Mutual Defense Assistance Program), totaled $12.53 billion, well in excess of $100 billion in current dollars. It was divided principally as shown in Table 3–2.

Conditional aid was the term used for American assistance designed to support the Western European Payments Agreement of 1948 and subsequent payments agreements. This aid financed trade between Western European countries and, therefore, unlike other forms of Marshall Aid, flowed among European nations. It allowed Western European nations to maximize the use of their own currencies rather than scarce dollars for trade. The ECA allocated grants and loans according to each country's dollar balance of payments deficit. Pursuant to agreements made under CEEC and OEEC auspices, each country drew up a requisition covering its annual requirements for dollar imports that the ECA used to make its calculations. Britain received 23 percent of total Marshall aid while France received 20 percent, in each case before taking account of inter-European transfers. Overall around a third of all

TABLE 3–2
PRINCIPAL ALLOCATION OF MARSHALL PLAN AID (U.S. $ BILLIONS)[a]

Grants	9.1994
Loans	1.1397
Conditional aid	1.5429
Total	11.8820

[a]Alan S. Milward, *The Reconstruction of Western Europe: 1945–1951.* (Berkeley, 1984), p. 95.

ERP imports were agricultural in nature, but imports of capital goods also proved crucial. Each country accumulated assets in local currency, known as "counterpart funds," from selling American-provided commodities. The U.S. government theoretically controlled the release of these funds, which were used largely to limit inflation and underwrite capital investment.[86] Many of the aid dollars remained in the United States. Countries wishing to procure products declared to be in surplus by the secretary of agriculture had to purchase them in the United States, while the original ERP legislation mandated that 25 percent of the total wheat or wheat products sent to Europe under the first ERP legislation had to be in the form of flour milled in the United States.[87]

American influence in Europe during Marshall Plan days extended far beyond the disbursement of aid. The ECA oversaw a multiplicity of projects. U.S. contractors under the supervision of the Army Corps of Engineers rebuilt the Corinth Canal in Greece. In Zonguldak, Turkey, American and Turkish engineers modernized mines. In Trieste twenty American technicians helped install U.S. equipment in an oil refinery. The ECA funded the Anglo-American Council on Productivity, which despite its name sent businessmen from Britain and other European nations to the United States to study American production techniques. The ECA also had a small-business division that distributed information and held counseling sessions. ECA employees did not neglect bread-and-butter issues, conducting economic surveys of Western Europe's infrastructure, evaluating Europe's demand for aid, managing agricultural shipments, and dealing with European officials.[88] On a broader level American officials attempted to shape European monetary and fiscal policy, especially in such areas as exchange rates and intra-European trade. Saving Western Europe included economically isolating the Soviet Union and its allies as well. The ECA managed export controls to the Soviet Union. This policy, designed to limit the flow of strategic goods to the Communist bloc, functioned on a cooperative basis among Washington and its Western European allies. The ECA also worked to acquire strategic materials for the United States.

Two large issues dominated most ERP debates. One was the future of Germany. American officials saw German recovery as essential. By contrast, France and Britain continued to demand and in some cases unilaterally to take reparations, which hurt the German economy. Indeed

Germany threatened to become a mere conduit for American aid to Britain and France. Once again the Soviet Union came to the rescue. The Berlin blockade subsumed the reparations debate. Berlin, located deep in the Soviet zone of Germany, had been divided into four separate zones of occupation. In June 1948, Soviet forces blocked ground access to that city, cutting off its lifelines. Rather than allow Communist forces control over the former German capital, American pilots supplied Berlin by air. That city became a symbol of Western resistance to the Soviet Union, while the confrontation led both the United States and France to take more conciliatory positions on German questions. By the time Stalin conceded defeat in May 1949, the same month as the American, British, and French zones merged to become West Germany (officially known as the Federal Republic of Germany), the reparations debate had faded in importance.[89] The Communist challenge allowed the rapid triumph of the American view of Germany's future.

The second question concerned the nature of European economic cooperation and integration. On this subject opinions ran the gamut, both in the United States and abroad. This issue had two dimensions. The first concerned the organization of ERP programs and the distribution of Marshall Plan aid. From the beginning American officials believed that multilateral European arrangements were a prerequisite for success. A joint plan would eliminate duplication and waste, maximize intra-European trade and transfers, and increase efficiency. The CEEC provided a beginning; its metamorphosis into the OEEC furnished a structural basis for the future. To this end participating countries made joint, multilateral pledges through the OEEC among themselves but signed one-to-one, bilateral agreements with the United States.

The more fundamental consideration was whether ERP should begin a process of Western European integration that would lead to economic and/or political union. European unity continued to appeal to Americans for several reasons, not the least of which was the conviction, tapping deep into the American psyche, that Europe's best course was to imitate the United States as closely as possible. These ideas had been featured in discussions prior to ERP's enactment, although they became far more important once the Marshall Plan became reality.[90]

While France, the Benelux countries, and Italy embraced the idea of European integration, Britain remained aloof. Neither British leaders nor the public regretted their wartime record nor needed to bury it in a new superstructure. That Britain had "won" the war also made it reluctant to see itself as the impoverished nation it had become. No continental country also possessed as strong economic ties with an empire or maintained a commonwealth. In fact, the decade immediately after the war was the most profitable for British imperial trading accounts. As a result, its leaders persisted in seeing Britain lodged within three interlocking circles: with the Continent, with the Empire and Commonwealth, and with the United States. To join a European union would be to favor one relationship to the detriment of others. Joining was out of the question.[91]

The British government's aversion to multilateralism could be carried to ridiculous extremes; for example, Chancellor of the Exchequer Sir Stafford Cripps almost refused to sign the original CEEC report on the grounds that it violated British sovereignty.[92] This attitude annoyed American officials. ECA administrators were in favor of integration, although they were not always sure what they meant by that term.[93] They had counted on Britain to lead the parade; London's refusal to fall in with their plans would be a great source of irritation over the next four years. After all, Britain, whose 1948 deficit was projected to be two and a half times that of France and Italy combined, presented the United States with its biggest economic headache.[94] In the event Britain did agree to join the European Payments Union, which liberalized trade and intra-European monetary arrangements. However, neither the Labour government nor the Churchill government that succeeded it in October 1951 could bring itself to join the European Coal and Steel Community (ECSC), the first of the European communities. The ECSC grew out of a plan proposed by French Foreign Minister Robert Schuman in May 1950 to merge the French and German steel and coal industries. It became reality two years later.

Well before the ECSC began functioning, another kind of unity had come about. In the autumn of 1947 Truman administration officials and others began to call for an American military alliance with Western Europe. The Soviet threat to Europe increasingly demanded a military as well as an economic response. As Ambassador Caffrey opined from

Paris in March 1948, "we are rapidly approaching the point where the hope of ERP will not be sufficient to eliminate the possibility of Communist success. . . . What Western Europe now needs is some assurance of a US security guarantee." One month later, Marshall, Lovett, Vandenberg, and John Foster Dulles met to discuss protecting Western Europe against Soviet attack.[95] Bevin had already grappled with the problem. On January 22, 1948, he proposed in the House of Commons a European defense alliance that would expand the Franco-British treaty signed at Dunkirk on March 4, 1947.[96] The result of the American and British initiatives, enshrined in a treaty signed in Washington on April 4, 1949, was the North Atlantic Treaty Organization (NATO), which joined the United States and most Western European countries in a permanent defense pact.

Western Europe's economic recovery ensured that the Marshall Plan would become the model for future Cold War foreign aid programs. Yet today historians debate its economic benefits.[97] While most accounts attribute to ERP the massive European recovery that far exceeded expectations, others assert that the 1947 emergency was a relatively minor payments crisis. What no one can deny is that during the years of ERP's existence, Western Europe's aggregate gross national product increased by 32 percent, agricultural production jumped 11 percent over the prewar level, and industrial output exceeded the 1938 figure by 40 percent. The Western Europe index of Gross National Product jumped from 87 in 1948 (1938 = 100) to 102 in 1950.[98]

The evidence also shows that both American and European officials in 1947 believed Europe desperately needed American assistance. In March 1948, Bevin and Cripps informed the British Cabinet that "it is an open question whether the Western European economy . . . can, even with the help of the European Recovery Program, recover to anything approaching the pre-war standard of living." Marshall aid quelled the fears and nourished the hopes of leaders and public alike. Sir Robert Hall, the director of the Economic Section of the British cabinet, declared that "the Marshall Plan was an absolutely essential operation." To another British Treasury official, Sir Leslie Rowan, the Marshall Plan was indispensable. For his part, Olivier Wormser, the French Foreign Office liaison with the OEEC, stated that the Marshall Plan not only "made it possible to avoid serious crisis and political upheavals in 1949" but "made for a degree of real prosperity due to great European efforts strongly supported by Marshall Plan aid."[99] It provided a climate of certainty—precisely the prerequisite for increased savings and investment. That some of the assumptions made in 1947 later turned out to be erroneous does not affect the role ERP played at the time. In this respect, the Marshall Plan was crucial.

Other results are not in dispute. The Marshall Plan provided the West with a tremendous victory. While this success did not roll back the Soviet Union's control over Eastern Europe, it affected sentiment in Western European countries, especially France, Italy, and the Western zones of Germany. "ERP was a form of psychological warfare," proclaimed Bohlen. Kennan's shrewd insistence on a European initiative defanged the Communist charge of American imperialism; continued American prosperity defused Moscow's prediction of an imminent American depression. Once the United States had adopted the policy of containment, propaganda played an ever-larger role in the superpower arsenal. In particular, Marshall had spent the summer and autumn of 1947 fuming at the Soviet Union's "brazen" propaganda; the Marshall Plan provided the perfect riposte. As Kennan recalled, "the psychological success at the outset was so amazing that we felt that the psychological effect was four-fifths accomplished before the first supplies arrived."[100] The buoyant Americans streaming to Europe in ERP's wake, imbued with the confidence generated by the World War II economic juggernaut and bearing dollars to burn, also offered a vibrant advertisement for the American way of life and a stunning reproach to the tide of gray that had overwhelmed Eastern Europe. Equally important was the Marshall Plan's role in reintegrating Germany into Europe and integrating Europe as a whole, economically and politically. The CEEC and OEEC gave European diplomats the impetus to work and plan together; American support for this trend carried it further along. In 1958 the six members of the ECSC inaugurated the European Economic Community (EEC), beginning the long march toward European unity. Just as significantly, the Marshall Plan paved the way for NATO and the four-decade-long Western alliance. As Sir Robert Hall put it, the Marshall Plan "brought America to the position of being more the leader and more trusted." The economist and financial diplomat Per Jacobssen told Allen Dulles that "the Marshall Plan . . . is a convenient

name for all the best that your country now means to Western Europe."
Its philosophical, charitable, and practical effects eroded decades of
distrust.[101]

Charitable considerations cannot be overlooked in an assessment
of the Marshall Plan. The plight of Europe was real and Americans
were genuinely moved. Furthermore, the Marshall Plan supplied an
idealism previously lacking in American foreign policy.[102] Domestic
political interest groups certainly played their part. The fervor of
businessmen and the enthusiasm of certain farm groups came at a
crucial moment. That self-interest nurtured their eagerness made it
no less valid. Indeed the Marshall Plan offers a case study in how a
nation does well by doing good. It provided the economic wherewithal for Western European nations to buy American products.
Beginning a pattern that would hold for the entire Cold War, many
ERP dollars stayed at home. Even without statutory buy-American
requirements, world economic conditions dictated a return of Marshall Plan dollars to the United States. When the United States went
into recession at the end of 1948, the Marshall Plan provided the
countercyclical infusion that kept the economic statistics from significantly deteriorating. The rise of unemployment was smaller than
many had feared, from 3.8 percent in 1948 to 5.9 percent in 1949.
New Deal prime-the-pump programs would not have been politically
feasible in 1948, but the anti-Communist, defense-inspired Marshall
Plan received the blessing of those who scorned federal domestic economic initiatives.[103] In this way also the Marshall Plan set the stage
for the Cold War world.

Yet these factors alone would not have brought about the Marshall
Plan. By mid-1947 the never-ending demand for dollars, on top of the
astronomical sums actually spent, combined with U.S. domestic economic concerns, had given Americans donor fatigue. While an inchoate
majority in Congress supported the Marshall Plan, a permanent and
determined minority, most of whose members were in the dominant
Republican party, opposed any more assistance. Two things combined to
make ERP reality. The first was the Cold War, which cheapened the cost
of foreign aid. The *New York Times* publisher Arthur Hays Sulzberger
put it well when he said "I preferred red ink to red blood."[104] Even Taft
conceded that the Marshall Plan "was justified by the threat of Russia

and Communism."[105] The Marshall Plan was conceived during the prelude to the Cold War, contributed to the outbreak of the Cold War, and then gave the United States an early victory.

Yet the equation "Marshall Plan equals victory in the Cold War" was not axiomatic. It took the bipartisan support mobilized by the administration to turn the Truman theorem into a definitive proof. During the 1940s the foreign policy establishment was in its fullest flower. Denied governmental authority during the interwar years, internationalists had seized it with enthusiasm after the fall of France in June 1940. Now they united behind the Marshall Plan, convinced it was the right approach at the right time. Fate also blessed the Marshall Plan with the support of Arthur Vandenberg. The 1946 elections might have empowered fervent isolationists. Without Vandenberg, who had connections to both camps but now gave his allegiance to the interventionists, the administration's ideas would never have become reality.[106] The success of the Marshall Plan convinced American planners that their faith in the efficacy of economic weapons to solve diplomatic problems was not misplaced. This triumph completely blotted out the failure of American economic diplomacy to affect Soviet policy.

Fortunately, the fathers of the Marshall Plan had aimed their economic weapons at economic problems that were susceptible to an economic solution. Harriman, writing to Clifford in 1953, warned "against undue preoccupation with economic concerns to the exclusion of others, and against the propensity of altogether too many people to think that if we solve the economic problem we automatically solve all others."[107] Western Europe provided the ideal setting for the American approach. The governing structure, infrastructure, and labor power availability previously existed. European governments lacked dollars; many craved American support. The Marshall Plan filled both deficiencies. American leaders, frightened themselves by the Communist threat and having alarmed the American public, used economic diplomacy in an unprecedented manner to an unheard of extent. The European Recovery Program remains a model of positive economic diplomacy. Because of American financial strength, the appropriations occasioned no domestic pain and indeed brought significant gain to certain industrial and agricultural sectors.[108] In this case economic diplomacy benefited both the United States and Western Europe, foreign and domestic interests. Only the Communist bloc, the target of American diplomacy, suffered.

The United States had brought about Western European economic recovery and political stability. It was a limited investment that paid incalculable dividends. A status quo favorable to American interests had been established. The deeper their economic recovery, the less appealing any Communist overture would be to Western European countries. Increasing prosperity filtering down the societal pecking order cemented political stability. Growing industrial capacity created steady orders for American goods while American farmers sold their production abroad as well. Among other things, the Marshall Plan was a method of funneling U.S. tax dollars to American sellers with Europe as the conduit. These funds laid the basis for the prosperity that would characterize the 1950s, at home and abroad.

4

The Fifties

Dwight David Eisenhower, who defined the American fifties, was the first professional soldier to become President since Ulysses Grant. A poor boy from Abilene, Kansas, he used the army as a means of social mobility, although his mother was a "passionate pacifist."[1] Starting World War II as a brigadier general, Eisenhower rose to command Allied forces in Europe, becoming one of the first five-star generals in American history. He showed an uncanny ability to get along with civilians as well as inspire loyalty among military men. Only in his brief stint as president of Columbia University did Eisenhower fail—his eighteen-month tenure proved disastrous. But most Americans did not share the negative opinions broadcast by Ivy League academics. Lacking an overt party allegiance, he was wooed by both Democrats and Republicans in 1948. In 1952, having made his GOP affiliation public, Eisenhower bested Robert Taft for the Republican nomination. The Korean War–induced anger, which dominated public opinion, and inflation ensured that any Republican would have the edge that year.

The image of Dwight D. Eisenhower dominated the 1950s. Safe, solid, middle-American, he promised security and safety in an anxious age. Ike had left his boyhood roots far behind and now surrounded himself with members of "the gang": wealthy individuals who took turns flying him to golfing and hunting vacations and presenting him with numerous gifts. While unable to repeal the New Deal, Eisenhower firmly believed in limiting government's role and cutting taxes. His ideas proved popular because unprecedented prosperity had relieved most Americans of the economic concerns that had besieged their parents. The positive role of defense spending was rarely noticed. Instead the United States, newly vulnerable to missile and airplane attack, worried about Communists—both external and within. Having a President who had vanquished the Nazi foe helped. Creating and funding a permanent military establishment that transformed the American idea of peacetime helped even more.

During the spring of 1950, the State Department's Policy Planning staff under the direction of Paul Nitze prepared a position paper for Truman. NSC 68 is one of the most frightening documents ever presented to an American president. It warned that American military strength was "becoming dangerously inadequate" and alleged that the Soviet Union was "developing the military capacity to support its design for world domination." Because the Soviet Union had the benefit of a new ideology "antithetical to our own," the United States must enlarge its own military commitment, which would require "significant domestic and financial economic adjustments." The United States would have to make a long-range commitment with a "bold and massive program of rebuilding the West's defensive potential to surpass that of the Soviet world and of meeting every fresh challenge promptly and unequivocally." During this "indefinite period of tension and danger," the U.S. government would preside over a situation "that should be defined less as a short-term crisis than as a permanent and fundamental alteration in the shape of international relations . . . the virtual abandonment by the United States of trying to distinguish between national and global security."[2] Such a program would not come cheaply: the authors of NSC 68 believed the United States needed to spend 20 percent of GNP on national defense. Just as the Truman administration had not initially embraced Winston Churchill's iron curtain speech, NSC 68 was contentiously received. But once again, domestic and international events soon converted a front-line position into orthodoxy.

NSC 68 came on the heels of a revolutionary alteration of the American way of life. Throughout its history the United States had eschewed a large standing army. In 1938 the U.S. army ranked behind the legions maintained by Romania and Greece. While wartime expansion created an armed service with twelve million men and women at its height, victory in Europe and Japan brought demobilization. The army began melting away, at least in 1945 and 1946. The Cold War quickly halted this decline. President Truman in 1947 signed the National Security Act to reorganize the executive branch for the new Cold War. The Army and Navy Departments merged with the War Department to form a new Department of Defense. The act also created a National Security Council charged with advising the President on international questions as well as the Central Intelligence Agency, whose job was to collect and analyze data from around the world.[3] Wartime had become all time.

The atmosphere of peril initiated by the crises of 1947 and 1948 worsened in 1949. In August the Soviet Union exploded an atomic bomb. Although U.S. scientists had long warned of such a weapon in Soviet hands, Truman's announcement stunned the American public. The Soviet success convinced the administration to go forward with the "super," or hydrogen, bomb. In October Communist forces led by Mao Zedong routed the Nationalist government from mainland China. Chiang Kai-shek, long America's favorite Asian, retreated to the offshore island of Taiwan (then known as Formosa) while Truman officials suffered Republican attacks for "losing China."

Republicans scored major gains in the 1950 midterm elections. The "Red Scare" at home was in full swing. Already in 1946 the Truman administration had begun a loyalty program, searching for internal subversion. Reports of atomic espionage and allegations that Alger Hiss, a high-ranking Roosevelt administration official, had spied for the Soviet Union set the tone. In fact, most historians now believe that Hiss was guilty. And evidence is emerging that at least two spies carried secrets of Los Alamos's Manhattan Project to Moscow during the race to build the bombs for Hiroshima and Nagasaki. One, Klaus Fuchs, came to Los Alamos from Britain. Another, as yet unidentified, may have come from Enrico Fermi's atomic laboratory in Chicago.[4] In general, we know that American Communists did take their orders from Moscow and some American Communists spied for the Soviet Union.[5] But the danger to the United States from internal subversion was minimal. Republicans nonetheless seized on the Communist issue. Wisconsin Senator Joseph McCarthy began his years of infamy by charging that there were 205 Communists in the State Department in a speech in Wheeling, Virginia, on February 9, 1950. McCarthy had completely made up these numbers.[6] The Red Scare went into overdrive; the administration found itself increasingly on the defensive.

On June 25 North Korea massively attacked South Korea across the demilitarized zone, setting off a panicked retreat by South Korean troops. Korea had been a Japanese colony since 1905, and was under Japanese influence long before that. In 1945 Soviet and American troops temporarily divided the country across the thirty-eighth parallel. Rival governments took power, each reflecting the ideology of its patron. In the north, Kim Il Sung set up a dreary police state, while the American-educated Syngman Rhee dominated the south in a capitalist, autocratic fashion. The Soviet Union blocked United Nations attempts at all-Korean elections.

The Truman administration, caught off-guard by the North Korean invasion, immediately responded militarily. Interpreting this aggression as a repetition of Munich, and not wanting to repeat the mistake of appeasing aggression, the President ordered the Seventh Fleet to the Formosa Straits and commanded General Douglas MacArthur, then the proconsul of the American occupation forces in Japan, to prepare his units for action. Most Americans supported the President although he had ordered the military action without first consulting Congress. The United States went to the United Nations for support, and with the Russian delegate absent, the Security Council approved an international war-making force. Eventually British, French, Canadian, Greek, and Turkish forces, among others, joined the overwhelmingly American UN command.

MacArthur guided the UN forces to an initial brilliant victory. The North Koreans had routed the South from Seoul, its capital. MacArthur landed troops behind enemy lines, outflanked his opponents, and liberated Seoul. Unfortunately his victory convinced the general and the administration to reject a return to the status quo and seek the rollback of the North's forces from all of Korea. Despite diplomatic warnings that Chinese troops would not tolerate the total defeat of North Korea, MacArthur pushed northward, assuring the President that Chinese troops would not cross the Yalu River. But on November 26, 200,000 Chinese troops counterattacked. Instead of being home by Christmas, as MacArthur had pledged, he and his men retreated back below the thirty-eighth parallel, once again fighting to retain South Korean territory.

By December 1950 the war had reached a bloody stalemate. The Soviet ambassador proposed a truce but MacArthur would have none of it. Instead he went behind Truman's back, attempting to sabotage truce discussions, then wrote Republican Speaker of the House Joseph Martin, drumming up opposition to negotiations. On April 12, 1951, Truman fired MacArthur. A cease-fire took hold in the summer of 1951 but the unresolved conflict cast a pall on American domestic and foreign politics.[7] From proving itself the strongest country in the world in 1945, the United States apparently could not win a limited war five years later. And the huge jump in inflation sparked by the Korean War, from 2 percent in 1950 to 8 percent in 1951, dramatically increased domestic discontent.[8] The American people groped for a solution.

Republicans clearly had the edge in the 1952 elections, but Eisenhower guaranteed victory by fighting a respectable campaign based on his promise to go to Korea should he win. It was left to vice-presidential nominee Richard Nixon to take the low road, spouting McCarthyite-type allegations against Democratic policies. Triumphing at the polls with coattails temporarily powerful enough to pull in congressional majorities in both houses, Eisenhower produced a purely public relations trip to South Korea in late November. Of more substance was his willingness to grasp any suggestion that would provide a solution to the war. The President in July 1953 accepted an armistice that restored the status quo, illustrating a basic point about Eisenhower's foreign policy: it represented a continuance of rather than a break with Democratic foreign policy. Documents have completely disproved the prevalent 1950s belief that the relationship between Eisenhower and Secretary of State John Foster Dulles was one of dummy and ventriloquist. While the President delegated authority in military fashion, he remained in complete charge of his administration.[9] For his part, one of Dulles's main preoccupations was to avoid creating a rift with Eisenhower of the kind that resulted in Woodrow Wilson's firing of Dulles's uncle, Robert Lansing, as secretary of state.[10]

Central to American foreign policy at midcentury was the Cold War. Eisenhower had campaigned on a platform of liberation of Eastern Europe and rollback of communism. Yet once in office the President and his secretary of state quietly adopted the Democratic policy of containment. To camouflage their retreat they kept up a relentless hardline anti-Communist rhetoric in public, disguising their more nuanced private opinions. The administration also gave Senator Joseph McCarthy and his confederates a wide berth to conduct witch hunts for what the right wing termed Communist subversives.

Abroad, Eisenhower and Dulles advocated a strategy of "massive retaliation," which the latter defined as the capability to "retaliate, instantly, by means and at places of our own choosing."[11] Nuclear weapons now became America's first line of defense. This was partly an economic doctrine, for by getting more bang for the buck American defense costs would be held in check.[12] It was also partly a doctrine for the faint of heart: democracies like to send pilots and missiles but hate to commit ground troops. Unfortunately, emphasizing a doomsday deterrent left little room for an American response to lesser confrontations. The administration was forced to resort to covert action and public relations campaigns to combat the Soviet Union in many parts of the world.

Dulles and Eisenhower agreed that the days of gunboat diplomacy were over. Covert action allowed them to keep the official record of American nonintervention pristine while simultaneously eliminating governments that Washington perceived as threatening to American interests. As the Iran coup of 1953 and the Guatemala coup the following year proved, covert operations offered a cheap solution to alleged Communist threats and allowed maximum American deniability. The latter factor was particularly important, given the continued American worship of the "court of world public opinion." Just as George Marshall and George Kennan had worried about propaganda victories, so too did their successors.

Both the Soviet Union and the United States now possessed very powerful nuclear arsenals. This reality produced an era of extreme caution amid continuing tension. True, there were repeated escalations of

Cold War confrontations, such as Chinese shelling of the Taiwanese islands of Quemoy and Matsu in 1958 and threatening Soviet noises over the future of Berlin the same year. But the United States and the Soviet Union, after 1955 led by Nikita Khrushchev, understood that successful brinkmanship required an appreciation of when to pull back. Neither side ever again threatened the vital interests of the other in Europe.

The end of the Korean War and the acceptance of the postwar division in Europe allowed Eisenhower to include economic constraints in his calculus of suitable defense policy. As he said in April 1953: "Every gun that is made, every warship launched, every rocket fired signifies, in the final sense, a theft from those who hunger and are not fed, those who are cold and are not clothed."[13] Eisenhower's determination contributed to the almost 25 percent plunge in military spending from 1954 to 1960. The President expounded his philosophy most fully in his farewell address, deriding the political economy of the national security state:

> This conjunction of an immense military establishment and a large arms industry is new in the American experience. . . . The total influence—economic, political, even spiritual—is felt in every city, every statehouse, every office of the federal government. . . . In the councils of government, we must guard against the acquisition of unwarranted influence, whether sought or unsought, by the military industrial complex. The potential for the disastrous rise of misplaced power exists and will persist.[14]

What the President failed to recognize was that it was precisely the American defense spending he condemned that brought unheard-of prosperity to the United States. Military spending continually primed the pump of the American economy, ensuring a steady stream of federal dollars into the civilian economy. The aerospace, communications, and computer industries especially benefited from government appropriations. Equally important, the postwar explosion in the Pacific region's wealth and population owed much to its disproportionate share of defense contracts.[15] The growth of military bases also fueled local economies in rural areas.

Eisenhower's domestic politics were unabashedly conservative. The President opposed the welfare state and intended to promote what he called opportunity and free enterprise over security. He once said, if you want security you should live in prison. Taking office after two decades of consistent federal government expansion, the President initially sought a rollback of New Deal programs. But domestic rollback proved no more attainable than the foreign variety. Instead Eisenhower accepted a minor expansion of federal government activity. (These expenditures came in the name of defense, reinforcing John Kenneth Galbraith's observation that defense spending was "the greatest of all exceptions to the general constraints on public expenditure."[16]) In 1956 Eisenhower endorsed the National Highway Act, which authorized the use of gasoline taxes for an interstate highway system because swift transportation was essential in case of Soviet attack. He also supported the building of the St. Lawrence Seaway between the United States and Canada.

In reality highways proved necessary because prosperous Americans continued to consummate their love affair with the automobile while the number of suburban developments exploded.[17] By the end of the 1950s one-quarter of Americans lived in suburbs.[18] This explosion had been made possible by the federal government's veteran's mortgage program, which granted mortgages with no down payment. Ridiculed by intellectuals, the subdivisions exemplified success to a generation of Americans who lived far better than their parents. The construction and furnishing of millions of new homes also helped keep the American economy growing. In fact the fifties boom was largely consumer driven. Hollywood and the nascent television networks parroted the virtues of consumption and encouraged Americans to welcome the notion of planned obsolescence. A new car stood at the heart of the American dream; American car manufacturers set the advertising and lifestyle for the 1950s. One out of seven Americans worked in jobs connected with the auto industry. The percentage of Americans owning cars jumped almost 20 percent from 1950 to 1955. Consumers snapped up other large purchases: only 3 percent of Americans with electricity owned televisions in 1948; 81 percent owned sets eight years later. The number of Americans owning washing machines increased 50 percent in the decade 1946 to 1956.[19] These changes reflected pent-up World War II purchasing power as well as the steady American economic growth rate of the early and mid-1950s. This new society received its name in John Kenneth Galbraith's 1958 best-seller, *The Affluent Society*.[20]

With the rest of the world still scrambling to recover from the wartime experience, American consumer dollars were spent on American products. Fears of foreign competition were risible. Without competition American workers successfully demanded wage increases that allowed skilled labor to live the American dream. Without competition management could grant increases, raise prices and dividends, and still retain market share. In this period of American market hegemony companies such as General Motors, General Electric, and U.S. Steel squandered their strength and grew complacent. The continuous casting process of steel manufacturing revolutionized steel making. Yet in the United States Big Steel refused to make the necessary capital investment to modernize its facilities. Automobile companies made few technological breakthroughs during the 1950s. Knowing they monopolized the market the Big Three—GM, Ford, and Chrysler—concentrated on style at the expensive of technology or production. Indeed in their drive to maximize profits the automobile companies during the 1950s spent most of their energy attempting to cut corners in production to reduce costs.

Corporate executives rarely paused to consider that American manufacturing hegemony, largely related to the war, would be ephemeral. Everyone seemed to believe that American was simply, by definition, the best. Squandering America's postwar lead in manufacturing and capital formation contributed to later economic woes. But we still could have it all—thanks to the interlocking international economic and security relationships that allowed the United States to play by its own rules. Our allies would continue to support us economically as long as we protected them militarily from the common threat. The American economy in this way received the extra cushion that allowed it to survive the complacent errors of the fifties.

Part of the problem at car companies reflected the reality that "car men"—those who worked in manufacturing—increasingly became the lower class at the Big Three. Finance boys became the dominant players. At Ford the so-called "whiz kids" took over the show for Henry Ford II. This cohort of young men, who had worked during World War II at the Pentagon, shared several characteristics: they had gone to prestigious schools, had no intrinsic interest in cars, and were destined for high places. Some, like Arjay Miller, stayed in the industry; Miller retired as president of Ford Motor Company. But Robert McNamara left a fifteen-year career at Ford, having risen to the presidency, to become Kennedy's secretary of defense. Under their tutelage automobile companies concentrated on the bottom line to the exclusion of long-term interests. Chrysler President Lynn Townsend summed up the fifties attitude when he told Ford car designer Gene Bordinant that all the public cared about was its stock splits.[21] Top management brushed aside potential improvements in manufacturing techniques. In the 1950s the audience for prophets such as W. Edwards Deming, one of the gurus of quality control, was almost exclusively Japanese.

The shift of power from manufacturer to managerial class was mirrored by the increasing white- and pink-collar dominance in employment. The postwar explosion of a college-educated working class owed much to federal largesse. The G.I. Bill of Rights aided returning veterans who wanted to continue or begin higher education, allowing millions of veterans to claim an education that they could never have afforded on their own. Given the historic resistance to federal aid to education, the G.I. Bill proved the most effective way of subsidizing higher education since the federal land grant system a century earlier.

The Soviet launch in 1957 of Sputnik, the first orbiting satellite, sparked more government aid to education—the 1958 National Defense Education Act, which generated munificent undergraduate loans and richly funded graduate fellowships dedicated to science, mathematics, and foreign languages.[22] Once again defense considerations motivated federal money for education, but not for countering the recession that struck in 1957 and 1958. Unemployment lagged at 5 percent, then rose to 7 percent. Eisenhower insisted on letting the recessions run their course, refusing to spend government funds to ameliorate the effects of the economic cycle.[23] He instead banked on a revival of consumer and business spending.[24] But the downturn made it difficult to view American consumer successes as a substitute for Soviet military technology.

Democrats, delighted with firm victories in the 1958 off-year elections, primed themselves for the 1960 presidential campaign. Men like Stuart Symington, Hubert Humphrey, and John F. Kennedy had first railed against Eisenhower for ignoring a "missile gap" in 1956. They charged that the United States had lagged behind the Soviet Union in the construction and stationing of nuclear missiles. The American space program did, in fact, have problems getting off the ground, even if there was no true missile gap. Eisenhower knew from classified information supplied by U-2 spy planes that the Soviet Union, not the United States, had the weaker armory. Having presided over an escalating ICBM and IRBM missile program, the President had a clear conscience, but he could not "belittle the importance of missiles" for political and psychological reasons.[25]

A balanced budget remained Eisenhower's yearly goal, although he managed this feat only three times in eight years. He succeeded in reducing military expenditures as a percentage of GNP from 13.8 percent in fiscal year 1953 to 9.1 percent in fiscal year 1961.[26] Eisenhower, of course, had the benefit of presiding over the United States during a period of stabilized threat when American soldiers were not engaged in combat. The President made it a top priority to fend off constant demands from the service chiefs to increase military spending. His military background gave him the proper pedigree to face them down. But with defense spending still at unprecedentedly high levels, the President became increasingly frustrated.

Eisenhower's drive to contain costs derived additional strength from his assumption that the stationing of hundreds of thousands of American troops in Europe was temporary. He sought help from European allies: Undersecretary of the Treasury C. Douglas Dillon and Treasury Secretary Robert Anderson journeyed to Europe to discuss burden sharing in the form of German contributions to American defense costs. The President during 1960 also attempted a different type of cost containment—a last-year push toward lowering superpower tensions, then at a high level. In November 1958 Khrushchev had announced that the Soviet Union might sign a separate peace treaty with East Germany. Such an action would imperil the status of West Berlin, which was surrounded by East Germany, and permanently freeze the division of Germany. Having set May 27, 1959, as the deadline for settling the issue, the Soviet premier triggered an uneasy period in international relations. General relief greeted Khrushchev's implicit backdown and agreement to a foreign ministers' conference. When this conference failed to produce an agreement, Khrushchev, rather than revive his ultimatum, agreed to visit the United States in 1959, and Eisenhower agreed to return the visit the following year.[27]

The Soviet premier's trip to the United States proved a colorful one. He appeared to enjoy himself, although American officials, for security reasons, denied his request to visit Disneyland. Khrushchev was allowed to meet John Wayne—his only other request—and engage him in a drinking contest. His two days at the presidential retreat produced newspaper descriptions of a peaceful "spirit of Camp David." Everyone anticipated the superpower summit scheduled for Geneva in May 1960. Eisenhower's growing hopes of a successful bipolar meeting that might produce the first nuclear test ban literally exploded in the flames of an American U-2 spy plane that crashed over the Soviet Union on May Day 1960. American officials, reassured by the CIA that the pilot could not have survived the crash, lied, saying that the downed aircraft was a weather plane. The Soviet production of Francis Gary Powers in Moscow proved the President a liar. Khrushchev walked out of the summit. The embarrassment of American officials, coupled with another recession, left many Americans dissatisfied with the current state of affairs, ready to respond to a new kind of leader.

5

The Suez Crisis

The British had no sooner invaded than they recognized immediately that they couldn't carry on a war of any scale without financial help; and in view of the U.S. position, taken promptly at the United Nations, we were not prepared to finance their war effort.

W. Randolph Burgess, Undersecretary of the Treasury

European borders solidified after 1949. The end of the Berlin blockade, the Soviet explosion of an atomic bomb, and the creation of NATO and its mirror image, the Warsaw Pact, made conflict in Europe too dangerous. Hot wars flared only on other continents. First came Asian strife: the Korean War of 1950–53 and the Indochinese conflict between the Viet Minh and a weak France supported by the United States. With the Geneva accords of 1954, the superpower rivalry moved to the Middle East. The Suez crisis of 1956, little remembered today, was the stuff of front-page headlines, worldwide tension, and, ultimately, of the inter-dependency of economic and military tactics. The accelerating disintegration of European empires put the contest between the United States and the Soviet Union for the allegiance of the newly independent nations on the front burner. With Moscow reaching out to the Middle East, Washington officials and their London counterparts offered American dollars in a bidding war to woo Egypt away from Communist influence.

The Middle East, in the 1950s still often referred to as the Near East, comprised the area stretching from Turkey eastward through the Per-

sian Gulf, including the northeast of Africa. Britain had long dominated the region; in the first decade of the postwar era, London
retained the most important outside role. For the British the fascina-
tion with the Middle East had practical as well as emotional and cultural roots. Economic factors played an increasingly important role in
focusing London's attention on the Empire in general and the Middle
East in particular. The decade 1945–1955 represented the most profitable period for the British Empire.[1] Trading with the Empire and
Commonwealth grew markedly, especially since such commerce did
not require dollars.

Growing British reliance on petroleum from Iran, then the largest
supplier of Middle Eastern oil, gave additional impetus to Britain's
interest in the region. Winston Churchill, to ensure a source of supply
for the Royal Navy, had bought 51 percent of the shares of the Anglo-
Persian Oil Company on behalf of the Admiralty. The 1950s accelerated Britain's metamorphosis into an automobile society and also
witnessed a significant conversion of British manufacturing from coal,
with its high labor costs, to less expensive and more reliable oil. But in
1951 Iran, Britain's chief source of petroleum, nationalized its oil properties. Britain and the United States responded by organizing a coup
that returned control of Iranian oil to Western companies. The message should have been clear: the days of Western control over colonial
resources were numbered.

The British government, led after 1951 by a Conservative cabinet
including Prime Minister Winston Churchill and Foreign Secretary
Anthony Eden, understood that maintaining an empire in the postwar
world required new tactics—rattling the saber would no longer make
foreign countries roll over. Eden had a reputation as a diplomat par
excellence. Having served as foreign secretary during the war, he
regained that position when the Conservatives returned to office and
also wore the mantle of Churchill's heir apparent. It was Eden who
actively sought cabinet permission to adopt a policy first espoused by
Ernest Bevin: "the conscious affirmation of the belief that intervention
would ultimately undermine rather than sustain British influence in
the Middle East."[2] The negotiations over the Suez Canal base during
1953 and 1954 illustrated the British government's adherence to this
policy.

Egypt had been a British protectorate since 1882. The Suez Canal base, the area on the other side of and including the canal, safeguarded the canal and more generally protected British interests in the region. This massive installation had once garrisoned 100,000 men and represented to both British and Egyptians Britain's hegemony in the region. But in 1952 a group of Egyptian army officers overthrew King Farouk and set up a military dictatorship. The new government, ostensibly led by General Mohammed Neguib, promised to revitalize Egyptian government and society and to eliminate all vestiges of colonialism. The base was its obvious first target. Eden successfully pushed for an evacuation, although, to Churchill, renouncing the base smacked of heresy. Britain was simply too poor, and Egypt too hostile, to keep it open. Dulles lauded the accord, signed on October 19, 1954: "I believe that the removal of this deterrent to closer cooperation will open a new approach to peaceful relations between the Near Eastern States and other nations of the free world."[3] It seemed to auger well for improved stability in the region.

By that time, tensions between Arabs and Jews made the Middle East infinitely more complicated. The Arab states and Israel were in a virtual state of war. Finally in 1954 the State Department was ready to join with the Foreign Office to find a solution to the problem. The result was Project Alpha—a blueprint for a settlement of the Arab-Israeli dispute: Washington and London would persuade Israel to cede a two-triangle corridor that would link Egypt with Jordan while inducing the Arab states to agree to an "over-all settlement" although not a peace treaty with Israel. Wrapping up the package, the British and American governments would guarantee the status quo and provide economic assistance. Diplomats in London and Washington began working on the plan's outline in 1954, and Dulles publicly unveiled it before the Council on Foreign Relations on August 26, 1955.[4] Concurrently heightened Cold War tensions in the region changed the nature of the Middle East forever.

Into the hornet's nest stepped Gamal Abdel Nasser, who in 1954 publicly took control of the Egyptian government. The Central Intelligence Agency favored Nasser over the revolution's titular head, Mohammed Neguib, establishing warm relations with him while the American ambassador dealt with Neguib.[5] The new president was only thirty-six, full of vigor and ambition. From a poor family, Nasser, like Eisenhower, had used the army as a means of social mobility. His obvious intelligence and personal charm attracted Western diplomats at the same time as it mesmerized Egyptians. Nasser broke with past practice and addressed his people in everyday Arabic rather than Classical Arabic. He was "one of their own . . . through and through."[6] Nasser's initial priorities were bolstering the army and improving the Egyptian economy. During late 1954 and early 1955 he negotiated with American officials to achieve the former while Egyptian officials met with British bankers and industrialists to assure the latter.

The British enterprise (actually a co-venture with German firms) that attracted the most attention was the idea of building a high dam at Aswan. Such an undertaking would provide hydroelectric power and irrigation water for the burgeoning Egyptian population. In the words of Jehan Sadat, whose husband, Anwar, was one of Nasser's closest colleagues, "The High Dam had lain at the heart of the Revolutionists' dreams for Egypt."[7] (That it would have damaging ecological effects was not an issue in the 1950s.) The British government saw this project as perfect—it would further improve Anglo-Egyptian relations and provide jobs for British firms. A working group of experts from the Bank of England, the Treasury, the Exports Credits Guarantee Department, and the English Electric Company began meeting on a regular basis.

British financial problems in the early 1950s, however, made it impossible for Britain by itself to fund the dam, estimated to be the most expensive hydroelectric project in history. The decade after 1945 saw London lurch from one financial crisis to the next; in fact Britain suffered a major crisis in each odd year during the decade. Time and time again American money came to the rescue. While Britain had devalued the pound in September 1949 from £1 = \$4.03 to £1 = \$2.80, the national budget remained precariously balanced. Continued high defense costs and large expenditures for social programs left little spare cash for foreign aid.

The British-based financial system had provided the anchor for the pre-1914 gold standard that made the City of London the world's leading financial center, and it left Britain with an important financial and foreign policy legacy. Maintaining and expanding the City's role became a driving force behind the British government's preference for a strong and stable pound—investors would not put their money in a weak, unsteady currency. Only thus could Britain continue to receive the income from loans, investments, and insurance (known as invisible exports) that supplied an increasing percentage of British foreign exchange and reserves.

As the British share of world manufactured goods continued the decline first apparent in the late nineteenth century, the importance of invisible exports to the British economy grew proportionately. In short, as Britain lost its real power, it increasingly craved the fringe benefits that power had conferred. That Britain had always been an importer of food was another influential consideration in the British preference for a strong currency. The Treasury and the Bank of England worked ceaselessly so the pound would retain its prewar status as a reserve currency that other countries would use as backing for their own currencies. This use of the pound occurred first and foremost in Sterling Area countries but was not confined to them. British policy also encouraged the utilization of the pound as a medium of international trading. Until 1960 the illusion of power held: the pound accounted for 40 percent of world trade, the dollar 25 percent. Never mind that artificially maintaining the value of the pound required high interest rates that damaged business and squeezed ordinary citizens.

After 1931 Empire and most Commonwealth countries (as well as some others) had linked their finances with those of Britain in the "Sterling Area"—those nations that used the pound as their currency or as reserves for their currency and kept their reserves of dollars and gold at the Bank of England. The Sterling Area served as glue for the Empire and ballast for the ephemeral Commonwealth of former colonies that were gaining their independence. Moreover, to British diplomats the Sterling Area seemed a counterweight to the genuine power wielded by the United States and the Soviet Union. Retaining it became a major foreign policy objective for British governments and a very costly indulgence.

Convinced of the need to woo Egypt but lacking its own resources, the British government turned to the United States. Yet, unlike its predecessor, the Eisenhower administration came to office believing that trade, not aid, would be the panacea for international financial problems. The leading spokesman for this position was Treasury Secretary George Humphrey, who assumed there were two kinds of foreign aid loans: those that went to unprofitable projects that would never be repaid and those given to profitable concerns that would become competitors of American industry. In either case, thought Humphrey, they were a mistake.

In September 1955 the British and American governments learned that the Soviet Union, through Czechoslovakia, had sold Egypt MiG fighters, Ilyushin bombers, and Stalin tanks in exchange for Egyptian cotton. For the first five years of the Cold War the Soviet Union remained virtually aloof from the Middle East. But at the end of 1952 Moscow reversed its earlier support of Israel and began to intervene actively on the Arab side during United Nations debates.[8] Both sides offered aid and military assistance to Egypt, initially in small amounts. Then, in April 1955, twenty-nine African and Asian nations held a conference in Bandung, Indonesia, where they declared themselves "non-aligned and neutral" in the struggle between East and West. Bandung marked Nasser's debut on the world stage, making his allegiance more valuable. The September Soviet arms deal thus caused great concern. Rather than rebuke Nasser, the United States and Britain joined in a bidding war for his support. One of the prime tools in the contest became the Aswan High Dam, which British Foreign Secretary Harold Macmillan characterized in October 1955 as "an essential move in the game."[9] Negotiations for the dam financing accelerated through autumn. British policy, in the words of the British ambassador to the United States Sir Roger Makins was "to lose no opportunity of trying to urge on the Americans the need to make up their minds quickly."[10] Humphrey was the largest stumbling block but eventually foreign policy imperatives overcame his financial objections. Both Washington and London radiated the conviction that the West must match the Soviet arms transaction. Under the circumstances funding the dam appeared to be the cheapest option. Western willingness to bankroll what would be the largest construction project in history for a country in the developing world was an unprecedented use of Western economic resources. It would also be less controversial in the United States than matching Soviet arms sales to Egypt. Not only would selling arms ignite a regional arms race but it would exacerbate demands for the United States to supply arms to Israel as well.

On December 16, 1955, the American and British governments, together with the World Bank, presented formal financing offers to Egyptian representatives. The documents called for the American and British governments to grant $54.6 million and $15.4 million, respectively, to Egypt. For its part the World Bank would loan $200 million at 5.5 percent interest for the first stage of the project and give "sympathetic attention" to a further loan for $130 million. In return Egypt would agree to raise the approximately $900 million balance of the dam's cost in its own currency. Ironically, during December the most difficult negotiations were between the British and American governments—$15.4 million proved almost too much for the British government, now headed by Anthony Eden as prime minister, to swallow. There remained problems with the deal. During January and February 1956 World Bank negotiators attempted to close the gaps in the two sides' thinking. The biggest stumbling blocks were the World Bank's attempt to limit future Egyptian arms sales in order to assure sufficient cash flow to repay the loan and the question of possible negative effects of the dam on the Sudan. The Sudan became independent in December 1955 and its new government refused to accept the previous allocation of Nile waters, which had greatly favored Egypt.[11]

The beginning of March found both the British and the American governments reconsidering their policy of wooing Nasser. Eden labeled Nasser "a man of limitless ambition" and took personally the stepped-up Egyptian propaganda campaign against British rule in Africa.[12] The British government also blamed Nasser for the firing by King Hussein of the British head of Jordan's army, General Sir John Glubb. The British and American governments had assumed that throwing money at Nasser would buy his allegiance to some if not all of their policy goals. They were wrong. To Eisenhower and Dulles, Nasser's major offense was his lack of enthusiasm for the Middle East shuttle diplomacy of Robert Anderson, Eisenhower's personal envoy to the region. Anderson made three missions to the Middle East, starting in November 1955, commuting between Cairo and Jerusalem to "explore the negotiability of differences" between the Egyptians and the Israelis as well as "to urge negotiations where negotiability will be feasible."[13] Nasser rejected Anderson's overtures, leaving Anderson to report to the President that "Nasser proved to be a complete stumbling block.

He is apparently seeking to be acknowledged as the political leader of the Arab World."[14]

The administration's relations with Congress now brought matters to a head. Foreign aid during the Eisenhower years never captured the allegiance of Congress in the way it had earlier, in part because of the administration's own lack of enthusiasm. During the first half of 1956 the Aswan project became a virtual legislative orphan. Resentment against Nasser's anti-Western attitude and fears of his military buildup against Israel, combined with the specter of growing competition for American farmers from Egyptian cotton nurtured by the dam's irrigation capabilities, undercut the administration's none-too-capable campaign in favor of the financing package. The administration had previously diverted fiscal year 1956 funds allocated to the Aswan project to other uses. In June 1956 the Senate Appropriations Committee in its report on the new foreign aid bill ordered the administration to consult with Congress prior to appropriating any fiscal year 1957 monies for the dam.[15]

Dulles, fully in charge of foreign policy at this point because of Eisenhower's ileitis attack, took this declaration as an unconstitutional usurpation of executive power. His reaction, the worst one possible, was to nullify the Senate Appropriations Committee's action by publicly announcing without delay that the administration would withdraw its offer to finance the dam. Any postponement was impossible, said Dulles to British Ambassador Sir Roger Makins, because he "was not prepared to let control of foreign policy pass to Congress."[16] As a result on July 19 Dulles gave Egyptian Ambassador Ahmad Hussein the bad news. Inexplicably Dulles chose not to blame Congress for this decision. Nor did the secretary refer to the Nile waters problem. Instead Dulles bluntly told Hussein that two reasons motivated the American decision to withdraw the offer: the fear that the enormous cost of the dam would engender anti-American resentment and a "feeling that the Egyptian government was working closely with those hostile to us who sought to injure us wherever they could."[17]

The American withdrawal automatically terminated the World Bank and British offers. While British officials would have preferred to spin matters out a bit longer, the "general view in London was the same."[18] Amazingly neither the British nor the American government saw the revocation as a serious matter. Newly appointed Assistant Secretary of State William Rountree speculated that in retaliation Nasser might refuse further American financial assistance.[19] Diplomats wondered if and when the Soviet Union would make an offer to fund the dam. What was conspicuously absent in both London and Washington was any concern that Nasser might retaliate against the West. Apparently, Western diplomats viewed third world peoples as passive characters to be acted upon but never capable of acting on their own.

But Nasser had an easy means of retaliation near at hand. The Suez Canal occupied both a real and a mythological position of vast importance. To the French who had engineered it and the British whose government owned 44 percent of the voting stock, possession of the canal and control of the Suez Canal Company remained a source of pride and security. Ships plying the Empire and Commonwealth trade depended on the canal. As Eden later said when asked about the canal, "Remember Australia."[20] Having grown up in the colonial era when Britain owned a quarter of the globe, he still viewed the canal as a necessity for imperial transport. Eden's comment showed that even progressive British officials retained the knee-jerk instincts that placed imperial communications at the forefront of geopolitics long after the underlying basis for their attitude had disappeared. Tankers laden with Middle Eastern oil for Western Europe made the canal their chief passageway—80 percent of Western Europe's oil came from the Middle East and 70 percent went through the Suez Canal. The Suez Canal Company's lease to run the canal expired in 1968; already in the mid-1950s British diplomats agonized over how to obtain an extension of the franchise.

Egyptian officials, for their part, intended to reclaim the canal as soon as they could. To them the Suez Canal Company represented imperialism at its worst. The company's management philosophy had not changed since the day the canal was built. The company discriminated against Egyptians working for the canal on salary, fringe benefits, and promotions. Company managers and directors made it very clear that they saw themselves above Egyptian law. Throughout early 1956 Egyptian government pressure on the Canal Company increased, particularly over the company's cash reserves. On June 18, when the last

British troops stationed at the Suez Canal base departed, the situation was ripe for trouble.[21]

Seizing the canal offered Nasser a perfect form of revenge against the West. He could enrich Egypt with the Canal Company's revenues, amounting to between $25 million and $35 million annually, secure in the knowledge that the British no longer possessed a military deterrent in the country.[22] Egyptians of every political persuasion would welcome the blow against imperialism. The United States was on record accepting the right of a country to nationalize companies provided due compensation followed, so he did not expect a particularly militant response from Washington. On July 26, Nasser appeared in Alexandria in an open car lit by a spotlight, making his way to a newly built speaker's platform. In front of a crowd of a quarter of a million people he announced that the "Compagnie Universelle du Maritime de Suez shall be nationalized as an Egyptian company and transferred to the state with all its assets."[23]

The reaction in London was swift and surprising. Informed of the nationalization while he was entertaining Iraqi King Faisal and Prime Minister Nuri al-Said, Eden immediately spoke of military action.[24] After a victorious election campaign in May 1955, the Eden government's fortunes had clearly declined. As a consequence commentators regularly speculated about Eden's possible resignation. Eden had staked his reputation on a conciliatory policy toward Nasser. When Nasser repudiated him, the prime minister turned against the Egyptian leader with vengeful fury. For their part French leaders, obsessed with Algeria, encouraged British belligerence. The rebellion against French control had reached major proportions. French Prime Minister Guy Mollet and Foreign Minister Christian Pineau took the comforting but erroneous position that removing Nasser, who supported the Algerian rebels, would end the Algerian rebellion. As Pineau said, "one successful battle in Egypt would be worth ten in North Africa."[25]

Nasser's revenge had caught Dulles in Peru. On his return the secretary of state and Eisenhower, now fully recovered, conferred at the White House. The President thought military action "was unwise."[26] Dulles concurred and unveiled his idea—an international conference to discuss control of the canal. Having attended such conferences for forty-eight years, Dulles viewed them as the answer to almost any diplomatic dilemma. Convening such a meeting would buy time as well as present the British and French governments with an alternative to military action. The secretary set off for London to convince his British and French counterparts of the wisdom of this course. At the same time Eisenhower urged Eden to delay military action. In his letter the President stressed the importance of world public opinion and the need to convince it "how earnestly all of us had tried to be just, fair and considerate," before undertaking any military action.[27]

During the first two weeks of August the State Department worked to assemble a conference in London. Dulles's frequently repeated assertion that Nasser must be forced "to disgorge" the canal allowed Eden and Mollet to believe that the United States envisioned the use of military action. By allowing the allies to retain an erroneous impression, Dulles bought time during the summer but laid the groundwork for later tragic misunderstandings.[28] The three Western nations sent out conference invitations to the signatories of the Convention of 1888, the treaty that governed the canal's operation, as well as to other major nations. Because Russia had been a signatory, the Soviet Union received one. Dulles desperately wanted to avoid setting a precedent that implied that countries with international canals had a right to object to foreign ownership—lest the Panamanian government get ideas. Accepting a Soviet delegation in London was a small price to pay for this protection.[29]

The Soviet Union understandably made the most of this imbroglio—applauding the nationalization and offering aid to Nasser to build the Aswan High Dam. Egypt welcomed the aid because Western economic sanctions against Egypt were already in force; the British ones, enacted on July 27, were the most far-ranging, virtually severing financial ties between Britain and Egypt. Since Egypt had been a British protectorate and had also been a member of the Sterling Area, its financial links with London were of great importance; the freezing of all Egyptian accounts, public and private, by the Bank of England was no small matter. As France followed the British example, neither the Egyptian government nor Egyptian citizens could now conduct business with their two traditional European bankers.[30]

The Eisenhower administration imposed sanctions on Egypt on July 31 after much internal debate. On that day the Egyptian government attempted to withdraw $10 million of a total $60 million of Egyptian government funds on deposit in the United States. The Treasury Department blocked the transfer while the President and his advisers debated what to do. CIA Director Allen Dulles worried that freezing Egyptian funds would lead to an Egyptian seizure of all American assets in Egypt. After some discussion, the conferees decided in favor of limited sanctions freezing existing American bank accounts of the Egyptian government, the National Bank of Egypt, and the Suez Canal Company, but left privately held assets unaffected. While military-related assistance stopped, general foreign assistance continued (a total of $62 million in fiscal 1956), albeit at a lesser pace.[31] The administration did not have high hopes that the economic sanctions would produce an Egyptian withdrawal, and their weak sanctions virtually admitted as much. As a National Security Council study concluded, "the resultant pressures upon the Nasir [sic] regime would probably not be sufficient within a year's time or even longer to threaten its survival."[32] In this respect—though later presidents tended to forget the lesson—they were correct. The main value of sanctions is almost always symbolic.

The first London conference convened on August 16. After a week of debate, a resolution calling on Nasser to transfer control of the canal to an international authority carried 18 to 4. Australian Prime Minister Sir Robert Menzies had the unenviable task of journeying to Egypt to put the proposal to Nasser. On his return from London on August 30 Dulles met with Eisenhower in the White House. The secretary reported that although the British and French governments had not renounced military action, he did not believe that "the situation was one which should be resolved by force."[33] Eisenhower completely concurred that "this was not the issue upon which to try to downgrade Nasser." Until then the President and the secretary of state had not entirely ruled out a public show of force. Now they decided that it was out of the question; from this point on, their task was to maintain continued good relations with the British and French governments while preventing them from doing what the two countries had decided was in their national self-interest.

Menzies's meeting with Nasser proved unavailing (no surprise there). Dulles now came up with another idea: the Suez Canal Users

Association (SCUA). User nations would station pilots at either end of the canal on small ships. The pilots would jump on incoming ships and guide them through the canal. From beginning to end the plan made no sense, something Dulles himself recognized when he labeled it "makeshift" and "not abounding in merit."[34] Its advantage was tactical. The administration believed that the passage of time would undercut the arguments in favor of force. Setting up yet another conference would buy that much more time. Basically Washington was ready to cede the canal to Egypt. The British and French governments went along with Dulles's scheme in the hope that acquiescence now would bring American support for a military venture later.

On September 14 the European pilots who had continued to work the canal passage walked off the job. Egypt replaced them with Egyptian and Communist-bloc recruits and the canal continued to operate. This success undercut the arguments against nationalization. As representatives from various nations reconvened in London on September 19, this time to discuss the SCUA plan, Britain and France brought the canal's nationalization before the UN Security Council. They were pushing for action and, unbeknown to the Eisenhower administration, had brought in a new player.

Virtually from the beginning of the Suez crisis the Eisenhower administration had worried about the role of Israel. To the Israeli government, led by Prime Minister David Ben-Gurion and Foreign Minister Golda Meir, the fuss about Nasser's action was somewhat comical. Since 1948 Egypt had illegally blocked Israeli ships and Israeli-bound shipping from using the canal. While the United Nations had passed a resolution condemning this action in 1951, neither the Suez Canal Company nor any nation had suggested using force to end the blockade. Despite its protestations and proximity to the canal, Israel was not invited to either London conference. Instead Dulles and Robert Anderson repeatedly urged the Israeli government to keep aloof from the entire subject and discouraged Israeli participation in the United Nations debates.[35]

The French government took a different tack. Since the early 1950s France had been the Israeli government's strongest supporter and its most significant arms supplier. During August and September French officials urged their Israeli counterparts to intervene militarily, in conjunction with an Anglo-French invasion. The Israeli government had strong reasons for heeding this appeal. The Soviet arms deal with Egypt frightened the Israeli government; with the Egyptian army not yet fully familiar with its new weaponry, the time to strike seemed at hand. That the French government was adamant about Israeli participation made it difficult for Ben-Gurion to say no—Israel could not afford to alienate Paris.[36]

When French diplomats proposed adding an Israeli dimension to the invasion plan, Eden and Foreign Secretary Selwyn Lloyd reacted with hostility. Relations were acrimonious between British officials who controlled Israel during the years of the Palestine mandate and Jews struggling for independence in the years before 1948. They had left a legacy of bitter resentment in Britain that, combined with traditional pro-Arab sentiment and upper-class anti-Semitism, offered little enthusiasm for any kind of cooperation. But Eden, in a decision kept from most of the cabinet, eventually acquiesced. On October 22, Ben-Gurion secretly met with Mollet and Lloyd in the French town of Sèvres. Over the next two days they negotiated the Sèvres protocol calling for an initial Israeli strike against Egypt to be followed by an Anglo-French ultimatum to Israel and Egypt to cease fighting. Thereafter the Anglo-French invasion, code-named Musketeer Revise, the purpose of which was ostensibly to separate the combatants, would be launched from both ground and air. The Sèvres agreement was to remain secret, allowing Britain to deny any cooperation with Israel.[37]

Eden decided not to inform the United States prior to launching any military action. His problem, however, was that he led a country whose military objectives were beyond its means. Not only did the Anglo-French plan call for the use of American-supplied jets, which by the terms of their governing agreements could be used only for NATO operations, but also the British government did not have the financial resources to carry on without American backing. The only explanation for Eden's irresponsible decision is that he hoped to box the United States into a corner whereby it would have no choice but to support its traditional ally.[38]

Israeli forces launched the invasion on October 29. It was only when British Ambassador to the United Nations Sir Pierson Dixon refused to join in an American démarche to the Security Council that the administration realized the British government had blessed the attack. Then the fury of betrayal knew no bounds—as Eisenhower said—"he did not see much value in an unworthy and unreliable ally and that the necessity to support them might not be as great as they believed."[39]

Several reasons account for the near-universal rage that swept over the administration. That "our closest ally" could have double-crossed the administration played a large part. Eisenhower and Dulles had repeatedly and clearly warned the British not to take any military action, especially before the presidential election scheduled for November 6. This impasse represented not a conspicuous failure to communicate but rather a failure on the British part to heed what American officials had said.

The jerry-built structure of the military plan added to the American anger. The Israeli invasion proved a great success—Israeli tanks raced into the Sinai, completing their occupation of Gaza and Sinai by November 2. The Anglo-French part of the plan was far less fruitful. On October 30, one day after the Israeli attack, the British and French governments demanded that both the Israeli and Egyptian governments allow British and French forces to enter Egypt to administer a cease-fire. Yet Musketeer Revise called for the first European troops to arrive on November 5 and the bulk of the force to land on November 6. This large gap allowed time for the United States to intervene. Had the invasion been a fait accompli, Eisenhower later acknowledged that the United States would have had no choice but to acquiesce.[40]

All these reasons pale in importance beside the most influential cause of the Eisenhower administration's wrath: the juxtaposition of the Suez invasion with the Hungarian crisis. During the spring of 1956, inspired by Soviet Premier Nikita Khrushchev's denunciation of Josef Stalin, Eastern European governments loosened their control over their societies. Six months of turmoil in the satellite states began. While Polish Prime Minister Wladyslaw Gomulka had backed down from a confrontation with Moscow, the new Hungarian government led by Imre Nagy announced its withdrawal from the Warsaw Pact on November 1. This step proved more than Moscow could tolerate. Three days later Soviet tanks rolled into Budapest and crushed the rebellion.

Eisenhower had campaigned on a platform of liberation and rollback and had allowed Radio Free Europe to encourage Eastern European uprisings. But now the administration had no choice but to stand idly by and watch the Soviet army smash the Hungarian freedom fighters. After all, short of atomic war, the American government's hands were tied. Therefore, Eisenhower and Dulles placed their reliance on the court of world public opinion. At the least, they comforted themselves, the Soviets would be exposed for the perfidious occupiers they were. The Suez crisis squashed this pale hope. Opinion in the United States and abroad, instead of focusing on the Hungarian crisis, condemned Britain and France as unreconstructed imperialists, exactly fitting the picture Soviet propaganda had long painted.

The administration decided to use the United Nations, with or without its erstwhile allies. When Britain and France blocked any attempt to obtain a Security Council resolution, the United States brought the Suez invasion before the General Assembly. On November 1, in front of the General Assembly, Dulles made what he considered his finest speech as he asked the General Assembly to intervene in Egypt. The General Assembly on November 4 approved resolutions calling for a cease-fire to be administered by a United Nations Emergency Force (UNEF), to take effect within twelve hours. On November 6, just after their troops had landed in Port Said, the British and French governments accepted the cease-fire. Eden and his colleagues acquiesced partly because they still misunderstood the American position, believing that the cease-fire would allow them to remain in Egypt, thereby achieving the goal of deposing Nasser.

But the American government had no intention of allowing its usual allies to claim a victory in the Suez crisis. Too much seemed at stake. As Dulles told Vice-President Richard Nixon, two factors made this moment a pivotal one in world history: "it is the beginning of the collapse of the Soviet Empire—the second is the idea is out that we can be dragged along at the heels of Britain and France in policies that are obsolete."[41] Fortunately for the administration the British government had placed in Washington's hands the perfect weapon with which to force Britain out of Egypt: money—specifically the pound sterling.

Maintaining the pound as an international trading currency had forced Britain to conduct its international economic policy on a starvation diet of reserves: in the years 1954–1957 British reserves of gold and convertible foreign exchange averaged only $2,322 million.[42]

American reserves, by contrast, were $22 billion. The paucity of British reserves made every year a perilous one for the Bank of England and Treasury Department. Exacerbating the situation, in February 1955 the Bank of England returned the pound to de facto convertibility for foreign transactions. From that point on, investors were able to freely convert their pounds into other currencies. This step was necessary because investors would not long hold pounds that could not be transferred into other currencies. But making the pound convertible meant the bank's reserves were always at risk should economic or political reasons drive foreign holders to cash in their sterling holdings. Because the exchange values of currencies were fixed rather than fluctuating, selling sterling was a no-lose proposition. If a devaluation occurred, investors who had bought other currencies would make significant profits. If the pound retained its value after a crisis, investors could repurchase sterling at the same price for which they had sold it, having lost nothing.

Any single political crisis in this environment became a sterling crisis as well. British officials knew that the Suez crisis would trigger problems for sterling. As Sir George Bolton, the director of the Bank of England, wrote on August 1, 1956, "If, however, we are unable to dislodge the Egyptians from full control of the canal, there will follow a collapse of the sterling exchange."[43] During August, September, and October the bank had officially lost $157 million in reserves, leaving it with $2,244 million. In actuality the Bank of England's loss was far greater; the sale of Trinidad Leasehold Company to American interests had provided $177 million to bolster sagging British reserves.[44] Several times in October British officials debated borrowing from the International Monetary Fund but decided against it, fearing that the announcement of such a loan would trigger the crisis that the loan was designed to avoid. Sure enough, after the Suez invasion, the Bank of England began to bleed reserves, losing $50 million in two days.[45] Chancellor of the Exchequer Harold Macmillan's statement informing his colleagues of a loss of British reserves of £100 million ($280 million) since the Suez invasion during the crucial cabinet meeting of November 6, which triggered the cabinet's agreement to the cease-fire, exemplifies the importance of the pound's status to the British government.[46]

In fact, Macmillan's statement was untrue. Britain would not lose that amount of reserves until the third week of November. As chancellor, he alone of ministers had access to the reserve figures. Either know-ingly or accidentally, Macmillan disregarded the facts when imploring his colleagues to accept the American cease-fire arrangement. Why he did so remains a mystery. Macmillan was one of the most resolute fig-ures in favor of military action, and his about-face carried great weight.[47] He, Eden, and their colleagues assumed at the least that once they had agreed to the cease-fire, American aid for the pound would readily flow, but Eisenhower used that moment to strike. The President and his officials made it clear that they had no intention of proffering any assistance for the pound until Britain actually withdrew from Egypt. During the second and third weeks of November dollars drained out of the Treasury. (The convertible status of the pound meant that the Bank of England had to give dollars back to investors who no longer wanted to hold pounds.) By November 27 the loss had reached close to the $280 million figure that Macmillan had produced on November 6.[48] The American government did not actually join the speculators who were selling sterling (a common allegation both at the time and later). Official holdings stood at £30 million on September 30 and £26 million on December 31.[49] Rather, the administration refused to discuss any kind of American credit for Britain and blocked the vital loan from the International Monetary Fund that Britain desperately needed.

The cutting-off of Western Europe's usual oil supplies exacerbated the British plight. In retaliation for the Israeli invasion, the Egyptian government had sunk 47 ships in the canal, thereby blocking it com-pletely by November 4. Concurrently, terrorists blew up pumping sta-tions for the Iraq Petroleum Company pipeline to the Mediterranean, the main such outlet for Europe. The United States controlled the bulk of the alternative sources of oil. As the President told Arthur Flem-ming, who was to chair the Middle East Emergency Committee, "he was inclined to think that those who began this operation should be left to work out their own oil problems—to boil in their own oil, so to speak."[50]

Time was running out for the pound. The British November reserve figures were scheduled to be released on December 3. If they showed British reserves to be below $2,000 million, the generally accepted min-imum level, without a simultaneous announcement of American and other aid, a run on the pound was a virtual certainty. Eden, racked by high fevers and drained by illness, left for Jamaica on November 23 to regain his shattered health. Macmillan and Lord Privy Seal R.A. Butler, by this point, understood that the United States had nothing to offer until a full British acquiescence. On December 3 the British government finally satisfied Eisenhower and Dulles that the cabinet had committed itself to an immediate withdrawal. (The French government quickly followed suit.[51]) The next day when Macmillan rose in the House of Commons to announce that the reserves had fallen to $1,965 million, he simultaneously reported that the United States would back a major British drawing (loan) from the IMF, as well as offer aid of its own.[52] The British government's request was for an IMF loan of $561,470,000 as well as a standby credit of $738,530,000. The American government announced that a line of credit of $500 million for the British government from the Export-Import Bank had been approved on December 21; the loan agreement itself was signed on February 25, 1957. Finally, the administration sponsored legislation amending the 1945 Anglo-American Loan Agreement permitting the British government to postpone annual repayments of principal and interest. The American government could rest content that it had taken the correct stand against an ally that, in the words of Treasury Secretary Humphrey, had "violated the basic principles in which we believe."[53]

Britain and France had tried to use offensive military power without any international consensus and without the support of the United States, the country that supplied their military hardware as well as economic sustenance. With grandiose aims but weak resources, they proved vulnerable to American economic diplomacy. But Nasser, on the other hand, although he led a country far poorer than its opponents, had a much easier task. He only needed to hang on to power. Economic diplomacy was insufficient to force his departure from Egypt's canal.

In the aftermath of the crisis the White House constructed what would come to be known as the Eisenhower Doctrine. Announced to Congress on January 5, it called for an additional appropriation of $200 million for American economic and military assistance in the Middle East to "any nation or group of nations which desires such aid" and asked for advance authorization to deploy American troops "to secure and protect the territorial integrity and political independence of such nations requesting such aid, against overt armed aggression from any nation controlled by International Communism."[54] Ironically the withdrawal of an American offer of $55 million to finance the Aswan High Dam had set in motion a train of events that caused Eisenhower to request the expenditure of far more money. This lesson was never fully learned: that small sums now can avert the need for larger sums later. The administration discarded its hopes of solving the Arab-Israeli conflict any time soon—as Dulles told his close aide Robert Bowie, "it did not make sense that he could solve problems which Moses and Joshua with Divine guidance could not solve."[55] It would take nearly four decades for peace efforts to come to fruition.

As Eisenhower strove for congressional approval of his package, the President and his aides attempted to end the Israeli occupation of Egyptian territory. Unfortunately, the Israeli government was not eager to relinquish freshly captured territory in the Straits of Tiran or in Gaza. The Egyptian government had used the former position to harass and block Israeli shipping from the port of Eilat while the latter location had been the site of terrorist activity against the Jewish state.

During January and into early February pressure from the Arab-Asian bloc in the United Nations for economic sanctions against Israel mounted. The administration had virtually stopped American aid ($24 million in fiscal 1957) to Israel immediately after the invasion.[56] What was at issue was the massive American private transfers to Israel, amounting to 35 percent of Israel's annual budget.[57] While the administration was cool toward Israel, congressional opinion was sympathetic. Senate majority leader Lyndon Johnson pointed out that the United Nations had neither slapped sanctions on the Soviet Union for the Hungarian invasion nor on India for its recent seizure of Kashmir. His Republican counterpart, William Knowland, told the administration that he wanted prior notice of any administration decision to vote in favor of sanctions against Israel so that he could resign from the American delegation to the United Nations.[58]

On February 11 Dulles presented Israeli Ambassador to Washington Abba Eban with an aide-mémoire that went some way toward recognizing the Israeli claim to the Straits of Tiran as an international waterway. When the Ben-Gurion government still refused to evacuate Egyptian territory, the administration decided on a two-level campaign, combining the threat of economic sanctions and the molding of public opinion. To accomplish the latter Dulles called up prominent Protestant clergymen such as Dr. Roswell Barnes, associate general secretary of the National Council of Churches, and Dr. Edward Elson of the National Presbyterian Church (who had baptized and confirmed the President in 1953), and asked them to preach sermons against American Jews to counteract "the Jewish influence here [which] is completely dominating the scene."[59] The secretary of state also urged the West German government to stop its restitution payments to Israel. These transfers, Israel's second-largest source of foreign exchange, arose from West Germany's attempt to atone for the Nazi Holocaust. On February 20 Eisenhower and Dulles met with congressional leaders and painted an apocalyptic picture of the stakes involved. As Dulles said, "if Israel should not withdraw there would be increased guerrilla warfare, stoppage of oil supplies, and growth of Russian influence."[60] The strong murmurings indicated that the administration's imposition of economic penalties against Israel would not go unchallenged; as Dulles told Henry Cabot Lodge, the U.S. ambassador to the United Nations, on February 12, "we were going to be in very serious trouble and indeed may lose our authority to impose sanctions."[61] Not surprisingly the administration decided to appeal to the public; the next evening the President addressed the nation to announce the threat of sanctions against Israel.

Still the Israeli government resisted. What tipped the balance was a French proposal made during the visit to Washington of Mollet and Pineau in late February: the French government agreed to deliver an aide-mémoire that would recognize Israel's right of self-defense in Gaza under specified conditions. France had thereby proposed a pledge that mirrored the American commitment vis-à-vis the Straits of Tiran. France was Israel's key arms supplier. Israel could not afford to alienate Paris and Washington simultaneously, particularly as France was now secretly beginning to supply Israel with nuclear technology. Once Mollet and Pineau had put the French idea on the table and the American government had accepted it, Ben-Gurion and his colleagues had no choice but to swallow the compromise and agree to withdraw all Israeli forces from Egyptian territory.[62]

The geopolitical consequences of the Suez crisis make this event a turning point in postwar history. British hegemony in the Middle East dissolved. Eden returned from Jamaica on December 14 and resigned from office on January 9, 1957. Macmillan, his successor, understood that British power derived from American support. Macmillan consequently moved very quickly to restore ruptured relations with the Eisenhower administration. During his close to seven years as prime minister, Macmillan assiduously consulted the American government and followed the American lead whenever necessary.

French leaders gleaned a different lesson from the Suez crisis. The American decision to force British and French troops out of Egypt confirmed French suspicions that the United States was not to be trusted. As a result Charles de Gaulle, who became president of the newly established Fifth French Republic in 1958, enjoyed widespread support for his decision to build an independent nuclear deterrent, the *force de frappe*, and ultimately withdraw from NATO's integrated military structure.

Egypt and Israel were the big winners in the Suez crisis. Although his forces met defeat in the field, the evacuation of British and French troops garnered Nasser enormous prestige in the Arab world. Overnight Nasser and Nasserism, a philosophy that appealed to Arab nationalism and unity, became the most potent force in the region.[63] And Israel's swift victories overturned the general assumption that the Jewish state's victory in the War of Independence was a fluke. Ben-Gurion's withdrawal from occupied territory nurtured an American sense of responsibility for Israel that steadily grew.

With its decision to intervene against its traditional allies and the creation of the Eisenhower Doctrine, the President and his officials embarked on a new path in the Middle East. No longer would the United States be content to follow the British lead. Instead the United States would control Western policy in the region. The results of the new look in the Middle East were seen in the President's decision to land army troops in Lebanon two years later during a period of regional turmoil—the only use of American troops in a combat situation during the Eisenhower presidency. Eisenhower ordered the American mission because he believed that in the wake of the 1958 revolution in Iraq, Western troops must support sympathetic regimes. This time the venture was Washington-born and -bred: when the crisis came, the United States could only do what the British had done.[64]

The case of sanctions and weapons sales to Egypt resembles the U.S. experience with the Soviet Union. Just as neither American economic carrots nor financial sticks bought diplomatic victories from Moscow, it seems obvious that any economic bonuses that Washington could offer Nasser would not have affected his policy. Economic diplomacy always works best when aimed toward economic rather than political or strategic goals. When attempted in the latter spheres, it is most effective if the target country's actions are minor matters. Obtaining arms was central to Nasser. He was not about to renounce his deal with the Soviets. The canal was almost as important to him. Sanctions would never have convinced him to renounce control.

Negative economic diplomacy never had a better set of litmus tests than those provided by the Suez crisis. Though they never seemed to learn the lesson, Western powers needed to ask three questions about sanctions: to what extent does the target country need the embargoed item? are there alternative sources? how important is the disputed action to the target country? If the challenged action is vital, economic sanctions, far from stopping the action, may have the opposite effect—engendering increased support for the target country's leadership.

Economic sanctions succeeded brilliantly during the Suez crisis—against Britain. London's British foreign policy perched on an inadequate economic base. As a result the British government teetered on the edge of a precipice. What was not comprehensible was the blithe British assumption that Eisenhower and Dulles and their colleagues would rescue Britain come what may. Financial crises had been gripping Britain virtually on a biannual basis since the end of World War II. It was obvious that any international confrontation over the Suez Canal would have led to financial strains for Britain. The United States provided the only source for British financial support. The lion's share of world capital markets was now in the United States. The U.S. government funded and controlled the World Bank and dominated the IMF. Communist sources were obviously unavailable. Yet the British government went ahead and launched a military invasion without attempting to ensure that American financial assistance for the pound would be forthcoming.

British writers then and since have alleged that the U.S. government dumped sterling in the millions. Such a step neither occurred nor was necessary. American passivity ensured British submission. In its decision to acquiesce, the British government, not for the first time nor for the last, put economic aspects of foreign policy ahead of other considerations. Britain, in other words, was a perfect target, susceptible to economic sanctions that always work best when levied by an ally. Its foreign and financial policy dictated that large reserves were absolutely necessary. No alternative sources of financial support existed. If the target country is a democracy, the need will always be greater because public opinion has to be taken into account. Finally, the Suez invasion, in the end, was not worth the candle to Britain. The cabinet ultimately decided against jettisoning a central tenet of British foreign policy to continue an ill-planned invasion of a country in support of a canal license that had only twelve years to run.

Egypt proved totally immune from American financial coercion. In 1956 it had a subsistence economy with little need for foreign reserves. It also possessed an alternative source of supply. The Soviet Union promised aid for the Aswan High Dam while the People's Republic of China actually sold sterling to provide funds for Egypt.[65] By nationalizing the canal Nasser also rallied all segments of Egpytian society behind him. In this case the target country's commitment to the questioned action could not have been higher. Economic hardship, to the limited extent it existed, only served to increase Nasser's popularity.

The degree of Israeli commitment to retaining the Egyptian land it had captured determined the Ben-Gurion government's decision to withdraw from the Straits of Tiran and the Gaza strip. Having won international protection in both areas, Israel had to weigh a partial loaf against the total enmity of the United States and rejection by France. The price was too high. As Dulles said to Lodge, Israeli officials "do not want to antagonize the Eisenhower Administration for four years. That is more important than any sanctions."[66]

Economic sanctions, however, have certain irresistible advantages that lead governments to use them irrespective of the effect they might have. One of the reasons that the Eisenhower administration embraced sanctions was that they required no congressional approval. Indeed, sanctions had long been the most executive of diplomatic courses. The freezing of assets fell under the 1917 Trading with the Enemy Act, which required only a presidential declaration of a national emergency for the President to possess full powers to impose such a step. As the national emergency declared in connection with the Korean War in 1950 had not been revoked, the Treasury was able to issue appropriate regulations. Economic sanctions were also attractive to the Eisenhower administration because in the 1950s they could be imposed with very little cost to the United States. In the case of Egypt sanctions also provided an easy way for the administration to demonstrate U.S. support to Britain and France without seriously harming Egypt or risking American interests abroad. Sanctions can "work" in many ways. Sometimes the government's real target is domestic public opinion. Other times foreign opinion, both governmental or general, is the target. In such cases sanctions can provide a useful tool. This is rarely publicly acknowledged by a government and is for that reason easily confused with the ostensible reason for the sanctions—to force a foreign country to change its objectionable ways. Unfortunately for Eisenhower's successors, the sui generis effect of American economic diplomacy on Britain presented a misleading example. Sanctions appeared to offer all the benefits of military action with none of the disadvantages. The price for this misinterpretation would be paid many times over.

6

The Sixties

On October 4, 1957, the Soviet Union shattered American self-confidence when it launched Sputnik, the first orbiting satellite.[1] Short of actually attacking the United States, there could hardly have been a more frightening revelation. True, the development of the long-range bomber in 1944 had already ended American invulnerability to air attack. But it was one thing to know that the United States was theoretically vulnerable; another to realize that every hour and a half a Soviet satellite passed over the United States beeping ominously. *Life* magazine, still the best barometer of American concerns, published an article entitled "Arguing the Case for Being Panicky." As Cyrus Vance later recalled, "throughout the country there was a feeling of a Communist threat with military overtones."[2] Americans questioned their achievements, their educational system, and their values.

In September 1959, when Soviet Premier Nikita Khrushchev visited the United States, President Dwight Eisenhower tried to even the score by taking the Soviet leader on a helicopter ride over suburban America, highlighting the extensive single-family houses and busy highways. But Khrushchev's present of a model of a missile called Lunik II, which had successfully traveled to the moon, at least momentarily overshad-owed suburbia. Although the United States clearly produced more consumer goods than the Soviet Union, its space program still lagged far behind the Soviet effort. Making matters worse, U.S. commentators began to bombard the media with predictions of a Soviet economy rapidly overtaking the United States. *Newsweek* warned its readers that the Soviet Union could be "on the high road to economic domination of the world." CIA chief Allen Dulles sounded the alarm in front of the Congressional Joint Economic Committee: "If the Soviet industrial growth rate persists at eight or nine percent per annum over the next decade, as is forecast, the gap between our two economies . . . will be dangerously narrowed."[3]

These predictions meant that the United States, with its annual growth rate hovering around 2.5 percent, could not even assume that its lead in domestic production would remain secure.[4] Maybe the Soviet Union, not the United States, would have the butter and the guns. As for the space race, the Soviet head start appeared practically insurmountable. John F. Kennedy exploited these fears in his 1960 pres-idential campaign. Throughout the race Kennedy lambasted Eisen-hower and his vice-president, now Republican presidential nominee, Richard Nixon, for spending too little money on defense, particularly harping on a supposed missile gap between the Soviet Union and the United States. At the same time Kennedy criticized Republican policies for failing to provide sufficient domestic economic growth.

During his administration Kennedy made international financial issues a higher priority than domestic economic initiatives. But Kennedy either would not or could not ignore the fact that the Ameri-can economy, as the hub of the Western international financial system, played a central international financial role as well as providing the basis for domestic American well-being. He succeeded in bolstering the position of the U.S. dollar and cutting the balance of payments deficit without sacrificing American control over the Western financial order. For one brief, shining moment, it seemed that the United States could have domestic prosperity while maintaining the integrity of the inter-national monetary system that it had created. Lyndon Johnson reversed the emphasis, putting foreign policy and foreign economic issues on the back burner and giving his attention to domestic political and economic concerns. In contrast to Kennedy, Johnson had little interest in foreign international financial questions. Johnson was cursed: he briefly saw the promised land of increased prosperity for all Americans but then had to watch the Vietnam War destroy much of what he had accomplished. After 1966, the accelerating American military commitment in Vietnam dictated a tax increase. But Johnson, loath to agree to the cuts in social spending that Congress demanded in exchange, postponed the inevitable. His failure to pay honestly for the war doomed the unprecedented American economic expansion of the mid-sixties to quick extinction.

Under the Bretton Woods system Washington backed the U.S. dollar with a commitment to sell gold at $35 per ounce to foreign governments. Equally important, the United States could not run a balance of payments deficit. The balance of payments reflects the difference between what a nation spends abroad and what it receives from other countries. This calculation includes government expenditures such as the cost of stationing NATO forces in Europe or foreign aid. When an American company set up a plant abroad, it damaged the balance of payments, as did the increasing numbers of American tourists flocking to Europe in the sixties. If a nation runs a large balance of payments deficit, other governments and private investors alike will lose faith in its currency. For any nation the consequences—the raising of interest rates (to attract investment that is fleeing) or devaluation—were serious. Because the dollar was at the center of the Bretton Woods system, a persistent American balance of payments deficit could spell disaster for America and its allies. Being the system's guarantor carried a large burden.

Foreign central banks—the banks for governments—now held growing amounts of American dollars that had flowed abroad from the United States. Besides holding dollars for themselves as reserves for their currencies, these central banks received dollars through foreign commercial transactions. When a U.S. company bought products abroad, it gave dollars to the foreign seller, who exchanged the dollars for local currency at the bank. The seller's bank then forwarded the dollars to its government. This process worked on a much larger scale when major transactions occurred: with dollars now the official currency of exchange, it was not surprising everyone abroad wanted them.

But foreign central banks and governments were entitled to exchange their holdings of dollars for gold held by the United States.

American gold stocks, which had held stable from 1945 to 1957, steadily declined thereafter. At the same time, the gap between American dollars in circulation and American reserves (the total of non-gold reserves and gold stocks) increased consistently through the period. After 1950 the U.S. balance of payments showed a deficit every year but one.[5] So just when Eisenhower and Kennedy were fearing a growing Soviet economy, the West seemed to be draining America's riches. But was it really? Following the intricacies of Bretton Woods, which is a bit like following a shell game between dollars and gold, suggests that America was always in a stronger position than it feared (just as the Soviets were weaker than Americans dreaded).

Although inaugurated in 1946, the Bretton Woods system never properly functioned until 1958. Immediately it showed signs of disintegration. For the first time since 1939 most European countries liberalized foreign exchange payments. Holders now had the option to convert one currency into another.[6] This development, necessary for the growth of world trade, had been envisioned as an immediate postwar reality, but the dislocations of World War II led to its postponement for over a decade. Once it occurred, Western European convertibility exacerbated the growing American balance of payments problem. In turn, the interconnected workings of the Bretton Woods structure ensured that Washington's financial problems would spill back to Western Europe. The dollar stood at the center of the world financial system, just as NATO put the United States military commitment to defend its allies at the center of Western security policy. The two obligations went hand and hand: what the United States was defending was the free market regime in the capitalist world.

The United States government guaranteed the gold price of its dollars. Each country within the system maintained a fixed value for its currency in relation to gold and therefore to the dollar ("par value"). Par values theoretically reflected the strength of the issuing country's economy and were supposed to reflect evenly purchasing power among nations ("purchasing power parity"). In other words, translated in terms of dollars or gold, the same item should cost the same amount in each country within the Bretton Woods system. However, governments did not set par values in a vacuum. Rather, a host of external influences helped determine monetary and fiscal policy. Some governments viewed a high par value as a matter of prestige. In particular, British officials associated a strong (expensive) currency with power in international affairs. A currency with a high par value also made purchasing imports easier. On the other hand, a strong currency made exports expensive, which led countries dependent on exports such as West Germany and Japan to embrace low par values. Their policy also curbed imports and dampened consumer consumption.

Dollars and gold served two functions: they guaranteed the integrity of the system but also provided a measuring stick for the value of each currency. Basing the Bretton Woods system on dollars caused the U.S. government to assume certain obligations. One was to maintain sufficient stocks of gold. Washington also had to keep the purchasing power of the dollar at $35/ounce. American inflation could threaten this promise: if the U.S. cost of living rose, dollars would be worth less at home than abroad. Americans would then purchase more exports, sending U.S. inflation through the system, affecting all its member countries. Increased American demand, coming at a time of European prosperity, would cause price rises in European countries, exacerbating European inflation.

Every system has built-in flaws, some worse than others. The great defect in the Bretton Woods system of the 1950s and 1960s came to be known as the Triffin Dilemma, after the Yale economist Robert Triffin: the world needed the United States to issue more dollars to foster growth. But an increase in dollars in circulation with no change in American productivity and gold reserves would both foster inflation and also undermine international faith in the dollar, which was the linchpin of the Bretton Woods system.[7] Everyone wanted dollars; but if they got them, the price of gold wouldn't hold. Here was the making of a shell game.

As soon as European convertibility resumed at the end of 1958, foreigners holding other currencies converted them into dollars. The dollars flowed to European central banks, which exchanged them for American gold, costing the United States $2.3 billion in gold reserves. It became clear the next year that this disturbing phenomenon was not a fluke when foreign governments on their own behalf and on behalf of their citizens drew a further $1 billion in gold.[8] Although the U.S. current account balance of payments improved, a deterioration in capital accounts continued. In 1960 private capital expenditure reached $3.5 billion. American companies, taking advantage of Marshall Plan–era tax incentives and lower foreign costs, were expanding overseas at an unprecedented rate.[9]

During the 1960 campaign, candidate Kennedy's comments about the need to increase both government spending and economic growth led to doubts about his commitment to "sound money." Suddenly the price of gold on the London market for private exchange leapt to an unprecedented $40 per ounce. In response, Kennedy publicly pledged that "if elected President I shall not devalue the dollar from the present rate. Rather I shall defend the present value and its soundness." What skeptics did not realize was that Kennedy had literally at his father's knee imbibed his belief in the evils of devaluation and the importance of the continued link between the dollar and gold at the present rate of $35 per ounce. Joseph Kennedy might have been a stock market speculator but he was a firm believer in traditional principles of conservative monetary finance.[10] Moreover, Kennedy believed that American financial leadership was a prerequisite for continued American global hegemony.

John Kennedy proved to have a strong personal commitment to the workings of the international financial system. But he was not blind to American domestic needs.[11] Indeed, it was the perceived stagnation of the American economy at the end of the Eisenhower years together with the recession of 1957 and the mini-slump of 1960 that partly sparked Kennedy's "we must get America moving again" campaign theme. Once in office he appointed Walter Heller, Kermit Gordon, and James Tobin to the Council of Economic Advisors (CEA). These economists had more influence on the American economy than anyone trained in that profession had ever previously enjoyed. While Treasury Secretary C. Douglas Dillon and Undersecretary of the Treasury Robert Roosa counseled balanced domestic budgets and a strong dollar, the CEA members took a very different approach. They read John Maynard Keynes to say that creating a small federal deficit by cutting taxes would substitute for lagging private investment and restore growth in the economy as a whole. This growth then would stimulate private investment, which would increase tax revenues. The happy result of increased revenues even with lower rates would cure the budget deficit within several years. It would also reduce unemployment, at a postwar high of almost 7 percent in 1962.[12] Here, in Keynesian guise, were the first supply-siders, who argued that tax cuts could pay for themselves by spurring growth.

Kennedy, for all his surface erudition, did not understand economics. He once told a friend that he remembered what monetary policy was only by recalling that the head of the Federal Reserve Board, William McChesney Martin, had a last name that also started with "m."[13] The President had begun his term by promising to balance the fiscal 1962 budget. Heller and company were dismayed; they felt that only a tax cut with its resulting purchasing power injection would reduce unemployment to 4 percent. While the President insisted that a tax cut was politically unacceptable, the Berlin crisis of 1961 accomplished the same fiscal stimulus that the economists had sought (at least the Keynesian part, if not the supply-side tax cut part). The additional military expenditures necessitated by the apparently heightened Soviet threat to West Germany, manifested by the building of the Berlin Wall in August 1961, led to increased defense expenditures. As a result the deficit for fiscal 1962 (July 1, 1961–June 30, 1962) was $6.5 billion, a long way toward the $10 million deficit that the CEA had sought.

In April 1962 the national contract between the huge steel companies and the United Steel Workers of America (USW) was up for renewal. Inflation concerned the CEA, which had set guidelines of 3 percent—the annual increase in productivity—for wage raises. Because steel was so important to the manufacturing sector of the economy, Heller informed the President that a steel contract settlement in excess of the guidelines could "upset the apple cart all by itself." Secretary of Labor Arthur Goldberg, a former lawyer for the USW, pressured the union to accept a settlement within the guidelines. The USW agreed and the administration assumed that the steel companies would keep their end of the unspoken bargain by holding their prices stable. But on April 10, Roger Blough, the president of U.S. Steel, announced an average price rise of 3.5 percent per ton. Other big steel companies immediately followed suit.

Kennedy was furious at the arrogance of the steel magnates and took their action as a personal betrayal. His private view, which soon became public (and long rankled businessmen), was, "My father always told me that all businessmen were sons-of-bitches but I never believed it till now." Accepting an inflationary increase would hurt both the domestic economy and the balance of payments. The President mustered all the weapons at his disposal. In a televised press conference he scolded the steel executives: "The American people will find it hard as I do, to accept a situation in which a tiny handful of steel executives whose pursuit of private power and profit exceeds their sense of public responsibility can show such utter contempt for the interests of 185 million Americans."[14] The administration and Congress launched investigations into price fixing and announced that the Pentagon would not purchase steel from companies that had raised prices. In the meantime White House officials urged smaller companies to refrain from increasing prices. Once Inland Steel agreed to exercise restraint, its Chicago competitor, Bethlehem Steel, rescinded its increase. By the night of April 13 U.S. Steel caved in.

Declaring war on the steel industry alienated businessmen; within weeks they had something more personal to blame the President for. A stock market panic on May 28, 1962, began a monthlong downward spiral that left the value of the stocks listed on the New York Stock Exchange 27 percent lower than they had been in December. Kennedy did his best to restore business confidence but concluded that nothing he could do would satisfy Wall Street. As he told Arthur Schlesinger and Ted Sorenson in early June, "I understand better every day why Roosevelt, who started out such a mild fellow, ended up so ferociously anti-business." Business antagonism simplified the task of Heller and the other CEA members, who were intent on eroding Kennedy's inbred financial conservatism. Slowly the President became comfortable with expansionist ideas.

Kennedy's resulting conversion to Keynesianism was apparent at his commencement address at Yale University on June 11. The President urged Yale's Elis to "move on from the reassuring repetition of stale phrases to a new, difficult but essential confrontation with reality." He attempted to expose the myth that the deficit was rapidly increasing, pointing out that it had declined since the war, both per person and as a percentage of gross national product. The recessions of 1952, 1954, 1958, and 1960 meant that the government must devote itself to "the practical management of a modern economy." The President reiterated the American postwar bargain: that the American middle and lower classes would not demand the cradle-to-grave economic security that democratic socialist governments had installed in Europe in the past fifteen years. Instead, if they would accept lower taxes and upward mobility, they could rely on the most unfettered capitalist system in the world to provide them with lives far better than their parents had enjoyed. So he proposed a tax cut. As for the system's glitches, the frequent recessions and high unemployment showed only that the managerial and governing classes had not kept their part of the bargain. The tax cut would rectify this failure not by changing the system but by making it work as intended.

In August Kennedy advertised his new economic ideas on television, announcing that he would ask Congress for comprehensive tax-cutting legislation in January 1963. In October 1962 Congress passed legislation permitting faster depreciation and other corporate tax benefits. Much to the President's surprise the business community leadership embraced his proposals. Ironically the stiffest opposition to the tax cut legislation came from two economists in Kennedy's circle: CEA member James Tobin and American Ambassador to India and noted economist John Kenneth Galbraith. Galbraith explained why the socialist Michael Harrington had attacked the tax cut as "reactionary Keynesianism": the taxpayer dollars would go for consumer fripperies rather than public works or investment that would benefit society as a whole. Galbraith, a skeptic when it came to the market's wisdom, believed that the government, through large-scale public works and investment projects, could invest the tax cut billions far more efficiently than the private sector.

But Kennedy remained a man of old-fashioned economic principles. Using fiscal policy to spur investment but leaving choices to the private sector was far more conservative than opting for increased government investment. The President's legislation, introduced in the new year, sought a personal tax cut that reduced rates by an average of 23 percent and a reduction of business taxes from 52 percent to 47 percent. In total his proposals would have cut $10 billion from personal taxes and $2.5 billion from corporate levies.[15] This would have been the most dramatic tax cut in American history. Business support remained enthusiastic, with key players such as Henry Ford II and executives of Standard Oil, American Can, and Con Edison joining together to form the Business Committee for Tax Reduction in 1963. But the bill became locked up in committee, where it remained at Kennedy's death on November 22, 1963.[16]

Before moving from Kennedy to Johnson we should look at Kennedy's Keynesian conversion and its relationship to his military and diplomatic views. The Cold War stood at the center of the new President's concerns. The widespread perception that the United States was lagging behind the Soviet Union prompted an aggressive administration defense posture exemplified by Kennedy's inaugural promise "to pay any price, bear any burden" in defense of freedom. As an issue, the missile gap evaporated once the President realized that the Soviet Union, not the United States, had the fewer missiles, yet American defense commitments drained an average of 9 percent of GNP during the years 1961–63.[17]

Kennedy's financial policy also began abroad. The price of gold and the stability of the financial system always remained one of Kennedy's two most important priorities throughout his tenure in office.[18] Selecting the investment banker C. Douglas Dillon, an undersecretary of state in the Eisenhower administration, as secretary of the Treasury further ensured a conservative foreign economic policy. Reducing the American balance of payments deficit and guarding the gold price and "soundness" of the dollar became pillars of American economic policy, foreign and domestic.

Dillon and Undersecretary of the Treasury for Monetary Affairs Robert Roosa crafted the American approach to the balance of payments problem. They cobbled together several safety nets that protected the international monetary system while leaving American control over the international monetary system intact. First was the Gold Pool, which cut by 50 percent the American responsibility to provide gold to the private market. The central banks of Belgium, France, Italy, the Netherlands, West Germany, and the United Kingdom together assumed the obligation to supply half of the demand in the London private market for gold, with the United States supplying the other half.[19] The U.S. government also began to borrow from foreign governments in their currency, promising to repay the loans in their currency. As a result holders of these so-called Roosa Bonds would not be hurt should the United States devalue the dollar. Equally important was the creation of a $6 billion line of credit, known as the General Arrangements to Borrow (GAB), which would be available to back up the IMF if its funds were insufficient to support one of the participants' currencies. In exchange for this commitment participants, including the United States, Canada, Britain, West Germany, France, Italy, Belgium, the Netherlands, Sweden, and Japan, received greater protection during financial crises.[20] The GAB members then formed the Group of Ten committee, which provided a forum for discussions of the future of the international monetary system.[21] They were also the leading members of the Organization for Economic Cooperation and Development (OECD), which in 1961 succeeded the old OEEC.

Kennedy's concentration on the U.S. balance of payments position also led to several programs designed to limit the outflow of American dollars. Under the aegis of the Cabinet Committee on the Balance of Payments, headed by Dillon, increasingly large amounts of American foreign aid were "tied" to purchases made in the United States. The Defense Department sought to buy as many military supplies as possible in the United States and cut the duty-free allowance for returning servicemen. It also increased the pressure on U.S. allies to aid the American bottom line. As the French and West Germans had large balance of payments surpluses, American officials thought they particularly should contribute to bolstering the international financial system and to the cost of both foreign aid and keeping American servicemen in Europe.[22]

Western European nations eventually accepted the need for Bretton Woods Band-Aids. But during 1961, they attempted to use the American desire for financial palliatives to force the United States to deal with its current accounts deficit. Ultimately, Washington's power and influence enabled it to bulldoze away allied objections and ideas. The willingness of foreign central banks to subscribe to borrowing agreements, to agree to swaps, and to buy Roosa Bonds accomplished one large objective: interlocking loan agreements now largely substituted for gold settlements.[23]

Why did the Europeans go along? Why did they get entangled in what were essentially American problems? The accommodation did not primarily derive from charity. Europeans, enjoying growth rates far higher than those of the United States, feared the possibility of a rapid end to U.S. balance of payments deficits because of the shock waves it would send through their own economies. They also remained shy of giving their currencies reserve status. Every system needs a large anchor, but no other country wanted that role. On a large scale, then, the Bretton Woods deals of the 1960s were just like local buying and selling—each side got what it needed from the transaction.

The U.S. balance of payments accounts improved impressively during 1962. Congress passed the Trade Expansion Act (TEA) of 1962, which granted the President authority to reduce tariffs by up to 50 percent on most goods and up to 100 percent on certain selected items under the aegis of the General Agreement on Tariffs and Trade (GATT).[24] The ideological roots of this measure, labeled by one historian "one of the greatest legislative accomplishments of Kennedy's presidency," lay in the long-held Democratic belief that tariff barriers were bad for both economic and foreign policy reasons.[25] Previously political concerns outweighed economic incentives, but now the recovery of Western Europe, the growth of the Common Market, and the problematic U.S. balance of payments position combined to elevate economic considerations in the calculus of American interests.[26] The TEA embodied the postwar consensus: a combination of free and fair trade would keep American consumer prices low and increase exports at the cost of limited damage to American manufacturers.[27]

Because administration officials remained apprehensive about the state of the international payments system, they debated taking preventive measures during this calm period in order to stave off another crisis in the future. A package of proposals known as the "interim international monetary arrangements" emerged in August 1962. The purpose of these plans, as Joseph Coppock, the director of the State Department's Foreign Economic Advisory Staff, summarized it, was to permit "the U.S. Government [to] be able to engage in expansionary policies without having to be concerned with the outflow of gold, with all of its psychological ramifications." Triffin's Dilemma loomed large. Moreover, as Heller advised Kennedy, "the confidence game is one you can't win." The CEA chief told the President that "your intervention with Roger Blough and the decline in the stock market were interpreted in some circles as bad for the dollar; but a steel price increase and a stock market boom would also have been regarded as unfavorable signals." Heller's conclusion: domestic economic priorities should trump foreign considerations every time.

Coppock, together with men such as the White House staffer Carl Kaysen, Budget Director Kermit Gordon and John Kenneth Galbraith, debated the idea of a unilateral Treasury announcement, without prior notification to U.S. allies, that the Treasury would no longer pay gold to foreign governments on demand. Another plank called for foreign governments to agree to a "standstill," which would make a very large percentage of their dollars no longer convertible. The advantages of either plan were obvious. Coppock, for one, thought the administration could sell this plan to U.S. allies by explaining that an ailing American domestic economy would both "weaken our political and psychological position vis-à-vis the Communists [and] lessen our economic capacity to support our military establishment." But the price of such freedom came too high: jettisoning the U.S. commitment to sell gold on demand at $35 per ounce to foreign governments would violate an ongoing American pledge to the IMF as well as Kennedy's repeated public promises. To men like Dillon, Roosa, and Federal Reserve Board Chairman William McChesney Martin, the interim arrangements were unthinkable.

Kennedy did authorize officials in late August to sound out French and other allied officials about "a more explicit understanding among the major European countries and ourselves on international monetary matters." The purpose of making an arrangement would be "to strengthen confidence in the dollar, limit unnecessary foreign takings of U.S. gold and strengthen the system of international monetary cooperation." But unlike administration suggestions, any interim arrangement proposed to the Europeans "should be a voluntary one undertaken on European initiative."[28]

In January 1963 Kaysen informed National Security Advisor McGeorge Bundy, "it is most unlikely that we can achieve the goal of balance in our international actions by the end of 1963. In fact, 1965 looks like the earliest realistic target year, and that may be optimistic." In February the President discussed balance of payments issues with former Secretary of State Dean Acheson, who advocated that the

United States stabilize its international accounts by borrowing $10 billion abroad, primarily in France or Germany. The next month Kennedy instructed the Cabinet Committee on the Balance of Payments to survey which foreign aid and defense programs significantly affected the balance of payments, to consider how to use tax policy to stimulate exports, and to calculate the financing of the U.S. payments deficit abroad.[29]

Various officials rehashed their solutions. Tobin, for his part, enthused about devaluing the dollar: "neither God nor the Constitution set the value of the dollar in gold or other currencies, and the world would not come to an end if it were changed." Galbraith took a different tack, proposing to slice American overseas commitments (military and civilian), end tariff negotiations, and implement capital controls blocking long-term American investment abroad for a period of six to nine months. This drastic medicine was necessary, thought Galbraith, to counteract the past habit of erring through optimism and the "desire to contract out of difficult action." While Galbraith cheerfully understood that the person who "commented responsibly" on the balance of payments problem "is a figure for popular execution," he feared that the consequence of inaction would be worse.[30]

As the *New York Times* pointed out in September, with an election around the corner Kennedy feared the political repercussions from failing to live up to his repeated pledges to cure the balance of payments problem.[31] Kennedy responded by delivering to Congress a new balance of payments message while simultaneously urging passage of his tax cut measure, which administration economists suggested would stimulate the economy, thereby attracting foreign investments. Kennedy's program included a $1 billion reduction in American dollar expenditure abroad, a $500 million IMF standby arrangement, and the imposition of an interest equalization tax (IET) designed to increase the cost to foreigners of borrowing in the United States by about 1 percent. The Federal Reserve Bank, hoping to attract foreign capital, immediately raised U.S. interest rates.[32] So at the end of his life, Kennedy still struggled with the obligations of financial world leadership. He had become a Keynesian who wanted tax cuts and was willing to accept deficits, but he continued to fret about the balance of payments. Shortly before he died Kennedy appeared to be reexamining his views about the importance of the dollar. But just as he would not have had the courage to exit from Vietnam, Kennedy could not have bucked his father's conventional wisdom that made a strong dollar the central financial god.

The heart of Lyndon Baines Johnson, President after November 22, 1963, lay in domestic policy, particularly the Great Society social programs that he initiated beginning in 1964. Johnson's tragedy and that of the country was that the Vietnam War increasingly swallowed up his presidency. Johnson, who had grown up poor in the impoverished South, was a child of Franklin Roosevelt's New Deal. As Johnson wrote in his memoirs, "My entire life, from boyhood on, had helped me recognize the work that needed to be done in America. My view of leadership had always been an activist one."[33] Johnson was one of the most skilled politicians of his generation. Now fate had given him his chance.

Johnson made Kennedy-era dreams reality. Combining his political ability with the opportunity for legislative accomplishment sparked by Kennedy's death, Johnson achieved passage of the giant tax cut in February 1964. He had compromised little. The final legislation reduced personal rates by an average of 21 percent over two years and clipped corporate levies down to 48 percent.[34] By slashing the federal budget to just under $100 billion he also robbed Republicans of the "sound economy" issue. In the short term Heller's optimistic predictions proved accurate. By September 1965 the tax cut had generated a $25 billion increase in gross national product and pushed the federal budget again into surplus. Unemployment fell to the historic low of 4.5 percent and kept falling. Moreover, at the end of fiscal 1965 the American economy had achieved an annual growth rate of 5.3 percent, as opposed to the average of 2.5 percent during the Eisenhower years.[35] The government-induced policy of wage-price moderation kept inflation in check as well—the rise in consumer prices for the years 1960–65 averaged 1.3 percent per year.[36] These were the great years of American prosperity. Moreover, the economic statistics for 1964 followed exactly the predictions made by the CEA. The prestige of the economics profession had never been higher.[37]

There was one hidden problem, however. Although it went unnoticed at the time, the 1960s would mark the end of a steady twenty-five-year period of working- and middle-class gains. American resources combined with war-driven (both World War II and Cold War) needs engineered rising prosperity for almost all sectors of society. During the period 1945–70 income distribution remained stable, with all classes sharing in the steady growth in American GNP. In fact the largest relative gains went to the working and poorer classes. Job security was an accepted fact.[38] Highly skilled manufacturing workers in heavy industry were able to buy their own houses and have two cars in their garages. Their children went to college. And then, just when these students of the sixties began to question the premises of the affluent society, its economic basis began to erode.

While Johnson was never willing to ask Congress for a declaration of war in Vietnam, in his first State of the Union address he declared "an unconditional war on poverty." Buoyed a year later by his landslide victory, during the 1965–66 session Johnson convinced Congress to pass legislation creating Medicare, multilevel federal aid to education, a model cities program, Operation Headstart, rent supplements, federal aid to mass transit, and a new housing act, not to mention the 1965 Voting Rights Act.[39] Families living in poverty declined from forty million in 1959 to twenty-five million in 1968. Black family income particularly increased.[40] Unfortunately 1965 also marked the beginning of an onslaught of Vietnam-related expenditures. While in fiscal year 1965 (July 1, 1964–June 30, 1965), fighting in Southeast Asia cost $100 million, just before that year ended, in May, Vietnam necessitated another $700 million. The President's August 1965 and January 1966 requests for Vietnam-related spending totaled $14 billion. Prudent economics dictated that Johnson seek a tax increase from Congress. Such an increase would not have overburdened American taxpayers—by 1966 the average of state and local taxation in the United States stood at 28 percent as compared with an average of 33.5 percent in Britain, West Germany, Italy, and France. But afraid of the domestic cuts enemies would attempt to extract and fearful of the public reaction at sacrificing for a war whose popularity was steadily declining, Johnson could not bring himself to ask for a tax increase until January 1967. Then he requested a 6 percent income tax surcharge but quickly withdrew the request when the economy appeared to slow down.[41]

The domestic economic costs of the Vietnam War were paid in the coin of inflation. While CEA members had feared that 1965 might bring an economic slowdown necessitating another tax cut, by December 1965 it became clear that the economy was dangerously close to "full employment." Once unemployment drops below 4 percent, too many employers chase too few workers. In order to capture them, managers bid up wages, then raise prices, unleashing inflation. A wage-price spiral begins as workers, faced with a higher cost of living, demand wage rises. By 1966 inflation, although only at 3.4 percent, already frightened Americans enough that they ranked it third among the nation's problems, behind only the Vietnam War and race relations.[42]

The CEA thought a tax increase might be needed in 1966. As it turned out, a previously scheduled rise in Social Security taxes combined with a credit crunch (an increase in interest rates mandated by the Federal Reserve Board) caused the economy to slow down. Inflation rose only 2.7 percent, not the predicted 4 percent. The first half of 1967 even saw a mini-recession. Having been wrong about every economic prediction during the past two years, the CEA was unprepared for the rapid economic reheating that began in July 1967. One month later Johnson sent to Congress a special message predicting that the Vietnam-induced deficit could start a "spiral of ruinous inflation" and asking for a temporary 10 percent income tax surcharge. In so doing he was following Keynesian economic advice: tax cuts were for a slow economy what a tax increase was to a rapidly overheating one. Unfortunately Wilbur Mills, the chairman of the House Ways and Means Committee, intended to exact a quid pro quo—no tax increase without significant cuts in domestic spending. Mills's committee voted on October 3 to put the tax bill aside until the administration proposed acceptable spending cuts. The administration could not budge him although in the fiscal years 1967 to 1968 American GNP devoted to military spending jumped from 7.9 percent to 9 percent.[43] As a result, the federal budget went into deficit.

The upshot: a brief Golden Age was wrecked by Vietnam and an overheated economy. Johnson was doubly obsessed by his troops in Southeast Asia and his economy at home. This double vision obscured the continuing problems of Triffin's Dilemma and the international exchanges. Eventually, the mutual problems of Vietnam guns and inflated butter would bring about the destruction of the original Bretton Woods order.

Johnson initially downgraded the priority of international economics. Gardner Ackley, the new chairman of the Council of Economic Advisors, wrote Johnson on December 10, 1964, that tax cuts and a "Great Society" budget would not hurt the gold system. "If jobs, income and profits keep moving up—and your well-established frugality image is maintained—such a deficit would *not* impair confidence [in the dollar both here and abroad]."[44] In February Johnson, reviewing the situation, told the cabinet that "I believe we can assure the people that no savings have been overlooked by the Federal Government."[45] With the administration equally determined to push forward on the so-called Kennedy Round of tariff reduction negotiations, the international economic skies seemed bright.

Yet doubts about the soundness of the Bretton Woods system persisted. In the summer of 1964, the Group of Ten issued a report on the international monetary system predicting that there would be a shortage of monetary reserves in the future, particularly if the United States balance of payments position strengthened.[46] The pace of gold production had not kept pace with public and private demand. The American pledge, made in 1964 to end U.S. payments deficits within the next five years, raised the urgency of the search for another mode of liquidity.[47] Washington provided a two-pronged response to external criticism. Johnson appointed a Foreign Economic Task Force in July 1964 while Secretary of the Treasury Dillon and other U.S. officials presided over a series of international conferences focusing on problems in the international financial system. To the disappointment of Dillon and CEA Chairman Walter Heller, the various meetings of the G-10 countries produced "more mouse than elephant."[48] The United States had pushed for a 50 percent increase in IMF member quotas—the annual subscriptions to the IMF that provided its working capital. French representatives adamantly resisted such a large increase.[49] The resulting 25 percent increase was a big setback.

In June 1965 President Johnson declared that it was necessary to "develop policies . . . with respect to the development of the international monetary and payments system and the role of the United States in the system." As a result Treasury Secretary Henry Fowler organized a special interdepartmental group in June 1965 to formulate American strategy, to be chaired by Frederick Deming, an undersecretary of the

Treasury for monetary affairs. Three months later the United States did an about-face and publicly supported the creation of a new reserve asset.[50] French President Charles de Gaulle had brought matters to a head in February 1965. Realizing that the United States would not cede dominance of the international payments system, he declared war against the gold exchange system. Other nations had to pay a price for payments deficits—if they lost reserves, the market would force them to raise interest rates, cut their deficits, obtain support credits, or devalue. De Gaulle resented the fact that no such constraints operated against the United States.[51]

Once Washington endorsed an altered reserve position, the French government did an about-face and balked at the idea. The French proposals had been at least partly designed to redistribute power in the international system and limit the freedom of the United States, as the reserve currency country, to print money with few international constraints. When the United States joined the reserve increase bandwagon, it did so on the condition that the distribution of new assets be made in the same ratio as IMF quotas. Such a calculation would allow the United States to maintain its dominance of the system. As de Gaulle pointed out: "what they [the United States] owe those countries they pay, at least in part, in dollars that they themselves can issue as they wish, instead of paying them totally in gold, which has a real value, and which one can possess only if one has earned it."

De Gaulle and French Minister of Finance and Economic Affairs Valéry Giscard d'Estaing instead advocated a true gold standard, which would make gold the only reserve against which currency could be issued. At the annual meetings of the Bretton Woods institutions in September 1965, Giscard chastised reserve currency countries (in other words, the United States and Great Britain) for their free ride on the backs of other OECD countries. Because of the trading and reserve position of dollars and sterling, these currencies stayed in demand notwithstanding the fiscal and monetary policies followed by Washington and London. In so doing, said the Frenchman, the United States, his main target, might "expose the world community which bears no responsibility therein, to a crisis which would be all the more serious as it would be sudden and unpredictable."[52]

The basic problem remained Europe's love-hate relationship with

American balance of payments deficits. European nations, particularly France, complained about American balance of payments deficits. They worried that the increasing amount of U.S. dollars in international circulation compared with American gold reserves would force the United States to end dollar convertibility. In such a case the billions of dollars in foreign government treasuries would drastically decline in value. At the same time, European officials could not push the United States too far. The easiest way for the United States to end its balance of payments deficits was to eliminate or significantly decrease the American defense commitment to Europe. Alternatively, the United States could jettison the Kennedy/Johnson push for greater free trade and erect tariff barriers that would keep more foreign goods out of the United States. Both these steps jeopardized Europe's interests at least as much as they threatened those of the United States.

Negotiations concerning the nature and definition of a new reserve asset continued through 1966 and into 1967. France continued to blame the United States for problems in the international monetary system and demanded that the United States ameliorate the gold shortage by increasing the price of gold. The Johnson administration firmly resisted this approach. Raising the price of gold entailed a devaluation of the dollar, and Washington refused to assume either the economic or the political consequences for such an act. No one in Washington wanted to grant the Soviet Union the windfall that a gold price increase would hand to the world's second-largest gold producer. That such a step necessitated congressional approval further increased its political unpopularity.

Not surprisingly then, it was not until September 1967 that the IMF members agreed on the outline of the plan that would generate Special Drawing Rights, or paper gold. The United States, with its gold supplies dwindling and its cupboard of quick fixes exhausted, pushed for the early creation of this new reserve asset, accepting several compromises designed to placate France. Instead of amounting to a new asset, the SDR's name indicated that it was more akin to a loan. "Not minted, not printed," SDRs existed only as computer entries.[53] The rules governing SDRs enabled the members of the European Community to block their usage if European nations voted as a group. Thirty percent of all SDR borrowings needed to be repaid by the country using them.

TABLE 6–1
OVERALL BALANCE OF PAYMENTS (U.S. $ BILLIONS)[a]

Year	U.S.	U.K.	France	Germany
1960	–3.4	–0.442	NA	2.25
1961	–1.35	0.109	NA	0.14
1962	–2.65	0.249	NA	–0.23
1963	–1.94	–0.372	NA	.72
1964	–1.53	–1.84	NA	0.22
1965	–1.29	–0.391	NA	–0.49
1966	0.24	–1.524	NA	0.61
1967	–3.38	–0.909	0.274	0
1968	1.67	–2.991	–3.632	1.81
1969	2.81	0.854	–1.038	–2.74
1970	–9.83	3.037	1.979	6.28
1971	–29.59	6.193	3.524	5.04

[a]Source: *International Financial Statistics*, series #7D8D (official settlements basis).
(Adapted from Volcker and Gyohten, p. 363.)

Originally it was thought that any new reserve asset had to be created against some real security but SDRs instead were to be issued only against the promise of IMF members to accept them. Each country received SDRs in proportion to its IMF quota, and, bowing to American desires, each SDR had a value in gold.[54] The complicated mechanics of changing the world's monetary order ensured that the first SDRs were not distributed until the beginning of 1970. By that time the fear that there was insufficient liquidity in the international system had been replaced by a growing belief that the outflow of American dollars abroad had created too much.[55]

The gold flow out of the United States continued. From reserves of $14.065 billion in 1965, American holdings of gold declined to $13.235 billion in 1966 and $12.065 billion at the end of 1967.[56] Washington tried to stem the tide by getting its allies to prepay debts owed to Uncle Sam and persuaded foreign officials to convert dollars into longer-term

TABLE 6–2
AMERICAN GOLD STOCKS (U.S. $ BILLIONS)[a]

Year	Gold
1957	22.857
1958	20.582
1959	19.507
1960	17.804
1961	16.947
1962	16.057
1963	15.596
1964	15.471
1965	14.065
1966	13.235
1967	12.065
1968	10.892
1969	11.859
1970	11.072
1971	10.206
1972	10.487
1973	11.652

[a]Source: IFS tape series #DIL, DIAN, D5 and D6.
(Adapted from Volcker and Gyohten, p. 366.)

dollar investments that did not count as part of the balance of payments deficit. In July 1965 the United States made its first borrowing from the International Monetary Fund.[57] For all the frequent American complaints about the burdens Bretton Woods entailed, Washington cheerfully took advantage of the benefits: its ability basically on demand to summon IMF monies to pay for the guns and butter of the 1960s.

The systemic Band-Aids developed in the early sixties did not prevent a crisis in March 1968. Accelerating American gold losses follow-

TABLE 6–3
U.S. FOREIGN ASSETS VS. LIABILITIES (U.S. $ BILLIONS)[a]

Year	Total Assets	External Liabilities	Balance
1960	24.6688	21.03	3.6388
1961	25.6029	22.93	2.6729
1962	24.5404	24.26	0.2894
1963	25.843	26.4	–0.557
1964	28.9124	29.35	–0.4376
1965	27.7	29.36	–1.86
1966	26.9117	31.02	–4.1083
1967	27.3602	35.66	–8.2998
1968	27.9899	38.47	–10.4801
1969	29.8936	45.9	–16.0064
1970	28.3569	46.95	–18.5931
1971	29.2546	67.8	–38.5454
1972	33.5803	82.87	–49.2897

[a]Source: IFS tape series #DIL, DIAN, D5 and D6.
(Adapted from Volcker and Gyohten, p. 366.)

ing Britain's sterling devaluation of November 1967 forced Washington to choose among various unattractive alternatives. Four options were debated: putting all American gold stocks on the line; shutting the "gold window" completely and ending American government sales of gold; establishing a more strictly controlled London private market for gold that the large countries would subsidize; and ending the Gold Pool and letting the market alone determine the price of gold for private transactions. Johnson administration officials chose the last option, which preserved the form of Bretton Woods while reducing American responsibility for the substance. Selecting this road required no congressional action and would draw less public attention than any of the other alternatives. What it did require was significant cooperation from Washington's allies. But American leverage over its allies made their

TABLE 6–4
U.S. FEDERAL BUDGET DEFICIT (U.S. $ BILLIONS)[a]

Year	Deficit
1965	–1.6
1966	–3.8
1967	–8.7
1968	–25.2

[a]Source: *Historical Abstract of the United States* (fiscal year).

agreement easier to obtain than congressional cooperation on tax legislation.

The administration had taken the least draconian of the options available to it. It had avoided the difficult domestic ramifications of raising the price of gold and devaluing the dollar, and it had rejected closing the gold window—in other words, renouncing the formal American obligation to buy and sell gold at $35 per ounce. Yet the chosen solution had further eaten away at the foundations of the Bretton Woods system. Washington's prior consultation with its allies limited some of the damage to the international system. Yet within the multilateral framework the administration had clearly taken a unilateral action that its allies could only swallow. For neither the first nor the last time, other members of the Western alliance showed themselves willing to accept American decisions—the price of rejecting them was too high.   Neither Kennedy nor Johnson was prepared to sacrifice either half of the equation. They were both dedicated anti-Communists. Kennedy saw the Cold War as the most important issue facing the United States. In the 1960s that meant equipping a military machine second to none, while appropriating significant sums for foreign assistance. Kennedy also counted maintaining the integrity of the dollar among his chief household gods. As his term progressed his commitment to stimulating the domestic economy steadily increased. But this was less of a change than it might appear. A strong domestic economy was necessary for its own sake but also to continue paying for anti-Communist guns and to prove to developing nations that the United

TABLE 6–5
NATIONAL DEFENSE OUTLAYS, 1960–94 (CONSTANT 1987 DOLLARS)[a]

Year	Defense Outlay as Percentage of Federal Outlay	Percentage of Gross Domestic Product
1960	52.2	9.5
1965	42.8	7.5
1966	43.2	7.9
1967	45.4	9.0
1968	46.0	9.7
1969	44.9	8.9
1970	41.8	8.3
1971	37.5	7.5
1972	34.3	6.9
1973	31.2	5.7
1974	29.5	5.7
1975	26.0	5.7
1976	24.1	5.3
1977	23.2	5.0
1978	23.8	5.1
1979	22.8	4.8
1980	22.7	5.1
1981	23.2	5.3
1982	24.9	5.9
1983	26.0	6.3
1984	26.7	6.2
1985	26.7	6.4
1986	27.6	6.5
1987	28.1	6.3
1988	27.3	6.0
1989	26.6	5.9
1990	23.9	5.5
1991	20.6	4.8
1992	21.6	5.0
1993	20.7	4.6
1994, est.	18.9	4.2

[a]*National Defense Outlays and Veterans Benefits: 1960–1994* (Washington, 1994), p. 352.

States had better economic answers than did the Soviet Union. In short, the domestic economy was as important to the battle for the hearts and minds of the third world as the Alliance for Progress.

Johnson viewed domestic issues as far more important than did Kennedy. The War on Poverty, not the Cold War, dominated his dreams. But trapped inside the containment consensus of his time, he could not escape the all-powerful ramifications of the bipolar confrontation. Not only was Johnson mired in Vietnam but the increasing deterioration in American financial accounts and its effect on the Bretton Woods system circumscribed both his domestic and foreign policy choices. Having it all became more expensive because in the sixties Americans and their elected leaders decided that they wanted more: more affluence, more government assistance (domestic and foreign), more defense. The wheels of the Bretton Woods car kept spinning faster and faster until Richard Nixon finally drove it off the road.

7

The Alliance for Progress

Latin America is the most critical area in the world.

John F. Kennedy, February 1963

Latin America was the site of the most dangerous superpower confrontation during the Cold War. The Soviet decision, publicly revealed in October 1962, to station nuclear missiles in Cuba, the island ninety-one miles away from the Florida coast, triggered an American ultimatum that brought the world to the edge of nuclear war. Since Fidel Castro assumed power in Cuba, the United States had followed a two-track policy toward Latin America. On the one hand, Washington attempted to remove Castro, who had evolved from a socialist when he took power into Moscow's most dedicated follower. On the other, the United States tried to woo the rest of Latin America into an anti-Communist and anti-Castro alliance. Economic diplomacy played a key role in both campaigns. The lessons of the Marshall Plan provided a model for the Western alliance: sanctions, despite their failure against Egypt, offered a cheap weapon against Castro. The Eisenhower and Kennedy administrations designed these policies to protect America's backyard. But Washington officials also believed that their initiatives would influence the legion of colonial states whose independence would change the face of the developing world. In sixties parlance, the contest was for the "hearts and minds" of the third world.

During the century after 1823 U.S. policy toward Latin America revolved around the Monroe Doctrine, which warned Europeans to stay out of hemispheric affairs and promised in return that the United States would not interfere in European matters. Theodore Roosevelt in 1904 proclaimed his own corollary: when "chronic wrongdoing in Latin America required outside intervention," the United States in the "exercise of an international police power" would prevent any outside power from interfering but would right the wrong itself. During the succeeding thirty years the United States intervened numerous times in Latin American affairs.

Teddy's relative Franklin D. Roosevelt proclaimed in 1933 a new deal for Latin America—the "good neighbor" policy. Admitting (at least by implication) that the United States had been a bad neighbor, this policy at its core recognized that no nation had the right to intervene in the internal affairs of another. U.S. troops would no longer appear in Latin American ports at any provocation. Yet the United States retained its traditional view that Latin America was Washington's special preserve.[1]

In 1947 the United States orchestrated the Rio Treaty, a regional security pact that bound the Latin and North American signatories to consider an armed attack by any country against an American state as an attack against all American states. The following year the American nations created the Organization of American States (OAS), a standing institution designed to handle inter-American issues. With most nations firmly under military or authoritarian control, little south of the border distracted the United States from more distant shores. As for the question of democracy, George Kennan best summed up the prevailing U.S. view during the beginning of the Cold War. A 1950 Latin American visit convinced him that in countries without vigorous indigenous local "concepts and traditions of popular government . . . harsh governmental measures of repression" might be the "only answer" to the Communist menace.[2] The great ideological conflicts of the twentieth century have produced a number of tragic ironies, none sadder than the large number of indefensible actions taken by Fascists and Communists in the name of antifascism and anticommunism.

The Eisenhower administration embraced and expanded Truman's policy. In accord with its general view on foreign assistance, officials rejected the notion of aid to Latin America. Their guiding principles were enshrined in National Security Council position paper 144/1, which proclaimed that a stable and secure hemisphere could be obtained by private assistance and American military aid combined with frequent warnings against forming any ties with Moscow.[3] During the first six years of the Eisenhower administration, officials closely adhered to these precepts. Secretary of the Treasury Humphrey summarily rejected a 1954 Latin American report spearheaded by Chilean Eduardo Frei that called for an Inter-American Fund for Development. Military assistance to the tune of $400 million constituted the Eisenhower administration's only significant aid program to Latin America. The President embraced this program, begun under the Truman administration, because he believed the United States needed Latin American strategic materials and because the United States could not alone defend South America should a war against Communists begin.[4]

The most notable American effort in those years was the CIA-sponsored coup in Guatemala in the summer of 1954, overthrowing the alleged Communist but certainly left-leaning government of Jacobo Arbenz Guzman in favor of the unmerciful General Carlos Castillo Armas. Arbenz had committed several unforgivable sins: although not a Communist, he retained strong ties to Guatemalan Communists, he purchased arms from Soviet-bloc nations, and he permitted the expropriation of the holdings of the United Fruit Company. Adding insult to injury, he offered the company as compensation only the undervalued sum the company had fabricated to avoid Guatemalan taxes. His constituents welcomed Arbenz's actions because United Fruit had run the nation as a private fief. But to Eisenhower and Dulles, the expropriation showed Arbenz to be at least a "fellow traveler," if not a closet Communist. While the Eisenhower administration had made it clear that explicit gunboat diplomacy was beyond the pale, it wholeheartedly embraced covert action. The Castillo Armas junta, needless to say, reversed the expropriation and trumpeted its anticommunism.[5] This was the era of "banana republics," CIA poison-pen attempts on Castro's life, and the dominant role in overt and covert U.S. policy toward Guatemala of a single corporation: the United Fruit Company, producers of Chiquita bananas.

Such blatant disregard for sovereignty could not last. When Vice-

President Nixon toured South America in 1958, he encountered continuous anti-American demonstrations. In Venezuela the confrontation turned violent. Nixon came under siege in Caracas and Eisenhower authorized preparations for an airborne rescue.[6] He managed to return unassisted to a hero's welcome and to the first genuine debate on Latin American policy since the administration had taken office in 1953. Leading the offensive against the status quo were the President's youngest brother, Dr. Milton Eisenhower, and C. Douglas Dillon. The latter, a prominent Wall Street investment banker and leading light of the Eastern internationalist wing of the Republican party, had served as ambassador to France and in 1957 became under-secretary of state with a special brief to concentrate on economic issues. Dillon's approach to foreign aid differed significantly from that of George Humphrey and Secretary of State John Foster Dulles; with Humphrey's exit from the government in 1957 and Dulles's death two years later, Dillon's role in the making of foreign economic policy steadily increased.

Concurrently Latin American diplomats intensified their pleas for American aid.[7] The period from 1940 to 1955 had been a prosperous one for most South American countries. World War II and the Korean War had raised the price of raw materials while wartime devastation placed a premium on farm products. These boom times ended after 1955. The return to normal production in Europe and Asia, combined with a decrease in demand for raw materials, drastically cut Latin American earnings while its population increased significantly. By the end of the 1950s the upper 5 percent of the populace accounted for 30 percent of consumption, while the bottom 50 percent of the region's people made do with only 20 percent of national income.[8]

The seminal Latin American proposal was "Operation Pan-America." Created by Brazil's president, Juscelino Kubitschek, in 1958, it called for the United States to pledge $40 billion in aid over the next two decades.[9] Dulles dismissed the Brazilian as "unreasonable," and no American official embraced Kubitschek's grand plan. But Latin American specialists from the Eisenhower administration such as John Moors Cabot and Thomas C. Mann joined Dillon and Milton Eisenhower in their quest for a new policy. In particular they questioned the assumption that military aid and succor for dictators was sufficient to make

Latin America safe from communism. For his part Cabot urged increased assistance "because the Latin Americans certainly were not going to clear up their own mess."[10] The effect of this slow evolution in American thinking became visible in NSC 5613/1, a special report on Latin America issued on November 26, 1958. The administration agreed to an Inter-American Development Bank, increased (if insignificantly) foreign aid to the region, and sent a parade of high-level visitors to call on various regional leaders.[11]

The ascent to power by Fidel Castro on New Year's Day 1959 gave further impetus to the Eisenhower administration's new conciliatory position. While it was not yet clear that Castro would throw in his lot with the Soviet Union, he was obviously determined to break the power over Cuba exercised by its corrupt government, native elite, and American business interests. Suddenly aid and security issues became strongly linked. In September Dillon represented the United States at the ministers' meeting of the OAS, which drafted the "Act of Bogota." In this milestone agreement, the United States formally accepted the linkage between economic and social development and eased its insistence that private capital alone should provide the money for Latin American development. Eisenhower's concurrent announcement that the United States would institute a $500 million Social Progress Trust Fund to invest in projects heretofore ineligible for U.S. support such as low-cost housing, schools, and health services increased American credibility.[12]

But the Eisenhower administration devoted far more attention during 1960 to honing a stick to use against Castro. Castro's dramatic march to power and his ouster of the corrupt Batista regime captured the attention of many Americans. Even though Nixon had professed himself convinced that Castro was not a Communist after meeting him in April 1959, the Eisenhower administration believed that the Cuban's loyalty lay far from Washington. (Christian Herter, who replaced Dulles as secretary of state, comforted himself that Castro was "very much like a child."[13]) Once Castro, early in 1960, agreed to sell sugar to the Soviet Union in return for oil and industrial products, the State Department told American oil companies in Cuba not to refine any Soviet oil. Castro nationalized the offending companies. Washington cut Cuba's sugar quota, the special exemption from American tariffs that permitted Cuba to sell sugar profitably in the United States, its chief market. (Before 1960, half of Cuba's sales of sugar were to the United States.) In August Eisenhower placed a partial embargo on Cuban products. The United States also raised the issue of Cuba at the OAS meeting and obtained a weak resolution criticizing Castro.

As the Soviet Union increased its sugar purchases, Castro nationalized all private property, domestic and foreign-owned. The U.S. government struck back by enacting further economic sanctions against Cuba on October 19. It reduced the Cuban sugar quota to zero, extended the embargo to foreign subsidiaries of U.S. companies, and mandated that vessels carrying cargo to and from Cuba could no longer carry goods financed by the U.S. government. Only medicine and some foods could pass through the economic barricades. Washington finally severed all diplomatic relations with Cuba in January 1961. But already in March 1960 the Eisenhower administration had authorized the CIA to begin planning Castro's overthrow.[14] The period 1960–61 marked the beginning of the most spectacularly failed economic embargo in history. For all that the United States was the dominant economy in its hemisphere and for all Cuba's lone, small-island status that made it an economic mouse in the American cat's paw, the Cuban sanctions lasted over thirty-five years with no effect on Castro's hold on power.

Candidate Kennedy made Castro a major issue during the 1960 campaign. According to Nixon biographer Stephen Ambrose, Cuba was one of the two issues on which the candidates apparently stood furthest apart. While Kennedy publicly advocated American action against Castro, Nixon, knowing of the Bay of Pigs invasion plans, found himself forced to prevaricate lest he endanger the operation. Kennedy, having proven himself as a hard-bitten anti-Communist, then made a speech on Latin America in October 1960 that promised an *Alianza para progresso*: a "great common effort to develop the resources of the entire hemisphere, strengthen forces of democracy and widen vocational and educational opportunities of every person in all the Americas."[15]

Crucial to the conception of the alliance was the work of Walt Rostow, a professor of economics at the Massachusetts Institute of Technology who was soon to join the administration. Rostow in 1960 had published *The Stages of Economic Growth*. Its thesis was simple and comforting. A healthy economy progressed through five stages of growth. For developing economies the second stage, the transition, and the third stage, the takeoff, were the crucial ones. Rostow suggested that outside forces could propel a developing country from the second to the third stage and thence to economic maturity. Once a third world country's economy had reached maturity, the energized middle class would establish democracy and civil liberties and institutionalize the preservation of human rights. This doctrine offered an intellectual counterweight to Communist ideology and a seemingly easy way to fight communism's spread. If the United States provided some seed money, the developing world's path to non-Communist economic development seemed inevitable.

Once elected, Kennedy created a plethora of prepresidential task forces, each assigned to tackle a different policy area. The Latin American task force, chaired by Adolf Berle, a veteran of Roosevelt's Good Neighbor policy, urged the embrace of "clear, consistent, moral, democratic principles" while stressing that the Communist threat required both a military and an economic response. It placed the principle of human freedom at the center of U.S. policy. Washington should always assume that only freely elected governments were legitimate and that these governments could be changed only in a peaceful fashion. Arguably the most important precept was the last: "American governments [should] not become either prisoners or tools of extra-American power politics." Here lay the key to the new American policy—communism must be kept out of the Americas.[16] In sum, the report laid out three goals for U.S. policy in Latin America: democracy, economic development, and containment. The task force apparently did not consider that these goals were mutually exclusive. Containment required stable governments in firm control of their populace, a difficult task for Latin American democracies, which usually lacked strong roots. Any attempt to redistribute wealth would antagonize both wealthy elites and American companies that had invested heavily in Latin America.

Kennedy administration officials, imbued with boundless self-confidence, felt empowered to carry out their goals. As the presidential aide and noted historian Arthur Schlesinger Jr. counseled the President, "Your accession to the Presidency creates a great opportunity. . . . You are a writer and historian. Your wife is a patron of the arts. You have appointed intellectuals to positions in your administration." And Latin America was "a continent seized by the course of revolutionary change."[17] Kennedy officials seemed confident that American money and know-how could channel newly apparent aspirations in a pro-Washington direction.

Kennedy's men drew special comfort from the legacy of the Marshall Plan. Many members of the new administration, such as Rostow, Berle, and Lincoln Gordon, had participated in the Marshall Plan. Berle indeed explicitly compared the Latin American situation in 1961 to that of Europe in 1947. The administration also seriously considered tapping Paul Hoffman, the former head of the Economic Cooperation Administration, to run its Latin American aid program.[18] Yet the most important parallel between the Marshall Plan and the incoming administration's nascent ideas about foreign aid was seldom alluded to publicly. Both initiatives were born of the fear of communism. As Edwin Vallon, the director of the State Department's Office of Caribbean and Mexican Affairs, told British diplomats in February 1961, "Questions of economic and trade policy can always be negotiated. But communist domination in this Hemisphere can never be negotiated."[19]

The passage of time has somewhat obscured the blatant Cold Warrior profile of the Kennedy administration. The bipartisan consensus on foreign affairs that gripped the United States after 1947 rendered dissent from unremitting anticommunism suspect and "Un-American." The only room for maneuver came on the right. As a result, in the years prior to 1960 Democratic aspirants for the presidency such as Hubert Humphrey, Stuart Symington, Lyndon Johnson, and Kennedy himself competed for the position of "most militant anti-Communist." Kennedy's campaign rhetoric was at the same fever pitch. Democratic accusations of who lost Cuba and allegations about a missile gap constantly reverberated. In his inaugural address Kennedy pledged that the United States would pay any price, bear any burden to wage the Cold War. The Alliance for Progress was to be an important component in the contest for the Americas.

Kennedy asked Richard Goodwin, a young speechwriter whose sole visit to Latin America had been "an orgiastic night just beyond the Texas border," to write the address launching the Alliance for Progress.[20] Kennedy delivered it on March 13 before an audience of

Latin American diplomats assembled at the White House. The speech favorably quoted Thomas Paine on revolution and proved stirring and pragmatic simultaneously. Kennedy embraced the need for massive changes to combat "staggering" problems. He espoused "a vast new Ten Year Plan for the Americas . . . a decade of democratic progress." The President's ten-point program specified a meeting of the Inter-American Economic and Social Council to launch the "massive planning effort which will be the head of the Alliance for Progress," expansion of the Food for Peace emergency aid program, U.S. cooperation on a case-by-case basis for commodity stabilization projects, expanded technical assistance, and an initial U.S. contribution of $500 million to the Social Progress Trust Fund. Were this program to succeed, proclaimed the President, by 1970 Latin America would no longer need substantial external assistance.[21]

Reaction to Kennedy's speech was positive on both sides of the border. In a succession of editorials the *New York Times* compared the "Kennedy Plan" to the Marshall Plan and stated that Kennedy's speech of March 13 and his message to Congress of March 14 had more "vital and hitherto ignored truths" than any other speech ever delivered in hemispheric history. The Republican *New York Herald Tribune* endorsed the plan while the *Philadelphia Inquirer* said it would "reinvigorate the Good Neighbor Policy." Predictably, the *Wall Street Journal* declined to join in the applause. Yet elements of the U.S. business community climbed on the bandwagon. Peter Nehemkis Jr., the Washington counsel for the Whirlpool Corporation, gave a strong endorsement to the plan at the Chicago World Trade Conference. It was three minutes to midnight, he declared. Either the United States backs peaceful revolution or another, much more dire kind would come.[22]

Kennedy followed up by sending to Congress a special message on foreign aid on March 22 that included both administrative reforms as well as a request for increased funding. He asked for $8.8 billion from Congress but also promised to tap funds from Western European allies. As the prepresidential task force report on foreign economic policy pointed out, the United States could no longer afford to be the Western world's sole donor nation.[23] Here was in Rostow's words the "new look" in foreign aid: a "turnaround from a defensive effort to shore up weak economies and to buy short-run political and military advantage, to a coordinated free world effort with enough resources to move forward those nations prepared to mobilize their own resources for development purposes.* The goal is to help other nations learn how to grow."

On April 17 a force of 1,500 Cuban exiles trained by the CIA landed on a Cuban beach. Denied American air cover and given erroneous intelligence, the Bay of Pigs invasion stood no chance against Cuban soldiers, who wiped out the invaders in one day. This failed attempt to invade Cuba, originated under Eisenhower but embraced by Kennedy, demonstrated what lay at the heart of the Kennedy administration's Latin American programs: anticommunism and the Monroe Doctrine's not-in-my-backyard edict.[24] The Alliance for Progress suddenly offered a fig leaf behind which the administration could hide during the heavy criticism that followed Kennedy's April 20 speech taking responsibility for the invasion attempt. Chile's Salvador Allende labeled the alliance a publicity ploy and he was right but it was an expensive ploy.[25] On May 8 the administration requested that the Organization of American States call for an economic conference at the ministerial level to discuss the plan. The President chose the veteran diplomat and Harvard professor Lincoln Gordon to coordinate American preparations. Gordon understood that comparisons with the Marshall Plan were "in most respects . . . misleading." The problems facing Latin America were greater and demanded much more in the way of institutional reform.[26]

Gordon also recognized that less money would be available for Latin America than was given to Europe at the beginning of the Cold War. The United States did not have the same financial advantages it possessed fifteen years earlier. Kennedy personally believed that the balance of payments was one of the two most important problems facing his administration.[27] As foreign aid constituted a major drain of dollars abroad, the administration became obsessed with husbanding its aid monies, and with drawing in allies and private corporations as partners.[28] Yet private investment seeks stability, and in Latin America stability usually came at the hands of an authoritarian regime and a landed oligarchy, the same group that, Schlesinger pointed out, "constitutes the chief barrier to the middle-class revolution."[29] Thus virtu-

---

*This term was a nod to Eisenhower's "new look" nuclear defense policy.

ally every attempt to make conditions amenable to external private investment weakened the thrust toward real change.[30]

During May and June task forces organized by the Inter-American Economic and Social Council convened in Washington to lay the groundwork for the forthcoming ministerial meeting to be held in Punta del Este, Uruguay. The Latin Americans, mainly technical experts, found their American counterparts poorly prepared. As the chairman of the task force on planning and development put it, "there was no philosophy, no thinking behind the U.S. position." The members of the American delegation who were closely associated with the President, Goodwin, and Schlesinger, at least seemed committed to the goal of genuine reform.[31] This sentiment found reflection in an administration position paper that proclaimed goals such as a major attack on illiteracy as well as decent housing for every urban family and a substantial and sustainable increase in economic growth. These lesser goals were all in the service of modernizing the social and economic life of the American republics "along lines of their own choice." (In fact, Washington would bless any Latin American government so long as it was neither Communist nor dominated by left-wing neutralists.) Neither then nor later did Washington officials address the issue that governments meeting their political criteria would not carry out their supposed economic and social goals.[32]

The Punta del Este Conference convened at the Uruguayan beach resort on August 5 and lasted twelve days. The chief American representative, Dillon, now secretary of the Treasury, electrified his audience with a pledge that the United States would contribute $20 billion in public and private funds over the next decade. The U.S. contribution amounted to 20 percent of the $100 billion it would probably take for Latin America to achieve an annual average growth rate of 5 percent of GNP. The administration had apparently put its money where its rhetoric was. But Dillon made this statement without presidential authorization; nor had the White House blessed Dillon's pledge that in the first year the administration would commit $1 billion. It would remain to be seen whether Kennedy would honor Dillon's promises.[33]

A public confrontation between Dillon and Cuban representative Che Guevara proved equally memorable. The two had been sparring during working committee meetings. Guevara then opted for a full frontal attack as he charged that the United States had constructed the Alliance for Progress as an "instrument of economic imperialism." Using his platform as a launching pad for attacks on the United States for its mistreatment of Cuba, Guevara then berated Washington for narrowly restricting the scope of the alliance. Predicting that Cuba would do far better than the rest of Latin America, he invited the judgment of history and urged the delegates to weigh the two approaches in twenty years.[34] Dillon responded with a calm defense of the Alliance for Progress together with a pledge that the United States would never recognize the legitimacy of the Castro regime. Here was the real meaning of the Alliance for Progress.[35]

The Punta del Este meetings produced a "Declaration to the Peoples of America" and the four titles, seven chapters, and appendix that followed. Since unity remained central to the drafters, the charter's language often remained vague; specificity would have made agreement impossible. The principles enshrined in the declaration were laudable: to improve and strengthen democratic traditions, to carry out rural and urban housing programs, to accelerate economic and social development, to assure fair wages, to increase public health programs, and to reform tax laws. But the provisions designed to implement the lofty goals were clearly insufficient to accomplish their mission. For that reason as well as others, the charter fell short of the encomium Schlesinger paid it—"the summons to a democratic revolution."[36]

Problems set in almost immediately. While the charter did not require Senate approval, Congress needed to authorize the appropriations for the alliance. Though Kennedy won his battle to combine existing bureaucracies into the new Agency for International Development (AID), legislators chipped away at the money tree. The alliance allocation of $3 billion over three years was cut by $600 million, and only the first year's appropriation was authorized.[37]

The issue of military aid supplied another area of complexity in the alliance equation. The President stated that "the policy of non-interference in the affairs of other nations does not bind us to non-action should our national interest require such action." Since the key threat in 1961 seemed to be "internal subversion of governments and military forces," the administration intended to mobilize money and labor power to win the loyalty of the Latin American military caste. During the

Kennedy years appropriations for military assistance steadily increased in real numbers, although military appropriations represented a smaller proportion of total aid to Latin America than previously.[38] Undersecretary of State Chester Bowles explained that "the objectives of the Alliance for Progress could not be accomplished without the assistance of an enlightened Latin American military establishment."

Just as important, the administration, using staff college visits and training programs as well as personal contacts, increased the connections between Latin American military officers and their U.S. counterparts. National Security Advisor McGeorge Bundy, in a national security action memorandum, summed up the administration's position in December 1962: "in the complex and rapidly shifting circumstances in Latin America it is essential that our military aid program be a carefully-tailored and constantly updated part of our overall strategy aimed at development and security in the hemisphere."[39] In other words, staving off the Communists required strong-armed friends. The results were predictable. Latin American democracies lost out as officers trained in the United States maneuvered against the civilian leadership of their own countries. American education provided an ideological justification for military takeovers, making it easier for officials in Washington to accept the coups.[40]

The Kennedy administration had apparently constructed the alliance as a joint venture between the United States and Latin America, but in fact the United States remained in the driver's seat. Brazilian President Jânio Quadros, who took office at the same time as Kennedy, harshly criticized the alliance for failing to involve Latin Americans themselves. Washington officials assumed that the combination of internal and external Communist threats with the democratization trend seen in Latin America during the 1950s would allow North American hopes to be fulfilled. As it turned out Latin American elites showed themselves far more wedded to their privileges than to democratic and societal changes.[41]

Brazil provided a troubling case in point during 1961. The region's largest country, occupying almost half of South America's land mass, it combined very rich mineral deposits with the continent's poorest region, the Northeast provinces. With a 2.7 percent annual growth rate it provided a key laboratory for the alliance. Kubitschek, the president from 1957 to 1961, had brought urgently needed economic progress to Brazil at the price of a large balance of payments deficit and soaring inflation. Concurrently a worldwide drop in the price of coffee, which provided over 50 percent of Brazil's foreign currency income and more than half of its dollars, intensified the economic crisis. The Kennedy administration viewed the establishment of close relations with Brazil as a top Latin American priority; many officials saw Brazil as an ideal counterweight to Cuba. Washington provided helpful financial relief during 1961 to Brazil: it supported an IMF loan, allowed the postponement of repayments from loans made by the U.S. government's Export Import (EXIM) Bank, and agreed to provide new credits in the amount of $338 million.

Yet political issues proved difficult. Quadros declared his independence by making supportive comments about Castro. When the president conferred Brazil's highest military decoration on Che Guevara, who was then returning home after the Punta del Este conference, the administration was appalled.[42] Quadros believed that Washington was insufficiently attuned to the needs of Latin Americans but wanted the United States to press harder for the reforms it had advocated at Punta del Este.[43] Then, on August 25 Quadros unexpectedly resigned the presidency and retreated to his home in São Paulo in the face of Brazil's worsening economic plight as well as military and right-wing criticism of his foreign policy. Apparently he hoped his departure would lead to an outpouring of loyalty similar to what Charles de Gaulle received from France in 1958.[44] The call to return never came.

Quadros's dramatic gesture took Washington totally by surprise. Secretary of State Rusk found it necessary to reassure Western ambassadors that the United States "had no hand" in Quadros's resignation.[45] In fact, from the American point of view, the Brazilian situation had gone from bad to worse. Quadros's successor, João Goulart, was viewed in Washington as a left-leaning politician with a penchant for anti-American statements. Goulart received the summons to office en route to Brazil from a visit to Beijing, at a time when the United States held to a strict policy of nonrecognition of the People's Republic of China; that summed up Goulart as far as Washington was concerned. Segments of Brazilian society, especially the military, felt the same way. For that reason Goulart could take office only after he agreed to an "Additional Act," which emasculated the president's role by transferring much of his power to a prime minister and Congress. Clearly, achieving American goals in Brazil would be very difficult, and each of Brazil's problems threatened to appear in other Latin American states.[46]

During early 1962 the Washington apparatus of various alliance programs began to fall into place. The Committee of Nine, designated in the charter to evaluate proposals, and now constituted, included Paul Rosenstein-Rodan and Harvey Peroloff of the United States, Felipe Pazos, the former president of the National Bank of Cuba, Hernando Agudelo Villa of Colombia, and Manuel Noriega Morales of Guatemala. U.S. officials including Teodoro Moscoso, in charge of administering alliance programs, and Goodwin visited Latin American countries to discuss possible uses of U.S. funds. Kennedy pressured them to show results—Moscoso recalled that the President continually asked him to explain why they were doing little and doing it slowly. But with no internal machinery and little planning experience, recipient countries had great trouble formulating their blueprints. Because the requirement to submit plans to the Committee of Nine would slow the process down even further, U.S. officials, stretching the charter's language, often bypassed the committee and allocated grants unilaterally. While time was of the essence, this fast-track approach doomed the multilateral aspect of the alliance, reducing it to a series of parallel bilateral American aid programs.[47]

AID Administrator Fowler Hamilton's outline of three agreements about to be concluded with Brazil, submitted to the President in February 1962, gives an indication of what the alliance was supporting: "(a) $33 million immediate impact loan grant program, (b) a $62 million long-range development program, and (c) a very substantial program for emergency food, wheat, corn, and dry milk." Fowler noted that these programs derived from recommendations made by the American survey team that visited Brazil in October 1961. There is, however, no indication that these disbursements were either part of a Brazilian plan or that they had been seen by the Committee of Nine.[48]

Meanwhile the administration used a second conference in Punta del Este in January 1962 to draw attention to what Kennedy officials saw as the chief Latin American issue—the problem of Castroism.

Washington wanted this conclave of OAS ministers to brand Castro an outlaw and exclude him from the hemispheric club. It became increasingly common to see the alliance as a thinly disguised bribe from Washington to buy support for its war against Castro.[49] Argentina, Brazil, and Mexico still opposed Castro's ostracism—they did not feel particularly threatened by the Cuban dictator. Indeed Mexican diplomats told their British counterparts that, rather than fear Castro, they welcomed him because Cuban policies had stimulated the United States to make Latin America a top priority. The administration toted up the population of Latin American countries on both sides of the sanctions question and found to its dismay that the pro-Castro population outweighed the pro-sanctions count by almost three to one.[50]

Eventually the conference produced a compromise falling short of the administration's goals. Only fourteen nations voted to make Castro a hemispheric pariah, although all twenty republics agreed that Cuba would be barred from the Inter-American Defense Board and agreed that the adoption of Marxist-Leninist ideology was irreconcilable with the inter-American system. Seventeen nations voted to end arms traffic with Cuba, and sixteen assented to a study of further trade embargo actions. As the administration had hoped for unanimous resolutions with real teeth in them, the result was obviously disappointing.[51]

The Bay of Pigs fiasco had not dimmed the Kennedy administration's eagerness to remove Castro from power. CIA operatives continued to dream up dirty tricks such as cigars exploding in Castro's face and depilatories to remove his beard, as well as exploring mob contacts to eliminate the Cuban dictator. American sanctions had little obvious effect on Castro's regime. The Soviet Union eagerly stepped into the breach the United States had left while Latin American nations generally refused to follow Washington's lead. Frustration over Cuba increased the administration's enthusiasm for military assistance programs that proved to be the smoothest-running part of the American assistance package. The need for stable Latin American governments increased proportionately. But these governments increasingly tended to be the more conservative if not authoritarian regimes that were reluctant, to say the least, to implement the reforms that American officials proclaimed were essential to the success of the alliance. The administration would have to choose between its goals.

Senator Bourke Hickenlooper forced the question after the nationalization by the Brazilian state of Rio Grande do Sul of an International Telephone and Telegraph subsidiary. His amendment to a foreign aid bill required the President to suspend all economic aid to any country that expropriated property owned by a U.S. company, disavowed any agreement with an American company, or levied discriminatory taxes on an American company unless the country took "effective steps" to provide due compensation to the company in "convertible foreign exchange" within six months. This requirement could not be waived and it covered any form of foreign assistance such as food donations and sugar quota provisions as well as standard alliance aid. To Hickenlooper any degree of leftism was too much. The proposed legislation infuriated Latin Americans, and the *New York Times* labeled it "backward progress."[52] The administration did not have the votes to defeat the amendment. Getting the 1962 foreign aid bill through Congress had taken all of the administration's skill. The $4.752 billion requested by the administration amounted to less than 1 percent of gross national product and almost $1 billion less than the authorization for space exploration for the comparable period.[53] Yet Congress almost balked. The nationalization question complicated alliance relations in many ways. American officials never comprehended that support for nationalization of basic industries was widespread in Latin America, and on this point American anticommunism was highly counterproductive.[54]

A more urgent problem was generating 50 percent of alliance funds, which the administration envisioned coming from private investment when Latin America experienced a net outflow of foreign capital.[55] The administration had assumed a 20 percent annual increase in American private investment in Latin America over the period 1958–60. Reports of various Latin American governments nationalizing foreign-held properties could only hurt this effort. Moreover, the administration had badly bungled its relations with business leaders from the start, not bringing them into the planning for Punta del Este until very late in the day.[56] The creation of a Commerce Department Committee for the Alliance for Progress (COMAP) in April 1962 was a step in the right direction but would not prove sufficient.

The question of nationalization could not be separated from a fundamental issue that lay at the heart of the alliance: how much reform would be required of participating Latin American countries. The economist Barbara Ward Jackson, writing in *Foreign Affairs* in October 1962, urged that "funds given as foreign aid have to be given within a framework that at least aims at a strategy for growth."[57] As former Colombian President Alberto Lleras Camargo wrote: if the Alliance for Progress came to be seen as just a traditional aid program, then "the governments and peoples south of the Rio Grande [would feel] that they were absolved from doing their share."[58] Yet one of the chief goals of the Kennedy administration was to use the Alliance for Progress as a propaganda weapon. If the administration held up its grants until major Latin reforms were accomplished, very little positive propaganda would be generated. While some Latin Americans lamented the lack of American pressure for structural change, Washington's enforcing of structural preconditions for aid would have been unpopular as well.[59]

Chilean land reform provided the best litmus test for the administration's policy during the spring. Probably no aspect of the Alliance for Progress created as much excitement in Latin America as the belief that it would foster agrarian reform.[60] But Chilean developments forced the administration to decide whether it should give aid to a regime that combined a plan for land reform with a military-led eviction of peasant squatters. Washington went along with Chile.[61] Another issue repeatedly drawing Washington's ire was the regressive tax system enforced by most Latin American countries. In March 1962, the alliance administrator Teodoro Moscoso warned that North Americans would not subsidize nations whose rich citizens were virtually immune from income taxation.[62] But Moscoso unfortunately spent almost as much time embroiled in counterproductive Washington infighting as he did dealing with alliance issues. In August a report on Brazil, Argentina, Chile, and Bolivia noted that "U.S. policies and programs are in a state of considerable disarray." It is no wonder that pessimism marked the first anniversary of the Charter.[63]

Events in Argentina during 1962 exacerbated the sense of gloom in Washington. After years of dictatorship, elections in 1958 had brought democracy to Argentina. The White House had been able to work with President Arturo Frondizi, although he took a less militant view toward Castroism than the administration desired.[64] Frondizi followed a policy of "developmentalism," encouraging foreign investment in capital-intensive industries such as steel and automobile manufacture.[65] He also reversed his earlier support for petroleum nationalization, which infuriated officers who supported a state monopoly. Unfortunately this center-leftist proved an inept governor who alienated conservatives by his foreign policy and liberals with his compromises on church/state issues. The always influential Argentine military tolerated Frondizi until early 1962, when neo-Peronist parties triumphed in regional elections. Military leaders responded by removing Frondizi from office in a bloodless coup on March 28, 1962. U.S. military attachés in Buenos Aires had advised against a coup, but the United States rapidly recognized the new government.[66] The rationale for a policy of continued engagement would remain an influential theory for the balance of the Cold War: denying aid would curtail American influence over the junta.[67] Argentina's strong pro-American stance during the Cuban missile crisis of October 1962, very different from Frondizi's quasi-neutralist position, and its assistance in the enforcement of the U.S. quarantine of Cuba, emphasized to many in Washington the wisdom of this approach. Kennedy believed that the twelve months succeeding the Cuban missile crisis would be "critical in Latin America with respect to renewed attempts at [Communist] penetration." So the crucial issue was not how much of the charter had been enacted but which side you were on.[68]

Washington initially took a harsher line against the perpetrators of a coup on July 18, 1962, which, using newly supplied American military equipment, ousted Peru's constitutional government. An American-trained military officer woke President Manuel Prado to inform him that a junta had taken over. Peru's leaders had taken a very strong position against Castro; Prime Minister Pedro Beltran in 1961 urged the administration to "mobiliz[e] with minimum delays against [the] Communist menace."[69] Now, the American ambassador to Peru, James Loeb, a founder of the liberal Americans for Democratic Action, urged Washington to withhold recognition of the regime and cancel all assistance. The administration agreed and Kennedy issued a statement calling the coup a serious setback for the Alliance for Progress.[70] Although nine countries joined in the American stance, one month after the coup, in part owing to strong pressure from the U.S. business community, the administration reversed itself. It resumed diplomatic relations and economic aid, although it continued to withhold military assistance until autumn.[71]

Brazilian developments in 1962 continued to disappoint administration optimists. Goulart was caught between extremists on both sides.[72] Brazil's balance of payments deficit and persistent inflation (an annual rate of 52 percent in 1962) jeopardized the country's economy. At the same time the prolonged political deadlock eviscerated Goulart's control over Congress and government spending. By August the State Department director of intelligence openly speculated that a coup was possible; the next month the same agency informed the secretary of state that the situation had gotten worse. Goulart had proved to be incompetent. In desperation he resorted increasingly to tactics that polarized Brazilian society. One of Brazil's important provincial leaders, São Paulo Governor Adhemar de Barros, told Kennedy that the nation's problems could be solved only by a military coup that would rid the nation of Goulart.

The U.S. business community reacted with alarm. The president of the São Paulo American Chamber of Commerce (also president of RCA Electorincal Brasileir) recommended to U.S. envoy William Draper Jr., who headed an interdepartmental mission to Brazil investigating the efficacy of American aid efforts, that Washington cut off all assistance. This action would trigger a coup that would allow the military to "correct the existing conditions." Brazil's financial plight became desperate. The former state secretary of finance Gastão Vidigal summed it up by telling Draper that Brazil's position "couldn't be worse." At the end of October the American embassy reported that the government needed at least $80 million to meet its current obligations through the end of the year and currently had no prospect of finding such sums.[73] The nexus of this crisis with the Alliance for Progress was clear. As Draper reported to the President, the financial emergency rendered it impossible for Brazil to meet any of its obligations under the charter. For that reason Draper recommended that the administration concentrate on economic stabilization and postpone the alliance program until after Brazil restored financial stability. Washington again chose the status quo, and proved willing to postpone reform for another day.[74]

The Cold War, which had gotten the United States into its alliance largesse, converted relations in the Americas into a bidding war. If you are against Moscow, we're with you. If you are a strongman and stabilizer who might calm down business and you're against Moscow, we're with you. For a Latin American dictator, the easiest way to demonstrate loyalty to the United States was to exhibit hostility to Castro, who remained the largest thorn in the American side. In the wake of the failed April 1961 Bay of Pigs invasion, Castro feared another invasion attempt by American troops. To protect himself he turned to the Soviet Union, declaring himself a Communist, which justified his urgent request for military aid. Soviet Premier Nikita Khrushchev responded by moving a variety of weapons to Cuba, including medium-range and intermediate-range nuclear missiles, as well as IL-28 nuclear bombers. Although Soviet Ambassador Anatoly Dobrynin reassured the Kennedy administration that Moscow had not placed nuclear weaponry in Cuba, during the summer of 1962 American intelligence sources picked up reports of Soviet missiles there. The CIA concluded on August 22 that "something new and different is taking place." On October 1 Secretary of Defense McNamara received evidence possibly indicating the installation of intermediate-range ballistic missiles. Two weeks later U-2 overflights revealed missile sites in Cuba. Kennedy realized that the missiles made little difference in the strategic balance but worried that the United States would be perceived to be weaker than the Soviet Union if the missiles remained adjacent to American shores.

The President and his advisers privately debated their options: an air strike, a diplomatic approach, or a blockade. When on October 22 Kennedy, in a television address to the nation, announced an American blockade of Cuba, the Cuban missile crisis was in full swing and Kennedy garnered the support of the U.S. public and also international opinion.* The President also ordered American nuclear forces to DEFCON 2, the highest alert short of war. Kennedy himself viewed Castro as "a symbol of Khrushchev's claim that communism was on the march, a beachhead for Soviet influence in Latin America, a lingering sign of his own failure at the Bay of Pigs." Still smarting from his weak

---

*Kennedy called the blockade a "quarantine" because a blockade is an act of war.

showing at the August 1961 Vienna summit with Khrushchev, the President needed publicly to force the Soviet missiles from Cuba. On October 24 Soviet ships stopped before crossing the "quarantine line." Four days later Khrushchev announced his order to withdraw the missiles, sending Castro into a towering fury because he had not been consulted. In return Kennedy privately agreed not to invade Cuba and to remove American missiles from Turkey.[75] The Soviet Union had been defeated, in part because of its nuclear inferiority; its isolation in the world community played a role as well.

The settlement of the Cuban missile crisis left the United States with no military option available against Castro. Only economic diplomacy remained. So while the administration lifted the blockade on November 20, it continued to tighten the economic screws. In October Congress gave Kennedy the power to cut off American aid to any country that allowed its flagships to transport goods to or from Cuba. In February the President encouraged maritime unions to boycott ships listed on the U.S. government blacklist for trading with Cuba. Four months later, invoking the Trading with the Enemy Act, the United States froze all Cuban assets in the United States ($33 million). While the administration pressured NATO allies to follow suit, it won agreement only to embargo military items. Western European countries otherwise continued to trade with the Castro government.[76] Combined with ongoing Soviet support of the island, this decision by NATO allies robbed American sanctions of any chance of determining Cuba's fate.

Once again the true point of the alliance was made clear. The President had planned to visit Brazil in November 1962, but the Cuban missile crisis intervened. His agenda, however, had included a "relaunching of the Alliance for Progress." That a program only fifteen months old needed to be "relaunched" illustrated the continuing muddle in administration policy. As a staff report prepared by the Bureau of the Budget in August 1962 concluded: "it appears to us that U.S. policies and programs are in a state of considerable disarray."[77] The future of the alliance had been the topic of meetings in the State Department and with Latin American diplomats throughout the summer and autumn. A resolution of the October meeting of the Inter-American Economic and Social Committee asked the council of the OAS to designate two leading Latin Americans to evaluate the alliance.

Appointed to the prestigious posts were former Presidents Kubitschek of Brazil and Camargo of Colombia. Kennedy met with them in December 1962 to lay out the American position. The President understood that the fall in commodities prices had damaged Latin American economies over the past two years. Unfortunately the United States could not increase its aid to make up the deficiency. The deteriorating U.S. balance of payments situation together with other demands on American resources made such an escalation impossible. Kubitschek informed the President that he felt money alone was not the problem. Rather, much of the difficulty lay in funding delays that, combined with the rising expectations generated by the announcement of the alliance, engendered growing disillusion with the administration's policies. Kennedy defended the alliance and blamed its problems on the workings of the American system, chiefly the need to consult Congress and the difficulties inherent in creating massive development programs.[78]

During the first week of February 1963, at his regular news conference, Kennedy proclaimed that "I regard Latin America as the most critical area in the world today." Yet the sense of fumbling in the administration's Latin American policy only increased as the second anniversary of the President's White House speech introducing the Alliance for Progress approached. Businessmen proved to be among the most ardent naysayers. J. Peter Grace, who had played a leading role in getting the administration to recognize the Peruvian junta, wrote that "I am convinced the Alliance for Progress is in an extremely precarious condition." David Rockefeller of the Chase Manhattan Bank and Walter Wriston, representing First National City Bank (now Citibank), both of whom served with Grace on the COMAP committee, believed that the methods for achieving the goals of the Alliance for Progress "must be radically changed."[79] Their opinions mirrored the business community's actions—during 1962 U.S. private investment in Latin America registered a net loss.

Grace had taken on the task of assembling the formal COMAP proposals for increased private investment in Latin America. The report, submitted to Secretary of Commerce Luther Hodges on December 20, 1962, documented the startling fall in private investment in the region. The chief reason for the change proved not to be the fear of nationalization; rather, the deterioration in the terms of trade had made Latin American investments unprofitable. Yet the COMAP proposals included a plea for a massive increase in U.S. government aid. As the report pointed out, while during 1961 American aid of all kinds in gross terms exceeded $1 billion, net of Latin American repayments on debt, it amounted to only $510 million, or half of what the United States pledged at Punta del Este. The report also called for changed tax treatment of U.S. investments in Latin America which would increase their profitability. Such a revision would amount to a different kind of U.S. Treasury subsidy to Latin America.[80]

The administration took a noncommittal view of the COMAP report, in part because it soon became clear that it did not have the endorsement of all twenty-five committee members. Simultaneously the White House addressed the problems caused by the Clay Committee report on foreign aid. During 1962 congressional support for foreign aid continued to erode. Convinced that without a public relations campaign, the 1963 legislation would be in jeopardy, the President appointed a blue ribbon panel of certified conservatives. Their job was to reassure a skeptical Congress and public of the need to continue the administration's aid effort. This was the fifth such committee appointed since 1950, each having been patterned on the Harriman Committee, which blessed the Marshall Plan. In picking a chair, the President took a calculated risk by appointing General Lucius Clay, who had won great prestige as commander of American forces in Berlin. But Kennedy lost his gamble. Deviating from their script, the members of the Clay Committee, in a report delivered in March 1963, insisted that "there is a feeling that we are trying to do too much for too many too soon, that we are overextended in resources and undercompensated in results, and that no end of foreign aid is either in sight or in mind." The report recommended a reduction in both civilian and military aid of half a billion dollars out of Kennedy's requested $4.5 billion sum. In view of the ongoing Cold War, Clay and his associates urged that the deeper cuts be made in civilian appropriations. The committee's recommendation that U.S. aid should not go to state-owned enterprises that compete with private endeavors was accepted by the administration but could prove problematic in the future.[81]

Kubitschek and Camargo submitted their reports on June 15, 1963.

They presented a sweeping critique, emphasizing that the alliance had not been granted sufficient resources and that it had lost the confidence of the Latin American peoples. Both men highlighted the need for a permanent Inter-American organization to carry out the tasks required by the Alliance for Progress to replace the ad hoc Wise Men committee of elder statesmen. For his part Kubitschek urged the administration to create an autonomous American agency to run the U.S. part of the program. Where Camargo concluded that "one cannot see anywhere in Latin America the spirit of enthusiasm" that the alliance required, Kubitschek laid most of the blame for the poor state of the alliance on the United States. The administration proved amenable to a committee on Inter-American development, but as Dillon wrote to the President, the Treasury worried about the congressional response should such a committee be empowered to make recommendations concerning the amount and nature of American aid. Dillon suggested that if the committee were given such authority, congressional approval of American representation on the committee should be considered.[82]

The public acknowledgment by the White House in August that it favored the creation of an Inter-American Development Committee occurred in the shadow of the emasculation by the Senate Foreign Relations Committee of the alliance's Social Progress Trust Fund. The committee not only slashed in half the administration's request for $200 million but approved an increase in the interest rate on loans from 3/4 of 1 percent to 2 percent, thereby circumscribing the amount of loans that a developing country could afford. It is no wonder that an outside research service began its appraisal of the alliance on the second anniversary of the Punta del Este meeting by stating that "doubt, disappointment and disdain color the second birthday of the Alliance for Progress."[83]

October saw coups in the Dominican Republic and Honduras, thereby bringing the total over the previous eighteen months to five. Assistant Secretary of State Edwin Martin concluded that the alliance's goal of development with democracy was unattainable because "in most of Latin America there is so little experience with the benefits of political legitimacy." He recommended that the United States continue to oppose coups but use force only "against intervention from outside the hemisphere by the international Communist conspiracy."[84] In effect this policy guaranteed success for Latin American *golpes* (coups).

White House officials, watching Congress further slash the foreign aid bill, might have been forgiven if they envied junta leaders. Kennedy had asked for a total of $4.5 billion in military and economic foreign aid appropriations. When the Senate reduced its appropriation to $3.72 billion (the lowest appropriation since 1947) and restricted the executive's discretionary power, the President on November 14 accused the Senate of interfering in foreign policy and severely limiting his ability to protect the national interest. His attack did not serve its purpose—the final aid bill, passed after a marathon session on New Year's Eve, further reduced that amount to $3 billion. Kennedy had originally requested $650 million for the alliance. The foreign aid program had been caught between the ire of conservatives, in particular House Subcommittee Chair Otto Passman, who detested all foreign aid, and liberals such as Senator Wayne Morse who assailed the current foreign aid program as a "shocking waste." Both men were Democrats. It took all of newly installed President Lyndon Johnson's legislative skill to get any bill passed; even Johnson's magic touch could not obtain a restoration of the foreign aid amounts originally authorized.

The assassination of John F. Kennedy on November 22, 1963, effectively buried the Alliance for Progress. His successor, Lyndon Johnson, believing that Kennedy's team was ineffectual, fired both Moscoso and Martin. On December 14 the new President appointed to the new post of assistant secretary of state for Inter-American affairs (combining the State Department and AID functions into one job) Thomas Mann, an assistant secretary of state for economic affairs under Eisenhower and the ambassador to Mexico during the Kennedy administration. On January 21 Johnson announced that he would request a total of only $3.4 billion in foreign economic and military assistance for fiscal 1965, the smallest such request in sixteen years.[85] In March 1964 Mann convened a three-day meeting of American ambassadors to Latin American countries to announce the precepts that would govern his regime. Known as the Mann Doctrine, his four principles were (1) to foster economic growth and be neutral on social reform;(2) to protect U.S. private investment in the hemisphere; (3) to show no preference, through aid or otherwise, for representative democratic institutions; and (4) to oppose Communism.[86]

Soon the alliance deteriorated into a catchphrase for American aid to Latin America that was given to any nation that showed itself to be sufficiently anti-Communist, regardless of its democratic or demographic status. The Johnson administration's enthusiastic response to the long-expected Brazilian coup in March 1964 illustrated its preference for military stability over democratic chaos. Washington's support for military regimes in turn discredited it further in many Latin American eyes.[87] Yet it would be unfair to accuse Johnson officials of jettisoning principles propounded by the Kennedy administration.

Measuring the alliance by the terms of its original charter yields a mixed balance sheet. American aid and private investment during the nineteen sixties, taken together with assistance from multilateral institutions, approached the $20 billion first announced by Dillon in August 1961. The increase in American private investment came primarily in the second half of the decade as the price of raw materials and foodstuffs began a sharp rise. The reversal of the terms of trade made investment in Latin America increasingly profitable.[88] Yet the actual amount of aid received by Latin America after taking account of government debt repayments was far lower. The efficacy of American aid must also be measured against the billions of Latin American capital that deserted the region each year. Observers estimated that between $500 million and $1 billion of Latin American capital fled the region in 1962 alone.[89]

In countries such as Brazil, where the increase in overall GNP did approximate the 2.5 percent figure laid out in the charter, the improvement did not reach the poor but instead fueled an increase in income for the middle and upper classes.[90] Instead of bolstering an endangered status quo as under the Marshall Plan, the Kennedy administration maintained that its goal was to alter the entire structure of Latin American society in a "revolutionary" manner. The charter envisioned an extremely ambitious program that would ameliorate structural poverty and launch massive social reforms. But its lofty and idealistic rhetoric provided an attractive surface with little substance. Few in the administration wanted to pay the price of a real revolution. For one thing such upheavals would jeopardize American private investment in Latin

America. Not only did alliance planners want to safeguard current investments, but their blueprints called for consistent increases in the private flow of funds from north to south. American and foreign investors had already been leaving Latin America—radical social and economic changes would only have accelerated this trend.

Latin American critics also alleged that the United States could not accept the economic changes that an Alliance for Progress genuinely dedicated to transformation would have entailed, in particular the severing of Latin reliance on U.S. markets and capital. Washington's decision to utilize private capital for the alliance certainly made it extremely difficult politically for the Kennedy administration to launch actions inimical to American overseas economic interests.[91] American economic ideology also created another flaw in the design of the alliance: many in Washington assumed that economic and social advancement would necessarily bring democratic political developments. Events in such countries as Chile, Argentina, Singapore, and Malaysia disproved this construct.[92]

American discourse always emphasized the need for an inter-American and democratic approach. Walt Rostow, for example, warned of the danger of encouraging the illusion that U.S. magic and money could solve Latin American problems.[93] Yet the United States did not want Latin American countries to find their own answers. Of key importance, Washington was not willing to stand by and watch left- and right-wing elements fight with centrist parties for control of the twenty governments at risk. Rather, the Kennedy administration intended the alliance to ensure the existence of governments that would always support American security goals.

As with the Marshall Plan, the alliance was meant to provide an answer to communism. But the Alliance for Progress was more ambitious. The Marshall Plan bolstered the status quo while the Alliance for Progress ostensibly sought to change it. Most Latin American countries were run by elites with little recognition of the need to share the wealth. The Latin American economist Raul Prebisch in 1961 observed that currents of social and economic reform were generally absent from Latin American governing circles.[94] By contrast, indigenous conditions in Europe allowed the United States to have it all. It could simultaneously provide the seed money for economic recovery, nurture democracy, and fight communism. American officials did not have to choose among their goals.

Latin America presented the United States with a far more difficult problem. Many Kennedy officials sincerely wanted to aid Latin American growth and development. Yet the bottom line remained the challenge from communism in general and Castro in particular. Communism and compassion proved contradictory; the United States could not have it all. Cold War logic forced Kennedy administration officials to tolerate undemocratic leaders so long as they toed the line on Castro. They remembered the equation, "chaos equals Communism," that had become conventional wisdom during the debates over the Marshall Plan. The messy Latin attempts at democratic governments during the 1960s struck fear in the hearts of American diplomats, who saw them as the prelude to Communist governments rather than as evidence of the growing pains of democracy.

But given Latin American conditions during the sixties, the Kennedy administration made the only practical choice. No amount of American money could have purchased the gains that the Marshall Plan brought to Western Europe. Neither the local elite nor the local infrastructure was sufficient. That being the case, Washington used limited resources to bolster hemispheric security at the height of the Cold War it was pledged to win.

TABLE 8–1
NET GOVERNMENTAL FOREIGN BALANCES OF
PAYMENTS AND RECEIPTS IN 1966 (U.S. $ MILLIONS)[a]

United States	−6,385
Great Britain	−1,288
Belgium/Luxembourg	−46
Sweden	−45
Netherlands	−42
Italy	−9
France	−1
Japan	+315
Germany	+339

[a]Sidney Pollard, *The Development of British Economy*, 3rd ed. (London, 1983), p. 364.

France in 1960 rode the crest of political and economic recovery. The Fourth Republic, established in 1946, disappeared in a virtual coup d'état twelve years later. Divisive politics at home and the Algerian revolt abroad motivated French military men to challenge civilian rule. Their replacement: the Fifth Republic headed by General Charles de Gaulle, whose leadership of the Free French forces had galvanized French resistance to Hitler. After the war, the resumption of party politics led him to flee to his country retreat of Colombey-les-Deux-Églises. There de Gaulle, whose ego more than matched his accomplishments, waited, confident that his moment would come. When it did, the general was ready. He demanded a new constitution with significant presidential powers. This arranged, de Gaulle set about his major reformation of the French government. He devalued the franc and began the painful process of disengaging from Algeria, which had actually been legally incorporated into metropolitan France. By 1960 the French economy began performing spectacularly. At the same time de Gaulle sought an enhanced position for France within the Western alliance. De Gaulle's view of European power politics had not altered from this summary that he had provided to Roosevelt's personal envoy, Harry Hopkins, in 1945:

[he] could not understand how they [the United States] can undertake to settle the fate of Europe in the absence of France. . . . The questions of the Rhine would not be settled by America any more than by Russia or by Great Britain. The solution could only be found one day by France or by Germany. Both had long sought it one against the other. Tomorrow they would discover it perhaps by joining together.[3]

As de Gaulle had envisioned, a Franco-German rapprochement formed the basis of French foreign policy. The European Economic Community, or Common Market, embodied this change of direction. The EEC, formed in 1958 by France, West Germany, Italy, and the Benelux countries, rested on the Franco-German axis. Its initial aim was economic, to eliminate trade barriers among its neighbors, but because of German willingness to support French dictation, its existence added ballast to French diplomatic endeavors.

In 1958 de Gaulle wrote to Eisenhower suggesting that NATO be governed under a tripartite Anglo-American-French directorship. Eisenhower was unenthusiastic. De Gaulle, however, did not abandon his negative attitude to the Atlantic Alliance. Indeed, his loathing of the NATO structure grew in tandem with French prosperity. The American rejection of de Gaulle's proposal, reiterated after Kennedy became President, only reinforced the French president's belief that "a small or medium-sized country must not stand too close to a very great power, without risk of being drawn into its orbit."[4] For this reason de Gaulle adamantly insisted on an independent French nuclear arsenal.

In response the Kennedy administration searched for an alternative that would placate France and include West Germany. The Federal Republic of Germany had been founded in 1949 by the union of the American, British, and French zones of Germany. Its economic success in the succeeding decade earned the term *wirtschaftswunder* as a prosperous German economy literally arose from ashes. In 1960 alone West Germany's official gold and foreign exchange reserves climbed by $2.4 billion.[5] In the same year, alarmed by the American gold outflow, the Eisenhower administration beseeched Bonn to contribute to American defense costs in Germany.

The Kennedy administration increased American pressure on West Germany to raise its financial contribution to NATO costs. The

Gilpatric "offset" agreement entered into by the United States and West Germany in October 1961 embodied this financial arrangement. Under this initial arrangement the German Defense Ministry pledged to order American military equipment, equaling in dollars U.S. dollar defense expenditures in West Germany during calendar years 1961 and 1962. Such purchases would negate, i.e., offset, the effect on the U.S. balance of payments of the American presence in Germany while at the same time assuring the U.S. defense industry of a steady stream of orders. West Germany, then in the process of upgrading and enlarging its army, would receive, in the words of an American official, "major equipment incorporating the latest technology at less cost and faster than is available [elsewhere]." As such the offset arrangement appeared beneficial to all parties.[6] It was renewed in 1963 and again in 1965.[7]

At the same time Washington attempted to alter NATO's defense structure. American officials opposed the independent nuclear force that Britain already possessed and France coveted. Their search for a gimmick to buy off all three Western allies led to the multilateral force, or MLF, an idea originally mooted during the 1950s, which then became a key part of American policy toward Western Europe well into the Johnson administration. The blueprints called for mixed crews to man nuclear-powered weapons with the United States always retaining a veto on the use of such weapons. While the British and West German governments went along with the scheme, albeit without enthusiasm, de Gaulle, realizing that "effective participation in control" was tantamount to no control at all, spurned it. Of course the Kennedy administration hoped that Germany would recompense it by increasing its share of Western defense costs. Not only did the price of NATO's defense remain high but American military commitments in Southeast Asia had begun their dramatic escalation. The number of American advisers in Vietnam, to take just one statistic, leapt from 800 in 1961 to 16,000 in 1963.

While the chief motivation behind the MLF was the need to find a place for an emergent Germany within the Western alliance, American officials had also hoped that the MLF would give Britain a graceful way to shed its superpower pretensions. The MLF structure would leave only Washington's hand on the nuclear button. American arrogance toward Britain's nuclear force partly stemmed from London's reliance on U.S. technology for its delivery system. A way to scuttle the British nuclear force apparently opened up at the end of 1962. The British government had developed its own Blue Streak delivery system, scheduled to go online in 1962–65. But in 1960 Blue Streak's mammoth estimated cost made it an easy target for elimination if a cheaper alternative could be found. Macmillan believed he had located one—the American Skybolt system. In March 1960 Eisenhower promised the British prime minister that Skybolt was available; the cabinet then scrapped Blue Streak. Macmillan's meeting notes also clearly state that "we could obtain Polaris [the other American delivery system], although at heavy cost, in some form or another if we might need it." When, in November 1962, cost overruns and system failures convinced the Pentagon to cancel Skybolt, American officials sought to use this opportunity to force Britain to renounce its nuclear deterrent. But during their Bermuda summit in December 1962, Macmillan convinced Kennedy that this would be an utter disaster. Instead the President promised Britain its own Polaris missiles. De Gaulle, once again left out of the Anglo-American partnership, used this agreement as a reason for announcing on January 14, 1963, his decision to veto the British application to join the Common Market.[8]

The financial problems facing Britain were far more acute than those occupying Washington. Britain's retention of the pound's reserve currency and trading status simultaneously with a large defense commitment on a diet of insufficient reserves doomed it to a knife-edged existence. Sterling, like the dollar, was constantly traded on world markets. This fact helped make London a leading financial center and increased Britain's invisible exports such as insurance. But foreign holders remained suspicious of the British government's ability to maintain the sterling parity of £1 = $2.80 set in 1949. For that reason they tended to sell sterling in favor of the dollar or gold, or, as the sixties continued, the French franc or deutsche mark, whenever any questionable British domestic economic or political news came over the wire. Typical harbingers of sterling problems included increases in the British balance of payments deficit, "large" wage settlements, or swelling British government social spending.

The Conservative party, in power since 1951, clung to the sterling parity but its dedication had not avoided a succession of sterling crises. A major emergency in 1961 was halted by temporary loans from European central banks totaling approximately $900 million, a $1.5 billion drawing from the IMF, and restrictive internal measures.[9] Pressure on sterling began again in 1963 and mounted during 1964. In February 1964 the British government began to consider a 1 percent rise in interest rates to stem the flow out of sterling. Such a rise was a typical first line of defense against the selling of a currency—an increase in the rate of return on deposits provided an incentive for foreign holders to purchase the beleaguered currency or change their minds about selling it. By making borrowing more expensive, raised interest rates also decreased imports, which improved the balance of payments, thereby further reassuring foreign holders of sterling. Unfortunately, it also dampened domestic economic growth.

In the complicated web of international economics, anybody's change in interest rates or currency rates affects everyone else. As Walter Heller, chairman of the Council of Economic Advisors, informed the President, the British rate boost would encourage other European countries to raise their rates, which would in turn put pressure on the United States to follow suit or find foreigners taking their dollar deposits elsewhere.[10] Visiting British Prime Minister Sir Alec Douglas-Home politely heard out Johnson when they conferred in Washington but British officials raised interest rates anyway.[11] Leaving the Oval Office, Home told reporters he believed that Johnson should not have criticized Britain for selling buses to Cuba. A furious Johnson never spoke to him again.[12]

The new Labour government headed by Prime Minister Harold Wilson that took office in October 1964 immediately faced a grave financial crisis. A former Oxford economics professor and wartime civil servant, Wilson had a reputation for being "fundamentally devious" and for "wanting to cut a dash on the stage." Wilson's decision to maintain the pound's value of $2.80 as the basis of his economic policy was good news for the United States. The pound was the first line of defense for the dollar. The Johnson administration, in turn, accepted the British emergency economic package announced on October 26, placing a 15 percent surcharge on most imports as the best alternative, although the British action violated various international trade agreements.[13] Britain did raise its bank rate in late November to 7 percent (twice the American discount rate), but the administration continued to support Wilson's decision even as Washington had to raise the American interest rate by .5 percent.[14] Monetary matters therefore ranked high on the agenda when Wilson paid his first visit as prime minister to Washington on December 7.

The briefing papers for this meeting reveal that Johnson's advisers were particularly concerned about the future of the Western alliance in general and the place of West Germany in particular. As former Secretary of State and presidential adviser Dean Acheson wrote Johnson, "the prime issue in the present European 'crisis' is, as it has been since 1870, Germany." Undersecretary of State George Ball listed two top goals for the Wilson visit: tying Germany irrevocably to the Western alliance and creating a pattern of collective nuclear defense rather than nuclear proliferation. At the same time American officials wanted to ensure a continued strong British defense role. As Secretary of State Dean Rusk told Foreign Secretary Patrick Gordon Walker and British Defense Minister Denis Healey, who had accompanied Wilson, "the UK role has a multiplying effect on our own role." The Johnson administration worried that the Labour party, whose left-wing members continued to be hostile to a strong defense policy, might diminish the British defense presence "East of Suez," i.e., Britain's global defense role that had left it with bases in Malaysia and Singapore and in the Persian Gulf. As Rusk pointedly stated: "The interests of the free world required [that] the US should play a role not only in terms of its own interests but in terms of the interests of the free world as a whole."[15] At the same time Johnson discussed the Vietnam conflict with his guest. Vietnam then and later proved a minefield for Wilson. A staunch anti-Communist himself, Wilson presided over a Labour party increasingly openly antagonistic to the growing American war effort. At the same time, the prime minister knew that Johnson would never stop urging a larger Vietnam role for Britain. But Wilson remained vague, intimating that he intended to disassociate Britain from any American bombing of North Vietnam.[16]

It was the same old story—the administration needed to juggle its Cold War priorities. The policy of military containment, slavishly adhered to throughout the Cold War, dictated that the United States contain the Soviet Union in Europe while waging the Vietnam War in Asia. Economic containment required a functioning capitalist international order with the United States at its center. Both strands of the Cold War proved increasingly expensive. But guns were not enough. Americans expected increasing slices of the pie and Johnson intended that they should have them. Far from cutting domestic spending to pay for foreign expenses, he raised nonmilitary expenditures, exponentially lifting American expectations in the process.

State Department officials crowed over the British Defense White Paper, made public on February 23, 1965, because for the first time this annual exercise recognized the threat that events in Southeast Asia and the Far East posed and called for a 2.3 percent increase in defense spending.[17] Rumors of a potential sterling devaluation flowed through New York markets during the spring. Wilson and his cabinet found the difficult balancing act a modern electorate demands impossible to manage. The Labour party was elected on its promise to improve the British economy, in general, and the lot of the British working class, in particular. At the same time the prime minister proved as wedded to Britain's traditional defense posture as his Conservative counterparts. The upshot was Federal Reserve Board Chairman William McChesney Martin's conclusion that the markets smelled trouble—was a devaluation imminent?[18] The problem with currency values is that they cannot be swept under the rug for long. Through late 1964 and into mid-1965, despite Britain's stopgap measures, a sterling crisis loomed. Britain's hold on great power status grew steadily weaker.

On July 7 Federal Reserve Bank of New York Vice-President Charles Coombs noted that the market had definitely turned against the pound. So important was the plight of sterling that it occupied the first place on Johnson's agenda when he met the so-called Wise Men foreign policy advisers (attendees included Acheson, Robert Lovett, John J. McCloy, and General Omar Bradley) later that day.[19] Three weeks later the mooted sterling crisis exploded. As usual, unpleasant choices faced Wilson and his colleagues. At the base of their planning lay the realization that Britain was still trapped on the "stop-go" treadmill: during the twentieth century whenever the British economy expanded, imports inevitably grew faster than exports. This trend called into question Britain's commitment to hold the sterling parity. Hemmed in by

their perceived need to avoid a devaluation, British postwar governments invariably responded by attempting to cut domestic demand by
raising interest rates, limiting consumer purchases made on the install-
ment [hire purchase] plan, and cutting government expenditures.
Even when the cure was successful, the concomitant recessionary side
effects always proved painful. On July 27 Chancellor of the Exchequer
James Callaghan informed the cabinet of the deflationary package that
he, together with the prime minister and George Brown, had worked
out. It included a moratorium on hospital, school, and housing construction, cuts in local government spending, restrictions on private
investment, and the jettisoning of plans to increase welfare state
expenditures.[20] Yet both British and American officials realized that the
pound would not be safe without external financial aid. Johnson met
with Treasury Secretary Henry Fowler as American officials caucused
to craft the administration's offer to the British and debate the quid pro
quo. Bundy's instinct was the toughest: "What I would like to say" was
that "a British Brigade in Vietnam would be worth a billion dollars at
the moment of truth for sterling." In preparation for the arrival of
British Cabinet Secretary Sir Burke Trend, the presidential adviser
Francis Bator created a list of Anglo-American goals: (1) to hold off
speculators in the short term and to manage the British balance of payments and domestic economy over the longer term; (2) Vietnam "—
with emphasis on what *he* might do"; (3) on East of Suez; (4) on
Germany, "especially the BAOR, [British forces stationed in West Ger-
many], nuclear arrangements and proliferation." On the East of Suez
issue Bator suggested informing Trend that "anything which could be
regarded as even a partial British withdrawal from overseas responsibilities is bound to lead to an agonizing reappraisal here."

Both Ball and Fowler believed that Wilson had gone as far as he
could on Vietnam. Ball told Bundy that suggesting a quid pro quo of a
British troop commitment in Vietnam during financial discussions
would make the British feel they were being cast as mercenaries. Ball
also asserted that if faced with that choice, the British would devalue.
Fowler agreed, believing that the United States should not seek additional British military commitments as the price for new American
aid. On the other hand, he saw nothing wrong with linking a British
rescue to London's promise to maintain its existing commitments.

Only Ackley dissented from the general view that the administration should tell the British government that "devaluation of the pound is unthinkable and cannot be permitted." Bator, in outlining the price the American government could exact for its aid, put his finger on the core issue:

> for Wilson there are some things worse than devaluation. If I'm wrong—if he makes an absolute objective of $2.80 [the current value of the pound]—then of course we are in the saddle and can impose whatever terms we wish when he comes for help on a Friday evening. But I am inclined to think that, even apart from extreme political demands, the proposition that devaluation would be a total and *certain* disaster for Wilson is wrong.[21]

The crisis persisted through August. Wilson continued his search for a Vietnam settlement. In April the British government, in its capacity as cochairman of the 1954 Geneva Conference, had asked the United States and other involved nations for a statement of each country's position on the worsening conflict.[22] The ensuing diplomatic maneuvers exasperated the President and his advisers and eroded their sympathy for Wilson. Yet international financial realities made American assistance to Britain virtually inevitable. Ball succinctly summed up the American worries: if the British devalued it would have serious effects on the American balance of payments and gold position both in the short run and the long run, and if the American government did not launch a rescue operation, the British would cut back on their worldwide defense commitments. Fowler kept urging a multilateral rescue package but added that the United States "should *insist on a wage-price-dividend freeze.*"

Indeed, the British government provided Washington with continual evidence of its seriousness. Minister for Economic Affairs George Brown called Bator on August 26, while "three management types and the union people" were in his office. Brown said he would keep them there until they agreed to a statutory wage-price program. Fowler told Callaghan that the trigger for the Martin/Cromer support package (named for Fed Chairman Martin and Lord Cromer, governor of the Bank of England) would be the announcement of the wage-price restraint legislation by the Labour government.[23]

At the end of August Fowler and Ball went to Europe to reassure nervous markets about the position of the dollar and to complete the British support package. In London Ball "really put it to the British on Singapore and our support of the pound." Bundy informed the President that "it took two talks for Wilson to agree to the association between our defense of the pound and their overseas commitments." Wilson's Rubicon was not East of Suez but a pledge on Vietnam; he did not have to cross this river because Johnson had decided that the American government would not link any British rescue with a British troop commitment in Vietnam.[24]

It took until September 10 for the sterling rescue package to be completed. Participating countries in the support credit, which amounted to about $1 billion, included Austria, Belgium, Canada, West Germany, the Netherlands, Italy, Japan, Sweden, and Switzerland, as well as the Bank for International Settlements. The United States put up about $400 million. British officials publicly emphasized the differences between this support operation and the crisis maneuvers of October and November 1964. The improved British balance of payments position and other Labour government programs, the prime minister pledged, would lead to balance of payments equilibrium in 1966. On September 16 Wilson unveiled the long-awaited National Plan, which in 239 pages laid out the path to two goals: an expansion of real GNP by 25 percent between 1964 and the end of the decade (an annual average of 3.8 percent) and a solution to the balance of payments problem. In an attempt to give concrete form to Wilson's repeated pledge to harness the "white heat of revolution" to the cause of improving British society, the plan also specified economic targets covering the whole gamut of government policy through 1970.[25] Temporarily the support operation was a big success. It offered Callaghan his first six-month period without the need to look at daily reports of sterling sales.[26]

As had become his habit, Wilson sought to visit Johnson in December. At the top of the agenda was the forthcoming annual British defense review. In exchange for agreeing to cuts in social spending during the summer, cabinet ministers had demanded and Wilson acquiesced in a target of a reduction in £100 million in defense expenditures. Bundy urged Trend to avoid any firm decisions until after the December meeting. The continued existence of the British independent nuclear arsenal was also on the agenda as well as possible Anglo-American action on Rhodesia. The white minority of that former self-governing British colony had unilaterally declared the country's independence in November. The administration already supported British economic sanctions; now Wilson sought to increase the pressure. As for the East of Suez issue, the administration "understood the [British] need to save foreign exchange. We have the same need. But neither they nor we can afford to skimp on overseas responsibilities."[27]

In early 1966 the administration followed closely the evolution of the U.K. defense review. To the relief of American officials the British defense statement of February 1966 "claim[ed] significant savings of money and foreign exchange against [a] comparatively small reduction [of] military capacity." The British ground force commitment in Germany would remain at about the same level. While the British government reiterated its decision to evacuate its Aden base in 1968, it intended to remain in Malaysia and Singapore.[28]

March brought good news for the Wilson government: new elections raised the Labour majority in Parliament from a razor-thin three votes to 97. Unfortunately, during the spring American policy in Vietnam notably raised Anglo-American tensions. The left wing of the Labour party, emboldened by its enlarged parliamentary presence, unceasingly lobbied Wilson to disassociate Britain from the growing American war effort. A majority of Labour's constituency parties, many trade unions, and the Labour Party Conference all supported the antiwar movement after 1966. These domestic political considerations squeezed Wilson just as the administration attempted to convince him to "maintain solidarity" with the United States on Vietnam.[29]

Before Wilson's scheduled July 29 visit to Washington another sterling crisis blew up. After the May gold and foreign exchange figures showed a large decline, speculative attacks on sterling forced Wilson and Callaghan back on the sterling watch treadmill. During June, as the balance of payments figures continued to deteriorate, the National Union of Seamen staged a walkout, challenging the government's wage-restraint policy, which had been a key part of the 1965 rescue package. Political discussions in London throughout July indicated that the cabinet consensus in favor of fighting an all-out battle against devaluation had begun to disintegrate. In part this change had to do with Europe. Ministers such as Roy Jenkins who were ardent advocates of Britain's joining the Common Market took to heart the advice of French Premier Georges Pompidou and French Foreign Minister Maurice Couve de Murville given on July 7 that British devaluation was a necessary precondition to entry into the Common Market. George Brown, the head of the Department of Economic Affairs, became a pro-devaluationist in 1965 because he preferred devaluation to the harsh measures that would be needed to avoid it.

But Wilson still soldiered on. In part he was motivated by memories of August 1931 when a sterling crisis led to the dissolution of the Labour cabinet and the formation of a National Government. He also believed that a devaluation would be harsh and remained avoidable. On July 19 Wilson, for the first and last time until the decision to devalue was taken some fifteen months later, allowed the cabinet to discuss the possibility of devaluation. He forced a cabinet vote and, using prime ministerial pressure, Wilson carried the day against devaluation by a vote of 17 to 6. He then announced on July 20 the most stringent set of economic measures ever issued in peacetime, including a six-month standstill on all wage and price increases, followed by a further six months of "severe restraints" on wages, and changes in expenditures and tax laws that would act to hold down British internal demand. These measures rendered the ambitious National Plan moot. As Wilson prepared to come to the United States, the Treasury Department confirmed that the market remained unconvinced that the British government could retain the $2.80 rate. In the two days July 20 and 21, the United States spent $106.3 million to support sterling on the New York foreign exchange market.[30]

Johnson had "deep and serious reservations" about receiving Wilson but concluded that the meeting was unavoidable. Yet Wilson still wanted very much to be on the closest of terms with the President.[31] Not surprisingly, American officials described Wilson as "beset by problems." The State Department evaluated the potential effects on the United States of the British economic crisis while Ball sent Johnson a twenty-five-page essay recommending that the United States convince Britain that "she is no longer the center of a world system." Ball thought Britain should be encouraged to accept a purely European role, join the Common Market, and renounce its independent nuclear deterrent. Fowler, for his part, wanted to help the British government "save itself," which would "prevent developments in the international, economic and financial sphere which would have very serious consequences for the United States, its entire foreign policy, and the continued stability of the free world financial system."[32] Bolstering Britain's financial position had enabled the United States to make international financial issues a low-priority item. With the Vietnam War steadily escalating, the last thing the United States wanted was a major international financial crisis.

In the end the summit followed the pattern of previous encounters: Johnson pushed Wilson to retain Britain's military commitments in Europe and elsewhere, to keep propping up the pound, and also to accept that Britain's future lay in Europe.[33] American officials did not comprehend that success on Johnson's third agenda item would undermine the Anglo-American assumptions upon which Wilson's adherence to the first two planks lay. If Britain made entry into the Common Market a top priority, it would become less interested in retaining either its quasi-superpower military commitments or the overvalued pound. But for all the difficulties, other events during 1966 increased Britain's importance to the United States.

Britain's place in the Western alliance was changing, but the identity of outlook between Washington and London remained constant. The Suez crisis put British leaders in their place. France, the other culprit in the Suez fiasco, followed a radically different course. When he was leader of the Free French Forces fighting Hitler's Germany, Charles de Gaulle proved a constant thorn in the American side, despite President Franklin Roosevelt's repeated attempts to marginalize him. He proved even more difficult to deal with once he became President of France in May 1958. When de Gaulle insultingly vetoed Britain's bid to join the Common Market on January 14, 1963, Ball responded by comparing de Gaulle to a Manchu emperor.[34] Ties between the two countries frayed further after Johnson became President: the American leader mistakenly believed that during their meeting on the night of Kennedy's funeral, de Gaulle had agreed to visit Washington.[35] But even had the two men got along splendidly, relations between the two nations would not have been easy. As de Gaulle told Johnson during their meeting of November 25, 1963, "France is trying to organize continental Europe from [an] economic point of view and after this [is] done perhaps also politically." The United States had a much diminished place in the Europe of de Gaulle's dreams.[36]

Financial questions between the two countries provided a bellwether of the steadily rising tensions.[37] During the first half of the sixties French prosperity continued. In 1962 France ran the largest ongoing balance of payments surplus in the world. The next year the French government began converting $34 million each month of its $900 million dollar holdings into gold. Adding to American unease was the fact that France had the legal right to purchase close to $2 billion of gold from the United States and thereby seriously damage the American effort to conserve its gold holdings.[38] Monetary matters remained at the heart of Franco-American difficulties for the next two years. De Gaulle took the position, as he publicly explained at a press conference on February 4, 1965, that the Bretton Woods vintage gold exchange system allowing dollars to serve the same function as gold gave the United States a free ride. It could finance balance of payments deficits by printing dollars that other countries would meekly accept. The merits of de Gaulle's case only irritated American officials, as did continuing French gold purchases. Additionally, during 1964 the U.S. government had begun its concerted attempt to reform the international payments system. The French government reacted recalcitrantly and in January 1965 announced that it would convert all new accruals of dollars to gold.[39]

French anger at American multinational expansion created additional difficulties. The climate in Paris during the 1960s prefigured the American response to Japanese investment in the United States two decades later. The French government viewed this process, in the words of a *Le Monde* correspondent, as a "Trojan horse" that would allow the surreptitious increase of American influence in France. It particularly annoyed French officials that the despised Bretton Woods gold exchange system facilitated American business expansion in their country.[40]

Foreign policy issues provided another area of discord. During 1965 Soviet-American relations still bore the stress marks caused by the removal of Nikita Khrushchev as First Secretary of the Communist party in October 1964. The idea of the MLF profoundly disturbed the Soviet Union, which saw it as a mechanism for giving West Germany nuclear capability.[41] After long advocating a tough anti-Soviet line, de Gaulle in 1964 began urging détente with Moscow. In June 1966 he made a much advertised if unproductive trip to Moscow. The French president clearly had begun to see himself at the head of a third force of nonaligned nations acting as the mediator between East and West with the goal of "creat[ing] European solidarity from the Atlantic to the Urals." That de Gaulle publicly labeled the growing American presence in Vietnam a grave error did nothing to nurture placid relations. His decision to recognize the People's Republic of China greatly irritated the administration.[42]

French defense policy frayed relations further. Kennedy administration officials had used the MLF to give France and West Germany the shadow of an increased European role without giving up any control over NATO policies, especially nuclear ones.[43] Because de Gaulle had rejected the notion of responsibility without power, he refused to participate. American officials appreciated neither the general's attitude nor the French construction of an independent nuclear arsenal. During 1965 it became clear that de Gaulle's dissatisfaction with NATO, which had its headquarters and major military installations in France, had increased geometrically. In January the well-informed *New York Times* correspondent C.L. Sulzberger reported that France would withdraw from the combined military structure of NATO in 1969. While Ball dismissed this report as coming "from the French who were more Gaullist than de Gaulle himself," in May de Gaulle told Ambassador Charles Bohlen that "after 1969 there will be no installation on French soil except those of French command."[44] At his September news conference the French leader publicly confirmed his opposition to NATO's integrated command structure, announcing his determination to alter it.

The administration kept its public response low-key. Rusk instructed Bohlen to make it clear to de Gaulle and French Foreign Minister Couve de Murville that the United States had no interest in the French proposal of a bilateral American/French agreement. At the same time the administration quietly began to consult with other NATO allies about the future. Paradoxically, the American dedication to NATO increased de Gaulle's freedom of movement: de Gaulle knew that a French withdrawal from NATO would not weaken European security in general or French security in particular. Wherever it was headquartered, the NATO umbrella would still shield France.[45] As he told the French diplomat Hervé Alphand, "It really doesn't matter. If things get bad—which I don't think they will—we'll find ourselves together all the same."[46]

Receiving substantially less than a majority in the French presidential election of December 1965 apparently increased de Gaulle's determination to strike out at NATO. On March 7, Couve de Murville met with Bohlen and handed him a two-and-a-half page handwritten note from de Gaulle to Johnson. Similar missives went to Wilson, Chancellor Ludwig Erhard of West Germany, and the Italian government. De Gaulle thereby informed his allies that "France proposes to recover entire exercise of her sovereignty over her territory, which is at present infringed by the permanent presence of allied military elements and no longer to place forces at the disposal of the Atlantic Organization." An official French aide-mémoire proclaimed that "the organization of the North Atlantic Treaty no longer responded . . . to the conditions which prevail in the world at the present time."[47]

In response the administration hid its annoyance with de Gaulle and played down the impasse, avoiding the danger, identified by Bator, of overdramatizing the situation. The President himself believed that de Gaulle, like Chairman Mao, was a great man but also an egomaniac and resolved not to give the French president the satisfaction of getting into a public quarrel. The President put it this way: "when a man asks you to leave his house, you tip your hat and go." As American officials began planning for NATO's coming eviction from French territory, Johnson wrote de Gaulle stressing American determination to "preserv[e] the deterrent system of NATO."[48] To obviate Republican criticism, Johnson continued to consult with former President Eisenhower. During the previous November, this former NATO commander had presciently advised an immediate acceptance of the 1969 deadline to depart from France and the construction of a new headquarters for NATO in Brussels. Now Eisenhower counseled avoiding "recrimination and open quarrelling . . . we should be 'sweet' in every note and statement, but completely firm in doing the things that the continued effectiveness of NATO requires." Johnson followed these precepts and drew comfort from reports that de Gaulle had little support outside of France.[49]

The logistics of evacuating NATO headquarters in Paris and disentangling French forces from NATO's joint command proved difficult. Moreover, de Gaulle's decision deprived NATO forces of their French storage and staging facilities and threw a giant monkey wrench into NATO's anti-Soviet strategic planning. Making matters worse, the French government sent another aide-mémoire on April 22 seeking to begin the practical measures necessary to accomplish this divorce. Negotiations continued throughout 1966. On July 1 French representatives left the military bodies of NATO, which moved to Brussels. Simultaneously the U.S. military command formally withdrew tactical nuclear weapons from French forces in Germany. On April 1, 1967, all American and Canadian forces evacuated French territory. After nettlesome discussions, de Gaulle condescended to allow NATO flights over French territory.[50]

Beneath the patina of surface harmony, American tempers boiled. Since administration officials saw the United States as the savior of France in two world wars, they found it hard to stomach the French position that U.S. military stocks could not remain in France nor could the United States be assured of the use of pipeline and telecommunications facilities located in France in the event of a new conflagration. In his memoirs Johnson merely stated that de Gaulle's actions were "ill-considered and dangerous." Privately the President used stronger language.[51] Continued French hostility to American positions on international financial questions during 1966 exacerbated tensions and, additionally, increased the importance of American relations with the Federal Republic of Germany during this difficult period.[52]

The American acceptance of an ongoing defense commitment to West Germany in October 1963 put security relations between the two nations on a permanent footing. At the same time, Washington intended to alter the financial nature of the links and increase West Germany's contribution to the Atlantic Alliance. The administration's insistence on financial recompense was not surprising. Both the deteriorating balance of payments position and ever-increasing German financial strength propelled the United States in that direction. In 1963 American military expenditures in Western Europe were $1.6 billion, of which military costs in West Germany and Berlin accounted for $734 million.[53]

When Johnson became President he sought meetings with most world leaders. His initial conference with West German Chancellor Ludwig Erhard took place on December 28 and 29, 1963. Erhard, an economist and postwar economic czar, had taken over from Konrad Adenauer two months earlier. Among the topics of discussion were East-West relations and offset arrangements.[54] During 1964, as the U.S. balance of payments position steadily improved, American supporters of the MLF attempted to interest Johnson in this solution to West Germany's future role in the Western alliance. As Ball told the President on April 10, 1964, it would "give the Germans a legitimate role in the defense of the Alliance but on a leash."[55]

In January 1963 German Chancellor Adenauer and French President de Gaulle had signed a historic treaty of rapprochement. De Gaulle intended to draw Germany into the French orbit: German economic might would be the engine of French diplomatic and economic hegemony in Europe. Bloody and bowed by World War II, German leaders dared not launch their own foreign policy. Economically, a French-German link made great sense. As both nations had balance of payments surpluses, their economic interests were in tandem. Because from the American viewpoint such an alliance would have been disastrous, it was for Johnson to woo West Germany away from the Gaullist embrace.[56]

While Johnson never exhibited the fervent concentration on Europe that characterized his predecessor, de Gaulle's policies elevated NATO's place on his agenda. This change became clear when Johnson and Erhard met on June 4, 1965. Because the American balance of payments position had strengthened during 1964, and Washington predicted a further improvement in 1965, the administration did not place the offset issue on the agenda.[57] In December 1965 Vietnam-induced balance of payments problems convinced American officials to raise the issue anew when Erhard visited Johnson. Ball urged the President to remind Erhard that "the U.S. will keep forces in Europe as long as they are needed and wanted, and the offset should also continue as long as needed." Erhard agreed that offset arrangements in the form of orders amounting to $1.35 billion by December 31, 1966, would continue. The two leaders also discussed nuclear sharing and the future of NATO.[58]

Economic matters remained at the forefront of American concerns.

Treasury Secretary Fowler emphasized the significance of the offset issue to the United States—it had become an "extremely important symbol of cooperation between the two countries." Fowler did not spell out a central American concern—the key role the offset arrangement played in countering congressional criticism of American troop commitments abroad. Legislative pressure grew steadily as Senate Majority Leader Mike Mansfield lobbied the Senate in favor of large cuts in American troops in Europe. The legislators did not question the need for the Cold War per se but wondered why after two decades Europe could not defend itself. Neither Mansfield nor equally influential Democratic Senator Stuart Symington showed any signs of accepting the administration's reassurances on the size of the American troop commitment or the generosity of the current offset arrangements.[59] That the road to Soviet-American détente began in 1966 increased domestic pressures on Johnson. Soviet First Secretary Leonid Brezhnev and Premier Aleksey Kosygin had replaced Khrushchev two years earlier. As relations with the People's Republic of China deteriorated through 1965 Brezhnev and Kosygin began to reach out to Washington. This thaw was welcomed by Johnson administration officials, in part because of a hope that Moscow could soften Hanoi's stance.[60]

Simultaneously, the offset issue had become equally important in German domestic politics. For the first time in its history the Federal Republic's gross national product had failed to rise. Tax revenues had consequently not met expectations, making Erhard's agreement to continue Federal Republic funding of dollar offset payments, no matter how beneficial ultimately, extremely problematic politically.[61] Erhard's own popularity dropped steadily through 1966. American prestige also declined. The intensification of the Vietnam conflict hurt American standing in Western Europe generally. Erhard's ability to continue American military procurement suffered as well from the Starfighter tragedy. Germany had purchased 700 of the American-made F-104G Starfighter planes. Sixty-six planes crashed in 1966 with thirty-eight pilot deaths.[62]

The operative offset arrangement expired in June 1967. After Erhard requested that Johnson sever the American connection between troops and offset, the administration decided to take another approach, designed to calm nervous British officials who had reacted to the collapse of Anglo-German talks by announcing BAOR troop with-drawals. On August 23 the President agreed to a trilateral approach: high-level officials from the United States, the Federal Republic, and Britain would seek a permanent solution to the problem.[63] This initia-tive would also allow "the Administration to retain control of its domestic political situation as regards the stationing of US troops in Europe." Erhard's meetings with Johnson on September 26–27 afforded American and German diplomats the opportunity to reassess their rela-tionship. As Bator told the President, both nations had a strong incen-tive to have the meetings end successfully.[64] But Erhard's domestic political position had worsened. Accused of being an American stooge, he responded by becoming increasingly belligerent toward the United States in public. Ambassador George C. McGhee, for his part, empha-sized the need to avoid unilateral American troop cuts that would be on the table if West Germany did not take steps to palliate congres-sional anger but also warned the President that the offset issue could bring down the Erhard government.

Erhard spent two hectic days in Washington. The chancellor believed that the warm relationship he had previously established with Johnson would allow him to win a political victory—the forgiving by the United States of up to a billion dollars of offset purchases required by the current agreement. He also sought further bilateral meetings rather than immediate tripartite meetings. The chancellor returned to Bonn empty-handed, dooming his attempt to cling to office. At the same time the United States was no closer to a solution of the offset problem.[65]

The trilateral meetings got under way at the end of October.[66] John-son's appointment of John J. McCloy to head the American delegation demonstrated the administration's desire to placate West German resentment at Washington's unyielding attitude and its insistence on three-party talks. The former high commissioner of Germany and certi-fied "Wiseman," McCloy was the German establishment's favorite American. The agenda included the parties' evaluation of the Soviet threat, the appropriate American and British troop levels necessary in Germany to combat this threat, and the nature and amount of offset arrangements that the West German government would enter into in exchange for the Anglo-American troop commitment. The figures in question were large: gross expenditures on U.S. forces in Germany (U.S. payments of cash dollars to Germany) in 1966 totaled $770 million at the current level of forces and were expected to rise to $850 million per annum during the next five years. By comparison the American balance of payments deficit in 1965 equalled $1.3 billion.[67] The offset paid by the German government for British forces in 1965 and 1966 was about $100 million per annum out of a total cost to Britain of $235 million per year. Given British financial difficulties, the amounts in question were even more politically sensitive.[68]

McCloy had also been asked to assess the American defense posture in Europe. Reporting to the President on November 21, he recommended that troop levels and offset questions be separated and no reduction in American forces be made.[69] As Johnson considered this advice, German political turmoil preempted the trilateral negotiations. The Erhard government was replaced by the so-called Grand Coalition government of the Christian Democratic party and the German Socialist party. The new chancellor, Kurt-Georg Kiesinger, had joined the Nazi party in 1933 but had been a firm supporter of the Federal Republic's democratic constitution.[70]

During January and into February, as the new German government decided whether to continue the trilateral discussions, the noises emanating from the other parties alarmed the administration. In particular German comments concerning Bonn's need to cut the British offset coming near the time of the annual British defense review dismayed Washington.[71] Congressional pressure had not ceased either; in December Mansfield reminded Undersecretary of State Eugene Rostow that the senator's resolution urging American troop cuts in Europe had widespread appeal among legislators.[72]

Johnson met with his advisers on February 25, 1967, to lay out the American positions for the soon-to-be-resumed trilateral discussions. Against a backdrop of an exploding American commitment to Vietnam and an overheated American economy, he emphasized his intent to hold troop cuts to a minimum but said that he wanted to assess the attitude of Congress before making any decisions on the level of U.S. forces in Europe. For that reason he decided to arrange a breakfast meeting with the congressional leadership as well as Secretaries Rusk and McNamara, and McCloy. While Johnson mulled over the possibility of congressional trouble, his advisers brought up another potential night-mare: de Gaulle's apparent attempt to use the trilateral impasse to mend the rift with West Germany that had occurred during the mid-sixties and bring the Federal Republic within the general's sphere of influence.[73]

Johnson's meeting with McCloy on March 1 highlighted the President's predicament. McCloy, acting more like Germany's representative in Washington than the reverse, chastised Johnson for changing the emphasis from American troop levels to the BAOR and offset payments. The President responded that Congress was three to one for troop cuts; only Republican Majority leader Everett Dirksen dissented ("he has German grandparents as I have," pointed out the President). The Germans "are as stingy as Hell," added Johnson as he instructed McCloy that "the Germans are the key; they have a new Government; if they can come up with something to help the British, then maybe we can hold the line." Johnson compared his position with Erhard's the year before—if "the Germans and the British will not play . . . then Mansfield and Dick Russell will tackle me." Just let Britain institute troop cuts, concluded the President, and, after waiting a little while, Mansfield will introduce his resolution, and Congress will "all gobble it up."[74]

In tandem with McCloy's meetings, the American Treasury conducted a series of discussions with the German government and the autonomous West German central bank, the Bundesbank, concerning the offset payments and major changes in the Bretton Woods system. The German government sought to make offset payments in another way, rather than simply buying military goods. Previously unenthusiastic, the administration welcomed a proposal for the Bundesbank to purchase U.S. Treasury notes, which would have the desired result of neutralizing the balance of payments effects of American expenditures in West Germany. The key remained the British offset situation: in mid-March a $40 million gap between Britain and Germany existed that threatened to bring down "the whole house of cards." In other words, if the British withdrew substantial troops from Germany, the administration could not withstand the domestic pressure to do the same. In that event, the Atlantic Alliance would be under serious threat.

Because the situation was so delicate and the potential financial promises by Germany so valuable, Johnson's advisers urged him to agree that the United States, if necessary, would make up the $40 million gap to Britain. The British now weighed in—Foreign Secretary George Brown informed the State Department on March 9 that his government was "publicly committed to getting 100% coverage of stationing costs." At the same time Brown reassured the Americans that if the $40 million were found, the British government needed only to withdraw a token brigade from Germany.

By the end of March the three sides concluded the financial discussions; during the next month the American and German negotiators settled the size of American redeployment. On May 2 the parties publicly unveiled a portion of their understandings: As promised, the British withdrew only one brigade from West Germany, a 5,000 cut out of 51,000 troops. The United States redeployed up to 35,000 military personnel out of a total commitment of 260,000. The redeployment would be done on a rotational basis with one of the three brigades of the 24th Infantry Division always remaining in Germany. Once a year all three brigades would conduct joint exercises in Germany. A similar rotational system would be undertaken for the three tactical fighter wings stationed in Germany. In this way the administration had mollified congressional critics and placated German fears.

West Germany agreed to furnish offset payments to the British in the amount of $137 million over the next year while the United States would procure in Britain another $19.6 million of military purchases during the same time frame. The balance of the $20 million British gap would be made up by the extra income the British would receive from relocating certain American units from France to Britain. The United States had conceded that Germany need offset only 80 percent of American costs.

The revolution came in the financial agreements between the United States and West Germany. The Bundesbank agreed to purchase U.S. government medium-term securities in the amount of $500 million in four equal quarterly installments beginning July 1, 1967. More important, in the so-called Blessing Letter (Blessing *Brief*) the Bundesbank promised in writing not to convert any dollars accruing out of German foreign exchange surpluses into gold from the U.S. Treasury. As Germany had the largest convertible exchange holdings of any

European country, this promise, made in perpetuity without any dollar cap, was of enormous importance. As Bator bragged to Johnson, it was "by far the most important part of the U.S.–German deal." Bator went on to inform the President that not only did the agreement put West Germany on a dollar standard, but "as long as we run our economy as responsibly as in the past few years, it will permit [us] to live with moderate deficits indefinitely." What Bator did not point out was that this agreement, as valuable as it was, undercut one of the basic premises of the Bretton Woods agreements: that the United States would always exchange gold for dollars presented at the U.S. Treasury. Once the largest holder of such dollars promised not to present them, the value of the American pledge had clearly declined. However, from the American point of view, no better price for the U.S. commitment in Europe could have been exacted.[75]

The trilateral negotiations achieved that rare denouement where each party received what it needed. West Germany had traded money for security while Wilson and his cabinet could face Parliament with a gap in the defense budget far smaller than seemed possible when the negotiations began. The United States achieved what it desired the most—ballast for the balance of payments and assurance in perpetuity that a German drain of gold from the United States Treasury would not occur. Of equal importance to Washington, the German agreements signified that Bonn had publicly aligned itself with Washington rather than Paris. The quid pro quo had been significant, although not really painful. True, the American agreement to discuss troop deployments with the Federal Republic prior to making any decisions acknowledged West Germany's elevation from client state to junior partner. But because Washington and Bonn agreed on the need for a strong U.S. defense presence in Western Europe, in general, and Germany, in particular, the administration had accepted an easily tenable bargain. Rather than turning American soldiers into German mercenaries, the trilateral agreements represented burden sharing at its best.

The trilateral agreements salvaged the American balance of payments position during 1967 but they were not sufficient to save the pound from devaluation. After the July 1966 cabinet discussions, Wilson once more put devaluation off limits. While Wilson's political standing had improved from July's low, during the autumn he was "on probation with the [Labour] Party and the people."[76] Financial policy lay at the heart of Wilson's travails. The July 1966 austerity package included a wage-price freeze followed by another six months of severe restraint that emasculated the promise of both Labour's 1964 and 1966 campaigns: that Labour's planned economy would produce increased British prosperity. Without the financial backing rendered impossible by the July 1966 measures, the Department of Economic Affairs, newly created in 1964, was without a purpose and the National Plan just so much paper. The Johnson administration remained sensitive to Britain's plight. When it became clear in November 1966 that Wilson needed a cash infusion to prevent British troop withdrawals from undercutting the trilateral discussions, the administration without delay arranged for an additional $35 million in offsetting American purchases in Britain.[77]

American generosity bought time for London and Washington. During early 1967 British economic and defense issues plagued both governments. Ironically the administration encouraged Wilson's decision in March 1967 to apply for British membership in the Common Market, not appreciating that a British turn toward Europe undermined its allegiance to the United States, to a worldwide defense commitment, and to the defense of the sterling parity.[78] De Gaulle needed to be convinced that Wilson would not be an American mole in Europe; even if Britain did not actually need to sever relations with the United States, applying to the Common Market undermined Wilson's incentive to sacrifice on behalf of the "special relationship." The French government had clearly stated its conviction that an "over-valued" pound and the existence of the Sterling Area constituted roadblocks to a British entry into Europe, further undercutting British allegiance to both.[79]

In exchange for the cuts in social spending contained in the July 1966 package, Wilson had agreed to a further reduction of £100 million in overseas spending, much of it to come out of defense expenditures. As a background paper prepared for National Security adviser Walt Rostow pointed out, after the July crisis, the severest since the 1949 devaluation, "more and more Englishmen are unable to find any real reason why their country should spend blood and treasure in far off places." The negotiating progress did not blind the administration to the fact that British defense expenditures were now under continuous review.[80] To the astonishment of presidential adviser William Bundy, the well-connected British journalist Henry Brandon informed him on April 11 that the Wilson cabinet stood on the verge of deciding to pull out East of Suez.[81] Johnson raised that point with Foreign Secretary Brown the next week and again when he met Wilson at the funeral of Konrad Adenauer on April 25. To increase the pressure on Wilson the administration requested that Australian and New Zealand diplomats attempt to persuade Britain not to cut its forces in Singapore and Malaysia by one-half by 1970–71 and evacuate totally in the mid-1970s.[82]

Wilson arrived for his regular spring visit to Washington on June 2. His focus remained on British domestic politics, specifically the fallout from the July 1966 austerity package. Advisers urged Johnson to apply all pressure possible to "keep Wilson on the right track" and persuade him to change his mind about Britain's East of Suez commitment.[83] In the event, the discussions focused on the Middle East—the tension between Israel and Egypt had reached the breaking point and war broke out on June 6.

The Six-Day War exacerbated pressures on sterling. As happened during the Suez crisis eleven years earlier, the disruption of the Suez Canal and Middle East shipping damaged British invisible exports and disrupted European oil supplies. According to Whitehall, the canal's closure cost Britain $200 million in the first six months.[84] During any crisis a weak reserve currency suffers the most of all as holders, fearing a devaluation, rush to sell the currency at the old rate. The existing fixed exchange rate system made such trading virtually risk-free, further raising the probability that it would occur.

By this time the White House had resigned itself to the British withdrawal from East of Suez, announced in the Supplemental Defense White Paper of July 18. Officials now focused their attention on the more important issue: the defense of sterling. An American idea for a 25-year loan to fund Britain's sterling area debts had circulated in February. It went nowhere, in part because the Johnson administration sought a British commitment to maintain an East of Suez defense role that the Wilson Cabinet was no longer willing to make. The dollar's worsening international position increased Washington's reliance on London to deflect investors' fears; in essence sterling served as a decoy that protected the dollar from the onslaught of the market. Walter Heller sent a comforting report on September 9: "there still seems to be a grim determination to avoid devaluation." The dock strike in September, which hurt exports much as the seamen's strike had done a year earlier, aggravated the financial crisis. Worse still, the rise in British economic activity triggered the customary deterioration in the British balance of payments. In response, on October 19 the Bank of England raised its interest rate to 6.5 percent.[85] The administration concurrently took measures to ameliorate sterling's difficulties.[86]

When the balance of payments deficit for October proved extremely large, the crisis worsened. As pressure on sterling heightened, on November 8 ministers began openly discussing devaluation. The cabinet knew that a severe clampdown on wages and prices together with a further rise in the bank rate would be needed to save the sterling parity. At the same time, if devaluation came, ministers would also need to devise harsh measures to offset the increased cost of imports and the attendant worsening of the balance of payments, which would accompany a cut in the international value of the pound.[87]

At this point the United States provided the only possible hope of rescue. Wilson considered a last-minute trip to Washington with Vietnam serving as the cover story. The timing proved impossible.[88] While during the first days of November the administration responded coolly to a rescue venture, on November 13 Rostow advised the President that "the risks for us are just too great to be worth the gamble—if it can be avoided through a good multilateral support operation." It was too late.[89] As Alfred Hayes, the president of the Federal Reserve Bank of New York, observed, "Britain chose to devalue."[90] On November 18 Chancellor of the Exchequer James Callaghan announced that the pound would be devalued 14 percent , from £1 = $2.80 to £1 = $2.40. It was left for the U.S. government to put the best possible face on the British action and brace for the storm against the dollar that was sure to follow.[91]

The interplay among the United States and its European allies during the 1960s illustrates the economic dimensions that lay at the heart of the Western alliance during the Cold War. Changes in the relative economic power of Western nations made the existing relationships among NATO nations obsolete and necessitated the creation of new rules to govern these connections. NATO had been erected on a foundation of American strength, aided by the British determination to continue defense and economic policies far beyond Britain's means. Both these pillars weakened during the 1960s. On the one hand, American financial strength could no longer sustain Western defense costs unaided. On the other hand, British ministers realized that, however strong their dedication to Empire, Commonwealth, and Sterling Area, the resources to uphold these commitments no longer existed. Ironically, as the British addiction to £1 = $2.80 and East of Suez waned, the American enthusiasm for both aspects of British foreign policy increased. For the first time, Washington officials now understood that the pound provided the first line of defense for the dollar. If the pound were devalued, speculators would attack the dollar, made vulnerable by the costs of running a war in Vietnam and a war on poverty simultaneously, without compensating tax increases. It was this realization, rather than the need to purchase British support for American policy in Vietnam, that motivated American support for the pound.

Absent the declaration of war and honest funding the President could never bring himself to request, the Vietnam War had stretched the American military machine past the point of no return. Administration officials believed that Western troops should remain in Southeast Asia and the Far East but would not do the job itself. Britain, in the view of the White House, should continue bearing the imperial burden. For a time the Labour government led by Harold Wilson followed the American script. The prime minister and his colleagues did not follow Washington's lead because they had surrendered to American pressure but because they shared the same aspirations. When British goals diverged from those in Washington, when Wilson no longer made an absolute fetish of $2.80, then disembarkation and devaluation quickly followed. While both countries had made the Cold War the basis of their foreign policies, in neither nation did public opinion support sacrificing the good life to fight the conflict. To the contrary, during the 1960s Western governments needed to produce prosperity to stay in power.

Fortunately for the future of the Western alliance, none of the major parties differed on the need to maintain a strong defense presence against the Soviet Union and the Warsaw Pact. This fact underwrote the success of the trilateral negotiations: neither the United States nor Britain nor West Germany could contemplate dismantling NATO. The Soviet arms buildup of the late sixties and the invasion of Czechoslovakia in August 1968 further reinforced these views. With all parties sharing the same overriding goal, only the details needed to be worked out.

The trilateral discussions settled the technicalities. None of the three relevant governments wanted to replace Anglo-American battalions with an enhanced German military machine. Instead Germany would become the money bags for the alliance, agreeing to buy U.S. Treasury bills, not purchase gold, and generally, as McCloy put it, take the United States off the hook on the balance of payments issue.[92] Gaining German financial support more than compensated the United States for the loss of the pound's international role that followed from the November 1967 devaluation. It further signified that in the clash between the United States and France, the United States would continue to command German loyalty. In this way the threat to the alliance from de Gaulle's maneuvers was successfully contained. The financial and defense arrangements made in 1967 eroded the original Cold War financial framework. It would be left for the next administration to complete the transformation.

9

The Seventies

Richard Nixon personified American Cold War society. His influence peaked during the period 1969–74, when he occupied the White House. It was fitting that he took office at the height of American postwar internal dissension because Nixon had come to fame by exploiting political and social divisions. Domestic economics, he believed, had cost him the 1960 election. Obsessed by the 1972 campaign from November 1968, Nixon pulled out all the stops to avoid becoming a one-term president: Watergate political dirty tricks and the derailment of Bretton Woods. Although his involvement in the Watergate scandal forced him to resign in disgrace on August 9, 1974, Nixon's specter haunted his successor, Gerald Ford. Indeed Ford's pardon of Nixon significantly contributed to his defeat in the 1976 election. Moreover, Nixon's economic gamesmanship gave full force to the inflation that cost Ford significant electoral support. The widespread revulsion against Nixon and Washington politics also played a part in the presidential campaign run by Jimmy Carter, one of the most anti-Washington candidates ever to seek national office. Carter's self-con-

sciously different presidency in turn brought Americans to Ronald Reagan, who promised economic and political renewal.

Nixon was a professional politician who used the anti-Red tide that swept the United States during the early years of the Cold War to make his name and to claim political leadership. He perfected the art of the smear, discrediting left-of-center candidates by linking them to Communists. Yet Nixon's instincts, as in the notorious Alger Hiss case, sometimes proved sounder than those of his opponents. Nixon's bad boy image also made him a useful running mate for Dwight Eisenhower in 1952. Ironically Nixon's success on the campaign trail, repeated four years later, earned him Eisenhower's disdain. During Nixon's eight years as vice-president, Ike never once invited him to the White House family quarters. Nixon's tactics and personality also garnered him widespread public dislike; being a Nixon hater was a popular occupation in liberal circles. That Nixon ultimately became President only engendered further contempt. In turn his unpopularity fed his growing paranoia. Two years after his 1960 defeat by John Kennedy, Nixon lost another race, this time for governor of California. Immediately after his concession speech Nixon told the press, his particular cross, that because he was quitting politics, "you won't have Nixon to kick around anymore."[1] But within two years Nixon returned to national politics. His ability to capture the center and enigmatic references to a secret plan to end the Vietnam War (mirroring Ike's promise to go to Korea sixteen years earlier) won him the presidency this time. But only just.

Nixon never forgot that he was a minority President, elected with 43.4 percent of the vote in a three-way race against Hubert Humphrey and George Wallace.[2] From election day 1968, Nixon began to plan his next campaign. In his favor was his intelligence, his cunning, and a concerted worldview of foreign policy. Another advantage was Nixon's willingness to sacrifice any principle whenever necessary. He also had able advisers on substantive matters.[3] (The skill of his political advisers proved dubious.) Nixon aimed his rhetoric at the "silent majority"— those who were not black, not young, and not liberal. But his domestic policies built on the revolution begun by Johnson. The Philadelphia Plan, at the time little celebrated, mandated what was in effect a federal quota system for minority hiring for federal contracts, an extension

of Johnson's 1965 Executive Order No. 11246, which first promulgated "affirmative action." Nixon also signed into law legislation linking automatic Social Security raises to upward increases in the Consumer Price Index. The bill had been promoted by Representative Wilbur Mills, who was running for president in 1972; Nixon, fearing the wrath of senior citizens, would not veto it. This legislation proved to be a crucial step in the creation of the entitlement society and also contributed to the acceleration of inflation in the early 1970s.[4] Most important, Nixon used the power of his office to ensure the best possible economic climate in 1972, indifferent to the havoc his decisions wreaked on the health of the economy.

The Vietnam War destroyed the containment consensus that had long dominated American foreign policy. Haggling over the proper number of American missiles and what kind of support to give a particular anti-Communist surrogate constituted the gamut of acceptable debate. No one in the mainstream, before Vietnam, discussed basic principles. They had been sealed in amber by the Berlin blockade and the Communist takeover of China. But the American ground war in Vietnam dissolved these assumptions, in direct proportion to the number of troops fighting in Southeast Asia. Opinion in America polarized between those who thought the war should be fought harder and those who wanted the United States to withdraw. Among the latter were principled opponents of the war as well as articulate, educated college students whose views received significant media attention. That the draft system largely exempted college students increased the determination of those subject to the draft to avoid the possibility of becoming a grim statistic. That the Vietnam War involved "a quarrel in a faraway country between people of whom we know little" (Neville Chamberlain's description of Czechoslovakia) did not increase its pull on the American conscience, nor did South Vietnam's unsavory series of military dictators.

National Security Adviser, later Secretary of State, Henry Kissinger shared command of foreign policy with Nixon, sometimes overshadowing the chief executive. A pragmatist of equal skill with the President, the German-born Harvard professor began 1968 advising Nixon's chief rival, Nelson Rockefeller, but by year's end had captured the ear of the President. They intended to implement a grand Metternichian global strategy to change the foreign policy parameters that

had been frozen for the past two decades.[5] Nixon and Kissinger saw Vietnam and the surrounding states of Cambodia and Laos as a sideshow and correctly appreciated that both Moscow and Beijing shared this view.[6] They sought a comprehensive agreement with First Secretary of the Soviet Communist Party Leonid Brezhnev covering outstanding bipolar issues, especially arms control. The Cuban missile crisis had sparked a massive Soviet missile buildup designed to achieve parity with the United States.[7] Soviet-American talks on an arms-limitation treaty had broken off in the wake of the Soviet invasion of Czechoslovakia in August 1968. Now Nixon intended to reopen these talks. To achieve the agreement he sought, Nixon decided upon a daring strategy—reaching out to the People's Republic of China (PRC). Since the Communist takeover in 1949, Washington had ostentatiously ostracized the Beijing government. Although clandestine talks were held from time to time in Warsaw, officially American administrations followed a one-China policy: the one China was Formosa (Taiwan), whose aging leader, Chiang Kai-shek, remained the darling of the American right.

The signs of a Sino-Soviet split had long been apparent. Unfortunately, domestic political concerns prevented American diplomats from taking advantage of the intra-Communist feuding until Nixon became President. His anti-Communist credentials shielded him from attack on the right, leaving left-wing politicians to watch helplessly as Nixon implemented their designs. During 1969 the United States signaled the PRC that Washington wanted to strengthen unofficial contacts; secret Warsaw talks soon resumed. During these conversations American diplomats indicated a willingness to downgrade U.S. military contacts with Taiwan, while the Chinese representatives agreed that a presidential envoy might visit Beijing. In October 1970 Nixon made his feelings clear, telling *Time* that "if there is anything I want to do before I die, it is to go to China." In April 1971 came the famous visit of the American ping-pong team to China. Three months later Kissinger, using the cover story of a trip to Pakistan, made his secret trip to China. The news proved electrifying, with critical domestic and international effects. American ties with the PRC pressured the Soviet Union at the negotiating table. Nixon gained tremendous domestic prestige for his daring diplomacy, which paid off during the 1972 campaign. At the same time grand strategy served to distract Americans from the Vietnam War, in which they were already fast losing interest.[8]

Nixon understood that Johnson's presidency had died in Vietnam. History would not repeat itself. The key, as this President saw it, was "Vietnamization"—returning the war to the South Vietnamese army (ARVN). On May 14, 1969, Nixon announced that soon "the South Vietnamese . . . will be able to take over some of the fighting." The President placed his policy shift within a broader context; the Nixon Doctrine, announced in Guam in July 1969, provided that the United States would aid "the defense and development of allies and friends" but "cannot—and will not—conceive all the plans, design all the programs, execute all the decisions and undertake all the defense of the free nations of the world." During the summer and fall Nixon ordered the withdrawal of sixty thousand American ground troops from Vietnam, reversing a buildup fifteen years in the making. The Nixon strategy was to combine the ground troop withdrawal with the provision to the ARVN of ample aid under a protective umbrella of American air and naval support. The White House believed that military forces on the ground remained essential to a political settlement of the war. Nixon remained stuck in the trap that had long bedeviled American leaders: he was unwilling to take the political consequences of agreeing to an obvious American withdrawal without victory, while Hanoi and its Viet Cong allies were prepared to outsuffer and outwait the Americans. After the Paris peace talks stalled, Nixon offered secret talks to North Vietnam. (It is a mark of Nixon's style that he attempted to keep these talks secret also from his secretary of state, William Rogers.)[9]

The following year, with Vietnam still an issue on college campuses and around coffee tables throughout the United States, Nixon and Kissinger launched a secret invasion of Cambodia, enlarging the war without congressional authorization. Nixon's "incursion," designed to eliminate North Vietnam's elusive major bases, led to further American polarization. Bloody protests racked college campuses (including four dead at Kent State University on May 4, 1970), while polls reflected that a majority of Americans supported the President. Vietnamization continued during 1971 and 1972; the Cambodian maneuver did not bring success to ARVN but, together with continued American saturation bombing of North and South Vietnam, it allowed further American troop withdrawals. The continuing arrival of Vietnam veterans stateside lowered the general temperature on Vietnam as did the decision by television networks at Nixon's behest to lessen their coverage of the conflict. Vietnam was the first television war. Watching simulcast American deaths hardened feelings against the war, as did various scenes of South Vietnamese brutality. (North Vietnamese brutality existed in abundance but did not make it onto American screens.) Nixon and his staff put enormous pressure on the television networks to eliminate what they saw as biased reporting just when media directors decided that the American public had tired of battle scenes. As Robert Northshield, a former executive producer for NBC News, put it, "[in 1972] the American voter is going to vote for Nixon now because the voter, who is also the viewer, thinks that Nixon has ended the war."[10]

During 1972 foreign policy came together for Nixon. Vietnam had been marginalized both in Washington and by Hanoi's allies in the Soviet Union and China. The President's week in China at the end of February allowed him to play the grand chess master to great public acclaim, proving to Nixon and Kissinger the advantages of their triangular strategy. At the end of May Nixon went to Moscow, inaugurating "détente" with the Soviet Union. He waxed lyrical over Brezhnev's "animal magnetism" and rejoiced that Soviet leaders seemed relatively indifferent to the interests of their satellite states.[11] Nixon's prize was the completion of the SALT I arms limitation treaty largely on American terms. The 1972 ABM treaty limited each signatory to two antiballistic missiles (ABMs) while the President also achieved a temporary agreement on offensive strategic weapons. Nixon used economic diplomacy to sweeten the deal for his adversaries, agreeing to a three-year $750 million credit that would enable the Soviet Union to purchase American wheat. Farm state voters embraced the pact and Nixon's stock rose. (Its negative effects became apparent the following year when it contributed to the inflation that savaged American food budgets.) Nixon's prestige rose to unprecedented heights. In November he triumphed with a landslide victory in 49 states. He completed his foreign policy sweep when, on January 23, 1973, the United States, South Vietnam, and North Vietnam signed the Paris Peace Accords, providing that a cease-fire would go into effect in Vietnam on January 27. The United States withdrew all American forces while North Vietnam released American prisoners of war. The political status of South Vietnam remained unresolved but America's longest war was almost over.[12]

Nixon and Kissinger had declared 1973 the "Year of [Western] Europe." The Nixon Doctrine's acceptance of the limits of American financial power coincided with growing European self-confidence. The enlarging of the European Economic Community, now called the European Community (EC), from six to nine members in January 1973 exemplified a growing allied thrust toward greater autonomy. Yet on both sides of the Atlantic, contradictions abounded. Washington urged continued European integration while expecting unquestioned obedience to U.S. orders. Europeans who craved deliverance from the American way still sought safety under the U.S. military umbrella. Of great substantive importance was German Chancellor Willy Brandt's move toward *Ostpolitik*: a reaching out to Eastern Europe in general and East Germany in particular. The administration still viewed Brandt's reversal of Adenauer's hard-line anti-Communism with suspicion but managed to accommodate it within its own push for détente.

Kissinger's brave declaration that 1973 would embody "new realities requiring new approaches" was meant to signal an all-out American-driven renewal of the NATO alliance. But a variety of difficulties dashed the attempt of Nixon and Kissinger to reenergize the Western alliance. Not one of the European big three—French President Georges Pompidou, German Chancellor Willy Brandt, and British Prime Minister Edward Heath—welcomed the opportunity offered by the White House. Political differences explained the reluctance of Pompidou and Brandt to take the leap; Heath proved "the most difficult British prime minister we [Kissinger and Nixon] had encountered." The September Yom Kippur War and the consequent oil shocks exploded the fiction of a unified EC mature enough to handle its own foreign policy. Instead of one for all and all for one, *sauve qui peut* ruled the day.[13]

Had the President been able to pay attention to foreign affairs, Nixon and Kissinger might have been able to rescue something from their abortive initiative. But Nixon spent most of 1973 fighting for his official life. As in a Greek tragedy, hubris sparked Nixon's fall at the height of his success. On June 17, 1972, several men burgled the Democratic party's national headquarters in the Watergate complex of

Washington, D.C. They belonged to a veritable empire of dirty trick-sters orchestrated by Nixon's staff and the Committee to Re-elect the President (CREEP), whose activities included wiretaps, break-ins, and disinformation campaigns. The President's masterminding of the cover-up of White House involvement in these and other crimes led to the progressive unraveling of his administration and the first presidential resignation in American history. Nothing could save the President from his fate, not lies, not sacrificial lambs, not foreign policy crises such as the 1973 Yom Kippur Middle Eastern War, which brought the United States to the highest military alert against the Soviet Union since the Cuban missile crisis.[14]

His successor, Gerald Ford, a former male model and Yale Law School graduate, inherited Nixon's policies and Henry Kissinger, who in September 1973 had become secretary of state.[15] Ford attempted to revive détente, which had been battered by Middle Eastern and other events. U.S. and Soviet negotiators reached an agreement placing a ceiling on large bombers and strategic nuclear missiles. In 1975 the United States and the Soviet Union joined thirty-three other nations in signing the Helsinki accords, which provided for four "baskets" of agreements. One mandated that force could not be used to change any country's borders. This guarantee of the Red Army's post–World War II conquests provided sufficient inducement for Moscow to agree to another basket affirming basic human rights for individuals. Indeed, Moscow welcomed this Western blessing of the Soviet sphere of influ-ence in Eastern Europe. But Kremlin leaders became alarmed at the surging number of dissidents who sought legitimacy under the "Basket Three" provisions. When Soviet citizens attempted to set up a Helsinki Watch in their homeland, they were brutalized; by May 1977 only four members of the Helsinki monitoring group's Soviet contingent were not incarcerated in labor camps or prisons.[16]

Ford presided over the shameful exit of the last Americans from Vietnam in April 1975, following a successful North Vietnamese and Viet Cong offensive. Nixon had promised South Vietnam's leaders that if they accepted the 1973 treaty, he would continue to support their regime and would "respond with full force" if North Vietnam violated the agreement. But Congress, wrenching control of foreign policy from the steadily weakening President, quickly scaled back aid for South

Vietnam. The ARVN may have been the world's fourth-largest army on paper in 1973 but it proved incapable of holding off its opponents two years later.[17] During early 1975 the administration futilely scurried to bolster the flagging South Vietnamese regime. As the last Americans fled in helicopters from the American Embassy in Saigon, Americans at home attempted to put the Vietnam War behind them.[18]

But domestic economic conditions during the 1970s provided little cheer. The era when American GNP doubled, when the American pie consistently grew, was over. Double-digit inflation became a reality in 1973 and 1974, eroding confidence in the President and faith in the future. A combination of domestic and foreign factors ended the knee-jerk years of the American dream: the erosion of relative American productivity and production advantages, the destruction of the fixed currency rates that kept inflation in check, the oil shocks, and widespread commodity price increases. During the first three quarters of 1974 GNP fell 2.5 percent and then declined another 3.2 percent in the winter of 1974–75. The American standard of living dropped from first to fifth in the world; West Germany, our former charity case, now ranked ahead of the United States.[19] Was having it all out of reach? Jimmy Carter seemed to think so.

Carter, a relatively unknown governor of Georgia, came to the attention of the elite as a member of the Trilateral Commission, a selective version of the Council on Foreign Relations.[20] He consciously campaigned as an outsider against Washington. The electorate, fed up with Nixon and Ford, responded by repudiating them at the polls. Carter vowed to banish traditional big power politics, slash the defense budget, and emphasize human rights issues. During his first two years in office Carter scored notable foreign policy triumphs. In March 1979 Israel and Egypt signed the Camp David accords, settling their conflicts, and normalizing diplomatic relations. This agreement marked the first peace treaty between Israel and an Arab country and represented an enormous advance in Middle Eastern diplomacy. Carter demonstrated equal conviction and political courage in his stewardship of the Panama Canal treaties, which in 1978 recognized the sovereignty of Panama over the canal territory and provided for the return of the canal to Panama in the year 2000.

But foreign policy issues fatally damaged Carter's credibility as President. Carter found it impossible to establish close relations with Western European leaders. (He was described by one British diplomat as "out of his depth, entirely honest, very scrupulous, but with no idea of how the world worked.") On the one hand, the President called for trilateralism—a tripartite relationship among Western Europe, Japan, and the United States. But on the other, he frightened NATO allies by attempting bilateral negotiations with the Soviet Union. Neither approach worked with Moscow. The Soviet announcement that it was deploying SS-20 nuclear missiles aimed at Western Europe led European allies and Washington hawks to charge Carter with undermining the NATO alliance. The United States then pledged to install 572 Pershing II missiles to counter the Soviet threat. This response triggered protests throughout Europe with no compensating approbation from allied leaders. The debate over the development of the neutron bomb also proved problematic for American decision makers. While West German Chancellor Helmut Schmidt supported the development of this weapon meant to be more lethal to people than buildings, Prime Minister James Callaghan of Great Britain and other European leaders told Carter they would refuse to permit neutron bombs to be stationed on their soil. Once again American policy pleased neither the antinuclear activists nor European political leaders.

The final nail in the coffin of Carter's strategy toward Moscow came with the Soviet invasion of Afghanistan in December 1979.[21] This first expansion by Soviet troops into a nation outside the borders of the Soviet bloc established in the 1940s led Carter to mouth rigid anti-Moscow rhetoric not heard in decades, to wit, announcing that the invasion was "the gravest threat to peace" since 1945. The President in his January 1980 State of the Union speech proclaimed the Carter Doctrine, maintaining that the United States would "repel by any means necessary, including military force," any "attempt by any outside force to gain control of the Persian Gulf region." Throughout the first half of 1980 Carter continually referred to the policy of containment. The SALT II treaty died as Carter shifted gears and aimed for nuclear superiority over the Soviets. Embodying the new hard-line administration tactics was Presidential Directive (PD) 59, which foresaw massive new forces fighting a prolonged, tactical nuclear war.[22] Foreign arms sales doubled between 1977 and 1980, while the military budget

soared. The precipitous rise in military spending then fed the unprecedented inflation that had become a feature of American life in the seventies. The President also announced a boycott of the 1980 Moscow
Olympics and an embargo on wheat sales. Carter called Soviet leader
Brezhnev a "liar" and informed the American people that "the action
of the Soviets has made a more dramatic change in my opinion of what
the Soviets' ultimate goals are than anything they've done in the previous time I've been in office." From attempting to promulgate a new foreign policy, Carter found himself echoing classic containment theory.
But this time only Britain, now led by Margaret Thatcher, strongly
backed the American decision to isolate the Soviet Union economically and diplomatically.[23]

The United States had long supported the Shah of Iran. His resignation and flight from Iran in January 1979 and the installation in
Teheran of a fundamentalist Islamic regime destroyed a pillar of American foreign policy in the Persian Gulf.[24] Fitful attempts at diplomacy
ended in October 1979 when Carter, under domestic pressure, agreed
to admit the fatally stricken Shah to the United States for medical
treatment. In retaliation radical students seized the American Embassy
in Teheran. The ensuing hostage crisis proved to be Carter's Waterloo.
The forcible detention of 51 Americans for 444 days led Carter, Secretary of State Cyrus Vance, and National Security Adviser Zbigniew
Brzezinski to attempt a variety of solutions. Standard diplomacy led
nowhere, and while far-reaching American economic sanctions,
notably a freeze of Iran's assets, proved damaging, they were not fatal to
Iran.[25]

Carter's actions fell under the International Emergency Economic
Powers Act, passed in 1977. Part of the post–Watergate burst of congressional self-assertion in foreign policy, IEEPA was intended to regu-
larize negative presidential economic diplomacy. But its broad
language, permitting in peacetime the sanctions and other actions previously allowed only in wartime or periods of national emergency, actually represented an expansion of presidential autonomy.[26]

Finally the administration launched a military strike that ended in a
humiliating embarrassment for the White House. Vance resigned but
the administration's credibility plummeted to zero. As ABC News
nightly reminded the public, America was held hostage. Ronald Rea-

gan rode to office promising that he would allow his fellow Americans to ride tall in the saddle once again.

Reagan's rhetoric also appealed to Americans frightened by the worsening economic malaise. Nearly 70 percent of the voters in the 1976 election named economic worries as their main concern. Carter had grievously disappointed them. Inflation rates again hit double digits, unemployment climbed to nearly 8 percent, and the second oil shock sent energy prices skyrocketing again. The dollar's international value plummeted—from September 1977 to October 1978 it dropped 40 percent against the yen and 13 percent against the deutsche mark.[27] Nor could the President from Plains, Georgia, supply emotional comfort. Instead he told Americans that they were responsible for the energy crisis because of their "self-indulgence and consumption." Reagan, by contrast, coming out of Hollywood's dream machine, offered a revived American dream: we could have it all.[28]

10

Bretton Woods Has a Great Fall

> There is widespread feeling in Europe that we have
> no interest or concern about the international finan-
> cial and economic system.
>
> Paul McCracken, Chairman, Council of Economic Advisors

Richard Nixon is famous for many things: for being the only President who resigned his office in disgrace, for his paranoia, for his triangular diplomacy, for his ardent anti-Communism. Yet few people
today realize that he was the destroyer of Bretton Woods. When Nixon
concluded that the price was too high, he pulled the plug. The President
wanted no systemic restraints on his power over the domestic economy.
Placing little value on international economic and monetary policy,
Nixon believed that increased global competition made a healthy balance of trade a nation's chief international economic priority. The
founding fathers of Bretton Woods, remembering Depression-era
autarky and secure in the knowledge of overweening American economic strength, assumed that a suitable foreign economic policy would
nurture the domestic economy. But Nixon, free from any systemic loyalty, believed that the United States could no longer afford the luxury of
supporting the Western economic system as a whole. He would do what
was best for the domestic economy and his own political future and let
the international economic system adapt to the United States.

The "Nixon shocks" of August 15, 1971, destroyed the Bretton

Woods system. Nixon severed the link between the dollar and gold. The great surprise was, nothing happened. Paradoxically, foreign currencies were now on a dollar standard. In his August 15 address the President had promised that in cooperation with the International Monetary Fund and American trading partners, "we will press for the necessary reforms to set up an urgently needed new international monetary system. Stability and equal treatment is in everybody's best interest." By mid-1973 Nixon and his advisers concluded that the nonsystem that had evolved over the previous twenty months actually suited the administration very well. The dollar standard preserved most of Washington's benefits from the Bretton Woods order at far less cost. The double-barreled strength of the American economic and security position made this alchemy possible.

Richard Nixon came to office wearing the mantle of fiscal responsibility and balanced budgets. Having served as Eisenhower's vice-president, he hardly needed to proclaim his fealty to conservative principles of finance. Yet Nixon proved far less interested in preserving a "sound dollar" and cultivating the confidence of foreign governments and investors than had either of his predecessors. Nixon's economic concerns were chiefly domestic. He believed that the 1960 recession had cost him the presidency. And he faced two obstacles in his obsession to present the electorate with a strong domestic economy in 1972. Given the cyclical nature of the American economy, the unprecedented economic growth of 1961–68 foreordained a downturn. The second problem was that during the later years of the Johnson administration, domestic and international factors had led to rapidly rising inflation: from 1 percent per year in 1961, inflation escalated to almost 6 percent in 1970.[1] While low by later standards, these rates frightened Americans unaccustomed to continually rising prices. As an antidote against the upward spiral, the Federal Reserve Board tightened money, raising interest rates to dampen the demand for goods and services that greatly contributed to rising inflation. Unfortunately the medicine had serious side effects—it slowed economic growth and raised unemployment, creating the new phenomenon of stagflation. Economists, whose prestige had soared during the sixties, found themselves increasingly perplexed by the worst-of-all-worlds combination of inflation and economic stagnation.

In January 1969 Nixon informed his newly appointed Treasury Secretary David M. Kennedy that "one of the objectives of this administration will be to move away from the system of controls over foreign
lending and investing."[2] At the same time Nixon prepared to discuss
foreign economic questions during his first trip to Europe as President.
Paul McCracken, the chairman of the Council of Economic Advisors,
told Nixon that "another crisis in the near future is quite conceivable."
In connection with this trip McCracken prepared a series of memoranda for the President on the international financial system. He
advised Nixon that rather than search for guilt, he should understand
that the strains in the Bretton Woods system occurred because various
countries put different objectives at the heart of their social and economic policies. Germany, given its hyperinflation during the 1920s,
believed that inflation was the greatest threat of all, while the British
Labour government found it hard to reduce government spending.
Unemployment headed the American list of economic ills to avoid.

McCracken's analysis of the strains within the system revealed the
real problem with the Bretton Woods order: it envisioned that the
United States would play a sui generis role. Alone of the world's governments, Washington needed to place systemic safety ahead of domestic economic concerns. McCracken, in company with the President
and administration officials, had obviously abandoned this mode of
thought. Nixon agreed with his advisers that the "preferred strategy, *if
possible*," was to "move ahead in 'calm discussion' with friends." However, the alternative to this approach, memorialized on February 20,
1969, was "unilateral action to suspend gold convertibility."[3] The European trip produced no new initiatives; unilateral action moved closer.[4]
In April 1969 the administration had begun the process of removing
controls on overseas American investment. This step paved the way for
capital flight from the United States unless the American rates rose
higher than European ones.[5]

Events soon forced limited changes in the system. The French government, still the least cooperative of the G-10 members, faced
another financial crisis. McCracken warned the President that a
French devaluation would hurt both the dollar and sterling. By June
the economist and long-time Nixon adviser Arthur Burns predicted
that the monetary situation appeared to be "approaching a critical

phase."[6] As White House staffer John Brown informed Nixon on June 25, the current climate provided reasons for Washington to urge substantive changes in the international monetary system: while high American interest rates had created a temporary improvement in the balance of payments position, lowering them would reverse the flow.[7] The administration did not seize this opportunity, but instead reacted passively when France devalued the franc 11.1 percent on August 8.[8]

With his eyes on the 1970 midterm election Nixon concentrated on domestic developments, seeking lower rates to counter the sluggish American economy. But the Federal Reserve Board, not Nixon, had the authority to change rates. Its power and autonomy indeed made it virtually a fourth branch of government. The previous head of the Fed, William McChesney Martin, had served under Eisenhower, Kennedy, and Johnson and during the first year of the Nixon administration. His ability to ignore political considerations endeared him to none of these Presidents. Martin's resignation, in January 1970, eased the President's task. The new Fed chairman, Arthur Burns, was a Nixon adviser who had coordinated Nixon's prepresidential task forces.[9]

Growing press criticism of the American domestic economic position in early 1970 ensured an imminent White House move. After reading the syndicated columnist Sylvia Porter's accusation that "the recession is already here and now," the President wrote that "(1) she wants it that way—(2) But this has some substance—it shows our problem." At the legislative leadership meeting of March 17, 1970, the President made clear his "intention of avoiding a recession at all costs and guarantee[d] some sort of upturn in the economy by election time."[10]

Nixon's fixation on electoral politics influenced not only the downward trend of domestic interest rates but the various fiscal and monetary decisions made by the administration. In October 1970 the President told his chief economic advisers—McCracken, Kennedy, and George P. Shultz, the director of the Office of Management and Budget—that he "wanted to keep the pressure on Arthur Burns to keep monetary policy expansive."[11] The official reserve transactions balance, one of the basic calculations of a country's international financial position, reflected Washington's sea change, deteriorating from a surplus of $1,641 billion at the end of 1968, a surplus of $2.739 billion at year end

1969, and then to a deficit of $9.839 billion at the end of 1970. A deficit of $3.4 billion in 1960 and 1967 sent the Kennedy and Johnson administrations frantically searching for quick cures. Nixon, by contrast, ignored the problem in favor of his more pressing concerns.[12] His attention to the domestic economy may have contributed to the Republican party's good showing in the midterm elections: a gain of two seats in the Senate and a loss of only nine in the House.

Nixon's focus on domestic issues continued after Election Day. The President worried that Arthur Burns was playing the same role Chairman Martin had done in 1960 when the latter did not lower interest rates. Low interest rates would stimulate housing and capital investment. The consequent American expansion would lead European rates to come down, ameliorating the dollar outflow.[13] Nixon understood the international consequences of his domestic economic policy. In a meeting with Burns and presidential aide John Ehrlichman on December 15, 1970, Nixon learned that the French government had requested $128 million of gold and West Germany $500 million. Burns said serious thought should be given either to increasing the gold price or to embargoing gold. The three men discussed whether the United States should "force a crisis." Politically, sooner was better than later because of the 1972 election. Nixon concluded the discussion by saying "let me know when—we'll do it." He would not have long to wait.[14]

The revolution in currency markets played an important role in shaping the events of 1969–73. During the 1950s enterprising bankers created an offshore market for dollars. Dollars could be deposited and traded in foreign banks or in foreign branches of American banks. Bankers could avoid regulation and control by government bodies in general and American regulatory and other decrees in particular. Additionally, until the Iran hostage crisis of 1979, it was assumed that these deposits would be immune if the American government decreed economic sanctions against the country in which the holder resided or where the deposit bank was located. What began as a trickle turned into a multibillion dollar flood by the 1970s as multinational corporations and individuals alike realized the benefits of these "Eurodollars."[15] Private holdings of dollars began significantly to affect governmental decisions. The success of currency traders—"speculators" in Nixon's parlance, the "gnomes of Zurich" to the British government—in forcing a sterling devaluation in 1967, a French franc devaluation in 1969, and the German mark float in 1971 increased private investors' confidence and weakened the ability of governments to adhere to Bretton Woods values.

In January 1971 Nixon appointed John Connally as secretary of the Treasury. Connally, a former Democratic Texas governor and victim of Lee Harvey Oswald, was a Johnson protégé who had switched parties. Nixon admired the handsome Texan, seeing him as a potential president. At one of his first meetings with the President Connally made it clear that he supported emphasizing domestic economic concerns. The President intended "to keep [the] heat" on Burns to achieve at least a 7 percent growth in the monetary supply to fuel domestic expansion. This policy was to be followed even though the country was experiencing unprecedented rises in wages and prices. Connally proclaimed himself a "low interest man" but pointed out to the President that the balance of payments position was "incredibly bad" and that bankers feared the administration's indifference.[16]

On March 9 McCracken addressed the Austrian National Bank in Vienna on the subject of "U.S. Economic Policy and the Requirements of Internal and External Stability." His visit came against a background of confused Western European ideas about the direction of American policy. As Secretary of State William Rogers had informed the President in January, NATO allies sought a more expansionary U.S. economic policy together with continued administration action against inflation.[17] McCracken's choice of venue was ironic—forty years before, the crash of the Austrian Creditanstalt Bank had triggered a general European financial collapse leading to the abandonment of the gold standard on both sides of the Atlantic. Not surprisingly McCracken declared that the administration was not placing domestic concerns ahead of international considerations and concluded that what was good for the United States was good for the international economy. But at home the administration made contingency plans for a financial crisis.

The Federal Reserve Board had begun planning for such an event during 1970; now Robert Solomon, the head of the Fed's International Division, accelerated the timetable. He assumed that "a crisis of confidence in the dollar could begin at any time." Foreigners and domestic investors, believing that a dollar devaluation was imminent, might rush to switch out of the dollar to avoid the pain and reap the benefits of the coming monetary change. Once such a process began, absent massive government intervention and sometimes despite it, a devaluation would be inescapable. Assistant Attorney General William Rehnquist informed McCracken that the President was not prohibited in any way from ending the right of foreign governments to exchange their dollars for gold but needed to obtain congressional authorization before "proposing or agreeing to any change in the par value of the United States dollar."[18]

A new executive branch agency, the Council on International Economic Policy (CIEP), under director Peter Peterson scouted out the future direction of American foreign economic policy. Its purpose was to coordinate executive branch international economic policy just as the National Security Council coordinated strategic and security policy. During the first meeting of CIEP, held on April 8, Nixon revealed his priorities. Notwithstanding a frightening hemorrhage of American dollars abroad, the President concentrated on questions relating to American trade. During Peterson's presentation, Nixon raised points concerning East-West trade and the prospects of the American motion picture industry abroad. He also announced that former Treasury Secretary David Kennedy would soon be going to Japan to discuss the issue of Japanese textile exports to the United States, then a growing political as well as economic issue.[19]

The predicted financial crisis arrived in May, not in the United States but in West Germany. The German mark had floated briefly in September 1969; one month later the Bundesbank fixed its value in a 9.39 percent upward revaluation. During 1970 many of the dollars leaving the United States were invested in DM, in anticipation of a further revaluation. The trend accelerated in the first quarter of 1971 when the United States recorded an unprecedented drain of $5.5 billion (which translated to $22 billion on an annual basis).[20] By March 26, German official reserves exceeded those of the United States, although German gold reserves were considerably smaller.[21] On Wednesday, May 4, over $2 billion fled into foreign official holdings of dollars before the shutdown of the foreign exchange markets of Austria, Belgium, Germany, the Netherlands, and Switzerland. The same day

Karl Klassen, the president of the Bundesbank, informed Burns that Germany was again under pressure. "Proposals have been made which I oppose of course, but which if they are pushed through will mean a change of the actual world monetary system. It is only possible to counter this if positive items can be said about the willingness for cooperation on your part."[22] During the Johnson years such a letter would certainly have brought urgent reassurance about American bona fides combined with veiled comments about American troop levels in Europe. Now Washington was silent.

Four days later the West German government announced that for the time being it would no longer maintain a fixed rate for the mark but would instead allow the market to determine its floating value vis-à-vis other currencies. The White House took a sanguine view of this major development. "Let them float their currency" was the consensus of a meeting among the President, Ehrlichman, and Shultz on May 6. The administration should not get excited because "only tourists are hurt." If the revaluation stuck, the administration could get rid of the capital controls program, which aggravated business and, as Nixon pointed out, increased the number of government employees.[23] The President ignored that American influence abroad had been partly based on Washington's willingness to run the Bretton Woods system. Abandoning this commitment could hurt American influence in other spheres. But Nixon refused to pay the domestic price for international economic stability.

The media shared the President's priorities. The network news broadcasts on Friday, May 8, placed the turmoil in the world's currency markets a dim second to the .1 percent rise in unemployment (to 6.1 percent) and the Democratic party's charge that "the Admin[istration] makes the same worn out promises that things will get better—and they're getting worse." The Vietnamization of the conflict in Southeast Asia had drawn the teeth from the war as a campaign issue. Now the economy emerged as easily the hottest potential issue of the 1972 campaign—Nixon had no intention of standing idly by and allowing his rivals to seize the initiative.[24]

In the meantime American officials welcomed the German decision to float the mark; McCracken opined that it was "a major success for our international economic policy." This action made American exports to Germany cheaper and raised the price of German imports in the United States. The administration had sought a realignment of parities without having to take the political heat for devaluing the dollar or the international responsibility for forcing various allies to take actions they believed were domestically disastrous. Now the market, with the help of the administration's benign neglect, apparently had begun the process in a relatively painless fashion.

McCracken, in Europe for various meetings during the week of May 9, informed the President that Europeans were indeed seizing on the phrase "benign neglect," which had recently appeared in two scholarly economic articles, to describe and condemn U.S. foreign economic policy. McCracken defended American policies as responsive to both domestic and international economic imperatives. Now he proposed to the President that the White House actively support better international economic coordination and send White House officials on the road discussing the world economy. Of course neither pious sermons nor low-key American visitations to foreign treasuries (another McCracken idea) would substitute for what European leaders really craved—an American government that put foreign economic policy as a first priority.[25]

By the beginning of June McCracken turned less sanguine. He therefore urged Nixon to promote a rapid implementation of IMF suggestions for increased flexibility in the international monetary system.[26] Congress also began to take a serious interest in the problem. In June Democratic Congressman Henry Reuss and Republican Senator Jacob Javits, who headed the Joint Subcommittee on International Exchange and Payments of the Joint Economic Committee, began hearings on American balance of payments problems. Witnesses streamed before the committee, each advocating reform of the international economic system although specific panaceas differed widely.[27]

On July 15 the President electrified the world with his announcement that National Security Adviser Henry Kissinger had been conducting secret negotiations with the People's Republic of China and that the President would soon be visiting the former pariah nation. One week later, equally momentously, Nixon privately agreed that it would probably be necessary for the United States to take "strong actions to redress the present competitive disadvantage of the United

States in the international economy." The administration leaned toward a general exchange rate adjustment of the dollar relative to other currencies. In other words, individual upward revaluations of the mark or the Swiss franc were no longer sufficient to curb the problem. Sparking the President's conclusion was not the future of the international financial system but rather the American balance of trade.

From 1896 until 1970 the United States ran a trade surplus. During the last years of the sixties the trade surplus began to dwindle alarmingly—in 1968 it was down to $70 million. While it climbed back up during 1969 and 1970, and again in the first quarter of 1971, during the second quarter of 1971 the United States ran a trade deficit of $804 million, almost certainly guaranteeing a deficit for the year. Alarmingly, this figure had not emerged during a boom, which typically encouraged large imports. The President's advisers found the explanation in an overvalued dollar that priced American products out of foreign markets and made imports cheaper than domestically manufactured goods. Forcing the dollar's value downward against other major currencies would solve the problem. As Nixon and McCracken agreed, such monetary action should be done as "a part of a broad program of U.S. leadership for the world looking toward a scaling down of barriers to trade generally in the industrial world." In this fashion the United States could "attack" the growing competition from the Common Market and Japan.[28]

On July 27 Nixon, Connally, and Peterson met to discuss "the growing balance of payments crisis and steps that might be taken on trade legislation as well as the monetary front." Domestic economic issues dominated the President's agenda. Right after the 1970 election he told his advisers, the "economy must *boom* beginning 7/72" (emphasis in the original). Inflation vied with unemployment as Nixon's chief domestic preoccupation. During 1970 stagflation established itself. As Herbert Stein, soon to become the chairman of the Council of Economic Advisors, put it, the "stubbornness of inflation was [the] real Achilles heel." Stein believed that inflation would soon drop but conceded that in the meantime it caused widespread public anxiety. With the media informing the public that a family car that cost $3,000 in 1969 cost $4,000 two years later, the anxiety level in the White House increased dramatically.[29] But Nixon proved unwilling to play the bad guy and veto a

Democratic tax cut removing Johnson's income tax surcharge or cut the budget. Instead he allowed the federal budget deficit to soar although he had railed against deficits during the 1968 campaign. Wholesale prices continued to increase in the first half of 1971, largely as a result of a growing world demand for commodities. Labor unions, responding to the inflationary environment, won wage hikes, further fueling inflation. Searching for answers, the President turned to Connally, whom he had designated as the "spokesman who would be the authoritative source" on economic issues, to come up with a solution to the domestic and international problems.

Peterson, for his part, met secretly with Shultz, Undersecretary of the Treasury Paul Volcker, and McCracken to "review alternative answers." Since February Peterson had been at work on a major reassessment of the American place in the changing world economy. His conclusions, which would be embodied in a searching report completed in December 1971, rested on the assumption that the United States up to that time had placed "security, military-political objectives and cold war tactics in a dominant position with economic policies largely shaped to serve these ends." Washington assumed that as its allies recovered they would "accept an increasing share of responsibility for the maintenance of security and economic order in the Free World" and would also expand their markets to American goods. As neither development had occurred, the United States, now relatively weaker than in past decades, would have to force the issues.[30]

A week later, on August 2, Connally spoke to the President, presenting the accelerating crisis as a "huge economic breakthrough based on the international monetary situation." Connally advocated "self-balancing" measures that would provide for closing the gold window, a floating of the dollar, a wage and price freeze for six months, and the imposition of a 10 percent import tax quota. On August 4 television broadcasters concentrated again on the domestic economy. The Dow Jones industrial average had lost 100 points since April, the prime rate (a key American bank lending rate) could rise to 6.5 percent, and unemployment, which had drifted downward, was inching back up to 6 percent. Correspondents reported that key Republicans were ready to break with the administration over economic policy. On the same day the President learned that the seasonally adjusted July increase in the wholesale industrial price index of 0.7 percent was the largest monthly rise since 1955. (The public would not hear these figures until the following week).[31]

Bad news poured into the White House. On Friday, August 6, the Treasury announced that American monetary reserves had declined by another $1 billion. Although he had planned to go home to Texas, Connally decided to stay in Washington for the weekend. Concurrently the Reuss Committee publicly concluded that a dollar devaluation was inescapable.[32] Foreign markets reflected these developments. The flow of speculative funds into Europe and Japan, steadily growing all year, accelerated wildly during the first week of August. France, for example, took in $120 million on August 4, and Japan gained $353 million in the week ending August 6.[33] On that same day Connally delivered a report to Nixon urging "total war on all economic fronts, including across-the-board wage and price controls." It was clear to Volcker that "we were on the brink of a market panic that willy-nilly would force us off gold." Not surprisingly McCracken advised Nixon on August 9 that "international monetary and financial developments have now become urgent and immediate policy problems."[34]

On Thursday, August 12, the White House told key officials to keep the weekend free. The next day helicopters flew top economic officials Connally, Burns, Shultz, McCracken, Volcker, Stein, and Peterson to Camp David for secret meetings with the President. Ehrlichman, H.R. Haldeman, and the presidential speechwriter William Safire also attended. That morning the British government had asked for gold cover for its $3 billion dollar holdings. Forty-eight hours later, at 9 p.m. on Sunday, August 15, the President emerged to unveil his New Economic Policy (a term Lenin had made famous) before television cameras and the American public.

The program was equally divided into domestic and foreign economic components. As late as July 22 Nixon had contemplated making John Kenneth Galbraith a "chief enemy" because he advocated government controls over the economy.[35] Now, jettisoning his principles for the second time in as many months, the President announced a ninety-day period of wage and price controls to be followed by a price review board. To stimulate the economy, he proposed a series of tax cuts designed to increase both business and consumer spending: a 10 percent, one-year job development tax credit, the repeal of the 7 percent excise tax on automobiles, and a one-year acceleration of personal income tax exemptions. To offset these cuts Nixon ordered a $4.7 billion reduction in federal spending, a 10 percent cut in foreign aid, and a three-month postponement of revenue sharing.

While the domestic portion of the New Economic Policy received greater public attention at the time, in retrospect the foreign economic aspects loom larger. The President proclaimed that the United States would close the gold window, suspending the U.S. promise on which the Bretton Woods system was based, to furnish gold in exchange for dollars presented by foreign governments or central banks.[36] This decision provoked the most discussion at Camp David. Burns opposed the monumental step, instead proposing to hold it in reserve. But the majority disagreed. As Connally had pointed out, the gold outflow was an immediate problem, the British government's request being the last straw.[37] Furthermore, the Treasury secretary asserted, there was no political risk in going all the way—Reuss wanted it done.[38] In any case, said Connally, "So the other countries don't like it. So what?" Stein and Shultz concurred, Stein advising the President to ignore the opposition of Charles Coombs, a vice-president of the New York Federal Reserve Bank, who had conjured up the specter of foreign chaos. It was that fear that paralyzed Herbert Hoover, concluded Stein. Closing the window would liberate the United States, and any subsequent public criticism would soon fade. When the President asked which foreign markets would be shaken by closing the gold window, Connally told him, "our friends." But Nixon understood that in the Cold War period the combined American security umbrella and economic predominance gave the country unprecedented leverage over its allies. Western Europe and Japan needed the United States more than it needed them. So the President decided to go ahead with an announcement that avoided "crisis rhetoric" but instead demanded a new realignment of the international monetary system, and railed against international money speculators. In this way, the most significant decision of all those taken at Camp David—the end of Bretton Woods—was quietly unveiled amid little discussion.

Closing the gold window solved the American gold drain but it did not address the question of overvaluation. Nixon's prescription: the simultaneous imposition of a 10 percent surcharge on all imports. The President's "long range goal [was] not to erect a 10 percent barrier around the US—that would be retrogressive—but to set a procedure that lets us go up and down with room for negotiation." In other words, Nixon would immediately raise the price of imports by 10 percent, which would temporarily accomplish the goal he had in mind—a change in the American trade position. The entire package was then wrapped within rhetorical ribbons emphasizing the need to create American prosperity without war and to fight the three great villains: unemployment, inflation, and international speculation. In his speech the President told Americans that "our best days lie ahead." Whether this prediction encapsulated the future of the international monetary order was unclear.[39]

In the days that followed U.S. officials met with their foreign counterparts to discuss the technical and substantive features of the new financial order. Volcker, meeting with British officials and bankers assembled near Victoria Station, "absolutely hedged" when asked whether the United States would reopen the gold window. The basis for the Bretton Woods financial system's rules and regulations no longer existed; substitutes needed to be invented. Of equal importance was the need to negotiate new ground rules. Volcker, who wanted to use the Nixon shock as a catalyst for the formation of a new economic world order, indicated to foreign counterparts that "the import surcharge could be taken off as soon as foreign countries took actions that could be expected to lead to a satisfactory improvement in our trade position." (It did not seem to trouble the administration that using the surtax as a lever for monetary change violated GATT rules.) It was still unclear to many foreign leaders what the United States had in mind. Connally's pronouncement on August 16 that "it would be a 'premature judgment' to say that the President's action amounted to a devaluation of the dollar" indicates the confusion that reigned in Washington.[40]

When markets opened on Tuesday, August 17, the price of the dollar against other major currencies reflected the changes that the administration sought. Sterling was up 2.3 percent over the old fixed rate, while the German mark traded at 8.3 percent over par. The Japanese government misunderstood the administration's goals and bought billions of dollars to keep the yen at its old rate against the dollar.[41] Nixon and his team rejoiced in their initial success. In the week after the President's announcement the Dow Jones industrial index rose 3 percent. Herbert Stein, acting chairman of the Council of Economic Advisors, estimated that the program would add $15 billion to the gross national product. More important, the Treasury concluded that "the President's NEP [New Economic Policy] has substantially changed the outlook for 1972." This happy conclusion meant that Nixon had accomplished his chief objective—improving his chances for victory fifteen months hence.

Public endorsements for the program were quickly forthcoming. Nixon had included something for everyone. The normally critical *New York Times* lauded the New Economic Policy. After "unhesitatingly applaud[ing] Nixon's boldness," the lead editorial on August 16 congratulated the President for abandoning the "do-nothing approach that immobilized the country and sapped the national will." McCracken informed Nixon on August 18 that polling data indicated that consumer confidence, in a slump all summer, had returned to May levels. Even better, all sectors of the public apparently endorsed the President's actions with some exceptions in the "professional class." Especially comforting to the administration was the attitude of blue-collar workers who, breaking away from the highly critical posture of AFL-CIO President George Meany, overwhelmingly backed the President's program. As these Nixon Democrats had been crucial to the President's victory in 1968, their reaction alone justified the switch to wage and price controls.[42]

But while clearly of secondary importance to the White House, the international ramifications of the NEP desperately needed to be addressed.[43] Key to the formulation of the preferred American policy was the calculation of what exchange rate would end the huge trade and payments deficits. The goal was to achieve a $7 billion improvement in the trade balance as well as a $2 billion improvement in the balance of payments. The Fed's staff worked out a set of calculations that led to an initial target of a 7.75 percent depreciation of the dollar, weighted by import shares with Japan, West Germany, and Canada, the chief targets. Moreover, U.S. economists calculated that for the American balance of payments to improve dramatically, the country needed to demand a global devaluation of the dollar and a global revaluation of all major currencies: it was not sufficient for foreign currencies to appreciate solely against the dollar. The firm Washington prejudice against further American sacrifices for the good of the system shone through.[44] Of course American trading partners had opposite goals. Fearing increased U.S. competition, they remained reluctant to revalue their currencies upward. The import surcharge was Washington's method of persuasion. The White House had in essence unilaterally devalued by a factor of 10 percent. Nixon and his team would not consider removing the surcharge without significant inducement. Although it was a crude tool, officials calculated that Japan and Canada were among the countries most affected by the surcharge. Moreover, this method avoided the ambush that a straight American devaluation might have created: a string of matching foreign devaluations.[45]

During the autumn the Western monetary order remained in flux. Some currencies, such as the Dutch guilder, floated completely while the British pound floated upward but had a fixed floor.[46] Japan, with the most undervalued currency, floated the yen at the end of August, which administration officials viewed as a major victory.[47] American diplomats repeated their willingness to reestablish convertibility but only when Washington was satisfied that other nations had made their fair share of sacrifices for the system.

As October ended, the chorus of praise for Nixon's program began to fade, to be replaced by doubts and disapproval. Domestic rumblings about the lack of muscle in the anti-inflation program coexisted with questions concerning the administration's heady confidence that it had OECD nations in a vise.[48] Behind the scenes European and Japanese ministers calculated the domestic political price of placating the United States. One thing was clear—no country was fully willing to trust the market to set exchange rates. Rather, finance ministries and central banks to a lesser or greater extent intended to control their country's currency level and trading, and insulate their economies from the invisible hand of the market. (For that reason these floats were known as "dirty floats," as opposed to "clean floats," which were purely market driven.) Equally apparent was the fact that while other countries were quick to criticize the United States for failing the world in its obligations to the Bretton Woods system, no other country or group of countries wished to assume the burdens that the United States had previously borne.[49]

In mid-November Phase I, the three-month period of mandatory wage and price controls, expired, to be replaced by the looser Phase II rules. The administration spread cheery economic news: inflation and interest rates were down and employment up. But doubts lingered. George Meany continued to berate the administration for its wage controls and, as Nixon put it at a Legislative Leadership session on November 16, "business men are bitching like hell." At that same meeting Connally said, "you can ride a good horse to death, and the world has been riding the U.S., a good horse, to death in the post-war years, and this has got to stop." The Treasury secretary noted that the United States took 30 percent of Japan's exports while Europe took only 5 percent because European tariff barriers kept Japanese goods out, whereas the United States allowed them in.[50]

A meeting of the G-10 nations had been scheduled for Rome for November 30. McCracken believed that "the United States in international policy stands at one of those crucial forks in history." McCracken reported to the President that OECD nations were increasingly worried about growing unemployment in their own nations. The administration had other problems. The constant White House harping on the theme of greedy Europe contributed to a nearly successful attempt by Congress to reduce unilaterally American troop levels in Europe. From time to time the administration alleged that half of the American balance of payments deficit of $11 billion was attributable to U.S. troops stationed abroad. This calculation was clearly erroneous and led to a situation where only the President's personal appeal to the Senate prevented a troop withdrawal.[51] Exacerbating American fears were the October trade figures, which, according to McCracken, "taken uncritically at face value, look[ed] ghastly."

By all accounts the Rome meetings were memorable as well as productive. Participants particularly recalled Connally's historic tour de force on the history and contributions of Roman civilization, done without notes, during his evening dinner speech. Indeed, Connally, who had previously garnered a "bull in the China shop" reputation, emerged from the European discussions with enhanced prestige. The G-10 finance ministers came to the meetings expecting the United

States to continue its obstructionism. With Connally's permission, Volcker speculated about a dollar devaluation and a gold price increase of 10 percent to 15 percent. Connally then uttered the words "All right, the issue had been raised, let's assume ten percent. What will your people do?" When the German representative, Karl Schiller, indicated that his government could accept a devaluation of between 10 and 12 percent, the ball had clearly come to the British and French governments.[52] McCracken later enthused to the Treasury secretary, "Your leadership at Rome quite literally started the world on toward an orderly reconstitution of the international economic system. The 'What if . . . "10 percent"' was an essential and brilliant ingredient." McCracken's praise was over the top but Connally had broken the impasse after months of stalemate.

On December 13 Nixon and President Georges Pompidou of France met in the Azores. Pompidou, a former banker, kept a close watch on financial negotiations. Prior to the actual discussions, Pompidou lectured Nixon on the virtues of gold and the evils of the dollar standard. The French president, who felt far more strongly about these issues than did Nixon, refused to permit the price of gold to rise above $38 per ounce, which translated into a dollar devaluation of 8.5 percent. National Security Adviser Henry Kissinger, who had accompanied Nixon to the Azores, advised the President that a failure to reach a settlement with Pompidou would fatally damage American relations with its allies and sabotage Western European economies. Anxious to end these tiresome discussions, Nixon assented to Pompidou's terms.[53]

The resulting communiqué publicly confirmed that the United States agreed to a change in the price of gold and a dollar devaluation. The decision was greeted with cheers in Washington. Congressman Henry Reuss, who had introduced a bill authorizing a gold price increase in Congress on November 18, termed the move "glorious." The Franco-American accord made a general agreement at the meetings of foreign governmental and financial officials set to begin on December 17 a virtual certainty.

One of the most important outstanding issues was the size of the Japanese revaluation of the yen. Connally's anger at the Japanese attitude led him, at dinner after the first day's negotiations, to attack Japan's trade practices. He made his dining companions turn over their plates to see the "made in Japan" label and observed that every camera in the room was Japanese. When Finance Minister Mikio Mizuta assented to a change of 16.88 percent, the Smithsonian agreement, as the accord came to be known, was almost complete. Of the major American trading partners, only Canada refused to return to a fixed rate for its currency. The other participants once again had rates for their currencies fixed against the dollar and against gold. The United States agreed to give up the dollar float but successfully resisted, at least for the moment, a return to dollar convertibility. Should Washington in the future agree to resume sales of gold to foreign governments and central banks, the price would be $38 per ounce. But Nixon refused to reopen the gold window now.

All parties compromised on important points on the Smithsonian agreement. The United States achieved a smaller dollar depreciation than it had desired—on a trade-weighted basis the new rates devalued the dollar only 8 percent. At the same time the United States agreed to remove the import surcharge. U.S. trading partners, already faced with growing unemployment, accepted currency appreciations in excess of what their domestic interest groups desired.[54] They agreed to wider bands between which currency levels could fluctuate, from the Bretton Woods limits of 1 percent either side of par (also known as the central rate) to 2.25 percent. For the time being they condoned the end to the convertibility of dollars held by governments into gold. This was no return to Bretton Woods. Yet most governments clearly longed for just that. Ironically, the result of the Nixon shocks was that instead of a quasi-gold standard, the Western world's finances had moved to a dollar standard. The American currency was even more central to the workings of the system. Even France, the most recalcitrant of the G-10 members and the most fixated on gold, was temporarily willing to live with a dollar standard to achieve monetary stability. The prevalent optimism led one administration official to opine on December 17 that "we could be leading the way into a new era of buoyant world trade, international investment and world economic growth." Standing beneath the Wright brothers' airplane, Nixon proclaimed the Smithsonian agreement the greatest monetary achievement in history.[55]

But it was not to last. In the aftermath of the Smithsonian accord, the G-10 nations prepared for negotiations intended to reform the international monetary system. Administration members again debated various proposals. Fed official Robert Solomon advocated that neither the dollar nor gold be placed at the center of the world monetary system. Rather he believed that Special Drawing Rights (SDRs) "should become the major, and possibly the only, reserve asset." This change would enable the United States "to preserve and extend an environment of freedom for world trade and investment." It would also preserve maximum flexibility for the United States to pursue its own goals. Connally and Volcker both publicly advocated a diminishing role for gold in the international monetary system. Even Burns, the most conservative of the President's advisers, believed that "the monetary role of gold [would] continue to diminish in the years ahead, while the role of special drawing rights increases." Burns, in keeping with his colleagues, cast serious doubt on a return to gold convertibility for the dollar. With foreign central bank holdings of dollars now exceeding $52 billion and American gold reserves amounting to only $12 billion, reopening the gold window hardly seemed feasible. But European bankers during February began to grow impatient with the American reluctance to discuss the subject.[56]

At the same time Western European nations and Japan agreed to commence long-term trade discussions with the United States in 1973 and made some immediate concessions that fell short of the American demands. Connally had previously linked a presidential blessing for the gold price increase bill to progress in the trade talks. But although the administration had little to show for its trouble, the White House deemed the progress sufficient to recommend that Congress act on the gold price legislation. In the meantime gold prices hit new highs as the dollar continued to depreciate against other currencies.[57] The commander-in-chief's goal remained to "do *everything* to help [the] expansion of the economy." Although he had developed doubts as to the wisdom of the domestic component of the August 15 bombshell, the President was sure that closing the gold window had been the correct decision. Shultz now advocated a radical change of the Bretton Woods system, rather than a "patch-up job," but suggested that it be undertaken incrementally. He proposed a small group to draft the U.S. negotiating position: Burns, Herbert Stein, and Secretary of State William Rogers, who would be "hurt if left out." The President commanded that the United States should "temporize" while "appear[ing] to be cooperative."

Nixon had not yet decided whether he wanted an eventual return to gold convertibility but he was adamant that the United States should "keep out of the hands of international bankers." At the same time Nixon intended to prevent Burns from dominating American decision making because the President believed that his central banker was too willing to "let the tail wag [the] dog" and overemphasize foreign economic policy at the expense of domestic concerns. And Nixon believed that "their crises don't mean that much to us." Kissinger, said the President, also should not be a part of this group. He was "too busy" for this job—"use him to make the big plays with European nations," commanded the President.[58]

During the spring the OECD nations agreed that the vehicle for the international monetary negotiations would be a "Committee of Twenty" (C-20) on which less developed nations would have representation. Developing nations hoped that the C-20 would also provide a mechanism for increasing foreign aid from the first world to the third. The United States had its own reasons for seeking the creation of a new forum for monetary reform discussions. In the administration's view the IMF Executive Board, the logical choice for such negotiations, was not of sufficient stature and was too much under the thumb of IMF officials.[59]

The new exchange rates already seemed shaky. Experts doubted the efficacy of the Smithsonian accord as speculators bet that the dollar would again be devalued.[60] By the end of May the free market price of gold had soared to $58 per ounce, or $20 over its official ceiling.[61] As it turned out it was the pound, not the dollar, that was devalued. In mid-June, speculators attacked sterling, motivated by the British economy's increasingly poor outlook. The usual culprits of a yawning trade deficit and growing inflation made the Smithsonian rate for the pound difficult to maintain. Exacerbating the situation was a looming dock strike and fears that the British entry into the European Community, scheduled for January 1, 1973, would have an adverse effect on the British economy, particularly on the cost of food. In contrast to previous years, the British government resisted the pressure for only a short period of time before announcing on June 23 that the pound would be permitted to float. In Britain, as in the United States, "respectable opinion" had turned against sacrificing the possibility of domestic growth for the sake of maintaining fixed rates. British newspapers hailed the decision, lauding Prime Minister Edward Heath for his courage, a far cry from the reaction that greeted Wilson's decision to devalue in 1967.[62] The Labour party also blessed the decision.[63] But Stein worried that a number of other countries would follow the British lead and devalue. This sort of competitive devaluation, where each country attempted to cheapen its exports at the expense of its trading partners, could jeopardize any improvement in the American statistics. Within six months the market had vitiated the Smithsonian accord; the question now was whether the wound was fatal.

Nixon officials drew several lessons from the British decision. To the economic adviser Peter Flanigan it showed "the wisdom of the U.S. refusal to consider convertibility until a new and stable monetary system is in place." Stein pointed out that the heavy trading in the dollar proved that its weakness had not dissipated. American officials also worried that the proliferation of exchange controls throughout Europe and Japan in the wake of the U.S. devaluation made the creation of a durable monetary order increasingly difficult.[64]

The administration team considering American strategy had a new Treasury secretary at the helm. Connally had resigned at the end of May, leaving behind him both supporters and detractors. Connally himself admitted that "I have sometimes heard the accusation that I have become a sort of bully boy on the manicured playing fields of international finance." George Shultz, the former dean of the business school at the University of Chicago and a Nixon stalwart, took over. By nature a conciliator, Shultz was the opposite of the pugnacious Connally. At the same time Shultz had a strong ideological commitment to floating exchange rates and no particular allegiance to the Bretton Woods system.[65]

Under Shultz's direction Volcker attempted to prepare a comprehensive reform plan for the international monetary system. The plan, featuring far more symmetrical obligations than the Bretton Woods blueprints had, was ready for unveiling by Nixon and Shultz at the September 1972 IMF meetings.[66] Harkening back to Keynes's wartime proposals, it placed obligations on countries running a balance of payments surplus while retaining Bretton Woods–vintage obligations on debtor nations. American officials had originally rejected Keynes's suggestions as amounting to a blank check on Washington's account. Now that the United States continued to run a deficit, which during the summer of 1972 steadily worsened, mandatory requirements on surplus nations seemed an attractive proposition.[67]

Nixon won a triumphant victory in November. Yet speculators continued to attack the dollar.[68] On February 12, Shultz publicly announced a dollar devaluation of 11.11 percent against the French franc and the German mark. This time Nixon confined himself to giving a noon radio address solely on the topic of international trade. To Ehrlichman and Shultz, Nixon wondered "when's the next crisis?" but did not try to prevent one from occurring. The administration's low-key approach indicated to speculators that Washington lacked a deep commitment to the new rates.[69]

Nonetheless the rates held, at least initially. Nixon applauded Shultz's "cool" handling of the monetary crisis, which he contrasted to the modus operandi of people like Henry Kissinger, who fomented a crisis atmosphere to "earn attention for themselves." (Nixon added that Kissinger would spark a crisis over Ecuador if Vietnam did not exist.) Apparently no longer interested in the fate of the dollar, he informed Shultz that "you have great delegation of authority" but told the Treasury secretary to "pour on the follow-up [and] hit the dollar-speculators." As the President pointed out, a "little jingoism" wouldn't hurt. To Congress Nixon justified the devaluation as a necessary step to curb the growing trade deficit resulting from the "new challenges in international competition." At a meeting with Sir Christopher Soames, the EEC trade negotiator, the President focused on the growing support for isolationism in the United States and the need to reassure Americans that "our products have a fair shake in world trade."[70]

By the last week in February, it was clear that the dollar was under siege. Funds flowed into strong currencies; the Swiss franc, for example, commanded a premium of 24 percent above its previous par value, and the demand for gold was strong. On Wednesday, February 28, a new dollar crisis began as the Dutch central bank purchased $150 million to keep the dollar from falling below its fixed rate less the permitted margin of 2.25 percent. The next day European central banks together used local currency equivalent to $4 billion to support the dollar with the Bundesbank alone expending $2.6 billion. The price of gold oscillated between $80 and $90 per ounce.[71]

On Saturday, March 3, Nixon met with Shultz, Burns, Stein, Budget Director Roy Ash, and Paul Volcker. Their topic: should the United States again intervene on behalf of the dollar, not to devalue but to support it? Shultz and Stein argued against such a step on the grounds "that it would give away what the Europeans wanted from us without getting what he wanted from them—reform." Burns, in opposition, stated that "our failure to offer to intervene would be taken in Europe as abdication of leadership and responsibility." Not surprisingly the President revealed himself to be in the anti-interventionist camp but requested that the group discuss the international political implications of this stance with Kissinger. The secretary of state recommended that the United States placate potential allied displeasure by consulting with major European nations and Japan.[72]

The G-10 countries, together with EC nations (a group now increased in size to nine nations from its original six members), agreed to meet in emergency session in Paris on March 9. In the meantime EC foreign exchange markets remained closed as "the nine" attempted to carve a single position for EC nations, concentrating on a possible joint float of their currencies. At the Paris meeting of March 9 and at a follow-up conclave one week later, conferees demonstrated their surprise at the sudden and total collapse of the amended Bretton Woods system. After blaming the crisis on the international speculators and blessing the propriety of current exchange rates, the participating nations admitted that at least for the time being the Bretton Woods system, in any incarnation, no longer existed. In fact no system did. Six members of the EC, including West Germany, France, and the Netherlands, as well as Sweden and Norway, agreed to maintain a joint float within 2.25 percent margins but would no longer support the previously agreed-upon dollar rates. In other words, these currencies would float together against the dollar. Britain, Italy, Japan, and Canada would separately float their currencies. All participants piously intoned their support for the continuing work of the Committee of Twenty. The official communiqué of March 16, which weakly supported government intervention in the markets, proved useless. The United States pledged to try to save the current dollar rate while concurrently ending exchange controls. Shultz's willingness to consider joint floating sympathetically put the final nail in the coffin of the revised Bretton Woods system. When the markets reopened on March 19, the international monetary system as it had existed from 1946 was history.[73]

On March 6, 1973, just as the fixed rate system entered its dying hours, Nixon addressed top American business leaders in the White House. As he had often done, the President stressed that the world economic situation in the 1970s was totally different from what it had been twenty-five years earlier:

> After World War II, economically the United States was so preeminent that we could afford to be generous and we were. But now the world has changed. We find now that [of] those we assisted, the Japanese are our second strongest competitor in the world, the Germans the third, and Western Europe, when joined together with Britain in the market, will be a formidable, certainly [sic], competitor indeed.

The administration needed to guarantee American businessmen the opportunity to compete on a fair basis with other countries. Domestic economic concerns could no longer be sacrificed for the good of the system as a whole. Nixon's dedication to free trade ensured that his emphasis would fall on the monetary side of the foreign economic policy equation. At the same time the United States required sufficient military strength to assure "peace and freedom in the years ahead."[74] Not stated was the connection between the two. That the United States still played the policeman for its allies gave its opinion increased weight in every sphere.

These ideas represented the evolution of themes that Nixon had been discussing since he took office. The Nixon Doctrine set forth a major qualification to the U.S. promise to aid "the defense and development of allies and friends": Washington could not and would not "conceive all the plans, design all the programs, execute all the decisions and undertake all the defense of the free nations of the world." In a speech in Kansas City on July 6, 1971, the President proclaimed the existence of "five great superpowers"—the United States, the Soviet Union, the People's Republic of China, Japan, and the EC—that would "determine the economic future and because economic power will be the key to other kinds of power, the future of the world in other ways in the last third of this century."[75]

Yet Nixon had no intention of relinquishing America's leadership of the Western alliance. He intended to make more out of less. By ending U.S. participation in the Vietnam War and by following a policy of détente with the Soviet Union and the People's Republic of China, the nation could reduce the defense budget. Anointing regional surrogates such as Iran would further reduce the cost of maintaining American influence. Washington could even turn a profit because Iran would need to buy sophisticated weapons system that the Pentagon and American defense contractors would be only too happy to sell. Nixon would make the relative American financial decline a source of new strength: by refusing some burdens and spreading others, Washington would improve its future economic position. Ironically Nixon's gamble in favor of détente purchased immediate fiscal relief at the price of extending the arms race. The CIA mistakenly believed that the Soviet economy's growth rate had consistently topped American statistics since 1951.[76] In reality détente provided the Soviet government with a welcome respite from the accelerating arms race of the 1960s. Without the pause, the Soviet economic implosion might have occurred earlier.

Nixon had gambled that the U.S. decision to end its support of the Bretton Woods system would not destroy American dominance of the Western alliance. The President's logic may have been flawed but his gamble paid off. Western nations still shared a common defense goal— to wage the Cold War—albeit now modified by Nixon's policy of détente. They considered the Soviet threat real and recognized that only the United States qualified to lead the alliance. Britain and France were too weak, Germany and Japan still discredited.[77] The continuity of Western support for the Cold War thus enabled the United States to retain its hegemony within the alliance. As a result OECD nations maintained their fealty to a United States whose systemic leadership would be far less disinterested than in previous years.

How, in retrospect, should we judge Nixon and the end of Bretton Woods? On June 28, 1971, Nixon waxed philosophical to his advisers, explaining the role of the President. After pointing out that he made a memorandum of every meeting he held (something that would play a large role during Watergate), the President told Messrs. Kissinger, Connally, and Shultz, among others, that "not one of you are responsible" for the government of the nation "—I am." I changed the course of American policy in foreign affairs and I am now "doing it in Econ[omics]."[78] Nixon believed that the domestic side of the economy was paramount, particularly the issues of unemployment and infla-tion.[79] In fact, in the service of his compulsion to achieve reelection, Nixon adopted a Keynesian expansionist economic policy that far exceeded the Kennedy and Johnson versions. That this policy would have considerable impact on America's foreign economic position was secondary.

Other factors contributed to a subordination of foreign economic policy under Nixon not seen since the beginning of the New Deal. Many administration members believed that the United States was unfairly saddled with the burden of being a reserve currency nation. Officials also suspected that foreigners delighted in American troubles. McCracken sent to Pete Peterson on June 28 a quotation from Will Rogers: "What would Europe do if we were in difficulties and needed help?. . . Europe would hold a celebration." As Connally less delicately put it, "foreigners are out to screw us. Our job is to screw them first."[80]

The Bretton Woods system, however, depended on America's assuming the burden of putting the system's well-being ahead of its own. Washington officials took on this obligation because they believed that the autarkic economic chaos of the Depression decade had con-tributed to the rise of Hitler and the coming of World War II. Given the enormous economic strength of the United States in 1945, the price of being the system's anchor seemed relatively cheap compared with the potential burdens. But by 1971, as the cost dramatically escalated, Nixon decided to put the domestic economy first and let the interna-tional chips fall where they might.

Central to this approach was the President's conviction that "as we move into the post–Vietnam world, military confrontation will be replaced by economic competition and we had to assure the competi-tive position of the United States."[81] Therefore increasing American industrial competitiveness headed the administration's foreign eco-nomic policy goals. A cheaper dollar would serve this purpose by mak-ing American products more salable abroad and pricing out imports. The 10 percent import surcharge served this purpose well. It would immediately curb imports by what in essence was a unilateral across-the-board devaluation while simultaneously serving as an excellent bargaining chip.

That last point is important. Nixon had adopted the postwar liberal free-trade consensus. At a time when protectionist sentiment had begun to regain respectability, the President continued to embrace international trade liberalization. His temporary surcharge was intended to improve the existing free trade system, not replace it. Indeed Nixon told McCracken that adjusting exchange rates would constitute "a way to deal with rapidly rising protectionist sentiment in the United States."[82] The President made his priorities clear in a letter to William McChesney Martin when he stated that in order to reestablish the strength and stability of the dollar, he had focused his efforts on improving the trade balance and the overall payments position. Martin doubtlessly thought Nixon had reversed the equation.[83]

But Nixon and his officials were reluctant to take the responsibility for devaluing the dollar. It was better to force the decision onto the laps of the foreigners who had ostensibly triggered it. Furthermore, in their deliberations Nixon and most of his advisers showed little allegiance to the Bretton Woods system. They had different priorities than Hull, Acheson, or Morgenthau. The prevailing attitude of the Nixon administration was summed up during a meeting of Shultz, John Ehrlichman, and Herbert Stein: "[We] can't let concern for bal[ance] of payments wreck our domestic economy." Shultz lacked any commitment to the Bretton Woods system as an antidote to financial autarky and as a bulwark against international anarchy and the rise of dictatorships. The idea of patching up the structure was quickly dismissed without a second thought, even though sixties inventions still in place such as swap lines and export controls might have handled the 1971 crisis. Only Burns demonstrated a loyalty to the Bretton Woods ideology; his views were ignored.[84]

The President also rejected the possibility of forming a multilateral consensus to accomplish the changes he sought. The administration did not consult with American allies prior to launching the New Economic Policy nor did a representative of the State Department or National Security Council even attend the Camp David meetings of August 13–15. This omission is even more surprising given the fact that

the Nixon Doctrine ostensibly depended on expanded U.S. cooperation with American allies. Actually the 1971 Nixon shocks seemed
more calculated to repel international cooperation than encourage it.
But the allies on which the Nixon-Kissinger approach depended such
as Iran, the Philippines, Saudi Arabia, and Israel were developing
nations eager to cooperate with the United States for reasons of their
own. Moreover, they were not the big losers of August 1971. It did not
really matter that Nixon's economic diplomacy helped torpedo the U.S.
attempt to reach out to NATO allies with the Year of Europe initiative
two years later. The United States held the important cards.

Of course a multilateral approach would not have ensured an out-
come acceptable to the United States. Volcker quotes the response of a
European Community official who, when asked what Europe would do
if the dollar were devalued, replied, "All European currencies would be
devalued by the same percentage on the same day." But given American clout within the Bretton Woods system, there existed a strong
chance that American views would have prevailed in a context that
did not make a mockery of the multilateral system that the United
States had embraced twenty-five years earlier. As the presidential
adviser Francis Bator pointed out to Johnson, "if the Europeans force a
crisis, our economic strength and real bargaining leverage will soon
become very clear to all concerned."[85] The OECD nations assented to
the American order at the Rambouillet summit in late 1975 and then
officially at the Jamaican IMF meeting in February 1976 because they
had no choice.[86] But the White House would not take the gamble.

Washington's unilateral decision making also represented a total
break from American practice during the previous decade. Unlike
Kennedy and Johnson, Nixon did not attempt to use U.S. military
power directly to obtain foreign economic concessions. Rather, he
harked back to the practice of an earlier president, Franklin D. Roosevelt, who agreed that the United States always came out the worst
from international conferences.

Whenever a politician invokes the classic dictum "Let justice be
done though the heavens fall," observers always sit on the edge of their
seats. Whenever that invocation is followed by a resounding silence,
something is wrong with the previous system. Such was the case with
Bretton Woods. It cost the United States quite a bit while providing no

more benefits that those the anarchy of the following years bestowed. The failure of the post–1971 search for order was a triumph for the Nixon administration. The floating rate system placed no restrictions on the President's ability to use fiscal and monetary tools to prime the domestic economy as he saw fit. During 1972 the United States recorded a 6 percent growth in real terms, while under the Phase II controls, wages and prices rose only 3 percent.[87] These rosy statistics, although hiding a powder keg, helped Nixon win the 1972 election, which to the President more than justified his strategy. The market theoretically provided a certain discipline but when traders sent the dollar lower, they accomplished the administration's goal with less political pain.

Key to Nixon's policy was his belief that "the only rule of international diplomacy that I know that works is the golden rule, and that is: 'Do unto others as they do unto you.'"[88]Going it alone seemed not only the proper pragmatic choice but politically and morally justifiable. (The Nixon administration underestimated the effects of the rampant inflation that began during the 1960s but escalated dramatically in 1973.)

The revolutionary changes in the international financial system logically should have cost the United States the financial leadership of the free world. Yet Washington retained its financial hegemony much as it had retained the political and military leadership of the Western alliance. One relevant factor was the sheer size of the American economy, which, by definition, gave it a large role. While the key currency country always benefits from this status, it also pays a price in the loss of domestic autonomy. Export-oriented nations like Germany and Japan would have paid a larger price than did the United States for such leadership, were they to have assumed the American role in the Western economic system, because of their greater dependence on trade. For this reason, neither country was eager to assume the role of international financial anchor. Indeed these countries and other Western European nations demonstrated even less devotion to the good of the world economy than had the Nixon administration. The lure of the free market and managed floating rates had captured their intellectuals as well. Making sacrifices for the fixed rate system seemed hard to justify and easy to avoid. While the American promise in 1944 to make concessions for the Bretton Woods system had been qualified, it exceeded the dedication shown by other countries twenty-five years later.

But even a nonsystem needs a leader, and it was left to the United States then to continue many of its Bretton Woods functions, although the Bretton Woods system no longer existed. No other nation stepped into the breach. While Nixon and his successors refrained from constantly playing the military card, the American role in the Western alliance cemented the dollar's central role. The United States had truly achieved the best of all possible worlds—the benefits of systemic leadership without many of the burdens. What had been a gold and dollar standard evolved into a pure dollar standard. As long as the Cold War lasted, this happy state of affairs would continue.

11

The Oil Shocks

Sorry, No Gas

Sign frequently posted in American gas stations during the winter of 1973–74

Just as coal dominated the nineteenth century, oil shaped the twentieth. The exponential expansion of civilian and military vehicles revolutionized every aspect of life, first and foremost in the United States. Its automobile industry adopted Henry Ford's mantra that the car should be not the plaything of the rich but a necessity for everyone. "See the USA in your Chevrolet" was the mantra of the early Cold War years. No longer a curiosity, the airplane also became a vital form of transportation. The military ramifications of these developments were important. Because armies of the future would depend on tanks and planes, strategists focused on securing reliable and accessible petroleum reserves.

Large multinational oil companies (MNOCs, or majors) dominated the oil industry. Sometimes referred to as the "seven sisters," several—Standard Oil of New York (later Mobil), Standard Oil of New Jersey (Esso, then Exxon), and Standard Oil of California (Socal or Chevron)—were children of John D. Rockefeller's Standard Oil Trust, which the Supreme Court ordered dissolved in 1911. Other American MNOCs were the Gulf Oil Company, controlled by the

Mellon family, and the Texas Oil Company (Texaco). British Petroleum (BP, formerly known as the Anglo-Persian and then the Anglo-
Iranian Oil Company) was of this group as was Royal Dutch Shell
(Shell), a result of the merger of the Royal Dutch Company with the
British Shell Oil Company. These companies were vertically integrated ones, controlling production, distribution, and sales of petroleum and its by-products. Even in countries with state-owned oil
companies the MNOCs' vast resources, both financial and oil-
related, ensured that they would retain significant influence over all
aspects of the petroleum industry. At the same time the nature of the
oil industry, with its rags-to-riches strikes, encouraged wildcatters
and small producers. These "independents," largely reliant on domestic American oil, cultivated ties with government officials whom they
lobbied for protection against the majors.

The history of oil in the American century is not only dominated by
the seven majors but also by a series of major mistakes. The first was
the assumption that plentiful oil supplies would be available even
though the demand for petroleum grew exponentially. To be sure, when
the United States became a net importer of oil in 1948, American officials and oil company executives made alarmed noises. But the discovery of tremendous new deposits in the 1950s and the subsequent oil
glut guaranteed complacency. Unfortunately these deposits were
located not in the United States, the home of earlier elephants (as
giant fields were known), but in the Middle East. Two other developments fed American self-satisfaction. The first was the discovery of the
large Alaskan oil field, which reinforced the American habit of assuming that domestic supplies could always make the difference. The second was the chimera of nuclear power. Spoken of in rapturous terms
("clean energy, " or "too cheap to matter"), atoms for peace (as Eisenhower termed this possibility) seemed the fountain of power—the eternal solution to energy needs. Its false promise explained the blasé
attitude the Johnson administration demonstrated when Arab oil producers attempted a boycott during the Six-Day War.[1] Only after the
Three Mile Island accident in 1979 and the Chernobyl disaster seven
years later did the dream definitively die.

A second mistake was the continued colonial attitude demonstrated
by Western nations and companies toward the oil-producing states.

The imperial mentality dies hard. Although European political empires disintegrated after 1945, Westerners assumed they could retain economic control over less developed nations. Nothing seemed to shake this gut-level presumption. Mexico had nationalized its oil deposits in 1938, Iran in 1951. Gamal Abdel Nasser seized the Suez Canal five years later. But oil company executives and the diplomats who advised them always thought: it can't happen here.

Allowing the seven sisters to dominate Western oil policy was another error. They had prescribed oil policy in the interwar period, but when World War II began some American government officials, notably Harold Ickes, Franklin Roosevelt's petroleum coordinator for national defense, believed that the federal government should itself obtain and control foreign oil reserves. These plans proved abortive; by the war's end, private enterprise remained firmly in the oil saddle.[2] Other countries at least had a state-owned oil company or controlled a private oil company; Britain, for example, held the majority of shares in BP. Only in the United States did private industry have a virtual monopoly over the most important national resource.

Delegation of public issue decision making to private companies has long been the American way. When Eisenhower-era Secretary of Defense Charles Wilson proclaimed "what's good for General Motors is good for America," he was enunciating a commonly held sentiment. Privatized foreign and economic policy is, at least initially, both financially and politically cheaper. Unfortunately companies put their needs first. And when the needs of private industry and the public no longer coincide, the public pays the price.

The "fifty-fifty" oil split shows how privatization worked in practice. In December 1950, Aramco (the Arab-American Oil Company— jointly owned by Socal, Texaco, Exxon, and Mobil), adopting an approach first implemented in Venezuela, agreed to split the profits from Saudi Arabian production with its monarchial government. The National Security Council in 1950 then blessed the arrangement as in America's best interests in the Middle East.[3] Of equal importance the U.S. Treasury in 1955, with the approval of the staff of the Joint Congressional Committee on Internal Revenue Taxation, declared that these payments would be treated as foreign taxes rather than business deductions for tax purposes. (The Saudi tax code had been prepared by the New York law firm of Sullivan & Cromwell, whose chief partner prior to January 1953 was John Foster Dulles.) As a result American MNOCs reduced their taxes virtually to zero and instead disbursed to oil-producing states in the Middle East and elsewhere payments generally exceeding U.S. official government foreign aid to the region.[4]

This "privatization" of foreign assistance had clear advantages for the administration of Dwight D. Eisenhower, who took office in January 1953. It allowed taxpayer dollars to be transferred from the U.S. Treasury to the treasuries of foreign governments without public discussion and debate. The lack of public scrutiny simplified a complex issue. Using the tax code to nurture the oil industry had a long American pedigree: the 27 percent oil depletion allowance was almost contemporaneous with the modern tax code. During the Eisenhower years the Justice Department also eased up on the so-called oil cartel case, which the Federal Trade Commission initiated in 1949 to prove that the MNOCs operated as a cartel in restraint of trade. Even during the Truman years the federal government had been split over the case. The State Department always took a benevolent view of oil combinations because they "serve the national interest."[5]

The fifty-fifty split also allowed the State and Defense Departments to avoid what they feared were the negative consequences of American support for the state of Israel. Both American diplomats and U.S. oil company executives believed that the Truman administration's decision in 1947 to support the creation of the state of Israel would irretrievably jeopardize American standing with the Arab Middle East, and they predicted that the 1948 Israeli War of Independence would suck U.S. troops into the region. These predictions proved false but MNOC executives and much of the American diplomatic establishment remained hostile to the Jewish state. That an Aramco vice-president could reply to a query at the Council on Foreign Relations as to whether the company employed any Jews by stating "No. We try to employ only Saudis and Americans" revealed the prevailing attitude.[6] As a result of the tax treatment of the fifty-fifty split, the amount of U.S. dollars flowing from the American Treasury to Arab oil producers dwarfed the amount of U.S. foreign aid to Israel from 1950 until 1973.

Why did the State Department adopt the oil company view of Israel? For one thing privatization of oil policy had a further twist: the revolving door between oil companies and government jobs was a constant in the postwar period. To take just one example, the Kerr-McGee oil company of Oklahoma sent Robert Kerr to the Senate while State Department official and oil expert George McGhee made his fortune in the Louisiana oil fields. Moreover, the State Department had a notorious record of anti-Semitism. It was the State Department, led by Assistant Secretary of State Breckenridge Long, that schemed to prevent European Jews fleeing the Nazi Final Solution from entering the United States. Loy Henderson, in charge of the Bureau of Near Eastern Affairs from 1945 to 1948, believed that American support for the creation of the state of Israel "corrupted the fundamental standards of self-determination and equality the United States stood for." (Interestingly, he did not see his participation in the CIA coup that overthrew the Iran government in 1953 as violating those standards.[7]) Of course, the seven sisters had good reasons to appease the Arabs. But those reasons did not justify the U.S. government's accepting oil company wisdom at face value.

The third mistake was the construction in the United States of a society that venerated the automobile and dwelt in suburban houses dependent on the perpetual supply of cheap energy. Postwar America found its ultimate expression in ever-larger American dream machines that guzzled gas as they ferried Americans from one far-flung location to another. Workplace, home, school, shopping center (the ur-creation of automobile America) depended on the automobile and the highway for their very existence. Unlike the mixed-income railroad suburbs of the nineteenth and early twentieth century, where everything remained in walking distance, Levittown and its successors became income-stratified bedroom communities. Individual houses expanded in size and energy consumption from earlier models. That the decisions of oil-producing states half a world away could puncture the American dream was inconceivable.

The beginning of the oil shocks made these mistakes painfully apparent. Oil-producer states had founded the Organization of Petroleum Exporting Countries (OPEC) in September 1960, in response to a series of oil company–mandated cuts in the posted (base) price, which had shrunk from $1.93/barrel (bbl) for Arabian Light in January 1956 to $1.80 for the same oil in September 1960.[8] Venezuela, Iran, and Iraq took the lead in crafting its first resolution, demanding that the MNOCs restore the cuts. But for eight years the continued oil glut kept OPEC impotent. The fifteenth OPEC Conference convened in January 1968 and accepted an agreement with the MNOCs that gave OPEC governments extra payments averaging one cent/bbl per year for seven years.[9] This was one of the last times that the seven sisters called the tune. Although unremarked at the time, two far more important events had occurred concurrently. Immediately after the fifteenth conference Saudi Arabia, Kuwait, and Libya founded the Organization of Arab Petroleum Exporting Countries (OAPEC). Designed as a complement to OPEC, its purpose was to coordinate the political use of the oil weapon. Britain evacuated all its forces from the key Aden base that year; in January 1969 the Wilson government announced the ending of British military commitments in the Persian Gulf. No longer would Britain undertake peacekeeping responsibilities in the region. A power vacuum in the region had now been created. The question was who would fill it.[10]

The key precipitating factor for the turmoil of the seventies lay in the Libyan revolution of September 1969, successfully led by Muammar al-Qadhafi. British troops stationed in Libya during the revolution chose not to intervene—King Idris had not endeared himself to the West and al-Qadhafi's ascent did not seem particularly ominous. Al-Qadhafi's first goal was to eject American troops from Wheelus Base, an outpost inherited from the British. This task accomplished, in 1970 al-Qadhafi set about changing the relationship between producer countries and MNOCs. With seven companies sharing the Libyan concession, he divided and conquered, changing rules of the game forever. al-Qadhafi won an increase in the posted price of oil and received retroactive payments back to 1965.

The MNOCs bungled their dealings with Libya. Al-Qadhafi had first targeted Occidental Petroleum, a company heavily dependent on Libyan crude and not one of the seven sisters. Rather than stand together with Oxy, the MNOCs allowed al-Qadhafi to defeat Armand Hammer's company. More important, the oil companies accepted al-Qadhafi's demand that the retroactive payments be made by changing the fifty-fifty split to fifty-five/forty-five. This decision proved utterly disastrous. By allowing a breach in the wall of the fifty-fifty agreement, the

MNOCs opened themselves up to challenges from other oil-producing states.[11]

Iran generated the next confrontation. The Shah was furious at being upstaged by an upstart. On November 14 the Iran producers' consortium agreed that the 55 percent rate would become the new base rate. Within one month the Venezuelan government passed a law mandating a tax rate of 60 percent and proclaiming that the government could raise oil prices at will. OPEC now demanded direct negotiations with the MNOCs. The Teheran Agreement of February 1971 embodied the new regime. It called for a general increase in the posted price of 35 cents and confirmed the basic 55 percent tax rate. In exchange for the new income the OPEC countries agreed to end leapfrogging (the process whereby each OPEC country would attempt to top the last agreement) and to forego any embargoes. The agreement was to be in effect for five years, until December 31, 1975.[12]

In 1972 OPEC found a new issue—"participation": the institution of the right of the producer countries to control their own oil production by obtaining an ever-larger equity interest (ownership) in their oil concessions and local companies. Although less radical than instant nationalization (implemented by Algeria in 1967), it spelled the beginning of the end of MNOC control over OPEC resources. In January 1972 Aramco, under great pressure, agreed to sell Saudi Arabia a 20 percent interest in the company. Iraq nationalized the Iraq Petroleum Company (IPC) holdings in the same year. In December 1972 OPEC and the MNOCs agreed that host governments would get a 25 percent participation in their concessions with their share gradually rising to 51 percent.[13] Venezuela passed legislation in 1971 and 1972 appropriating full ownership in its oil concessions by 1975, while the Shah insisted that he receive the best deal given to any other country.

Libya, for its part, instituted strict production controls in 1971. Having recognized that oil was by nature a dwindling asset and having discovered that he could raise income while simultaneously reducing production, Gadhafi cut oil production in 1972 to 32 percent less than the amount permitted in 1970 and reduced it again in 1973 and 1974. As these fiats came during a time of growing shortage, the stage was set for a successful boycott.[14] In short, merely through OPEC's flexing of oligopolistic muscles, between 1969 and 1972 the majors lost control over price and production and were losing the ownership of their foreign concessions. The era of Western domination of the world's oil was drawing to a close. Adding impetus to this shift was the spiraling dollar inflation. With oil prices calculated in dollars, the erosion of American purchasing power decreased the real value of the money oil producers received for their products. OPEC nations resolved to take action.

Richard Nixon, who took office in January 1969, had a problem. As a CEA analysis explained: "there was no excess capacity outside the Persian Gulf, the non-OAPEC short-run supply elasticity was low, stocks were relatively low, world demand had been increasing at a rapid rate, and there were no short-run substitutes for oil."[15] Moreover, mandatory import limits had kept American oil prices above the world price; heating oil prices in New England, for example, had gone up 25 percent in the period 1958 to 1969 while world prices had declined. In response, New England legislators pressed the President to take quick action to reverse the trend. Nixon designated Labor Secretary George Shultz to head a presidential inquiry into the ten-year-old program.[16] The Nixon administration also monitored the 1970 and 1971 negotiations between the OPEC nations and the MNOCs. Although in 1971 less than 5 percent of American oil came from the Middle East, administration projections estimated that U.S. imports of oil from the "Eastern Hemisphere" would rise from 305,000 bbl/day in 1970 to 2,620,000 bbl/day in 1980. In April 1971 the presidential aide Peter Flanigan raised the possibility of an "energy crisis."

At this point, the administration made yet another mistake that would plague American policy in the Middle East for decades. The Shah, returned to his throne in 1953 by a CIA coup, had long been a bulwark of America's Middle Eastern policy. Rather than confront the Shah, one of OPEC's principal hawks, Nixon and his National Security Adviser Henry Kissinger anointed the Shah as a pillar of the Nixon Doctrine. They blessed his willingness to assume the policeman's role in the Persian Gulf renounced by Britain. In May 1972 the two Americans visited Teheran and promised the Shah the keys to the American arms cupboard so that the Shah's army could meet its new role. They were not deterred by reports that "the Shah [has] embarked on another course designed to reinforce his self-styled role as leader and originator of ideas in OPEC." A CIA report written in August 1972 provided reassurance that "a continuing and growing supply of oil from *Iran* appears as certain as anyt[h]ing can be in an uncertain world."[17] Thus the new pattern: pick a Middle Eastern ally; grow dependent on him; give him what he wants; wait for inevitable disaster.

At the end of 1972 the Shah rejected the June agreement and demanded that the consortium of Western oil companies that controlled the sale of Iranian oil sell all its properties and rights in Iran to the National Iranian Oil Company (NIOC). A Nixon administration memorandum recommended that "the Companies should search for a new and alternative solution to the problem that could both satisfy the Shah's objectives and be acceptable to the Companies." It also advocated that the consortium realize the "seriousness of the situation" and obtain the "active support" of the respective MNOC governments. On January 15, 1973 Vice-President Spiro Agnew met with Iranian Minister of the Economy Hushang Ansari and "made a strong pitch that the Iranian give the oil companies a fair opportunity to plead their case." Ansari replied by predicting that in five years Iran's GNP would equal Great Britain's and made it clear that Iran would take full control of its oil industry. He also rejected the arguments that such a result would upset arrangements with Saudi Arabia and Kuwait.[18] Flanigan and Kissinger advised the President that the "companies have a good case." Worried that confiscation by Iran would set a precedent not only for OPEC but for other extractive industries, they informed Nixon that "we have taken a hard line with the Iranians."

Saudi Arabia in 1972 presented a more amenable face to Washington. In October the administration toyed with a Saudi offer proposing a "'special relationship'" between Saudi Arabia and the United States for the supply of oil coupled with sharply increased Saudi investments in the United States to offset the balance of payments drain. But Iran was still America's favored regional partner. After suggesting that the Saudi government was primarily interested in American political protection, the State Department drafted a negative reply. Shortly after his second inaugural Nixon wrote King Faisal of Saudi Arabia assuring the king of Washington's friendship and congratulating him on the new Saudi agreements with the MNOCs. After expressing his concern over the Middle East situation, the President requested that Saudi Arabia keep the Arab-Israeli conflict separate from the Saudi-American relation-ship.[19] American MNOCs rejected this advice. Their spokesman and lobbyist, John J. McCloy, attempted to end the administration's tilt toward Israel. McCloy trumpeted the Aramco line that if the United States did not change course, it would bear the brunt of the worsening oil shortage. Oil company officials immediately conferred with Assistant Secretary of State Joseph Sisco and Kissinger deputy Brent Scow-croft after King Faisal informed Aramco officials in May 1973 that if the United States did not pressure Israel to return unilaterally territory conquered during the Six-Day War, the Americans "may lose every-thing," i.e., the Aramco concessions.[20] The congruence between MNOC and State Department policy illustrates the important role MNOCs played in both American business and diplomacy. But oil company executives seldom separated their best interests from those of the country as a whole.

Turning up the heat on the administration, oil companies promoted their views directly to the public. For example, at the end of June, Mobil warned in a newspaper advertisement that "in the last analysis, political considerations may become the critical element in Saudi Ara-bia's decisions because we will need the oil more than Saudi Arabia will need the money." Otto Miller, CEO of Socal, wrote his 300,000 share-holders and employees the next month, informing them that "it is highly important at this time that the United States should work more closely with the Arab governments to build up and enhance our rela-tions with the Arab people. . . . There must be understanding on our part of the aspirations of the Arab people, and more positive support of their efforts toward peace in the Middle East."[21] Miller's carefully coded words conveyed his aim: to drum up public pressure to eviscerate American support for Israel.

In September 1972 the growing shortage of gasoline and the decrease of home heating oil inventories led Nixon, on Flanigan's rec-ommendation, to increase the permissible levels of 1972 oil imports for the second time that year. Here lay the issue that separated the inter-ests of the majors from the needs of the independents—the smaller American companies. The independents had long fought for the con-tinuance of American oil import quotas—without these limits on cheap, imported oil, independents, who depended on more expensive domestic production, could not compete in the American market. Even ultra–free market Presidents such as Dwight Eisenhower had acquiesced in this system. His rationale: national security demanded that the United States retain its domestic oil industry. His decision: institute mandatory oil import quotas in 1959 limiting imported oil to around 9 percent of American annual usage.

But the quota system kept the U.S. price of oil above the market. Without their consent consumers paid for their domestic oil industry. As long as the price of energy remained low, protests remained muffled. That changed now. Three months later a National Petroleum Council report predicted a growing American reliance on oil and gas imports. As the report assumed that "substantial changes in life-style between now and 1985 are precluded by existing mores and habits," it placed little faith in conservation as a way to control the need for increasing imports. To increase domestic supplies, the report urged the continuation of oil import quotas and advocated an expanded use of coal and uranium sources.[22]

When a group of Northeast legislators discussed the "energy crisis" with James V. Akins, head of the Office of Fuel and Energy, in February 1973, he agreed that the quota system was unwieldy but resisted major changes. Akins viewed as problematic their request for oil company production and cost data, raising objections to the idea of stockpiling as a means of protecting against a boycott. He pointed out that buying and storing one barrel of oil cost around $5.00 initially (at a time when the posted price hovered around $3.00/bbl) and the annual maintenance and capital cost for that barrel would add another $.60. Akins also expounded on the difficulties of paying for storage facilities: neither Congress nor the oil companies wanted to be the villain who would pass the cost onto the consumer.

Other aspects of the energy issue troubled the administration; for example, what would be the effect of increased energy imports on the balance of payments position and how badly would a rise in gasoline taxes damage the President's fight against inflation? By spring the energy crisis merited an eighteen-page presidential message to Congress. Nixon announced the end of quantitative controls on oil imports, established a National Energy Office, and ordered an acceleration of oil leases for new drilling on the Outer

Continental Shelf. Furthermore, he asked Congress to remove price controls on domestic natural gas, to permit work on the trans-Alaska pipeline, and to allow the licensing of deep water ocean ports to make it easier for the new, larger tankers to use U.S. ports. Crude oil prices in May rose 4.2 percent while refined products were up 4.7 percent for the month and 24.8 percent over the previous 12 months.[23] The sense of crisis grew.

In August 1972 the CIA produced a report on the medium-term outlook for oil supplies. Analysts understood that the renewal of hostilities between Arab states and Israel might trigger the collective Arab use of the oil weapon. The report also pointed out that while during past crises oil companies had been able to maintain a disinterested position,

> recently, however, both the companies and some producer governments have encouraged increased US government involvement in oil matters; hereafter, the companies and some producer governments may find themselves more closely associated than before in Arab minds with US policy on the Arab-Israeli question and hence more exposed to direct punitive actions from Arab countries.

At a minimum, the CIA officials concluded, if another war began some of the Arab states would attempt to embargo oil shipments to the United States.[24]

The settlement of the Suez crisis in March 1957 had left United Nations Emergency Forces (UNEF) patrolling border areas between Egypt and Israel. During the following decade Soviet arms poured into Egypt and Syria. The United States attempted to avoid matching these shipments. While John Kennedy agreed to ship Hawk missiles to Israel, France remained Israel's major supplier.[25] In May 1967, Egyptian President Nasser, emboldened by his large weapons stocks, demanded that UNEF troops depart Egyptian territory. Tensions escalated as Washington scrambled to forestall another Middle Eastern conflict. On June 6, taking matters into their own hands, Israeli armed forces attacked Egypt, Jordan, and Syria. Six days later Israel controlled the West Bank of the Jordan River, East Jerusalem, the Golan Heights, Gaza, and the West Bank of the Sinai. French President Charles de Gaulle, irritated that Israel had ignored his warnings against a preemptive campaign, ended French support for the Jewish state; the United States assumed this role and became Israel's chief ally. American diplomats obtained passage of United Nations Security Council Resolution 242 of November 1967, which called on Israel to withdraw "from territories occupied in the recent conflict" and recognized the right of all states in the region to "live in peace with secure and recognized boundaries." With Arab states adamantly retaining their state of war with Israel and the Jewish state holding captured Jordanian, Syrian, and Egyptian territory, the area remained a tinderbox. It exploded on the afternoon of October 6, 1973, as Jews began their observance of Yom Kippur, the most sacred day of the Jewish calendar. Egyptian and Syrian forces struck Israel; within two days Egyptian forces had crossed the Suez Canal and advanced fifteen miles past Israeli lines. Syrian troops made similar progress into the Golan Heights. Israeli troops counterattacked on October 8 and found themselves locked in a bitterly contested battle.

During the second week of the war, as Soviet supplies poured into Egypt and Syria, the United States delayed shipments to Israel, hoping that a cease-fire would make any arms transfers unnecessary. Nixon and Kissinger, now secretary of state, believed that a quick halt to hostilities might even end the Arab-Israeli deadlock, which, among other things, endangered Western oil supplies. Their allies locked in fierce combat, the United States and the Soviet Union found themselves dragged toward a confrontation neither had sought. On October 12 after Egyptian President Anwar Sadat, flush with Soviet arms, refused a cease-fire, Nixon decided that Israel must be immediately resupplied. Rather than accept the Pentagon recommendation for only limited shipments, Nixon told Kissinger, "Goddam it, use every [plane] we have. Tell them to send everything that can fly!"[26] The administration neither consulted NATO allies nor sought their approval. Western European countries, fearful of endangering their own oil supplies, responded by refusing the use of their bases for refueling. Only Portugal acquiesced.

A week after the airlift began, Saudi Arabia announced an embargo on oil destined for the United States. In mid-September OPEC held its 35th Conference in Vienna: Resolution XXXB.160 summoned MNOCs to renegotiate the Teheran Agreement on October 8. That conference took place against the somber background of the Yom Kippur War. The Persian Gulf states summarily rejected the MNOC offer of an inflation-linked index and a general increase of 15 percent, or $.45/bbl, and demanded a doubling of the posted price (a $3/bbl increase), as well as the inflation index and a sulfur premium. After MNOCs requested a recess to consult with their governments, on October 16, OPEC unilaterally announced a price rise of $2/bbl. An era had ended. No longer would OPEC negotiate with the MNOCs. From now on the companies and their home governments would simply receive the dictates of OPEC members. While the OAPEC embargo and cutbacks were not directly part of the OPEC revolution, it took the two concurrent events—the boycott and the price explosion—to create the 1973 crisis. The OAPEC actions tightened the market, forcing OECD members to scramble for extra sources of oil, in turn further constricting supplies and driving up prices, to the benefit of OPEC. The Yom Kippur War merely accelerated the already-breaking OPEC revolution.[27]

The American oil embargo was launched by the Conference of Arab Oil Ministers, a separate group from OPEC but one consisting only of OPEC members who were also members of OAPEC. This group also decided in October to embargo supplies to South Africa, the Netherlands, and Portugal and to institute a series of supply reductions of 5 percent per month based on September 1973 sales until Israel returned to its 1967 borders and restored the "legitimate rights" of the Palestinian people. Kissinger's arrangement of a cease-fire on October 24 did not affect these decisions. The oil weapon was now a reality.

Although not immune, the United States was in the best position to withstand the embargo because of its limited use of Arab supplies. The boycott meant a reduction of between one and two million bbl/day, equaling 17 percent of U.S. imports, or 6 percent of total consumption. However, the general production cutbacks also ate into American supplies of imported refined products. Ironically, the MNOCs inherited the unpleasant job of allocating available supplies among their customers, sharing the pain as equitably as possible. Facing opprobrium from consumers and governments alike, the MNOCs performed their unenviable task in an expeditious and fair manner.[28]

Administration officials debated how to deal with the shortage.

They had limited enthusiasm for foisting rationing or other consumption curbs on the American people. Flanigan, for one, resisted the idea of mentioning washing in cold water because he thought "we will be laughed at if we say this publicly." Another official opposed the idea of imposing a 25 percent cut in the amount of available airplane fuel because it would have a disastrous effect on airline economics and might spark a recession. Clearly curbing automobile use was crucial but the White House avoided forced changes in the American lifestyle. Instead, the President asked state and local officials to encourage voluntary action such as the use of car pools, reduced highway speeds, and set-aside bus lanes.[29]

Walter Wriston, chief executive officer of Citibank, described the atmosphere in Washington as reeking of "hysteria." Nixon, embattled in the Watergate crisis, made two television addresses on the energy crisis during November. On November 7 he sought voluntary conservation measures and congressional action. Three weeks later, he announced draft legislation curtailing the hours of service stations, imposing a lower maximum nationwide highway speed, and cutting jet fuel allocation, reduced 10 percent in early November, an additional 15 percent. The administration still avoided crucial issues such as lifting oil and gas controls, allowing market pricing for domestic oil, and using tax policy to change oil consumption. Each dilemma pitted interest groups against each other. Should consumers be favored over producers? Should domestic use come before business needs? How should the cost of conservation be allocated? CEA Chairman Herbert Stein's cal-

FIGURE 11-1
HISTORICALLY SPEAKING, GASOLINE PRICES ARE LOW
Average Annual Service-Station Price for a Nonpremium Gallon of Gasoline, Including Taxes

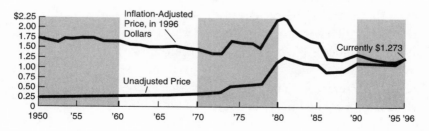

The New York Times, May 3, 1996.

culation that the embargo would reduce American GNP during the first quarter of 1974 between 1 and 2 percent showed the American stakes.[30]

On December 22 OPEC's Persian Gulf subcommittee met in Teheran. The Shah sparked a new price rise—now each government would receive $7/bbl for each barrel of oil, making for a posted price of $11.65/bbl. It did not faze the Shah that this escalation meant the posted price had jumped almost five times in one year (it was $2.90 in mid-1973). Indeed, he proclaimed that the new price reflected his "kindness and generosity," observing that the new posted price was far less than the recent Teheran auction prices of spot oil, which had escalated to $17.04.[31]

This represented a sudden, massive transfer of wealth. Using the October 16 price increase as a basis for his calculations, the American official Samuel Pizer estimated that if production held at the 1973 levels, the gross revenues of oil-producing states during 1974 would jump to $20 billion from less than $10 billion in 1972.[32] The resulting positive impact on the balance of payments of oil-producer nations would be mirrored by a negative impact on the economies of oil-importing nations. Japan, the hardest hit of the OECD countries, could record a 500 percent increase in its balance of payments deficit. The administration estimated that after the December price rise, the total annual OECD oil import bill in 1974 would increase by $56.3 billion.[33]

The serious consequences of this new financial order would not, of course, be felt in the industrialized world alone. Developing nations not blessed with oil deposits also saw their oil import bills rise astronomically. Nascent Western concern about their plight vied with fears that these typically primary producer states might decide to emulate OPEC and create producer cartels to raise the prices of their raw materials. Given that a major component of the post–1971 inflation had been a price rise in such commodities, this fear was not an idle one.

On December 4 Nixon announced that he had asked Congress to create a Federal Energy Office. In the meantime, he appointed Deputy Treasury Secretary William Simon to oversee energy questions as executive director of the Energy Emergency Action Group (Nixon assumed the chairmanship). Two weeks later the President pledged to ask Congress to enact an emergency windfall profits tax on domestic oil production. At the same time Nixon and his advisers debated unraveling the decades-old system of oil price and production controls. Free market prices would encourage both new exploration and conservation, as George Shultz, now Treasury secretary, pointed out at a meeting with the President on December 7. Administration officials also discussed the possibility of oil ration coupons. Stein suggested to Simon that the government could sell advertising space on the backs of the coupons, thereby garnering extra federal revenue. Another frequently debated issue was whether to leave in place or temporarily waive environmental regulations limiting coal and nuclear fuel usage.[34]

On January 9 the administration invited major oil-consuming nations to discuss the energy crisis in Washington on February 11 and informed OPEC members of this conference.[35] The energy crisis had greatly expanded the cracks in the Western alliance. Hard-hit members of the European Community had already succumbed to Arab pressure. When Arab oil ministers announced on November 4, 1973, that they would cut production to ensure that December's exports of Arab oil would be about 30 percent less than those in September, EC countries quickly urged Israel to withdraw its troops from Egyptian land. OAPEC responded by announcing on November 18 that as a reward the EC would be exempted from the December 5 percent production cutback. The EC issued a further pro-Arab statement on December 16; officials also proclaimed their support for Palestinian rights. The EC began a series of joint meetings with Arab representatives, the most important of which was a 1974 meeting with the Arab League and the Palestine Liberation Organization. The Japanese government on November 22 also publicly backed the Arab position. But European and Japanese appeasement of the Arab bloc yielded few tangible price rewards.[36] By contrast Kissinger told Saudi Arabian Minister of Petroleum and Mineral Resources Sheikh Ahmed Zaki Yamani and Algerian oil minister Belaid Abdesselam that the boycott would not alter American policy. (His forthright statement exaggerated American firmness. The United States actually pressured Israel to reach a settlement allowing Sadat to retire his armies from the field, honor intact, and Kissinger began a period of intense shuttle diplomacy, crafting cease-fire agreements between Israel and the various Arab combatants.[37])

Kissinger spoke for the United States at the Washington conference.

His stressed trilevel cooperation—among the consumer nations, between the consumer and producer nations, and with the developing world. His main points—the need for conservation, research, emergency sharing provisions, and aid to impoverished nations—were not especially controversial. The official communiqué ending the conference on February 13 embodied these points and announced that the conferees would establish an international coordinating body that started life as the Energy Coordination Group and quickly became the International Energy Agency (IEA). It set up shop in Paris, notwithstanding a continued French refusal to join.[38]

Kissinger's shuttle diplomacy continued, using the framework of UN Resolution 338 of October 1973 reiterating and reapplying the United Nations 1967 Resolution 242. As a result Israel signed disengagement agreements with Egypt in January and Syria in May. The secretary of state flattered Arab leaders by including many Mideast capitals on his whirlwind tours. Most important, the administration wooed Saudi Arabia.[39] Washington offered the carrot of expanded access to the American weapons arsenal. In response Arab governments lifted the oil boycott in mid-March. Nixon made a goodwill tour of the region in the spring, visiting Jordan, Egypt, and Saudi Arabia as well as Israel. The President also trimmed his heretofore ardent support for the Jewish state, telling congressional leaders in June 1974 that aid to Israel from now on must be "balanced."[40]

The oil boycott was over, but the massive oil price hikes (by a factor of four) still stood. The administration grappled with the domestic consequences of the more than fourfold rise in oil prices. One important initiative was Project Independence. Simon spearheaded this program, which was designed to achieve "national self-sufficiency" in energy by 1980.[41] The goal was clear, but the means to achieve it were not. A key issue was whether government fiat or free market action should lead the way. Adopting a free market approach would necessitate price decontrol. That was the only way to make new exploration and development profitable as well as make feasible previously uneconomic sources of energy. But such a large increase in energy prices would have dramatic effects, both good and bad, on the American economy.[42]

Most directly affected by the administration's plans for Project Independence were the MNOCs and the independents. The independents chafed at continued price control and resented their lack of maneuvering room. The MNOCs' world had collapsed. Their virtual hegemony over the oil industry vanished. The continued OPEC demand for participation spelled the demise of their ownership interest in the massive foreign fields—in the future they would be mere middlemen. In the meantime MNOC earnings soared: in the first quarter of 1974 reported profits of the leading major oil companies rose 76 percent over first-quarter 1973 figures, with domestic profits rising 37 percent and profits from foreign operations soaring 119 percent.[43] While American legislation in place in January 1974 limited oil company profits on imported oil to $.45/barrel, in practice MNOCs benefited from the crisis in several ways. The foreign tax credit provisions meant that the increased payments to OPEC members would enable each MNOC to receive a dollar-for-dollar credit against its American taxes for increased tax (royalty) payments abroad. The tightening of supplies gave the MNOCs an advantage over the smaller independents, which did not have the long-term contracts with OPEC members and were therefore much more dependent on the market for so-called spot oil purchases. MNOCs could also charge the new, higher price for oil that they had previously purchased and held in inventory. MNOC–owned gas stations could then undercut independent operations and win a larger market share. Outside the United States MNOCs could charge whatever they could get. As a result CEA staffers observed "there appears to be a commonality of interests between OPEC and the producers." The MNOCs understood whom they wanted to appease. Advocating the Arab line in the Middle East became a top priority. Their spokesman, John J. McCloy, continued pressing the administration, joining oil company officials for a meeting with Kissinger on March 29.[44]

Congress attempted to assert its own influence over American energy policy. The hearings on MNOCs and foreign policy led by Senator Frank Church and those conducted by Senator Henry Jackson as head of the Senate Permanent Committee on Investigations were the most visible sign of legislative concern. A parade of witnesses from the oil industry and the federal government allowed senators to vent the public's anger to executives who managed to be complacent and defensive simultaneously.[45] These hearings spawned legislation cutting the oil depletion and foreign tax credit allowances. During the same period

Congress, following Nixon's suggestion, authorized the Trans-Alaska pipeline to deliver Alaskan oil to the lower forty-eight states. Lawmakers also supported price rollbacks and continued energy price control. Simon and other administration spokesmen attempted to block such ideas, with little success. As a result Nixon vetoed the Energy Emergency legislation passed by Congress in February 1974.[46]

During the spring and summer of 1974 Nixon concentrated not on the energy crisis but on saving himself from impeachment. By contrast his staff fought the deepening, clearly energy-related recession. As Flanigan pointed out in June, for the first time in decades the major industrialized nations experienced a simultaneous drop in industrial output. For the six-month period from November 1973 to March 1974, American industrial production declined 3.1 percent while Japanese figures dipped 2.9 percent and those for Britain fell by 4.6 percent.[47] Upon Nixon's resignation on August 8, 1974, Gerald Ford faced the tasks of decreasing American reliance on imported sources of energy, creating a free market in energy, maintaining consumer purchasing power at pretax rates, and providing funds for domestic energy initiatives.[48] At least Ford had the opportunity to craft domestic policy within the context of four years of stable OPEC prices. In December 1974 the posted price/bbl stood at $11.25; four years later it was $12.70.[49]

The size of the federal gasoline tax and the issue of fuel economy loomed large in these debates. A 1974 Federal Energy Administration study showed that while the U.S. tax per gallon stood at $.12, in Western Europe comparable assessments ranged from a low of $.53 in Britain to a high of $1.16 in Italy; in Japan it stood at $.46. Higher gas taxes would decrease consumption, in turn reducing American demand for imported petroleum. For an administration pledged to energy independence, raising taxes seemed an obvious step. But equally important was general American economic health. Unfortunately, the economic environment could not have been less auspicious. Unemployment during January 1975 increased by 1 percent to 8.2 percent, its highest level in thirty-five years. A recession gripped the United States simultaneously with double-digit inflation. "Stagflation" drove down American confidence in the future to levels not seen since the Depression. Raising taxes during a severe recession made neither economic nor political sense. Moreover, it would be difficult to persuade the American people to accept a tax program that ran counter to the basic American assumption of a right to cheap gasoline.

Increasing fuel efficiency posed other problems. While in the United States cars on the average got 14 miles per gallon, in Western Europe average mileage ranged from 20 to 26 miles per gallon.[50] The importance of the automobile to the American economy as a whole increased the difficulty faced by Ford as he struggled with these decisions: at the end of 1974 the motor vehicle and associated industries accounted for 18 percent of total U.S. gross national product.[51]

Ford unveiled much of his energy package in his State of the Union message of January 1975, sending thirteen bills to Congress in the same month. Project Independence remained at the center of the program. Ford's blueprint called for a ten-year plan that would build 200 nuclear power plants, 250 major coal mines, 30 major oil refineries, and 20 major synthetic fuel plants. The administration's central goal was to cut imports by at least one million bbl/day. But Ford officials reported that "the chances of the energy program getting through Congress in its present form are doubtful. . . . it imposes a burden on the American people—and Congress doesn't like to impose burdens."

One year later it became clear that presidential politics doomed the passage of significant energy legislation. Indeed the subject was so controversial that Ford's advisers were divided as to whether he should even discuss energy in his election speeches.[52] In the event, Ford lost the closely fought election. He bequeathed to Jimmy Carter a White House commitment to energy legislation unmatched by achievement. The intricate energy laws dealing with oil and gas price regulation remained on the books. Congress's desire to placate consumer outrage at the rise in energy prices and the perceived need to stimulate conservation and energy independence clashed constantly.[53]

Only one of Ford's proposals had a major, lasting impact. In 1975, the federal government set fuel efficiency standards for the automobile industry that mandated a doubling of new car fuel efficiency within the next decade. Even this battle was a difficult one—Henry Ford II, the chairman and chief executive officer of the car company that bore his grandfather's name, informed the President in January 1975 that he would only reluctantly accept voluntary fuel economy improvement standards and then asked, as a quid pro quo, that automobiles be exempted from proposed new emission standards.[54]

Carter, who came to the nation's highest office largely in response to the Watergate scandal, was avowedly anti-Washington. Unlike his predecessor, he was comfortable with injecting concepts of morality into public discourse. An engineer by training, the President from Plains, Georgia, declared that energy would be his number-one priority. He appointed as energy secretary James Schlesinger, holder of a doctorate in economics, who had served Nixon as chairman of the Atomic Energy Commission, director of the Central Intelligence Agency, and lastly, secretary of defense. Schlesinger shared Carter's views, especially on the centrality of conservation in any energy package.

The President unveiled his program in April 1977, within the ninety-day deadline he had set himself. Sitting before a fire, clothed in a cardigan, Carter labeled his energy campaign the "moral equivalent of war." He rejected the postwar consumer consensus, instead asking the American people to embrace a more frugal lifestyle. Carter's Republican predecessors, understanding the electorate far better than he, avoided such draconian rhetoric. In actuality, Carter's program mirrored many of the Nixon/Ford proposals, including the so-far unattainable quest of rationalized oil prices. In emphasis, however, the Carter-Schlesinger proposals relied more heavily on conservation than Republican initiatives had.[55]

Not surprisingly the President's attempt to substitute an energy crusade for the American dream flopped badly. Fading public perceptions of an energy crisis combined with unprecedented inflation generated a negative reaction to Carter's call for sacrifice. By January 1978, close to half of the respondents in a CBS News/New York Times poll agreed that the energy crisis was a figment of Carter's imagination.[56] At the end of 1978, the President had achieved little. The exploration and development oil rush had spawned a connected demand for oil-related equipment such as drilling rigs and tankers. The massive price rises had rendered economic previously unprofitable reserves in the United States and abroad.[57] But the amount of American oil imports steadily rose as did the percentage of those exports from OAPEC countries; in the period from the oil boycott through mid-1976, the share of American imports from Arab OPEC members climbed from 22 percent to 37 percent.[58] American conservation efforts did not keep pace; among other reasons, continued price controls removed much of the economic incentive.

Walter Levy, one of the gurus of oil forecasting, predicted that oil prices would remain stable from 1977 through 1981.[59] He was wrong; in 1979 new oil price rises dwarfed the 1973–74 escalation. The explanation lay not in OPEC decisions but in the panicked reaction of Western buyers to the possible effects on the oil market of the overthrow of the Shah of Iran and his replacement by the relentlessly anti-American Ayatollah Ruholla Khomeini. Here was the disaster waiting to happen to American Middle East policy. Because Iran had become part of the backbone of both Washington's Middle East and its petroleum policies, the United States felt the brunt of the Iran crisis.

America's relationship with the Shah steadily intensified during the Nixon years. Both the President and Secretary of State Kissinger considered the Shah trustworthy, notwithstanding his central role in the oil price explosion. They fell all over themselves attempting to furnish the military hardware that had a special place in the Shah's heart. American companies, both defense contractors and those selling consumer products, benefited as the Shah increased Iran's military budget 680 percent from 1972 to 1977.[60] Unfortunately the new prosperity flowing into Iran was distributed neither equally nor productively. Instead Iranian society suffered a vast dislocation that undermined its traditional culture at the same time as members of the new ruling elite became progressively more disenchanted with the Shah's autocratic and brutal dictates.

Carter accepted the inherited U.S. connection with the Shah. Perhaps the most embarrassing moment of his presidency came at a New Year's banquet in Teheran on December 31, 1977, when he said that "Iran, because of the great leadership of the Shah, is an island of stability in one of the more troubled areas of the world."[61] During 1978 American officials belatedly realized that the Shah's hold over the country had become extremely precarious; on January 16, 1979, he fled Teheran, never to return. Power in Iran now lay with the Ayatollah Ruhollah Khomeini, a fundamentalist Islamic cleric. Khomeini and his associates unleashed a revolution in Iran whose circles continue to spin outward. His policies had two immediate effects: they destroyed a

major component of American Middle East policy while simultaneously setting into motion the second oil shock.

Beginning in December 1978, when Iranian oil exports ceased, oil
prices almost trebled in three years, to $34.00/bbl in December 1981.[62]
Various factors explain the climb. The Iranian revolution removed
about two million bbl/day from production, creating an actual although
not insuperable shortage. Fear fueled further scarcity—companies and
consumers alike panicked and rushed to build inventories. This under-
standable reaction led to a doubling of the shortage as demand for oil
mushroomed by an additional three million bbl/day. MNOCs viewed
the second oil shock from a different vantage point than five years earlier. The Saudi government, for example, now totally owned all of
Aramco's properties, concession rights, and petroleum production. The
four American partners—Exxon, Mobil, Socal, and Texaco—merely
performed such transportation and distribution tasks as the Saudi government allotted them. Even this middleman role had eroded as oil-
producing nations sought to control where and under what terms their
oil would be sold. The new rules in turn exacerbated the anxiety.

Oil-producer nations rushed to take advantage of the situation.
Ironically, the potential for profits destroyed OPEC solidarity as each
producing state sold oil at the highest price. Saudi Arabia, in particular,
raised production after 1978: "We engineered the glut and we want to
see it in order to stabilize the price," explained Sheik Yamani. Consum-
ing nations also took an autarkic attitude. The IEA's emergency allocation plan was never put into effect. Various European nations singled
out Japan's massive trading companies for special blame; their panic
bidding had worsened the already difficult situation.[63]

The second oil shock with its attendant gasoline shortage should
have provided an impetus to Carter's energy program. Yet the President's initial decisions, to decontrol oil prices and institute a windfall
profits tax on "excess" oil company profits, infuriated both liberals and
conservatives. The American public reacted poorly to his decision to
frame his proposal for a massive synthetic fuels program within the context of what he called "America's crisis of confidence." By autumn,
Carter's focus on Iran had altered from the energy implications of the
revolution to the crisis in his own presidency, sparked by the Iranian
seizure of American Embassy employees on November 4, 1979, and

their subsequent fourteen-month captivity. While America may not have been held hostage (a phrase popularized by ABC television news), Carter certainly was. In the Iran crisis lay the ashes of his administration.[64]

The oil supershock continued into the first years of the Reagan administration. The Iran-Iraq war, which began on September 22, 1980, sent a further wave of fear through world oil markets. Uncertainty again lay at the heart of the problem—no one knew what the effect of a war between two oil-producing states would be. Continuing high oil prices contributed to another recession within OECD nations from 1979 to 1983.[65] In turn the recession (as well as the increased energy prices) cut demand. The search for alternative sources of supply and new forms of energy usage received yet another boost. Then from 1983 to 1985, oil prices softened and in 1986 they began a free fall, which left them at $19.00/bbl at the end of that year. In December 1988 the posted price of a barrel stood at $18.00; in March 1994 it was less than $14.00/bbl. It only climbed past the $19.00 mark in 1996.[66]

Incongruously, while this development spelled immediate relief for the American consumer, it proved catastrophic for national energy initiatives. Cheap imported oil priced new domestic exploration as well as alternative sources of energy out of the market. As early as 1982 various synthetic fuels programs in OECD nations had lost political favor as governments, wary of the enormous expense of these programs and mindful of their promises to cut taxes, axed most of the initiatives begun in the previous decade. Conservation measures, especially those of the more painful variety, also became less attractive.

The energy crisis of the 1970s illuminated the strengths and weaknesses of the Western alliance. Cheap and plentiful energy was fundamental to the Cold War. By the 1950s giving free rein to the automobile had become as American as apple pie. The federal government nurtured these developments by offering subsidized mortgages to veterans and then constructing the interstate highway system criss-crossing the nation. Western European nations played catch-up, providing their citizens with scaled-down versions of the American dream. At the same time Washington and its allies relied on cheap energy to fuel a gas-guzzling state-of-the-art defense program.

It was not a classified fact that the growing addiction to cheap

energy could not be satisfied forever. Yet throughout the fifties and sixties Washington remained complacent. Most important, Washington
allowed MNOCs to dominate energy policy decision making. Their
stewardship permitted the U.S. government to substitute the requirements of one particular industry for a myriad of interest group
demands. The men who guided the MNOCs, for example, John J.
McCloy, George McGhee, and Robert Kerr, were often former and
future government appointees or close associates of politicians and
bureaucrats.

Domestic American policy during the seventies featured big plans
that came to very little. Energy independence was indeed possible, not
least because throughout the period 1973 through 1987 the United
States ranked as the first- or second-largest producer of crude oil and
coal.[67] The United States had a real choice about its energy future. The
simplest option was to adopt a stringent conservation program to
achieve energy self-sufficiency. Alternatively, through public or private
action or a combination of both, the United States could have implemented Project Independence or another crash program. But the
Nixon and Ford administrations never dared ask Americans to accept
fundamental changes in their lifestyle. They largely chose to rely on
market forces to increase energy conservation. Carter's bold attempt to
downsize the American dream also failed. The drop in oil prices after
1983 spelled the end of any serious effort toward energy autonomy. The
American public was unwilling to pay the triple price that would be
required for the United States to live within its energy means: economic, political, and societal.

American strategic reserves increased in the years after the oil
shocks. Indeed the significant stockpile laid down by Washington,
almost 600 million barrels in 1990, allowed the Desert Shield coalition
to withstand Saddam Hussein's attempted use of the oil weapon during
the Persian Gulf War.[68] The oil shocks also altered American consumption patterns: "by 1985 the United States was 25 percent more energy
efficient and 32 percent more oil efficient than it had been in 1973."[69]
The growing environmental movement contributed to this progress.
For the first time in decades it became chic as well as virtuous to save
energy. Yet these improvements proved insufficient to stop the continued growth in American dependence on foreign reserves. These policy

failures cannot be laid at the door of MNOCs, OPEC, or the various administrations. The American public had gotten the policy it wanted.

The oil shocks spelled the end of MNOC control over the international petroleum industry. Since the beginning of the century, the MNOCs had occupied the villain's role in American folklore. Yet their performance during the postwar era deserves not an unqualified thumb's down but rather a mixed grade. On the one hand, the actions of the American MNOCs allowed successive Washington administrations to have their cake and eat it too. The federal government could follow a neutral or pro-Israel policy, all the while knowing that its private arm would pursue a very different agenda. That this delegation was antidemocratic should not be blamed on the MNOCs but on the government officials who blessed the arrangement.

The early Cold War era's stalwart faith in the efficacy and virtuousness of private enterprise increased Washington's willingness to leave the MNOCs unhampered. Failing to prosecute the oil cartel cases and the National Security Council's decision blessing the fifty-fifty arrangement, validated by the IRS and congressional committee alike, increased MNOC influence over American foreign policy. With the permission of a succession of attorneys general, oil companies flouted antitrust laws, joining forces for ostensibly limited purposes but no doubt discussing other matters as well. U.S. policy bolstered the position of MNOCs in oil-producing states, at the same time subsidizing client governments and sparing the executive branch from messy, unpredictable fights with Congress over foreign aid. The frequent trading of jobs by MNOC executives and State Department officials eased the cooperation between the public and private sectors: both sides used each other. But MNOC influence was not sufficient to alter significantly Washington's policy toward Israel. It was one thing to follow the MNOC lead on oil questions but quite another to transform American security policy at their bidding.

Pragmatic reasons supported the privatization of foreign energy policy, although it cost the public control over a part of American Middle East policy. The market generally proved effective in allocating costs and responding to the energy environment. While the MNOCs short-sightedly failed to recognize the clear signals of an impending producers' revolution, most diplomats missed the signs as well. The indications were there; in 1960 a CIA assessment concluded that "the terms and conditions of Middle East oil concessions are likely to be considerably changed. The position of Western oil companies will be further weakened by erosion of the fifty/fifty profit sharing formula and by joint efforts of the producing countries to control prices."[70] But such evidence in the main was ignored. In particular, once the oil shocks came, the MNOCs' allocation program worked at least as well as any other program would have, sharing the OPEC-induced pain as equally as possible. Although forward planning could not have prevented the oil shocks, earlier anticipation might have eased the pain.

American foreign policy proved inconclusive. Being a superpower did not insulate the United States from the oil shocks, although its economic strength and domestic reserves allowed it to surmount the crises more easily. Moreover, that oil was priced in dollars gave the United States significant protection against the pain of oil price hikes. Confusion between two separate problems—the Arab oil boycott and the OPEC price rises—complicated decision making. The boycott was a short-lived phenomenon that, had it lasted, could have been dealt with in an orderly fashion. The Arab use of sanctions against the United States proved no more successful than the American use of economic sanctions against various Arab nations—Egypt during the Suez crisis or Iraq during Operations Desert Shield and Storm.

Washington based its Middle Eastern diplomacy on its relationship with the Shah of Iran. When the Iranian revolution ended this relationship, the United States, rather than reexamine its basic premises, merely substituted one oil-rich despot for another. Now Saudi Arabia, the possessor of the world's largest proven deposits, became the foundation for American regional policy. While the American-Saudi relationship goes back to the 1930s, its intimacy intensified markedly after the Shah's demise.[71] Until 1991, the kingdom successfully hid evidence of how close these ties had become, but Saddam Hussein's invasion of Kuwait terrified the Saudi government. Faced with Saddam's threats, the Saudi government needed a visible American deterrent. The success of Operation Desert Storm provided immediate vindication of this policy. But recent developments indicate that this regional ally may ultimately prove no more reliable than Iran.

More problematic were the oil price rises and production limits. The decision by OPEC members to control their oil fields sent shock waves through Western economies, putting an end to the era of ever cheaper energy. The somewhat feeble attempts by Nixon and Kissinger to rally the West against OPEC and OAPEC faltered. Cold War suzerainty did not guarantee the United States NATO support in the confrontation with OAPEC. Because OECD countries saw the oil shocks as separable from the Cold War, they had few qualms about pursing a policy that diverged from that proposed by Washington. In particular, European nations quickly reduced their support for Israel rather than carving out a NATO position on the subject. The Ford administration envisioned the IEA as a vehicle for multilateral action. Yet its member nations refused to activate its emergency allocation plan when the second oil shock occurred. One policy option never seriously debated was the use of force to obtain energy supplies. Few people had any illusions that gunboats could solve the energy crisis.

The role of the Soviet Union in the energy shocks proved an opportunistic one. Moscow controlled huge oil, coal, and gas reserves—until the chaos of the late 1980s the Soviet Union ranked first, second, and third in the respective production from those energy sources.[72] The U.S. government had long feared the effect of Soviet production on the "orderly" oil market. Once the Soviet Union began marketing its oil internationally, during the sixties, American administrations followed a double-barreled strategy against Moscow. Kennedy and his successors waived the antitrust laws and permitted MNOCs to discuss jointly how to handle this threat, while U.S. officials pressured Western European nations not to purchase energy from the Soviet Union.[73]

While the Soviet Union steadily increased its influence in the Middle East during the 1960s, the Cold War did not cause the oil shocks. The Soviet Union became the free rider—it could raise its energy prices to match those levied by OPEC and obtain new customers in Western Europe eager to diversify their source of supply. At their height, during the period 1982–85, Soviet exports supplied Western Europe with 16–20 percent of its oil requirements as well as significant amounts of natural gas.[74] Intermittent American objections to these transactions proved unavailing.[75] Moscow derived benefits of a different sort from the energy crisis. The enormous increase in revenues granted the faltering Soviet economy a stay of execution. The huge rise in disposable income flowing to OPEC producers provided plenty of spare money that could be channeled into the purchase of Soviet arms. Between 1971 and 1981 energy ran second only to arms sales as a source of Soviet hard currency earnings.[76] Many of these sales were to the Middle East, stoking the various conflicts that devastated the region in the Cold War years.

The Arab-Israeli confrontation remained the most important of these contests. The Six Day and Yom Kippur Wars provided igniting points for Arab oil boycotts: oil became OAPEC's main weapon in its battle against Israel. But the power shift from MNOCs and their governments to oil-producing states was an inexorable one that would have occurred irrespective of the Arab-Israeli conflict. While the oil weapon helped convince Western European states to alter their position vis-à-vis the Arab-Israeli question, their gyrations produced limited results. The most important effect of this transformation was to widen various fissures within the NATO alliance. Although American officials criticized Western Europe for appeasing OAPEC members, their own diplomacy exhibited some of the same sins. Because of its superpower position, the United States retained good relations with Iran until the Shah's fall and with Saudi Arabia thereafter, despite America's pro-Israeli stand. Washington, again through the private sector, also took the lead in attempting to recapture for the United States as many of the petrodollars as possible. It was the cheapest alternative.

12

Public Becomes Private

Petrodollar Recycling and Third World Debt

Countries do not fail to exist.

Walter Wriston, Chief Executive Officer, Citibank

It was spring 1982. A reputable Mexican government borrower, NAFINSA, approached banks around the world, seeking $1.2 billion to fund Mexican public projects. The spread, which is to say, the banks' profit on the loan (the difference between the amount the NAFINSA paid in interest and the amount the banks paid to their depositors), was rich and the borrower deemed reliable. Over a hundred banks scrambled to get a piece of the action. They were from all over—the United States, the Middle East, Europe, and Japan. Faith in third world debt deals was still strong. Many Japanese banks simply asked if the Bank of Tokyo was in. When told that it was, they gave their approval. Several banks, it transpired, had never seen any documents for the loan. Never mind, said the bankers, we will put up our $5 million or $10 million or $20 million.[1] In retrospect, the spring of 1982 marked the end of an era when the term "third world debt" was not an insult. So many deals had been made with such seductive spreads, and so little scrutiny. But although this tragedy ends in the mire of Latin American lending, the story begins in the world of oil.

The fourfold increase in oil prices during 1973–74 had a massive

253

effect on the international monetary system. In January 1974 the CIA predicted that the oil bill for the free world would increase by $70 billion during the year; in early 1975 experts estimated OPEC cash surpluses for 1974 at $55–60 million. Transfers of this magnitude translated into a loss of purchasing power of about 3 percent of GNP in Western Europe and Japan.[2] Representative Henry Gonzalez, an increasingly influential member of the House Banking Committee, cited a study estimating that by 1980 OPEC members would own 70 percent of international monetary reserves. CIA analysts feared that only a small part of the transfers could be offset by purchases by oil-producing nations from consumer nations, while any attempt to ameliorate the deterioration in OECD economies could spark a trade war. Raised on the writings of John Maynard Keynes, who thought much smaller transfers of capital would be catastrophic for the international financial order, worried economists studied such topics as "the absorbative capacity of the OPEC countries" and pondered whether OPEC was responsible for various dips and rises in the dollar's value. The breakdown of the Bretton Woods system and the brave new world of floating currencies, which had barely begun when the first oil shock hit, intensified the uncertainty facing governments and international institutions.

Events did not justify the panicked reaction to the first oil shock. Roughly half of OPEC's 1974 surplus found its way into OECD member banks. U.S. government securities attracted petrodollars (the dollars oil-producing countries receive from selling petroleum) as well.[3] Of equal importance, during the period 1975 to 1989 OPEC imports grew at an average of 15 percent in real terms. These stabilizing decisions made by OPEC nations allowed the international financial system to acclimatize to the changed circumstances. Then the Iranian revolution triggered the second oil shock. Current account balances of OPEC nations surged from $5 billion in 1978 to $65 billion one year later. It would take half a decade for the new imbalance to level out.[4]

Beginning in 1974 Western governments responded in various ways to OPEC surpluses. As described in Chapter 11, governments attempted to limit the possibility of future oil price increases. At the same time OECD officials discussed the "need to arouse in the oil producers a full recognition of their responsibilities in ameliorating the hardships they are causing."[5] To the extent that OPEC nations wished to aid poorer countries, OECD members welcomed their help. On the other hand, developed nations showed little desire to use the oil shocks as an impetus to speed up efforts to reform the international financial system. Instead the oil shocks became an excuse for largely ending these efforts. For their part Arab nations, in particular Saudi Arabia, Kuwait, Libya, and the United Arab Emirates (UAE), created networks of investment institutions designed to manage their burgeoning foreign holdings. Kuwait, which had a payments surplus since the early 1960s, had the most sophisticated managers while Saudi Arabian institutions, constrained by conservative King Faisal's personal views, were "backward and not well suited for efficient asset management." But Saudi Arabia rapidly changed its policies, by April 1974 welcoming investment to accelerate its previously stately pace of development.[6]

In company with other Western nations, Washington attempted to entice oil-producing nations into spending their new riches in the United States. In early January 1974, Undersecretary of the Treasury Paul Volcker sent to Federal Reserve Board Chairman Arthur Burns a list of possible drawing cards for oil country surpluses, including new investment funds, a special reserve asset, and various new kinds of investment banks. A working group of the Council on International Economic Policy (CIEP) had focused on this problem since the end of 1973; by July 1974 it had prepared a multifaceted agenda, encompassing the monitoring of Arab investments by U.S. intelligence agencies, continued government study of the problem, and increasing the Commerce Department's efforts to promote American goods and services to Saudi Arabia. William Simon, then secretary of the Treasury, personally discussed arrangements with the Saudi Arabian government for substantial investments ($8–12 billion) in U.S. Treasury securities.[7]

Luring Arab governments to purchase American goods and services and invest in the United States presented difficult issues. American policymakers knew they had to overcome Arab suspicions that U.S. intentions were nefarious. Saudi Arabian Prince Faisal expressed a prevalent sentiment that Washington was encouraging investment "so that Arab assets could be nationalized if oil was used as a political weapon." The potentially major profits and important ties to be garnered by the sale of American weaponry loomed large.[8] Many Middle Eastern nations were eager to direct their new wealth toward American high-tech military equipment. American defense companies just as eagerly sought these sales. White House officials justified such transactions on the grounds that supplying weaponry would improve America's relations with its traditional friends in the region as well as benefit American producers and the balance of payments. But the Nixon administration retained a commitment to Israeli security, raising the question of what, if any, additional protection the U.S. government should then offer to Israel to offset the effect of such sales. Nor did Washington pause to consider that supplying U.S. weapons to Middle Eastern countries might lessen rather than increase American power over events.

The Ford administration eagerly sought OPEC business. One possible approach discussed was bartering Iranian oil for American arms. Secretary of State Henry Kissinger discussed with the Shah transactions worth $13 billion over a period of five years.[9] A vexing issue was the treatment of OPEC investments in the United States. Throughout the nineteenth century foreigners owned significant chunks of American industry as well as U.S. land and natural resources. The explosion of American financial strength at the beginning of the twentieth century, together with the effects of the two world wars, cost foreigners much of their U.S. economic presence. OPEC surpluses threatened to turn the clock back. Nixon and Ford administration officials clearly saw the advantages of attracting OPEC capital to the United States. But both within and without the government, foreign ownership of American industry and assets remained controversial. As a White House staffer, Geoff Shepard, wrote, the "specter of foreign oil profits being used to buy control of U.S. companies is understandably frightening to the average American citizen." He worried that this issue "would lend itself to demagoguery and simplistic solutions by headline hunting politicians."

It was obvious that Congress would become involved; by early 1975 a number of bills had been introduced to restrict foreign investment in the United States. But the administration welcomed the return of petrodollars to the United States; as L. William Seidman explained, administration strategy reaffirmed "our traditional policy which opposes any new restrictions on foreign investment in the U.S. except where absolutely essential on national security grounds or to protect an essential national interest." Seidman, in company with other administration officials, believed that existing laws were sufficient to deal with any potential problems. However, growing public resentment at Arab investment in the United States convinced the administration that only a White House initiative could block unwanted congressional legislation.

Helping to push Ford and his colleagues to this conclusion was the Pan Am case. At the end of 1974 the Iranian government conducted serious negotiations with Pan American World Airways to purchase a share in the carrier. Once America's leading airline, its financial situation had soured as a result of its lack of domestic feeders for international routes and the eruption in airplane fuel costs. Iranian cash would solve its financial crisis and avoid a potential government bailout, but Pan Am's visibility and symbolic importance in the United States made the issue a tricky one.

The Ford administration's approval of the purchase in February 1975 lent impetus to the White House decision to promulgate an executive order on foreign investment in the United States. Signed on May 7, 1975, it established a senior committee "to review major issues related to foreign investment in this country, including specific major acquisitions of equity or debt by foreign sources." At the same time the White House announced that it expected foreign governments would consult informally with Washington before making large official investments in the United States (defined as those made by official foreign government entities), exceeding $40 million. During the next year the Treasury and Commerce Departments completed exhaustive studies of foreign portfolio and direct investments in the United States; investments by official agencies of foreign governments in American corporate stocks and securities of state and local governments amounted to $3.3 billion in fiscal 1976. Oil-producing countries purchased $3.1 billion of longer-term marketable U.S. Treasury securities during the same period.[10] Ultimately no action was taken against any of these transactions—but in the meantime many politicians spoke ominously of foreign domination.

Another area of concern proved to be the Arab boycott. First instituted in 1948, it represented the attempt by various Arab nations to isolate Israel economically. No one disputed the right of Arab nations to refrain from trading with the Israeli government or Israeli companies. But the Arab Boycott Office over the years attempted to expand the boycott much further. Arab nations, many of which had expelled their Jewish citizens after World War II, made it clear that foreign Jews were not welcome to work on Western-run projects. The boycott office instituted a secondary boycott, blacklisting companies that did business with Israeli companies or the Israeli government and then began a tertiary boycott against companies that did business with companies doing business with Israel. Obviously, at the secondary and tertiary levels, these actions constituted interference with domestic trade of Western nations.

U.S. policy was governed by the Export Administration Act of 1969, which expressed the opposition of the United States to boycotts but did not forbid American citizens from participating in them. The newly found OPEC wealth raised the importance of the Arab boycott. Arab nations were not shy about using this leverage. By early 1975 it became clear that some Arab nations had insisted on excluding banks with prominent Jewish officials or owners from lending syndicates. Eager bankers quickly acquiesced to pressure from potential borrowers. The London merchant bankers Kleinwort, Benson openly proclaimed it would willingly follow the wishes of any Arab client seeking prior approval of all participants in its transactions. Firms with Jewish directors or officers who individually had supported Israel were particularly at risk. Lazard Frères found itself excluded from various transactions as did N.M. Rothschild and Sons. In the United States, reports circulated that some Arab nationals had offered to make deposits in U.S. banks based on conditions concerning the exclusion of Jews from the management or ownership of the banks.

Ford administration officials again walked a tightrope. They were anxious to placate Arab investors and to keep as much OPEC money as possible in the United States. American officials were well aware that their European and Japanese counterparts would not be taking legal action to thwart the boycott. National Security Council staffer Robert B. Oakley advised opposition to proposed legislation

> on the grounds that (a) it is doubtful if it could be enforced and is in part inconsistent with certain actions of the United States Government; (b) enactment of the Bill would not put an end to sanctions against Israel while our exports would suffer because the Arabs could turn to other

sources of supply if US firms were prohibited from complying with boy-cott; (c) H.R. 5246 would be interpreted as a major shift in U.S. foreign policy.

But the White House knew that if it did not seize the high ground, Congress, already holding hearings, would pass tough legislation that would be politically difficult to veto.

Ford unveiled his initiative at his press conference of February 26, 1975. The President proclaimed that any religious discrimination "is totally contrary to the American tradition and repugnant to American principles." He added that "any allegations of discrimination will be fully investigated and appropriate action taken under the laws of the United States." The following week, the President sent a copy of this statement to the secretaries of state, Treasury, defense, and commerce and to the attorney general, directing them to do their "utmost" to fol-low through on his pledge to investigate and prosecute any such cases that violate American laws. The Justice Department opened an inves-tigation into discrimination within the international banking commu-nity. The comptroller of the currency notified national banks that his office intended to secure adherence to American laws, and the Securi-ties and Exchange Commission investigated the issue of discrimina-tion.[11] Under President Jimmy Carter the Arab boycott remained a thorny issue. Congress passed stronger antiboycott legislation in 1979 that remains in effect. Violations continued in succeeding years amid charges that the federal government had been less than zealous in pros-ecuting these cases.[12]

The accelerated flow of resources from OECD members to OPEC countries had grave consequences for developing nations without oil deposits of their own. They found themselves in need of extra capital to finance oil imports at the same time as they sought external funding for general development purposes. During the fifties and sixties West and East used foreign aid to woo the allegiance of these nations. But the oil shocks, in combination with the devastating recession of the mid-sev-enties, demolished available resources of donor nations. Into the vac-uum stepped private banking institutions that proved willing to serve as the middlemen between oil-rich nations with spare capital and developing nations in financial difficulties.

Every emerging country seeks foreign capital to finance its growth and development. For their part, outside investors, searching for an El Dorado, eagerly embrace overseas opportunities. During the era of imperialism European colonial powers invested heavily in their colonies. At the same time bankers in the City of London, the center of the world financial system, funded improvements in the United States and Latin America. After World War I, as New York City came to rival London as a financial center, American bankers began to lend to Europe and to less developed nations as well. The loans made in the 1920s, however, were primarily in the form of bonds. Individuals would contact investment bankers who formed groups known as syndicates to finance projects such as railways, utilities, and mines. Many but not all of the project borrowers were government entities, either national government or various local authorities. This activity abruptly halted after the Depression took hold in the early 1930s. During that decade sovereign borrowers throughout Central Europe and Latin America defaulted, failing to make the required payments of principal and interest on their debts. As a result transnational sovereign borrowing in the international capital markets virtually ended.

The Bretton Woods architects understood the need for capital in the underdeveloped world. They designated the International Bank for Reconstruction and Development (IBRD, or World Bank) as a multilateral entity to fund such development, supplementing private institutions. As John Maynard Keynes explained, "We feel very strongly indeed that loans from creditor to debtor countries in the early postwar period are essential to avoid widespread economic chaos and much needless human suffering." But the World Bank would not just lend money. In the words of its second president, Eugene Black, this institution would also "speak frankly to these countries and insist upon them carrying out their proper policies."[13] Yet the World Bank, in company with the International Monetary Fund, got off to a slow start. During the 1950s, its largest planned project was the Aswan High Dam, which came to nothing when the United States and Britain withdrew their coordinated offers to fund it. The situation began to change in the sixties, which President Kennedy labeled the Development Decade. The most important spur to assistance programs was the explosion in the number of newly independent states after 1960. The Cold War magnified the impact of sheer numbers; both the United States and the Soviet Union used foreign aid as a means of buying the allegiance of these new nations. U.S. officials, who continued to view the World Bank, always with an American president, as a U.S. government institution by another name, encouraged the expansion in its lending, which began during the sixties. Many of its projects exhibited the same "edifice complex"—bigger is always better—as did private capital projects during the optimistic decades that preceded the oil shocks. At the same time the World Bank proved instrumental in funding India's impressive agricultural revolution and in the positive development of other poor nations. The World Bank now had two affiliated organizations, the first of which, the International Finance Corporation (IFC), invested in joint ventures and did stock underwriting with private enterprises. The International Development Association (IDA) funded the same kind of projects supported by the World Bank but on much easier terms: the loans ran for fifty years and did not bear interest.[14]

Direct American aid to less developed nations (LDCs) began in earnest in 1949 with the Point Four program, which President Truman intended to use to funnel American science and technology to "underdeveloped areas." Under Eisenhower the United States gave limited aid to such nations as India, Pakistan, Iran, and Egypt.[15] Kennedy officials took a more aggressive attitude toward foreign aid embodied in the Alliance for Progress.[16] Moreover, the United States funded the Upper Volta Dam in Ghana, a quintessential Cold War–motivated project. Ghana's leader, Kwame Nkrumah, who had been in power since Ghana received its independence in 1957, had steadily tilted more toward the Soviet Union. Kennedy considered not funding the dam but relented, fearing that Moscow would enter the resulting vacuum as it had in Egypt.[17] The United Nations, then in its period of explosive growth, participated in organizing the international aid regime. In 1964, as an outgrowth of the UN Conference on Trade and Development (UNCTAD), the United Nations established the United Nations Trade and Development Board, thereby signaling a new commitment to LDCs. Among other things, the initial meeting of UNCTAD focused attention on the "commodity problem." Of the eighty or so LDCs in 1965, "more than thirty depend for more than half their foreign exchange earnings on exports of a single crop or commodity."[18] Such one-crop economies were particularly vulnerable to economic, climatic, or market crises. The developed world took up much of the challenge. In 1970 foreign aid accounted for 48 percent of all foreign capital received by LDCs. Government aid officials worked on the assumption that if all developed countries donated 0.7 percent of their GNP as aid (the United Nations official target), the needs of LDCs could be met. Buoyed by academic theorists, they shared the optimistic sixties feeling that money could solve any problem.[19]

Through the work of the Committee of Twenty, which from 1971 to 1974 sought to rework the international monetary system, the IMF put itself right at the center of issues involving the developing world. LDCs hoped that among other things the C-20 deliberations would "establish a link between SDR allocations and development assistance."[20] C-20 deliberations focused at length on the dire need for capital in the less developed world. Originally some members of the C-20 desired that SDRs be used to fill the void. Yet the capital gap, which increased after the oil shocks, proved too large to satisfy by government or multilateral institutions alone.

By the end of 1973, officials of OECD countries realized that the oil shocks could well trigger the total impoverishment of oil-poor LDCs. Of course, the first priority of industrialized nations was to solve their own problems: how to finance their increased oil bill as well as the concurrent rise in commodity prices, which, among other things, significantly increased the price of food. Indeed prices of cotton, wool, rubber, and other agricultural materials had doubled from the start of 1972 through the middle of 1973. Grain prices went up 50 percent during the same period while metal prices rose 30 percent.[21] Fertilizer costs also escalated. But LDCs faced the same problems with far smaller resources. Aggravating the crisis, LDC exports sharply dropped as the oil shock turned the fragile economic recovery in OECD countries into a deep recession in the developing world. In April 1974, Nixon administration officials estimated the initial LDC shortfall at $14 billion. The hardest-hit LDCs were the poorest of the poor: countries without oil that also lacked an exportable commodity whose price had recently risen or countries whose fragile economies could not cope with any blow whatsoever. They included Bangladesh, Botswana, Guyana, Lesotho, Senegal, Niger, Upper Volta (Burkina Faso), and Vietnam.[22]

Immediately after the December 1973 oil price escalation the IMF's executive director, H. Johannes Witteveen, proposed a special arrangement whereby the IMF would manage a fund to provide loans to oil-importing LDCs on terms far easier than its normal loans. The IMF had never taken such a step but Witteveen believed that the alternative would be a return to the autarkic policies of the thirties. U.S. officials evinced little enthusiasm. Treasury Secretary George Shultz and his successor, William Simon, feared that LDCs would not be able to repay any such loans and that eventually they would ask the United States for aid. Initially the United States took the position that "a reduction of prices is, of course, the first answer to the problems facing the LDCs." Officials further maintained that oil prices would come down through market forces or outside pressures. German Finance Minister (later Chancellor) Helmut Schmidt instead advocated working toward a common energy policy rather than setting up a charity fund. But by late spring 1974, LDC pressure and continued high energy prices persuaded the United States to soften its objections. Having forgone protesting the oil price rise, they were looking for ways to finance the increased costs. For their part, LDCs admired the OPEC strike at the West, only hoping that they could emulate it by forming producer cartels of their own. Yet even in July 1974 the CIEP Executive Committee argued that "the U.S. should resist pressures in multilateral forums for overall schemes and solutions requiring special country contributions."[23] In other words, the United States should foil the primary producer nations' attempt at blackmail.

The oil facility, established on June 13, 1974, proved a dramatic shift for the IMF. Instead of relying on quotas to raise money, the IMF now began to operate like a bank, borrowing from surplus countries and lending to debtor nations. By August the IMF had arranged to borrow IMF Special Drawing Rights (SDR) 3.0 billion (worth somewhat over $3.6 billion) from the central banks of Canada, the Netherlands, Iran, Kuwait, Oman, Saudi Arabia, the United Arab Emirates, Venezuela, and (sometime later) Nigeria for the 1974 oil facility. Interest was to be paid by the borrowers at an annual rate of 7.7 percent. Borrowers were eligible if they had a balance of payments deficit they could not finance out of existing resources. The first customers—Bangladesh, Chile, Haiti, Kenya, South Korea, Pakistan, Sri Lanka, Sudan, and Tanzania—

received loans by September 6; six more LDCs received loans by September 29, as did Greece, Yugoslavia, and the hardest-hit developed nation, Italy. Ultimately forty countries borrowed under the 1974 facility.

In 1975 the IMF approved a second oil facility. Again U.S. officials initially objected, maintaining that LDCs should solve their oil problems through conservation. Other nations discounted American views, pointing out that the large American domestic oil production gave the United States a cushion unavailable to other nations. Washington's lack of progress on the conservation front further diminished its credibility. The 1975 facility totaled SDR 3,855.5 million. This time the Bundesbank contributed as well as the central banks or governments of Switzerland, Sweden, and Belgium. The oil-producing nations that provided the 1974 funds donated funds again, although with some reluctance because their surpluses were smaller than they had anticipated. More borrowers took loans this time. The list included Britain, Finland, Greece, New Zealand, and Spain, as well as developing countries such as Argentina, Egypt, Zaire, and Zambia. Indeed Britain's share amounted to SDR 1,000 million while SDR 780 million went to Italy.[24]

Three years later, the second round of oil price increases did not spawn comparable facilities. Financial officials now viewed large energy costs as a permanent rather than temporary phenomenon. IMF loans to help with the cost of the second oil shock were given on the normal, conditional basis: the IMF made its loans only if the borrower promised to meet various financial conditions such as accepting the pain of a balanced budget, cutting deficit spending, and controlling inflation. (The oil facilities largely eschewed conditionality.) Mitigating the position of LDCs was the Witteveen facility, operative in March 1979, a $10 billion fund designed to help countries with severe balance of payments problems.[25]

The Ford administration displayed the typical American lack of enthusiasm for multilateral efforts not orchestrated by the United States. Yet political and economic changes during the mid-seventies forced the administration to participate in multilateral discussions between the rich "North" and the poorer "South" countries. After the first oil shock direct American foreign aid, in company with that granted by other developed nations, failed to keep pace with LDC demands for assistance with normal development programs as well as oil-driven costs. Increasing LDC populations combined with prevalent government mismanagement of LDC resources ensured that aid requests would always increase. That LDC elites tended to spirit their wealth out of their countries rather than invest internally exacerbated funding problems. By 1978 aid made up 30 percent of capital flows to LDCs, down from 44 percent in 1970. Industrial countries during that year gave only 0.35 percent of their GNP, one-half of the UN target. The next year American aid declined to 0.2 percent of GNP. By the late seventies the lion's share of U.S. aid went to Egypt and Israel, with Pakistan and Central America gaining much of the rest.[26]

What was happening was simple. Poorer nations that had grown accustomed to assistance programs in the heady days of the fifties and sixties became addicted to foreign aid. They used the Cold War balancing act of red against red, white, and blue to get it. Now the actions of OPEC emboldened them further. But the United States, as the dominant economic and military power, resisted the growing demands that it met at international gatherings. The South G-77 group had begun what American officials labeled a "strategy of confrontation" at the Sixth Special Session of the General Assembly in April 1974. At the insistence of LDCs, the General Assembly approved a "New International Economic Order" and a "Charter of Economic Rights and Duties." The administration grew increasingly concerned at what it viewed as the LDCs' bellicosity. Kissinger took them to task in a speech in Kansas City in May 1975 where he denounced their demand for a new financial order. When the UN Seventh Special Session convened in New York in September 1975, the stage was set for a showdown between the United States and the LDCs. But Washington realized it had no support from its allies for such a stance and beat a tactical retreat. Instead of spewing anger and explanations, Kissinger proposed increasing funds to LDCs, expanded world food production, and increased LDC exports to the United States. In response the LDCs agreed to back away from demands for a total international financial restructuring and also jettisoned their insistence on indexing commodities prices to inflation in Western countries.

The United States then agreed to attend a Conference on International Cooperation (CIEC) with twenty-seven countries, nineteen from the developing world and eight from industrialized nations. Having lost its battle to limit CIEC discussions to energy issues, U.S. officials attempted to avoid any links between energy, commodity prices, and other issues on the grounds that linkage would only politicize the dialogue. However, once American diplomats decided that the discussions would accomplish little of substantive value, they stopped resisting a broader approach, since "we [could] not be pressured into going further in the other commissions than we would otherwise go." Instead U.S. negotiators intended "to continue to assert U.S. leadership in North-South relations." Other aims included limiting OPEC's unilateral control over oil prices, breaking the growing link between OPEC nations and other LDCs, and keeping OECD nations toeing the American line in the International Energy Authority.

The conference was held in Paris from December 16 to 19, 1975. It established separate commissions that would meet on a monthly basis on raw materials, energy, development, and related financial and monetary issues. LDCs would hold ten of the fifteen seats on each commission. Undersecretary of State for Economic Affairs Charles W. Robinson wrote to Kissinger that the secretary's contribution had made possible "the official launching of 'North-South' détente." Robinson was particularly pleased that the United States had been able to "exploit" differences between OPEC and other LDCs. It augured poorly for the CIEC's effectiveness that delegates spent more time jockeying for position than discussing substantive issues.[27]

The North-South dialogue continued as a further UNCTAD meeting convened in Nairobi in May 1976. After considerable dithering Kissinger, concluding that his absence would prove dangerous, attended. In his speech the secretary of state suggested a comprehensive plan addressing major commodities, measures to facilitate technology transfer to LDCs, and efforts to help developing nations with balance of payments and debt problems. Of the greatest importance was Kissinger's suggestion to establish a multilateral bank run as an arm of the World Bank to channel private capital raised through the sale of bonds into mineral resource development. At the same time American delegates resisted pressure for LDC debt relief or for a multilateral conference on LDC indebtedness and rebuffed attempts to link commodity prices to prices of industrial products.[28] In retrospect Nairobi marked the high point of LDC influence. The brief period when it looked like the sheer force of LDC numbers would exert change in the international financial system passed. OECD nations, propelled by firm American resistance to LDC pressure, refused to cave in to LDC demands. The Soviet Union, already locked in the downward economic spiral that would cause its collapse, would not step into the breach. LDC nations were left dependent on Darwinian "survival of the fittest" logic. Some, such as South Korea, would move from the ranks of LDCs to developed nations, while others, such as Argentina, would see their relative economic position decline over time.

OPEC nations individually and in concert expanded their links with less developed nations during this period. The Kuwait Development Fund proved a very active lender—Egypt, Tunisia, and Sudan being prime beneficiaries. Other OPEC–funded institutions included the Arab Fund for Economic and Social Development, the Islamic Development Fund, and the African Development Bank. OPEC development ministers created a development fund to help less fortunate LDCs. Iran and Venezuela had suggested a $5 billion pool empowered to make five-year loans. In the event, the fund contained only $800 million at its start. Iran and Saudi Arabia each donated in excess of $200 million, with eight other oil-producing states contributing the balance. OPEC nations also began making investments in LDCs; during the second half of the seventies, Brazil was one popular choice.[29] However, both multilateral-generated government funds and direct OPEC investments were of little importance compared with the role played by another source.

When OPEC members decided not to hand their surplus monies to LDC nations, they still faced the problem of investing these surplus funds. The lack of sophisticated banking systems in most OPEC members forced these newly affluent states to deposit their funds elsewhere. Western money-center banks provided the logical home. Bankers welcomed the funds but having accepted the deposits, they then looked feverishly for likely borrowers. The deep recession of the Ford-Carter years, combined with the erosion of industrial customers who had found cheaper sources of funding, forced lenders to look abroad, something they had refused to do for three decades after the Great Depression.

The massive international defaults of the 1930s scared private U.S. bankers from foreign markets until the 1960s. That Brazil rescheduled its government debt in 1961 and 1964, Argentina in 1962 and 1965, and Peru in 1968 (among others) should have further dampened the climate for private LDC loans. But push and pull factors brought about a changing lending environment in the mid-1960s. Mexico led the way for other LDCs in 1965, altering its laws to enable public and private borrowers to obtain access to foreign private bank loans. Its government overcame traditional scruples as it tried to shed the bad reputation it had garnered from defaults earlier in the century. Bank lending came to be seen as a method for Mexico to obtain external funds to develop and expand its economy and infrastructure without the strings that came with foreign assistance or the loss of control produced by foreign direct investment. Brazil's decision to follow Mexico's lead signaled the beginning of a major trend.

The equal and opposite response in bank boardrooms was waiting. The retirement of bankers who remembered the massive international defaults played a crucial role. Members of the younger generation coming to power became intrigued by the specter of whole new capital markets to conquer. Since individual compensation increasingly depended on a banker's ability to create new assets that, in the case of banks, means the generation of new loans, personal financial imperatives encouraged expansion as well. Dramatic changes in capital markets after 1970 intensified these tendencies. Large corporations, the bread and butter borrowers from American banks, had discovered cheaper ways to raise money. Nixon-era deregulation facilitated their move to the commercial paper market. When they deigned to borrow, domestic companies bargained down the spread to almost nothing. By contrast an American bank lending in Brazil after 1967 could lend to its local branch, tacking on a significant spread of perhaps 2 percent over its costs of funds. The local branch could then lend to a local borrower, charging another 2 to 4 percent spread. No wonder to many bankers foreign countries seemed to offer a promised land.[30]

These bankers would be lending mainly dollars—both those recorded on the books of banks in the United States and "Eurodollars," those booked abroad.[31] Many of them were found in OPEC coffers.[32] Religious reasons (the Islamic prohibition against interest-bearing loans) and historical factors had prevented Arab nations, which owned much of the newly transferred wealth, from developing significant indigenous banking networks. OPEC deposits in Western banks needed to be invested somewhere—why not in developing countries that were hungry for the money and would pay the highest rates to get it?[33]

The chief exponent of the brave new world of international lending was Walter Wriston, chief executive officer of Citicorp, the largest U.S. bank for much of this period. In company with other bank CEOs coming into their own in the seventies, he advised, "Go foreign, young man." Wriston believed that because countries could not go out of business, lending to foreign nations carried fewer risks than other kinds of loans.[34] It proved irrelevant that this optimism completely ignored historical experience or recent reschedulings in countries such as Indonesia and Turkey. The first oil shock led to massive increases in LDC balance of payments deficits. Worsening the plight of poor nations was the deep recession in the industrialized world. This economic slow-down meant that LDCs could not trade their way back into surplus. Multilateral organizations could fill some of the gap but not all of it. Here Wriston and his fellow bankers, not only in the United States, saw an opportunity: they would make loans for straight balance of payments purposes, in other words, extend credit to make up the shortfall between a country's income from its external relations and its expenditures with the rest of the world. The risk factor traditionally scared bankers. If a country kept borrowing each year to make its international ends meet, it would start each new year ever deeper in debt. Only continued loans could keep the cycle going, but bankers at some point would find the situation too perilous to continue. This logic convinced bankers during the fifties and sixties to confine their LDC lending to trade receivables that were secured by the exports the sale of which they financed.

However, in the mid-seventies a new sense of optimism reigned. International lending grew each year in the decade; by the end of 1975 the Bank for International Settlements estimated that non–oil-producing LDCs had borrowed $63 billion. At that point balance sheets read better than might have been expected—most Asian and African countries remained creditors of the banks. In 1976 bank lending went up again—over $9 billion of new loans were made as opposed to fewer than $2 billion in 1972. As the LDCs had managed their increased debt burden without major problems, no side issues clouded the sky. More important, banks continued flush with cash, with no place to invest the money. Lending to needy LDCs seemed the perfect solution for every-one.[35]

During the period 1974–77 bankers who maintained that loans to the developing world were safer than those to domestic borrowers had evidence to back up their claims. The big problems for U.S. financial institutions in that decade—the collapse of Penn Central and the bailouts of Lockheed, Chrysler, and New York City—origi-nated at home. Yet the banks intended to have their cake and eat it too. Maintaining to their governments that LDC loans were safe, they concurrently charged the LDCs a "risk premium" for the loans—an increased interest rate to account for the greater risk to the lender making the loans. Not only did this risk premium exist but between 1974 and 1976 it rose steadily.[36] The shape of the Eurodol-lar market also carried two time bombs. Eurodollar deposits were typically of six months' duration, while banks made short-term, medium-term, and long-term loans. As a result every six months banks needed to go to the market and refund their loans: they bor-rowed short to lend long. If anything should happen to scare deposi-tors so that the next six months' supply of funds dried up, the banks could be caught short.[37] The borrower, who had contracted to pay the lender its spread above a floating interest rate, also bore the risk of rising market rates.[38]

The Federal Reserve Board grew increasingly concerned about these loans. As the guardian of the integrity of the U.S. banking system, the Fed's role was crucial. Board Chairman Arthur Burns worried about the implications for the American banking system of a major interna-tional default: "we ought to drop the word 'recycling' from our vocabu-lary. . . . What it means is piling debt on top of debt, and more realistically bad debt on top of good debt." Federal Reserve official Ralph W. Smith informed Burns, "banks have evidently found it more desirable to make these BOP [Balance of Payment] loans . . . than to reduce interest rates by enough to stimulate domestic loan demand." Smith added, "whether the additional risk in some of these foreign B[alance] O[f] P[ayment] loans is sufficiently compensated for by the additional interest charge or 'risk premium' is a question which can be answered definitively only ex post." The chairman's fears led him to have staff officials analyze what would be the impact on the income of major American banks if LDC borrowers stopped making their interest payments.[39]

In early 1977 Federal Reserve Board officials undertook a survey of the domestic and foreign loan loss ratio of major American banks. Their statistics revealed that in both 1975 and 1976 the losses for foreign loans were significantly smaller than those for domestic loans. Yet American officials were not reassured. For that reason the Fed in mid-1977 discussed a proposal for "official pre-screening of large international credits" in all G-10 countries. Although this idea came to nothing, the Senate Subcommittee on Foreign Economic Policy produced in September 1977 a report analyzing international debt, the banks, and U.S. foreign policy. The study confirmed that both the OPEC surplus and the LDC international debt position posed difficult problems.[40]

Burns, together with Fed officials and foreign counterparts, now came up with another idea—requiring developed and developing countries to supply detailed and timely data on indebtedness. The policy of disclosure, the underpinning of American securities laws, had never been effectively applied to foreign borrowers. Had these ideas been implemented, the next few years would have been much easier for officials. But Congress turned it into something very different, attempting to garner information concerning the location and size of Arab deposits in U.S. banks. Indeed Burns, sharing the fears of American bankers that meaningful depositor disclosure laws would drive Arab deposits abroad, vigorously fought efforts led by Senator Frank Church to obtain such information. Instead, in the spring of 1976 the Fed published a report detailing the aggregate deposits of Middle Eastern and North African OPEC states with the six largest American banks, revealing that 5.7 percent of these institutions' total deposits came from those nations.[41]

LDC borrowing steadily expanded during 1978. In March 1977 David Rockefeller, chairman of the Chase Manhattan Bank, warned that "bank debt to a number of these countries has been expanding at a rate that should not—and cannot—be sustained."[42] But the second oil shock left the international banking system even more awash with cash. The renewed and enlarged OPEC surpluses had given vast pools of money to nations unable to invest their largesse at home—again much of the money went to Western banks that sent it on to LDC borrowers, whose repayments generated the interest bankers paid to depositors. Adding to the expansion of the market was the decision by many small banks to enter the international market. Motivated by the need to increase their earnings and swayed by the romance of playing in the big leagues with the prospect of larger than normal profits, unsophisticated regional and small-town institutions joined the gravy train. To their later sorrow, they relied on money center banks to provide the knowledge that they themselves lacked.

As a result banks continued to face a debtors' market. Borrowers, taking advantage of this situation, rushed to prepay existing loans and borrow at more favorable rates. By mid-1978 private bank lending to LDCs equaled $165 billion.[43] Much of this money could never be repaid by LDC borrowers. Banks were now locked in: they would have to keep lending new money so that their customers could repay their old debts. With interest rates continuing low in comparison with inflation, the burden on LDC borrowers was still bearable. Whether borrowers could meet their needs in a different environment had yet to be seen. The better-than-expected LDC track record in part derived from the high inflation rates then prevailing, which rendered interest rates cheap and indeed sometimes nonexistent. (The real interest rate is calculated by subtracting the inflation rate from the interest rate. If the result is a negative number, the lender, not the borrower, is paying for the loan.)

Much of their business was in Latin America. For example, in 1976 a Federal Reserve Board study found that about one-half of total U.S. bank loans to LDCs were made to borrowers in Mexico and Brazil, and three-quarters of the total American LDC loans went to Latin America. The reasons were obvious—Latin America's proximity had nurtured close ties with American banks that were further strengthened because many members of Latin American ruling elites had been educated in the United States. The encouraging progress made by Latin America during the sixties and seventies also provided a basis for confidence. The region's total GDP grew from $147 billion in 1960 to $420 million in 1978. Literacy and life expectancy both improved remarkably during the same period. Unfortunately Latin American economies had been badly hurt by the oil shocks and world recession: in 1977 real

GDP in Latin America grew an average of 4.5 percent, a far cry from the regional average of 7.2 percent that held true from 1968 until 1974. Debtors made up the shortfall with foreign loans that bankers remained eager to provide.[44]

The end was near—and its trigger was oil. The huge jump in oil prices from the end of 1978 into mid-1979 triggered an escalation in the combined current account deficit of the world's poorer countries of about $40 billion for 1979. Every time the price of oil rose by $1 per barrel, non–oil-producing LDCs needed to find nearly $2 billion more per year. Without an IMF special oil facility, banks presented the only available source of funds. Indeed the World Bank calculated that 45 percent of LDC capital requirements during the 1980s would be met by banks. (The financial plight of LDCs had persuaded the World Bank's Board of Governors in 1980 to double the bank's capital stock.) By 1981 commercial banks supplied 42 percent of total net credit flows to all developing countries, while official development sources donated 37 percent.[45] Prime Minister Margaret Thatcher expressed the newly ascendant conservative view of multilateral aid, rejecting any multilateral assistance as a "handout."[46]

The cycle of heavy bank lending continued for the next three years. Poor countries grew increasingly dependent on bank loans to meet their external needs. Financial incentives on both sides of the lending transactions kept the merry-go-round turning. Between mid-1978 and mid-1982, Mexico's debts to foreign banks tripled, Brazil's indebtedness doubled, while Argentina and Chile each increased its indebtedness almost 500 percent. Changes in the American regulatory system made it easier for banks to lend to different entities owned by foreign governments; American tax code provisions magnified the attractiveness of foreign lending.[47] At the time, these loans appeared to be a no-lose proposition. The LDCs would receive the money they needed, the OPEC surpluses would be recycled, governments would not need to tackle these problems, and the banks would make money. From the top of the major money center banks—Citibank, Bank of America, Manufacturers Hanover—the word came down: lend abroad. Bankers plied their trade with abandon. Many bankers seemed to live by Henry Ford's adage: "history is bunk." They continued to ignore not only lending disasters of long ago but such recent experiences as the balance of payments problems experienced by such major debtors as Argentina and Brazil during the sixties. These men (few women were then involved) often failed even to glance at loan documents. Why should we read them?, they would ask. If Morgan Guaranty [the lead bank] says it's okay, we can give our five million. After all, the debtor is a sovereign borrower.[48] In fact this unrealistic faith in the reliability of sovereign borrowers played a major part in the debacle that followed. Obviously a nation does not go out of business nor does it file for bankruptcy protection. But what bankers often overlooked was the reality that they had little recourse should a government borrower decide to renege on its debts.

During this period imports to developed nations fell, a devastating development for LDCs. Conversely, richer countries, notably the United States and Japan, at this time saw their exports climb dramatically. In the United States, for example, during the second half of 1979 exports grew at an annual rate of 19.8 percent.[49] At the same time the Federal Reserve Board, under its new chairman, Paul Volcker, determined to tackle inflation, which had reached record levels in the United States during the seventies. While inflation had made it easier for the United States to pay its spiraling oil bill, it had demoralized Americans and despoiled American economic stability. Volcker utilized the classic remedy of raising American interest rates to squeeze excess demand out of the economy. Those rates more than doubled between 1978 and 1981, reaching 17.4 percent and staying near that level during Ronald Reagan's next year in office. Unfortunately for foreign borrowers, most LDC loans were made in dollars with floating interest rates that were wholly or partially determined by American interest rates. Wriston's charge that Volcker had caused the debt crisis was an exaggeration but it had some basis in fact. The dramatic spike in interest rates escalated the cost of LDC debt service. Moreover, the success of Volcker's tactics created further problems for LDSs—a decline in worldwide inflation boosted real interest rates on their loans.[50]

High American interest rates also encouraged capital flight from Latin America. Official assessments were that $50 billion flowed out of the continent between 1978 and 1982. The Federal Reserve Board estimated that over one-third of the $252 billion increase in the debt of Argentina, Brazil, Chile, Mexico, and Venezuela was deposited in foreign bank accounts or was used to buy foreign assets, and calculated that during the period 1974–82 for the eight major debtor nations, private capital export was the second-largest use of foreign exchange (debt service came first). LDC banks themselves borrowed money from foreign lenders that they then re-lent abroad, making a profit on the difference. In Brazil, for example, $1.6 billion received from foreign loans was frozen when Poland declared a moratorium on its debts on March 5, 1981.[51]

The end was at hand. The Falkland War of May 1982 triggered the collapse. Bankers always avoid political problems; the war between Britain and Argentina not only increased the political risk of lending to Argentina but began a process drying up long-term loans to the whole region. Underlying bankers' attitudes was the sense that many Latin American countries were overextended. For example, the Amex Bank Review estimated in May 1982 that the debt service ratio of developing nations (repayments of principal and interest on loans calculated as a percentage of export earnings) leapt from 32 percent in 1977 to 50 percent in 1981. Further proof of the region's precarious state came from Latin America's 1981 balance sheet: the region borrowed a net $34.6 billion but paid interest of $28.2 billion, leaving a net benefit of $6.4 billion.[52]

At the beginning of August 1982, Volcker, then on vacation, learned that the bankruptcy of an obscure but highflying Oklahoma bank had jeopardized the solvency of Continental Illinois. On August 12 he found out that Mexico was virtually broke. In response Volcker mobilized the influence and resources of the Federal Reserve System. The U.S. Treasury had ignored the hints dropped in July by Mexican Finance Minister Jesús Silva Herzog that Mexico was in serious trouble. But early in the week of August 9, Herzog and his deputy Angel Gurria announced that Mexico's financial cupboard was bare. With American banks heavily at risk, Volcker spearheaded the U.S. response, orchestrating an interim solution: (1) the U.S. government agreed to make immediate payments to Mexico in the amount of $1 billion from the Treasury Department's exchange stabilization fund to be repaid by the Department of Energy's payment to Mexico for oil deliveries for the strategic oil reserve; (2) the Treasury and the Fed arranged "swap facilities" for Mexico; (3) the Bank for International Settlements made a short-term loan to Mexico; and (4) the banks agreed not to call in their loans.[53] Mexico, with its large oil deposits (its reserves were estimated at 60 billion bbl), was not among the poorer borrowers. In fact, its oil deposits had encouraged bankers to make it one of the two largest LDC borrowers. But in 1982 the price of oil began to decline. This news, good for some borrowers, devastated the Mexican economy, which depended on the sale of petroleum (accounting for 70 percent of Mexican exports) to pay its debt service.[54]

Mexico's action sparked a chain reaction—by spring 1983 virtually every Latin American country had sought relief and rescheduling of its debts. American and other international banks, at the prodding of their governments and the IMF, concluded that their only way out was to continue lending borrowers money with which to repay enough on old loans to make them current, i.e., not overdue. For that reason by the end of February 1983 banks reached agreements worth $9.5 billion with Mexico and Brazil.[55] A pattern of restructuring emerged. In the first instance borrowers contacted the IMF. The debt crisis gave the IMF unprecedented prominence. Headed since 1979 by Jacques de Larosière, the IMF now stood at the apex of the refinancing triangle, becoming "part of the domestic regulatory mechanism of U.S. banking." It arranged support credits for borrowers in exchange for their commitment to meet certain conditions (the "conditionality" requirement) designed to nurture stable economies. These conditions included cutting government deficits and curbing imports by, among other actions, devaluing overvalued currencies and squeezing out inflation. In this way the IMF took over the work of assessing the position of the borrowers and ensuring their fiscal responsibility that banks should have done by themselves.[56]

The concept of conditionality predated the debt crisis. Former IMF Executive Director Witteveen defended conditionality not as a quid pro quo but rather as "an essential complement to the assistance [the IMF] provides." The rationale was appealing: it made no sense to lend new money without simultaneously attempting to cure the problems that triggered the defaults.[57] What was new was the IMF's insistence that its new loans also be tied to the lending of new money and the restructuring of old loans by the banks. By forcing both sides to compromise, the IMF prevented the ultimate calamity: a default by a major borrower sparking a chain reaction of bank failures that in turn could have brought down the entire international monetary system. As with any good compromise, all sides received something. Borrowers acquired some new money and avoided being locked out indefinitely from the commercial market. In exchange, they agreed to use much, if not all, of the new loans to pay debt service on the old loans.

Banks derived more benefits from these transactions, known as reschedulings. Ironically, the money center banks that had led, managed, and agented the large syndicates of bank lending groups made out the best, although they bore the most responsibility for the crisis. Every new loan generated new fees for lead banks that under then applicable accounting rules could be taken into income immediately. Therefore at a time when many loans were in deep trouble, the balance sheets of money center banks actually boasted increased earnings. Money center banks dominated the lenders' committees that ran the reschedulings. As restructurings needed to be unanimous to be effective, the organizing work proved enormously complex. Mexico's $5 billion jumbo credit agreement received the blessing of 530 commercial banks.[58] Smaller banks, which did not receive the rich fee income generated by these transactions, often proved unenthusiastic about participating in restructurings. But the bank committees that soon sprouted up for each impecunious country, together with the Fed and its counterparts abroad, pressured recalcitrants to cave in and go along. Holdouts, any one of which could have collapsed the whole house of cards, received the carrot-and-stick treatment. Because the agreements required the new money to be used to repay old loans, the banks could view their old loans as repaid. They would not have to report losses, nor did they need to create reserves against these loans, that is, put aside income from earnings in anticipation of bad loans. Banks therefore avoided much of the negative effect on their balance sheets and credit ratings that unpaid or defaulted loans would require. But the threat of increased attention from regulatory authorities to rebellious banks always loomed as well.[59]

The reschedulings proved such a great success that they allowed bankers to tell the world and themselves that the crisis was only temporary. Debtors shared this optimism; both Mexico and Brazil planned early returns to the market. From August 1982 to the end of 1984 the

IMF lent $22 billion in support of economic adjustment programs in seventy countries. One year after the crisis began, Mexico's economy had improved dramatically. Mexico had a $6.5 billion trade surplus for the first half of the year and was husbanding some of its IMF credits.[60] The Pollyanna approach to the condition of Latin America generally continued into 1984. Rescheduling seemed to be satisfying the needs of all parties.[61] Additionally, Latin American business could be very profitable. Citibank, for example, in 1983 generated 19.5 percent of its profits in Brazil.[62]

But in May 1984, depositors again pulled out of Continental Illinois, one of America's largest banks. Their panic was triggered partly by Continental's huge Latin American exposure. The Federal Reserve Board intervened, providing sufficient resources to avoid a bank panic. Depositors now ran scared generally. Manufacturers Hanover (today, with Chemical Bank, part of the Chase Bank), the leading U.S. lender to Latin America, had Latin American loans exceeding 250 percent of shareholders' equity. The other eight largest U.S. banks had Latin American exposure equal to or in excess of 150 percent of shareholders' equity. Only by demolishing earnings could these banks have created reserves against possible losses to protect themselves. For example, had each large bank taken a 10 percent reserve against losses on loans to Argentina, Brazil, Venezuela, and Mexico in 1983, Bank of America and Manufacturers Hanover would have posted losses for the year and other major American banks would have seen their earnings drop between 60 and 95 percent.[63]

In May 1984 the presidents of Argentina, Brazil, Colombia, and Brazil jointly condemned high world interest rates. One month later representatives of eleven Latin American nations convened at Cartagena, Colombia, where they drafted a charter demanding lower interest rates, the reduction of loan spreads, and the elimination of commissions. While Secretary of State George Shultz worried about the effect of a domino of defaults, ultimately the debtors' cartel had little impact. For the fourth consecutive year, Latin America transferred more money abroad than was invested in the region; in that year the difference was $30 billion. As a consequence the region's debt, after adjusting for inflation, actually fell, although it still stood at a whopping $368 billion. The rescheduling treadmill was wearing thin. Mexico, for example, from 1983 through 1986 entered into four rescheduling packages covering in total $119.7 billion as well as new loans of $16.5 billion.[64]

These statistics, combined with borrowers' complaints and lenders' fears, impelled American Treasury Secretary James Baker III to make a three-part proposal to place LDC finances on a more even keel in late 1985.[65] The Baker Plan consisted of a proposal to provide $21 billion from private banks ($13 billion from banks outside the United States), $9 billion from the World Bank and the Inter-American Development Bank, and an IMF re-lending of the $2.7 billion it expected to be repaid within the next six years to go to the fifteen poorest countries with continued balance of payments problems (ten of the fifteen were in Latin America). The bargain was simple: if debtors agreed to keep repaying their loans, Western governments and banks would lend them enough money to climb out of recession. His initiative also emphasized the need to prevent LDC capital flight and urged debtor countries to continue to tighten their belts. The Baker Plan never worked as well as the secretary had hoped, mainly because banks believed that it asked too much from them and delivered too little. Yet during the period $28.6 billion flowed to the "Baker Fifteen." These countries, as well as two others similarly situated, saw their foreign debts rise from $446 billion at the end of 1985 to $485 billion three years later. Banks steadily disengaged from LDC lending, obtaining repayment, at least in some cases, from monies made available by OECD governments and multilateral institutions.[66]

Pushed by their regulators and less inhibited by their stock markets, European and Japanese banks during the mid-1980s wrote down the value of their loans. But U.S. banks, attempting to avoid drastic reductions in their earnings and stock prices, kept postponing the morning after. In 1987 American, Japanese, British, and other OECD regulators produced an agreement to phase in bank capital requirements within the next three to five years. Finally, in May 1987, Citicorp, the largest American bank, faced the inevitable and announced it would increase its bad loan reserves by 150 percent. As a result it took a loss of $1 billion in 1987. While other large U.S. banks did not follow suit, they did take steps to limit their risk, for example, swapping loans in the secondary market and purchasing bonds in exchange for loans.[67]

In 1989, newly installed Treasury Secretary Nicholas Brady

launched yet another rescue plan. The time was clearly right for a comprehensive attempt to end the crisis. Having established reserves for bad debts, banks could absorb significant debt write-offs without triggering a general systemic crisis. Many banks had already sold off their LDC loans, at a substantial discount, or swapped them for equity. The outstanding loans of the nine largest U.S. banks to Latin America fell from 177 percent of capital in 1982 to 84 percent by 1988. The Brady Plan therefore called for banks to agree to voluntary debt reduction and to receive in exchange the right to select their compensation from a variety of options. Borrowers would agree to reduce their inflation rates and open their economies to international markets. The IMF now began to uncouple itself from private LDC lending, ending a linkage that began seven years earlier. In essence the Brady Plan coopted the various private bank solutions that had been developed by individual banks in preceding years. The first Brady Plan package went into effect in 1989; five years later Brazil, the last major holdout, signed an accord with 750 creditor banks. The third world debt crisis of the 1980s was finally over.[68] By that time LDCs had again begun to attract massive amounts of OECD capital, in the process laying the groundwork for yet another debt crisis.

In the end there was no catastrophe, only some bad years for big banks and some bad feelings toward Latin American defaulters. What lessons were learned? First, oil was a many-tentacled monster. The oil shocks of the seventies presented successive administrations with a massive problem of financial substance and organization. The first oil shock immediately succeeded the collapse of the Bretton Woods system. Nixon's blows to the international financial order prevented the United States from leading OECD nations toward a solution of the three-pronged financial disruption: to the industrialized world, to the LDCs, and to the international financial system. Nor did any other nation or any multilateral organization prove equal to the challenge of orchestrating a concerted international public-sector response.

While U.S. officials worked with the IMF and other nations to create assistance programs for LDCs, Washington lacked the will to generate large-scale aid to bridge the gap between LDC resources and needs. The stunted development of UNCTAD illustrates the lack of interest of G-7 nations, facing their own period of adjustment, in the North-

South problem. Only a perceived threat to the first world's way of life would have motivated a different response. Here was the second lesson. The financial problems of LDCs posed no such threat; the plight of poor nations never rose to the top of the U.S. agenda in the way the condition of Western Europe did in the late 1940s or the situation of Latin America did in the 1960s. If the Soviet Union had sought to take advantage of the debt crisis, another story might have emerged. Although the Soviet Union did not possess significant hard currency reserves, it had resources with which to outbid the West, notably oil and gas. After all, it had entered just such a contest at the end of the 1950s and into the following decade. But preoccupied by its own financial problems and the need to compete with American defense expenditures, the Soviet Union played little part in the crisis.

The third lesson emerged in the mid-seventies—if governments won't take on international financial problems, private sector lenders will happily fill the void, as long as the price seems right. Their eagerness proved a mixed blessing, even if it maintained America's leading international role. Private bankers eagerly stepped in where governments feared to tread. Flush with cash, no longer fearful of the perils of loans to developing nations, bankers eagerly embraced the opportunity to recycle petrodollars. This privatized economic diplomacy suited all parties until the early eighties. Not only was the private sector put in charge of these transactions but government supervision of loans was lax. The Federal Reserve Board changed its rules to allow banks to increase their loans to each country. Banks, with the knowledge of regulatory authorities, repeatedly exceeded their legal lending limits to foreign governments and borrowers.[69]

Then the environment changed. The cost of loans skyrocketed just when the price of commodities fell. The decline of inflation caused the real price to borrowers of their loans to escalate dramatically, curtailing drastically the ability of borrowers to service their debts. A massive crisis ensued. Fearful of an international banking collapse such as had occurred in the 1930s, government entities, both national and multilateral, entered the picture. The fourth lesson: governments can never say never. The Federal Reserve Board and its foreign counterparts, together with the IMF, ensured that the restructuring of LDC debt would proceed in an orderly manner. While U.S. American financial institutions failed because of bad real estate and development loans, no bank collapsed because of its LDC debt. For this result the Federal Reserve Board and the IMF deserve much credit. While IMF packages often proved painful to borrowers, given their generally oligarchical governments, most LDCs would not have enjoyed a fair distribution of economic pain in any event. The IMF requirements of anti-inflation programs and open markets at least offered hope of a better economic tomorrow, which is more than many countries offered their poorer citizens.

The imbroglio demonstrated the failure of either the banks or government entities to monitor the nature and number of LDC loans.[70] Banks lent abroad on the basis of minimal and sometimes nonexistent disclosure, in complete contradiction of the principles that governed their domestic lending. The regulatory laxity in the years before the crisis encouraged the widespread belief that Washington would bail out the money center banks should their solvency be jeopardized. Supporting this belief was the fact that in the early 1980s three-quarters of the international indebtedness was denominated in dollars with U.S. banks providing most of the loans. In fact Arthur Burns did his best to supervise these loans. He received no help from bankers who resented his attempts at governance. Stricter controls went against the American ethos in favor of unbridled free enterprise.[71]

In the event, once Mexico defaulted, Washington acted just as many had predicted. The Federal Reserve led the way in orchestrating a decade of reschedulings. For the U.S. taxpayer, it must be said, this denouement proved much cheaper than the savings and loan fiasco. The drawn-out reschedulings allowed banks to write off their losses over a lengthy period of time. The U.S. tax code's provisions that allow banks to offset losses against profits allocated some of the cost of the debt crisis from the banks to the taxpayer. The stretched-out solution shielded the OECD economies from a devastating blow that could not have easily been accommodated. International financial developments during the two decades after 1973 also contributed to the ability of the international financial system to withstand the effects of petrodollar recycling.

So the best lesson of all was that the nonsystem that succeeded the Bretton Woods era proved resilient, as did Western economies. As OPEC became unable to sustain high prices, oil-importing nations could reduce their oil bills, allowing their economies to cope with losses run up by major money center banks. The cycle was complete. The United States and other OECD nations abdicated responsibility to the private sector for petrodollar recycling and the worsening LDC plight. Bankers took charge, demonstrating their inherent strengths and weaknesses. When the crisis came in August 1982, the public sector rescued the banks but required them to contribute to their salvage. The burden had been allocated as fairly as was politically feasible. The hybrid solution to the debt crisis, with its public and private aspects, may have been the only way the American public would have stomached a transfer of resources from the United States to LDCs. That the shareholders of American banks ultimately paid a significant price for the bailout was only just, considering that it was the banks that began the crisis. U.S. officials also used the IMF and other multilateral organizations as conduits to channel American aid to LDCs. The piece of the puzzle glaringly absent from this picture is the role of Congress. The debt crisis highlighted the ability of the Fed, the most unaccountable part of the U.S. government, to coordinate an international financial rescue with the help of the executive branch, multilateral organizations, and private banks but with little assistance from the American public's elected representatives. No doubt, it would have been difficult to sell Congress on the bailout that was accomplished. Perhaps fortunately, no one tried.

Neither OPEC nations nor LDCs could successfully challenge the Western economic structure. The Communist bloc no longer provided a viable alternative, while newly enriched OPEC nations proved more eager to join the international economic order than to fight it. Washington officials found sufficient monies to rescue the system, both at home and abroad, without the necessity of first creating a political consensus in favor of foreign aid. American leadership was offered and accepted. The Cold War international consensus benefited Washington and its allies, even as the LDCs carried a painful burden.

13

The Eighties

Ronald Reagan, a former "B"-movie actor, first came to prominence on the national political scene during the 1964 Republican
national convention when he nominated Barry Goldwater for President. Having served two terms as governor of California, he challenged Gerald Ford for the Republican presidential nomination in
1976. Four years later Reagan triumphed. The American economy
had foundered during the Carter years, racked by the second oil
shock and double-digit inflation. Reagan promised to lift the malaise
weighing down Americans. He believed "that America's greatest
years were ahead of it, that we had to look at the things that had
made it the greatest, richest and most progressive country on earth in
the first place, decide what had gone wrong, and then put it back on
course."[1] Economic issues became his first priority but the President
also stressed his commitment to battle the Soviet Union—in his
term, the "evil empire." The Reagan Doctrine, as explicated by the
President in his 1985 State of the Union message, proclaimed that
"Our mission is to nourish and defend freedom and democracy, and to
communicate these ideals everywhere we can. . . " Cold War rhetoric

during Reagan's first term escalated to its highest level in a generation. What no one realized was that this flare-up of Soviet-American
tensions signaled not the latest acceleration of the superpower rivalry
but the last.

Riding the crest of the same antisocialist wave that brought Margaret Thatcher to power in Britain, Reagan continually railed against
"encroaching government control." Yet Reagan was not really an ideological President. David Stockman, Reagan's first head of the Office of
Management and Budget, concluded that "he had no concrete program to dislocate and traumatize the here-and-now of American society." Moreover, Reagan's idol was Franklin Roosevelt. The New Deal
President's programs provided Reagan's father and brother with jobs in
1933, saving the family from penury. Roosevelt and Reagan also shared
a passion for communication, and both understood that a chief executive's ability to motivate the electorate was as important a task as devis-
ing a legislative agenda.[2]

Economic issues remained at the heart of Reagan's worldview
throughout his first term.[3] The Reagan team, initially led by Stockman
and Secretary of the Treasury Donald Regan, embraced supply-side
economics: a belief popular among conservative academic economists
that high marginal tax rates and burdensome government regulations
had stifled the incentives for business to produce goods and suppressed
the means for consumers to buy them. At the heart of Reagan's campaign rhetoric was his pledge to balance the federal budget. But when
the administration unveiled its "Reaganomics" blueprint in February
1981, it omitted this promise. Instead the Republican package to cure
American economic woes called for cutting the growth in federal
spending, reducing personal income taxes and regulatory relief, and (in
cooperation with the Fed) implementing a monetary policy that would
bring stability to the dollar and international currency markets. The
state of the American economy continued to decline; a deep recession
gripped the country in mid-1981. Unemployment surged to a postwar
high of 11 percent. Yet Federal Reserve Board Chairman Paul Volcker
(in office since 1979) refused to lower rates because high rates were the
key to winning the battle against the double-digit inflation that had
devastated Americans economically and psychologically at the end of
the Carter years.[4] A debate began in intellectual circles as to whether

the United States, like Germany before it, was overly concerned with the problem of inflation.

By 1983 the economy had embarked on its longest peacetime expansion. While many tax preferences were eliminated and the tax base broadened, the marginal rate had been more than cut in half to 33 percent. Inflation rapidly declined; by 1986 it was only 1.9 percent. Between 1983 and 1986 GNP grew at an average rate of 4.1 percent. The dollar, which had hit record lows during the Carter administration, began to soar to levels unheard of for two decades. Global uncertainty played a part as investors, afraid of political currents abroad, sought the safe haven of the United States. Of equal importance were American interest rates, which remained high throughout the Reagan years. Volcker's policies partly explain the stickiness of American rates. The Reagan team bore its share of responsibility. Choosing to cut taxes while concurrently launching a massive rearmament program necessitated wildly increased federal borrowing. The national deficit rose by over $1 trillion between 1981 and 1987. Reagan accumulated more government debt in six years than all Presidents combined in the preceding 190 years. For the first time since World War II the federal deficit exceeded 5 percent of gross domestic product. The Treasury made up the gap between federal expenditures and federal revenues by borrowing, driving all American interest rates higher.[5] (See Table 13–1.)

Reagan won the 1984 election in a landslide, proclaiming that it was morning in America. Everyone felt the economic picture was indeed sunny. Overlooked at first was the dramatic transformation of American international accounts. In 1985 the United States became a debtor nation, a status it left behind during World War I. The dollar's rapid trajectory sucked foreign goods into the United States while pricing American exports out of foreign markets. Solving the problem proved difficult. Treasury Secretary James Baker successfully managed an orderly decline of the dollar through two international agreements (the Plaza and Louvre accords), but they increased the cost of the imports to which Americans had become addicted. The hoped-for surge in U.S. exports failed to come—Americans proved loath to renounce their Japanese cars or electronic gadgets. By 1987 doubts began to grow about Reaganite economic policies. Then came the stock market crash of October 1987. As the Dow Jones industrial average plummeted over

TABLE 13–1
FEDERAL SURPLUS OR DEFICIT AS A PERCENTAGE OF GROSS DOMESTIC PRODUCT, 1945–96[a]

Fiscal Year of Period	Surplus or Deficit (–)
1945	–22.4
1946	–7.5
1947	1.8
1948	4.8
1949	0.2
1950	–1.2
1951	1.9
1952	–0.4
1953	–1.8
1954	–0.3
1955	–0.8
1956	0.9
1957	0.8
1958	–0.6
1959	–2.7
1960	0.1
1961	–0.6
1962	–1.3
1963	–0.8
1964	–0.9
1965	–0.2
1966	–0.5
1967	–1.1
1968	–3.0
1969	0.4
1970	–0.3
1971	–2.2
1972	–2.0
1973	–1.2
1974	–0.4
1975	–3.5
1976	–4.4
(Transition quarter)	–3.3
1977	–2.8
1978	–2.7

TABLE 13–1 *continued*

Fiscal Year of Period	Surplus or Deficit (–)
1979	–1.7
1980	–2.8
1981	–2.7
1982	–4.1
1983	–6.3
1984	–5.0
1985	–5.4
1986	–5.2
1987	–3.4
1988	–3.2
1989	–2.9
1990	–4.0
1991	–4.7
1992	–4.9
1993	–4.1
1994	–3.1
1995*	–2.7
1996*	–2.7

* Estimates

Note: Through fiscal year 1976, the fiscal year was on a July 1–June 30 basis; beginning October 1976 (fiscal year 1977), the fiscal year is on an October 1–Septenber 30 basis. The 3-month period from July 1, 1976 through September 30, 1976 is a separate fiscal period known as the transition quarter.

aSource: *Economic Report of the President: February 1995* (Washington, 1995).

five hundred points in one day, Reagan's assurance of American strength suddenly sounded like hubris. *Newsweek*'s December cover story proclaiming that "the eighties are over" reflected a widespread belief that the prosperity of the past four years had been illusory.

In retrospect, the October crash was much more of a temporary correction than a harbinger of doom. Reagan's economic expansion continued, albeit more slowly, into his successor George Bush's single term. Eventually it set records for peacetime expansion with continuous growth from 1982 until 1990. Only at the end of 1991 and the first two quarters of 1992 did a recession hit—hard enough to drive Bush from office. These economic boom times gave Reagan the opportunity to implement an expensive defense policy designed to counteract the Soviet Union. At his first presidential press conference he proclaimed that the Communists "reserve unto themselves the right to commit any crime, to lie, to cheat, in order to attain [their goals]. . . . we operate on a different set of standards."[6] Certainly his administration produced more hawkish rhetoric than had been heard since the days of John F. Kennedy (who was Reagan's contemporary). Secretary of Defense Casper Weinberger presided over a renewed arms race. Military spending climbed from Carter's five-year projection of $1.1 trillion to $1.5 trillion. The navy especially benefited from this bounty. In 1983 the United States launched the Strategic Defense Initiative (known as SDI, or "star wars"), intended to provide a high-tech protective umbrella spread out in the skies above the United States and its allies.[7]

Washington officials quickly divided the world into friend and foe. Reversing Carter's emphasis on human rights concerns, the Reagan administration adopted Ambassador to the United Nations Jeane Kirkpatrick's distinction between totalitarian, Communist regimes and authoritarian, anti-Communist ones. In her view, the latter regimes merited U.S. support because they retained economic freedoms, backed the United States on the international stage, and had the potential to evolve into democracies. At the same time the United States gave increasing support for covert actions far and near against Communist regimes. In Pakistan American money funded mujahideen guerrilla groups to fight Soviet soldiers in neighboring Afghanistan. Washington funneled money to anti-Communist forces in Angola and Mozambique. Closer to home, the Reagan administration embarked on a major campaign against the Communist Sandinista regime that had taken power in Nicaragua in 1979. Reagan warned the American people of their possible peril by pointing out that Managua practically bordered El Paso and followed up his words by ordering the mining of Managua's harbors, in violation of international law.

Events in Europe soon overshadowed Latin American developments. The Soviet Union during Reagan's first term was led by a gerontocracy. Leonid Brezhnev, in power since Johnson's time, ruled an increasingly sclerotic regime until his death in 1982. His successor, seventy-eight-year-old Yuri Andropov, used his control over the KGB to reach the top of the Soviet government. Andropov, also in his seventies, governed for fewer than two years. His main accomplishment was enabling his young protégé, Mikhail Gorbachev, to assume the leadership of the Soviet Union less than a year after his death. Gorbachev was unlike any Soviet leader in three decades. He had relative youth (he was fifty-four in 1985), originality, and energy on his side. Driving him was the knowledge that he had two choices: reform his dying regime or watch it decline into oblivion. Gorbachev knew, as American officials did not, how precarious the political and economic health of the Soviet Union was. A committed Communist, he destroyed the traditional boundaries of Soviet society not to end the Communist system but to save it.

Gorbachev launched a double-barreled domestic program. "*Perestroika*" would rescue the domestic economic system by liberalizing the socialist rules that had governed Soviet society for seventy years. Previous leaders had believed that Soviet military might alone would suffice to retain superpower status. Gorbachev reversed his predecessors' priorities, understanding that only by reviving the faltering Soviet economy could Moscow continue to retain its international position.[8] "*Glasnost*" permitted open discussions unheard of in Russia, either under czars or Communist rulers. Newspapers and television stations launched unprecedented, open debates while political prisoners began returning from the Gulag. Western media, truly international by virtue of satellite, cable, and fax machine, obtained ever greater exposure behind the iron curtain. But with the economy continuing in free fall, the freedom to discuss economic and other issues raised tensions and became the freedom to call the whole system into question.

Foreign policy proved far more rewarding. The Reagan administration initially viewed Gorbachev with suspicion. But just as the conservative hawk Richard Nixon was able to open relations with China, superhawk Reagan was able to negotiate with Gorbachev. Reagan came to appreciate that Gorbachev "was different in style [and] in substance . . . from previous Soviet leaders. He [was] a man who takes chances and that is what you need for progress." In October 1986 at the Reykjavik summit, Reagan and Gorbachev discussed the previously unmentionable subject of an end to all nuclear and ballistic missiles.[9]

Gorbachev needed to slow down if not end the arms race, which was bankrupting the Soviet Union. Whatever its technical merits, the SDI had raised the ante too high for Moscow. At first blush Reagan, having come to office determined to vanquish the Soviet Union, would appear to have been the wrong president at the right time. But Reagan's lack of intellectual preconceptions and his reliance on instinct actually allowed him to comprehend the changes in the international landscape during the second half of the eighties before many of his more sophisticated advisers. Soon the two leaders were corresponding regularly. The fruit of their relationship was the Intermediate Nuclear Forces (INF) treaty banning all intermediate-range missiles in Europe to the Urals. Reagan later recalled, "I told [Gorbachev] that there was a very unique situation. I said, 'Here are the two of us in a room and probably the only two people in the world who could have started World War III. And we're also the only two people, perhaps in the world that could prevent World War III.'" Reagan and Gorbachev made more bilateral progress than any of their predecessors could have imagined.[10]

Bush's election victory allowed him, together with Secretary of State James Baker, to midwife a peaceful end to the Cold War. During the summer of 1989, an endless stream of refugees left Communist Eastern European states for Western nations. By autumn it was clear that the Soviet Union would not intervene. As the historian Martin Malia wrote, "The chain reaction of events leading from the Polish elections of June throughout the collapse of the Berlin Wall in November to the fall of [Romanian dictator Nicolai] Ceausescu in December is the most stunning episode in the disintegration of Communism."[11] When the Berlin Wall came down on November 9, 1989, the Cold War virtually ended. Gorbachev, struggling to save the Soviet Union, could not hold on to the satellites. Bush and Baker, thereafter, concentrated on the peaceful reunification of Germany and the reintegration of Eastern Europe into Western society. In October 1990 Germany officially became one country again. But fourteen months later, the world moved beyond Gorbachev's rule and Bush's expectation: the Soviet Union disintegrated. Bush and Baker had embraced Gorbachev. He was the kind of man they liked to deal with: articulate, helpful, decisive. "Better the devil you know" summed up their worldview. Washington officials turned a blind eye to any evidence of growing Soviet decomposition.

When the Baltic republics (Lithuania, Latvia, Estonia) signaled their intention to secede from the Soviet Union, they received little succor from the administration, although the United States had never officially recognized their incorporation in 1940 into the Soviet Union. Gorbachev's decision to use force to reconquer media centers in Latvia and Lithuania in January 1991, during the run-up to Desert Storm, brought only token protest from Bush and Baker. By the Soviet Union's last year of existence, Washington was paying as much attention to supporting its former foe as it had once done to containing it.

All the while, Gorbachev's prestige at home was declining. The disintegration of Communist party control left a state with a crumbling political system and a chaotic economy. Disgruntled apparatchiks attempted a coup against Gorbachev in August 1991. The hero of the hour was not Gorbachev but the newly elected Russian president, Boris Yeltsin, also a former Communist. Four months later, on Christmas Day, Gorbachev resigned. The Soviet Union was history. Fifteen independent nations replaced the Soviet empire. Some, such as Lithuania, had known periods of great historical prominence. Others, such as Belarus, had never been independent nations. Bush proudly proclaimed his allegiance to a "new world order." The United States, the world's only superpower, would be the world's policeman. His administration had faced an unexpected problem—the disintegration of nations. Bush and Baker turned out to be ardent defenders of the nation-states that existed when they took office. But events moved beyond their control.

14

Free Trade Forever?

> If we are to have full post war employment, America's
> tremendous productive capacity must have markets
> . . . foreign markets.
>
> Advertisement for the Alcoa Steamship Company, *Time*, June 4, 1945

George Bush wanted to win a second term as President. He first thought that the American victory in the Persian Gulf War would assure his reelection, but its importance quickly paled, washed out by the ever stronger recession. To improve his electoral chances, Bush traveled to Japan in December 1991. He had planned an international journey that would advertise his foreign policy prowess. But with polls showing that Americans were interested in domestic economic issues, particularly the deepening recession, not great power politics, he reoriented his approach. The President's choice of destination was not frivolous. During the Cold War relations between Tokyo and Washington were central to American foreign economic and security policy as well as to U.S. internal economic policy. In earlier decades American presidents welcomed Japanese imports and financial sustenance. But Japan's continually rising balance of trade and payments surpluses had become difficult to tolerate during the deepening American recession. Bush had said that his goal was "jobs, jobs, jobs." Wedded to the Cold War free trade consensus, he sought voluntary Japanese trade policy concessions to undermine growing protectionist sentiment and jump-start the

American economy in the coming election year. To show that he meant business, Bush invited the leaders of General Motors, Ford, and Chrysler to accompany him. Yet the visit produced little of substance— its highlight turned out to be unexpected, when Bush vomited on Prime Minister Kiichi Miyazawa at a state dinner.

The quantity and quality of America's resources and the nature of its immigrant labor force gave the United States a unique perspective on trade issues. Unlike other great powers, its economy was not dependent on foreign imports. Food, fuel, factories—America possessed them in abundance. Just as their country's geographic isolation gave Americans unparalleled freedom to debate political and diplomatic policy, U.S. economic strength provided them the luxury of discussing whether they wanted to join their markets to those abroad. By the end of World War II American internationalists had become convinced that trade walls not only made for bad neighbors but encouraged the slide toward war.[1] As *Life* recorded in 1947, "suicidal trade policies can . . . push a world toward war. . . . The economic policies of the 1930s may not have caused World War II and wrecked the League of Nations, but they certainly helped prepare the ground."[2]

America's new status as the world's leading industrial power encouraged liberal trade sentiments. Self-confident corporate executives were willing to sacrifice American tariff walls if other nations would knock down theirs. Insecurity also strengthened free trade sentiment; many in the agricultural and business communities feared that without new overseas markets, the United States would face a repetition of the cruel postwar recession that followed World War I. The growing Soviet threat further nourished antitariff sentiment. Communism fed on poverty and the absence of hope. Lessening trade barriers would increase international economic prosperity, wiping out the attraction of Marxist ideology, all at little cost to the American taxpayer. During the debate on the Marshall Plan Allen Dulles, together with others active in the Committee to Support the Marshall Plan, linked free trade to the American aid program, pointing out that increased Western European trade could dramatically lessen the need for U.S. assistance. The visible abundance of American material life would also provide an antidote to communism. Free trade, rather than the closed Communist world, would produce for other nations what the United States already enjoyed. A tariff-free world, opined an editorial writer of *Life*, should "be made to work so well that even the Russians will come to see that one sure way for them to approach a standard of living above the sub-human is to join in the fun."[3]

Yet significant dissenters to these newly fashionable American views remained. Small businessmen and manufacturers, fearing foreign competition, vociferously protested a liberalized U.S. trade policy. They found champions on the Republican side of the aisle. Indeed in the early postwar period debates over trade policy were conducted largely within the Republican party. Franklin Roosevelt, burdened by wartime and anticipated postwar problems, devoted one of his last messages to Congress to a plea for renewal of the Reciprocal Trade Agreements Act (RTAA), allowing the President to enter into bilateral tariff-cutting treaties. "This is essential to the substantial increase in our foreign trade which is necessary for full employment and improved standards of living," proclaimed Roosevelt.[4] But Republican stalwarts continued to view low tariffs as anathema.[5] As a result the administration won the 1945 RTAA extension only by pledging to include an escape clause protecting domestic producers in any future trade agreement and by promising not to negotiate agreements damaging to any portion of U.S. business, labor, or agriculture.[6] This contradictory mandate mirrored public opinion. In 1946 pollsters reported that 57 percent of the general public saw no connection between high tariffs and war, while 46 percent of the general public thought that increased imports would make no difference to them personally, and 13 percent believed that increased imports would be detrimental. Yet 64 percent of those polled believed that the United States must "buy in order to sell."[7]

"Two steps forward, one step back" continued to characterize the progress of the American crusade for freer trade during the next fifteen years. In October 1947 President Harry Truman used his authority under the RTAA to join the General Agreement on Tariffs and Trade (GATT), which represented the first successful postwar multilateral codification of free trade principles. The original twenty-three contracting countries pledged to conduct their trade on a multilateral basis without favor to particular countries and to reduce or abolish trade barriers and quotas. The signatories also agreed to discuss tariff levels as well as exceptions at successive "rounds" of negotiations. GATT was only a provisional agreement, and it allowed each country to maintain escape clauses to protect its domestic producers.[8] But the failure of Congress to approve the International Trade Organization the next year sparked GATT's evolution into a permanent framework for tariff reductions.[9]

Even convinced Republican interventionists such as Arthur Vandenberg and Henry Cabot Lodge, Jr., voted against RTAA's extension in 1948. When Republicans returned to the White House in 1953, President Dwight Eisenhower and his colleagues could not avoid dealing with their party's divisions on trade. The White House strenuously advocated increased trade rather than aid to newly independent and impoverished countries. As secretary of state, John Foster Dulles told the Senate Finance Committee in 1958 that the RTAA was also a key weapon in the war against communism. Countries with increased access to export markets could improve their citizens' standard of living, thereby immunizing them against Communist influence.[10] But senior Republicans in Congress still opposed lowering trade barriers. As a result the battles during the 1950s to renew the RTAA were bloody. Indeed Eisenhower won the 1955 renewal only by agreeing to circumscribe his independent authority.[11]

The advent of a Democratic administration again signaled a more active trade policy. John F. Kennedy convinced Congress in 1962 to pass the Trade Expansion Act (TEA), designed to stimulate American growth, reduce the American balance of payments deficit, and strengthen economic relations with other countries. Behind the President's initiative lay the growing conviction that American economic growth had lagged behind Soviet results. Officials hoped that increased foreign trade would provide a jump start enabling American growth statistics to surpass the figures reported by Moscow. The emergence of the European Economic Community (EC) also increased the relevance of trade talks. In 1958 six major European nations linked themselves in a Common Market, characterized by no tariffs within the system and sturdy tariff walls against all others. While American diplomats had long supported such an organization and continued to advocate British membership in the body, they now feared its effect on American exports. For the first time since World War II, the United States had lost export markets to foreign competitors.[12] As Kennedy said in explaining the need for the TEA, "The two great Atlantic markets will either mark the beginning of a new chapter in the alliance of free nations—or a threat to the growth of Western unity."[13]

Yet the TEA embodied a fair trade as well as free trade stance. While free trade is purely market-driven, fair trade allows a nation to balance the need for international free trade with domestic economic and political interests. The President could offer the succor of raised tariffs, quotas, or appropriate compensatory market arrangements with other nations—all permissible steps under GATT rules.[14] Kennedy's legislation gave the President the power and political headache of striking the balance among domestic interest groups and between internal and international considerations. It continued the postwar tendency of increasing the executive's power by creating the office of Special Trade Representative.

The first round of GATT negotiations after the passage of the TEA, the so-called Kennedy round, concluded in 1967. The United States agreed to a balanced set of cuts eliminating American tariffs on about $4.5 billion of industrial and agricultural imports, in exchange for reductions on about the same amount of exports. The success of the Kennedy round allowed Johnson administration officials to plan their next trade initiative. Secretary of State Dean Rusk stressed the need to maintain the American export surplus; the still healthy trade surplus offset the worrisome American balance of payments deficit.[15] Rusk's planning benefited from the widespread assumption that the free and fair trade position had decisively triumphed over protectionism. But just two years later, when Richard Nixon became President, the American landscape looked very different.

The key to the changing trade landscape was the decline in the U.S. balance of trade surplus and the meteoric rise in Japanese exports. The 1960s brought Japan's complete integration into the Western alliance. Its economy began to take off, protected by an American-drawn constitution that prohibited offensive military actions, and by Washington's security guarantee. Japan joined the Organization of Economic Cooperation and Development (OECD) in 1964; the next year it signed a peace treaty with South Korea, easing decades of hostility. In 1965 as well Japan enlisted in and helped fund the American-sponsored Asian Development Bank. Beginning in 1964 U.S. officials began urging their Japanese counterparts to grant aid to LDCs and make offsetting payments to the United States to pay for American military expenses in Japan, much the same way West Germany did. The United States also began to press Japan to increase the size of the Self-Defense Forces, as the Japanese army was called.[16] During the Vietnam War Japan made the leap from a deficit to a surplus country; no longer a poor relation, it was now an economic power. From 1954 to 1971 Japan's economy grew 500 percent. By 1956 it had become the world's largest shipbuilding nation; in 1962 its economy exceeded Britain's in size, while in 1967 it topped West Germany to move into third place.[17] (See Table 14–1.)

Japanese exports to the United States consisted mainly of consumer goods. American imports into Japan by contrast in 1968 were limited by 122 quantitative or quota restrictions (QRs), which violated GATT rules. They were also hindered by the yen/dollar exchange rate, which during the first half of 1971 stood at $1 = Y358, the same level since 1953. The characteristics of the market for heavy electronic goods was typical: both the United States and Japan were leading exporters and producers of such equipment, but while the United States also imported electronic equipment, much of it Japanese, Japan imported almost nothing.[18] (See Table 14–2.)

Richard Nixon firmly belonged to the trade, not aid, camp. Moreover, he had imbibed the Eastern Republican free trade ideology. Yet the trade landscape had drastically changed. The United States had

TABLE 14–1
JAPAN'S BALANCE OF PAYMENTS ON
CURRENT ACCOUNT, 1964–71[a] (U.S. $ BILLIONS)

Year	Balance of Payments
1964	$ – 480
1969	$2,119
1970	$1,190
1971	$5,797

[a]Dillon Read & Co. Archives, New York, New York,
Prospectus, the Japan Development Bank, March 1975.

TABLE 14–2
CHANGES IN JAPANESE-AMERICAN TRADE[a]

U.S. Imports from Japan, 1966–70:	U.S. Exports to the World, 1966–70:	U.S. Trade Deficit with Japan: Prior to 1965,
Up 98 percent	Up 42 percent	None
U.S. Exports to Japan, 1966–70:	U.S. Imports from the World, 1966–70:	U.S. Trade Deficit with Japan, 1970,
Up 96 percent	Up 56 percent	$1.2 billion

[a]NP, McCracken Papers, Box 11, "Basic Developments in U.S.–Japan Trade Relationships, 1966–1971," November 1, 1971.

long run a positive balance of trade with the rest of the world: Americans sold more to foreign countries than they bought from foreign manufacturers. During the 1960s the combination of an overvalued dollar (which made U.S. exports expensive and cheapened the price of imports), foreign rivals' lower manufacturing costs, specifically in West Germany and Japan, and the effect of protectionist Common Market farm policies led to a steady erosion of the balance of trade surplus and its total disappearance in 1971.

Rather than mounting an all-out protectionist campaign, the White House took a more complex approach. To buy time, Nixon appointed a presidential commission on international trade and investment to be headed by Albert Williams, the chairman of the Executive Committee of the Board of Directors of IBM. American diplomats also encouraged foreign countries to purchase U.S. exports and pushed for the elimination of nontariff barriers. Secretary of Commerce Maurice H. Stans, who would later become famous for his bribe carrying during the Watergate scandal, stressed the four economic freedoms: freedom to trade, travel, invest, and exchange technology, as he toured the world seeking opportunities for American business.[19] The effect of Nixonian trade policy found its clearest expression in the President's policy toward the country that produced the knottiest trade problems—Japan.

The Nixon Doctrine, enunciated by the President in 1969, recognized that the United States, no longer able to afford its original Cold War strategy, must delegate some of the responsibility for the Western alliance. Détente with the Soviet Union and the opening of relations with the People's Republic of China represented the other half of the walnut. By lessening Cold War tensions, the United States could cut American defense expenditures further. Japan's position now became anomalous. It was less a strategic partner than an economic competitor. Indeed Nixon told Chinese dictator Mao Zedong that the United States was following a dual containment policy in Asia: against the Soviet Union and Japan.[20]

But economic ties now tightly bound Washington and Tokyo. Japan in 1970 was the second-largest customer for American goods after Canada, accounting for 11 percent of total American exports, which also equaled 29.2 percent of Japanese imports. By the same token the United States took 31 percent of Japanese exports, which accounted for 15 percent of U.S. imports. Cotton textile imports were covered by a bilateral agreement under the multilateral Long-Term Cotton Textile Agreement of 1962. During 1970 and 1971 wool and synthetic fibers became an important bilateral issue. Forced to adapt to a deficit, at least temporarily, American officials expressed increased frustration with Japanese policy. Guiding their sentiments was the knowledge, in the words of the CIA's intelligence directorate, that "the liberalization of restrictions on imports and inflows of direct foreign investment by Japan has been largely illusory." CIEP official Ernie Shrenzel wrote in June 1971 that "Japan Inc., continues to roll on, at the expense of US markets and US industry. And we continued to fuel their fires, by our own acts of commission, and omission." For their part, increasingly confident Japanese business leaders began to blame the United States for its problems. Kenichiro Komai, the president of Hitachi, observed that "if it is true that American manufacturers suffered damage, they should improve their own setup."

From the moment he became President, Nixon took an active part in textile negotiations. He was contemptuous of State Department officials, believing that they "will settle for anything." He also faced heavy domestic pressure to take a vigorous role. The South was crucial to Nixon's 1972 strategy and the textile industry played a key role in the new South. Raising the stakes, Democrat Wilbur Mills, the chairman of the powerful House Ways and Means Committee, kept nipping at the President's heels. Mills introduced legislation in the spring of 1970 that would impose mandatory quotas on wool and synthetic imports. On July 16, 1971, Nixon wrote Prime Minister Eisaku Sato of Japan as well as President Chung Hee Park of South Korea "to personally reaffirm to [them] the very great importance which I attach to settling the textile issue."[21] The President, in common with other members of his administration, worried that the increasing anger generated by these imports would undermine American support for a liberal trade policy. On the other hand, by 1971 Nixon made it clear that he did not want doctrinaire free traders in his administration.[22]

Linked to the issue of textiles was the question of Okinawa, the largest of the Japanese Ryukyu Islands, which the United States had occupied since the end of World War II. While the pro-American Sato termed its retention a symbol of Japan's defeat and an obstacle to better relations with the United States, the Pentagon proclaimed the bases indispensable to American defense needs.[23] At their first summit held in Hawaii in 1969, Nixon, without specifying a firm date, promised Sato that the United States would return the islands. During this meeting Nixon apparently won Sato's agreement to significant voluntary textile restraints. Unfortunately, having run into stiff opposition from Japan's powerful Ministry of Technology and Industry (MITI) and textile companies, Sato could not deliver on his promises.[24] This incident caused much resentment in Washington.[25] However, in June 1971, the United States and Japan signed the return agreement providing that the United States would relinquish control over Okinawa the following year, although the Pentagon retained the huge Kadean air base.[26]

Nixon's subsequent dismissive attitude toward Japan was much in evidence during 1971, the summer of the "Nixon shocks." First, in July, the President announced the end of the American quarantine of the People's Republic of China. Japan, having slavishly mimicked the American nonrecognition policy, reeled at the sudden and unexpected about-face, made by Washington without any private explanation. As Nixon blandly recorded in his memoirs, "the Japanese presented a particularly difficult problem."[27] Nixon's decision announced on August 15 to sever the link between the dollar and gold and impose a 10 percent across-the-board surcharge on imports to the United States proved equally stunning. The use of the 10 percent surcharge, in clear violation of GATT rules, further illustrates Nixon's basic approach to governance: the ends always justify the means and rules are made to be broken. U.S. officials failed to provide Tokyo with prior warning. Japan depended on the United States for a third of its exports; the 10 percent surcharge affected 94 percent of exports to the United States and could have been devastating. Indeed Japan's central bank, the Bank of Japan, spent millions of dollars in a futile and unwanted (by the United States) attempt to bolster the dollar's rate against the yen.[28]

Tellingly, one of the issues occupying the President's time just before the crucial weekend was current American policy on textile imports. White House economic adviser Pete Peterson had explained to the President on August 6 that textile industry leaders were due to meet in one week. Unless Nixon provided tangible assistance to textiles manufacturers fighting Japanese competition, the industry would turn to congressional leader Wilbur Mills, already chasing after the 1972 Democratic presidential nomination. Peter Flanigan elucidated the underlying point: the charge that the President "did not deliver" to the textile industry needed to be proved "demonstrably false" by election day, 1972.

The Nixon economic shock concentrated Japanese attention on textile issues and broke the stalemate. On October 15 the United States and Japan reached the "Kennedy Agreement" (named after American Ambassador at Large and former Treasury Secretary David Kennedy), which the *Washington Post* described as a "Japanese capitulation." (Ironically, by that time the textile issue was no longer really important—the steadily increasing number of Japanese cars was the real issue.) American-Japanese talks continued into the winter as the United States made it clear it hoped to achieve a billion-dollar improvement in the trade balance between the United States and Japan before it would consider lifting the import surcharge. Japan also participated in the Smithsonian Agreement of December 1971, which resulted in a general dollar devaluation of about 8 percent relative to the world's major currencies.[29]

Yet during the next two years as the dollar/yen rate dropped from $1 = Y358 to $1 = Y302, Japanese industry quickly rebounded.[30] Exports to the United States consistently increased. In September 1972 Treasury Undersecretary Paul Volcker in testimony to Congress labeled Japan's continued balance of payments surplus the "major single force of disequilibrium in the world economy." Japanese QRs had fallen in number but the Japanese market remained no more accessible to American manufacturers and farmers. In fact as P. Kuwayama of the Federal Reserve Bank of New York's research division pointed out, "the Japanese import market in the postwar period has probably been the most highly protected among those of all industrial countries." As Kuwayama further explained, Japanese restrictions included QRs, tariffs, and the hugely important "administrative guidance"—pressure emanating from MITI and the Ministry of Finance, ensuring that large corporations favored domestic sources for their requirements.[31]

By contrast, Japanese imports entered the United States in increasing quantities. In 1975 imported passenger cars captured 18.3 percent of the market; half of them came from Japan.[32] As for small electronics, by 1980 the American industry that pioneered mass market radio and television and invented VCRs had virtually become extinct. In 1965 Japanese production was 13 percent of U.S. totals; five years later the portion had increased to 37 percent.[33] Sony, Hitachi, and Panasonic became household words in the United States. According to a CIA report issued in January 1972, Japanese policy concentrated on a small number of export industries at one time, thereby allowing the newcomers to achieve significant and rapid market penetration. The Japanese government acquiesced in significant U.S. export controls—by 1972 40 percent of Japanese trade was covered by some sort of restraint. But these agreements generally came after Japanese companies had already achieved a significant market base. As Table 14–3 illustrates, these controls did not significantly restrict export growth. Because the European Community had been more successful at limiting Japanese imports, Japanese pressure to export into the United States continued to grow.[34]

That the impressive Japanese performance occurred against the backdrop of the two oil shocks and the severe recession of 1974–75 emphasizes the greatness of the achievement. Japan, in 1970 the world's largest importer of oil, was extremely vulnerable to Arab pressure. The Arab oil boycott's initial impact was severe: in November 1973 the CIA estimated that by the end of the year Japan would lose about 9 percent of its normal oil supplies.[35] The Japanese government responded to the changed oil landscape both diplomatically and eco-

TABLE 14–3
MAJOR JAPANESE EXPORTS RESTRAINED IN THE UNITED STATES[a]

Product and Year of Restraint	Increase in Imports in Year Following Restraints (percent)
Steel, 1969	6
Transistors, 1960	12
Cotton textiles, 1956	7
Sewing machines, 1961	8
Metal flatware, 1958	17
Ball bearings, NA	31
Manmade textiles, 1971	—

[a]DD–16G, CIA Intelligence Memorandum, "The Nature of Japanese Export Controls: Some Implications for the United States," January 1972.

nomically. Tokyo adopted a blatant pro-Arab tilt and offered new government loans to Middle Eastern states while rushing consideration of already pending aid proposals, hoping to receive special treatment from Arab oil producers.[36] Concurrently, MITI and other Japanese agencies oversaw a massive conservation drive resulting in an enormous increase in Japanese efficiency and fuel usage.[37] Japanese officials also rapidly steered companies away from energy-hogging industries such as iron and steel, already under competitive pressure from newly emergent countries such as South Korea, to more energy-sparing high-technology production.[38] As a result of this three-pronged strategy, Japan was better able than other OECD nations to withstand the second oil crisis, bouncing back rapidly from the initial severe effects.

The bureaucrats running Japanese policy at the behest of Liberal Democratic Party (LDP) politicians, who contented themselves with dividing up the political spoils, took as their chief goal the maintenance and increase of foreign markets, especially American. What could have been catastrophic instead brought stunning success. An official from the Japanese Ministry of Finance described Japanese strategy during the 1970s as "a policy of appropriate policy management and stringent self-control." The U.S. view was different. Robert Aliber of the University of Chicago Business School posed the question to Undersecretary of the Treasury Volcker: how was it that in 1973 Japan's oil import bill was $5 billion and Japan had a current account surplus of several hundred million dollars, while in 1976 Japan's oil bill was $20 billion and Japan had a current account surplus of several billion dollars?[39] Finding the correct response would become a preoccupation of American administrations thereafter.

American economic statistics, by contrast, during the 1970s made depressing reading. Imports rose while exports fell—the steel belt became the rust belt. Indeed the history of the steel industry illuminated the prevailing pattern. The self-confidence of postwar American executives had turned to arrogance. Complacent companies refused to reinvest their profits, especially the expensive but worthwhile continuous-casting process. Plants like Sparrows Point in Baltimore and the great Homestead Works in Pittsburgh continued to use the same open-hearth methods that had been cutting edge in 1900. Confident that the sellers' market in steel would continue indefinitely, manufacturers granted wage increases to their workers and high dividends to themselves, which were in turn paid for by consistent increases in steel prices. Unfortunately West Germany and Japan, albeit out of necessity, brought on stream new plants producing higher-quality steel at much less cost. As a result, during the deep recession of 1974–75, plant after American plant closed. A similar transformation took place in the automobile industry. Since the phrase "made in Japan" had been synonymous with shoddy merchandise and bad workmanship in the years following upon World War II, the first Japanese cars seemed like curiosities. But within twenty years an amazing reversal had occurred. Just as Detroit earned the reputation of producing lemons, Japanese cars gained popularity with their enviable record of efficiency, quality, and low price.

These developments, coupled with skyrocketing U.S. consumer imports, eroded the prevailing American faith in free trade policies. Nixon engineered his August 15 dollar shock to improve America's trading position. Elite opinion in the United States remained firmly in favor of free trade. The League of Women Voters, for example, urged Nixon in October 1971 to recant his "growing ransom list of demands made of our trading partners." Nixon told his Commission on International Trade and Investment Policy that the United States could remain competitive with "sacrifice and hard work as well as some old policy initiatives."[40] But during 1972 the trade position deteriorated again, ensuring that trade would remain a political hot potato. Wilbur Mills, talking to the President in February 1973, suggested that Nixon impose a new import surcharge "to stop the flood of imports." Private petitions for escape clause treatment, antidumping measures, counter-vailing duties, and other forms of import restrictions grew steadily. Yet Nixon, in February 1974, committed himself to "move forward in a multi-national attempt to reduce trade barriers."[41]

The steadily eroding American economic position had convinced Nixon officials to introduce a new trade bill that reached Capitol Hill in April 1973. For the first time in Cold War history Americans debated a trade bill from the perspective of a nation running a balance of trade deficit; the 1972 U.S. deficit was the worst of the twentieth century. The legislation strove for a balance between Nixon's international priorities and domestic political imperatives, sharpened by the worsening recession and deteriorating trade balance. The President requested renewed authority to negotiate on tariffs and nontariff barriers, as well as relief for import-damaged industries, preferences for LDCs, and most-favored-nation status for the Soviet Union (the commitment to give the Soviet Union the same treatment as other countries received). Instead of speedy passage, Nixon's proposal stalled in Congress. The Senate did not consider it until early 1974, by which time the oil shocks had wrecked economic expectations. Moreover, Senator Henry Jackson (D. Wash.) delayed the bill by using it as a vehicle to further his presidential ambitions. Jackson sought to employ most-favored-nation preferential tariff status for the Soviet Union as a lever to pry Soviet permission for Jews to emigrate, while Secretary of State Kissinger adamantly refused to jeopardize détente in this fashion. By the time the Trade Act of 1974 became law (it lost the word "Reform" along the way), Nixon was no longer President. His successor received circumscribed power to reduce or eliminate tariffs, but Congress had the final say on nontariff barriers (NTBs). The Tariff Commission became the International Trade Commission (ITC). Congressional input strengthened the industry and worker protection, which the President's draft already had expanded from the TEA model.[42]

The fading of détente during the Carter years gave a boost to the flagging Japanese-American relationship. Once again the Washington-Tokyo alliance, with its network of military bases, seemed vital. But growing American economic woes dragged the President into domestic trade politics. While he theoretically hewed to the Democratically molded bipartisan consensus in favor of free and fair trade, he could not ignore the domestic cries for protection sparked by the rising American trade deficit. That 250,000 autoworkers were out of work had to be weighed against prevailing elite sentiment such as a December 1980 *New York Times* editorial, which lectured Americans that "the obvious problems that have beset autos, steel and a few other industries are exceptions, not the rule."[43] In 1977 Federal Reserve Board official E.M. Truman urged progress on the Tokyo round of GATT negotiations. The Trade Act had authorized full American participation in multilateral talks dedicated to expanding the opportunities for free trade. Truman, however, pointed out that tariff cuts would probably increase American imports as much as they did exports. What made the discussions particularly difficult was their focus on NTBs such as favorable tax treatment of exports, export guaranties, and provision of export insurance. Carter appointed as special trade representative (STR) Robert Strauss, lawyer and well-known Democratic party leader. Strauss presided over the Multilateral Trade Negotiations, playing a major role in the agreement reached in July 1978 on a "framework of understanding on the Tokyo Round." Tariff reductions of about 30 percent soon followed, with Congress easily approving NTB agreements the following year.[44]

But the Trade Act forced Carter to deal personally with industry complaints. Unlike its predecessor, the Tariff Commission, the ITC rapidly reached a determination of import-driven damage. In January 1977 it ruled that such damage had affected the nonrubber footwear industry, while in March it reached the same conclusion with respect to color television sets. The Trade Act gave the President sixty days after the ITC's recommendation of relief to decide on appropriate action to take, but Congress could override the decision. In both cases Carter strove for the middle ground, rejecting tariff increases but negotiating orderly market arrangements with Taiwan and South Korea on shoes and Japan on color televisions. The administration also began a reference price system for steel, designed to prevent dumping. But despite bilateral Japanese-American negotiations, Japan's trade surplus with the United States grew until the temporary brake of the second oil shock.[45]

The petroleum price rises of 1978–79 delivered another serious blow to the reeling American economy. But the pressure of Japanese imports continued. By the end of the seventies American consumer products' companies had ceded whole areas of production to Japanese competitors, while Nissan, Toyota, and Honda cars were in great demand. The *Wall Street Journal* proclaimed: "The reason we are not alarmed by a $25 billion trade deficit is that it will be the result of consenting adults trading their wares in the private market place," but others were not as sanguine.[46] Within the ambit of the overall commitment to freer trade, American officials attempted to cope with their continuing problem. As early as September 1971 the American delegation to the Eighth Japan–U.S. Businessmen's Conference had "made the point that the imbalance in our bilateral trade relations could no longer be sustained and that economic problems can quickly cause political reactions." The growing concern that the United States was in danger of losing crucial market share in such key areas as semiconductors and electronics led to a spate of congressional hearings. Legislation concerning trade and export associations came up for discussion; some senators argued that the Webb-Pomerene Act emphasized antitrust concerns at the expense of competitiveness. The constant refrain that exporters faced U.S. government disincentives produced particularly effective headlines. Japanese-American economic relations provided the spark for a more general discussion of U.S. trade issues. But no consensus on a replacement for American free and fair trade policy surfaced.[47]

A variety of choices existed. Washington could step up its efforts to open the Japanese market to American manufacturers. As the CIA had reported in September 1971, "Since the early 1960s, Tokyo has promised repeatedly to remove its trade and investment barriers." Progress remained glacial.[48] Foreigners found it virtually impossible to make meaningful direct investments in Japanese companies. Tokyo continually clung to an undervalued yen so that Japanese products would remain cheap in the United States while American products could not compete in Japanese markets. (See Table 14–4.) The Japanese postwar bargain was different from the American one. Cheap,

TABLE 14-4
U.S. AND JAPAN TRADE BALANCES (FOB, U.S. $ BILLIONS)[a]

Year	U.S. Trade Balance	Japanese Trade Balance
1973	0.91	3.64
1974	−5.51	1.35
1975	8.9	4.94
1976	−9.47	9.8
1977	−31.11	17.16
1978	−33.94	24.3
1979	−27.54	1.74
1980	−25.5	2.13
1981	−27.99	19.96
1982	−36.44	18.08
1983	−67.08	31.46
1984	−112.51	44.26
1985	−122.16	55.99
1986	−145.05	92.82
1987	−159.49	96.42
1988	−126.97	95
1989	−114.87	76.85

[a]Volcker and Gyohten, *op. cit.*, p. 368.

abundant consumer goods ranked at the bottom. Instead the Japanese people continued to support or at least tolerate a persisting emphasis on export growth and jobs for life combined with a low standard of living relative to national wealth. The rising Japanese trade surplus with both the United States and the rest of the world reflected this emphasis. By the same token the standard of living in Japan continued to lag far behind that of other OECD countries. When recovery came to Japan in 1976, Japan's trade surplus continued to rise; recovery in the United States had the opposite effect.

GATT and other treaties limited the American government's unilateral power to cut Japanese imports, although Nixon had shown how such "technicalities" could be ignored. Alternatives existed. The Federal Reserve Board could raise interest rates, thereby limiting the ability of Americans to undertake discretionary purchases, many of them Japanese consumer goods. But the already record high interest rates of the seventies and early eighties prohibited such a step. The Fed could also lower the amount of consumer credit available, a choice frequently utilized by the British government. Congress and the President could agree on tax increases to suck consumption dollars out of the American economy. Any of these choices would automatically limit purchases of imported goods. But no domestic political consensus supported taking such measures. On the contrary, the post–World War II bargain between the American elites and the mass of Americans rested on the development and continuance of a consumption economy. The good life would be possible for everyone, one that came supplied with a growing number of material possessions such as several cars, televisions, and stereos. American government officials never tested the willingness of their constituents to fight the Cold War if it meant curbing their lifestyles. Indeed American living standards had risen throughout the fifties and sixties. When the pie stopped growing in the next decade, cheap imports became vital—they supplied the bread and circuses that kept the American empire in business.

After 1971, successive administrations found this balancing act more difficult to sustain. Changes in global economic patterns had eroded the American government's ability simultaneously to run the Western economic system, lead the Cold War military alliance, and deliver consumer heaven to voters. Administrations needed to square the circle. An obvious solution was to curtail the U.S. consumption economy. But that would have taken a major revolution in American thought, which, as the various debates over energy policy had shown, was not forthcoming. The stagnation in U.S. incomes beginning in the seventies might have revolutionized spending habits. But Japanese and other imported goods forestalled such an unhappy turn of events. In fact the steady fall in the cost of many consumer products allowed families during these years to continue to accumulate more products while their net income stagnated or declined.

Knowledge that Japanese products supplied this safety valve added an extra dimension to Japanese-American negotiations. American officials had no trouble developing "to-do lists" for their Japanese counterparts. Such a list prepared for FRB Chairman Arthur Burns in October 1977 included Japan's relaxing quota restrictions on imports, making the Japanese market more accessible to foreign suppliers, and liberalizing the purchasing policies of government and government-related enterprises following a strict buy-Japanese policy. U.S. officials advocated these measures because "despite the removal of most formal import restrictions, the Japanese domestic market remains almost impervious to many forms of foreign competition."[49] Tokyo responded with a two-part strategy: on the surface diplomats evinced a compliant attitude, replete with promises that seemed to answer American complaints. Yet the accessibility of the Japanese market never really improved.

Ronald Reagan came to office pledged to fight the Soviet evil empire. His ardent anticommunism further cemented American relations with Japan, our faithful ally in the Pacific. Reagan's huge defense expenditures also provided a new economic nexus for the relationship. Having cut taxes and boosted defense spending, the Reagan administration depended on borrowed money to keep the federal budget afloat. Increasingly these funds came from Japanese investors who, like the Arabs during the previous decade, recycled dollars back to the United States.

In the face of a growing U.S. deficit with Japan, Reagan's Chicago-school economic principles kept him true to the trade policies of the past three decades. The administration pursued the familiar two-layered free and fair formula with the weight increasingly on the latter half. Officials participated in GATT negotiations while simultaneously opting for voluntary restraint programs that had the opposite effect. Under these accords, major trading countries agreed to limit exports of various products to each other; about one-third of American manufactured goods were covered by voluntary quotas and other quantitative restrictions.[50] During Reagan's first term negotiators reached the Third Multifiber Arrangement (MFA), which, in the *Economist*'s description, "turns the world clothing market into a large cartel." At the same time U.S. negotiators strove to cut the share of steel imports to the American market from over 30 percent to less than 20 percent, while the number of Japanese cars annually imported into the United States remained fixed at 1.8 million. The new but already imperiled American semiconductor industry became a favored child. The divided reaction to the comprehensive third agreement on semiconductors, reached in 1986, revealed the complexity of trade issues. Semiconductor producers seeking government protection were ranged against computer manufacturers and consumer groups who wanted to preserve access to low-cost Japanese supplies. The Reagan administration responded to apparent Japanese violations of the agreement with sanctions the following year.[51]

Reaganomics proved as important to Japanese-American relations as specific trade policies. FRB Chairman Paul Volcker's inflation-crushing program featuring high real interest rates drew an influx of foreign money into the United States from investors rushing to reap sizable profits at little risk. As a consequence the dollar's value against foreign currencies rose steadily. Americans went on an immense international shopping spree. Federal tax cuts further fueled the import boom and increased the federal deficit. Washington's borrowing in turn sparked further interest rate hikes. Japanese lenders invested heavily in U.S. government securities. These policies contributed in no small measure to the success of Reagan's 1984 feel-good campaign message. But his optimistic portrait concealed real costs to the American present and future. At the dollar's 1980s peak, reached on February 25, 1985, it equaled the West German DM 3.47 and Y263.05.[52] The increase in the dollar's exchange rate made American goods too expensive for foreigners. Industry and agriculture lost customers to foreign suppliers whose prices had not been affected by the dollar's rise in value. During the early eighties U.S. farmers had enjoyed record sales abroad; the dollar's rise proved painful. American producers declined to follow the Japanese model, adjusting their prices downward, and sacrificing profit for market share.[53]

Instead Washington came to their rescue. Early in Reagan's second term Washington officials decided to halt the dollar's rise. Secretary of the Treasury James Baker convened a meeting of the Group of Five—the finance ministers of the United States, Japan, West Germany, France, and Britain—in New York. On September 22, 1985, they reached the Plaza Accord, issuing a communiqué stating their intent that other currencies should rise in value against the dollar. While the ministers set no fixed rate for the dollar against the mark or yen, they agreed to spend $18 billion to drive the dollar down. These leaders reconvened in Paris, reaching the Louvre Agreement in February 1987, which adopted the principle of central rates (target currency levels), set at $1 = DM 1.85120 and $1 = Y153.50.[54] But these rates did not hold; instead the dollar/yen ratio declined by half, from $1 = Y254.2 in January 1985 to $1 = Y127.6 three years later. Officials predicted that this drop would cut both the American trade and payments deficits. Yet Japanese goods continued to pour into the country. Unlike their American counterparts Japanese businesses traded profits for continued market share, avoiding the catastrophic loss of U.S. market share that had accompanied the rise of the dollar in the first half of the eighties. Every time dollars bought fewer yen, making Japanese goods more expensive, Japanese manufacturers cut their profits to keep the dollar price of their goods stable.

But the decline in the dollar's value during the second half of the eighties had a major effect on Japanese investment policies. All of a sudden Japanese yen bought twice as many dollar-priced goods as they had before. At the same time Japanese investors who had bought U.S. Treasury notes and other dollar-denominated securities saw the yen value of their investments cut in half. Their strategy changed. Instead of investing in dollar securities, they went on a massive shopping spree. Unlike the one Americans had indulged in, Japanese investors bought flagship assets: Universal studios, CBS records, MCA entertainment, and, most memorably, Rockefeller Center. Japanese investment in the United States had grown at a breathtaking rate during the Reagan years: "foreign ownership of U.S. assets more than quadrupled from $500 billion in 1980 to $2.1 trillion in 1989, equivalent to more than six percent of U.S. wealth."[55] (That these investments came at the top of the market would not be apparent for several years.) At the same time Toyota, Nissan, and other Japanese companies built manufacturing plants in the United States.

States and localities fell all over themselves wooing these potential employers and taxpayers. Particularly in the automobile industry, workers agreed to sacrifice unions in return for new and scarce manufacturing jobs. This strategy also gave Japanese manufacturers a fallback

FIGURE 14–1
ACQUISITIONS AND NEW ESTABLISHMENTS BY JAPANESE FIRMS
Number and Value of Transactions, 1984–1990

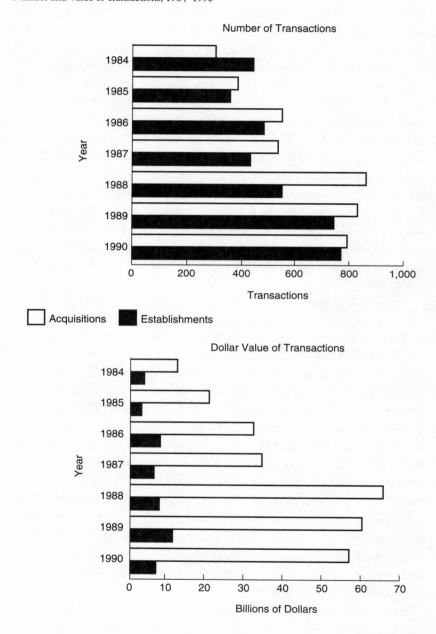

Source: U.S. Department of Commerce, *Survey of Current Business*, 71 (May 1991), p. 30.

position no matter how trade talks turned out. By producing in the United States, they would be shielded from protectionist strands in American trade policy.[56] The bidding war for Japanese investment in the United States also tempered politicians' protectionist calls; anyone wishing to lure a Japanese factory to his or her district would think twice about criticizing Tokyo too vociferously. These changes in the American scene reflected by such developments significantly contributed to the "decline" debate that swept the United States during the second half of the eighties.

Congress proved more willing to express American antagonism toward Japan. When Toshiba sold state of-the-art submarine machine tools to the Soviet Union, irate legislators smashed Toshiba radios and televisions on the steps of the Capitol. The Senate approved legislation banning various Toshiba products from the United States. Congress routinely passed resolutions threatening to impose quotas on Japanese imports unless Tokyo increased defense spending or paid a portion of American Cold War defense costs.

Against this background trade discussions continued without pause.[57] American negotiators tried to open Japanese markets to American goods while Tokyo's diplomats stalled significant U.S. penetration of Japanese markets and ducked tough U.S. legislation. Voluntary restraint agreements remained the order of the day.[58] But given the increasing friction between the two countries, not all congressional legislation could be circumvented. In 1988 Congress passed a bill targeted at Japan (although not by name). It required the U.S. trade representative to identify specific countries discriminating against American producers of goods and services and enumerate the nature of the restrictions. The trade representative was then required to seek negotiations with the offenders. If changes did not occur, the act empowered the President to limit access to the American market.

Japan loomed even larger in the changed trade universe that George Bush found himself facing. The economic barriers separating East and West collapsed. Between 1945 and 1947 Stalin had made it clear that neither the Soviet Union nor the satellite states would participate in an American-run financial order. Beginning with the Battle Act, passed under President Truman, the United States reciprocated by attempting to place an economic wall around the free world. Washington officials spent much time and energy attempting to prevent or curtail their allies' trade with Communist states as well. During periods of détente, trade between East and West would grow, only to reverse course when tensions increased. American sales of grain to the Soviet Union, for instance, rose through the 1970s, even as political issues, such as Soviet Jewish emigration, undermined trade relations.[59] Emblematic of the American approach was President Ford's observation at the Rambouillet summit of November 1975:

> the development of strong economic ties with the countries of Eastern Europe, the Soviet Union and the People's Republic of China represents an essential element in our overall policy. Close economic ties and increased trade enhance our ability to foster restraint and cooperation in the behavior of the communist countries.[60]

But when the Soviet Union invaded Afghanistan in December 1979, President Carter cut off American grain sales. These transactions had become so important to the U.S. market that when the imposition of martial law in Poland in 1981 raised the possibility of yet another American embargo of food sales to the Soviet Union, grain prices fell 10 percent within a few days. The Polish crisis led to a particularly controversial instance of American economic sanctions: the attempt of the Reagan administration in 1982 to create a secondary level of sanctions to block various Western European companies from constructing a Siberian pipeline for the Soviet Union. U.S. officials attempted to halt not only American exports of equipment and technical data but also European reexports of American products. With European governments stridently objecting to the extraterritoriality and retroactivity of American actions, it took intense negotiations before a compromise was reached.[61] Suddenly the fall of the Berlin Wall consigned these issues to the dustbin of history. Now integrating formerly Communist countries into the world economy became the top priority.

The members of the European Community had agreed, in the Single European Act of 1986 and the Maastricht Treaty of 1991, to eliminate all trade barriers within its twelve-nation boundary and form a single market while retaining trade barriers outside the community's borders. The Maastricht Treaty envisioned European monetary union by 1999 at the latest. Regional groupings suddenly became the order of the day: the North American Free Trade Agreement (NAFTA), linking Canada, the United States, and Mexico; the Asia-Pacific Economic Cooperation (APEC) summit series also included the United States. GATT negotiations continued as well. The Uruguay round, begun in 1986, focused on agricultural subsidies and the treatment of the entertainment and service industries. As manufacturing jobs fled to developing nations, the treatment of intangibles and cultural products loomed larger. The United States, with its virtual lock on mass entertainment, bitterly fought against subsidies for local film and television industries.

American trade negotiations with Japan never stopped. Many U.S. executives proved far better at beating up Japan in Congress than at besting Japanese competitors in the marketplace. Lee Iacocca, the chief executive officer of Chrysler, made lambasting Japan part of his regular patter. As Iacocca's autobiography was a best-selling nonfiction book of the 1980s, his constant criticism, verging on xenophobia, could not be ignored. Yet the pattern of Japanese-American negotiations did not change radically. Japanese leaders would promise to open their markets but then did not deliver. Protected by their network of informal restrictions, Japanese corporations continued to dominate their home markets. At the same time much of Iacocca's talk was bluster, designed to obfuscate the uncomfortable reality that Japanese carmakers generally produced better cars at a cheaper price. Conversely, had all government-imposed barriers to American sales to Japan vanished, American companies would have found it difficult to match Japanese sales in the United States. Still too complacent, few U.S. companies were prepared to put in the years of patient effort that had borne such rewards for their Japanese counterparts.[62] The Bush administration now emphasized quantitative targets for American sales in Japan. That the Japanese recession during the eighties and early nineties was more severe than the American version gave Tokyo an excuse for procrastination.[63]

At the same time the American-Japanese relationship changed in significant ways. The Cold War's end in 1989 undermined the security nexus that held the two countries together, creating new tensions. The Exon-Florio provision of the Omnibus Trade and Competitiveness Act of 1988 granted the President the authority to block foreign acquisitions of U.S. firms that threatened to impair the national security. This measure reflected concerns that foreign companies might gain control of critical technologies through acquisitions of U.S. firms. A number of legislative proposals were introduced in the 101st Congress advancing a policy of "strategic investment" that would chart a departure from the neutral policy of previous administrations. Eventually Semantech, a computer chip joint venture between the federal government and various high-tech companies received funding.[64]

The tricky negotiations between Washington and Tokyo during the Persian Gulf War provided further evidence of the changing geopolitical situation. Without really subscribing to the American decision to force Saddam Hussein from Kuwait, Japan eventually pledged $10.74 billion to Desert Shield and Storm. But this subsidy came only after congressional pressure and diplomatic arm twisting.[65] At the same time Japan pressured Bush to break his "read my lips, no new taxes" pledge. Blaming Washington for its economic woes, Tokyo pushed the United States to put its house in order. Bush gave in, partly to convince Japan to embark on the economic stimulus package that Americans hoped would increase U.S. imports to Japan.

The post–Cold War era proved unkind to Japanese-American relations. The collapse of the Liberal Democratic party, which had ruled Japan since the departure of the American occupation government, left a large vacuum. Moreover, Japanese businessmen and writers demonstrated a more hostile attitude toward the United States. *The Japan That Can Say NO: Why Japan Will Be First Among Equals* by LDP politician Shintaro Ishihara received the most press.[66] An anti-American polemic, it exuded superiority as it urged Japanese officials to end their practice of accommodating Washington. "Americans should realize that the modern era is over," preached Ishihara as he urged American businessmen to "adjust" to Japanese practices instead of complaining about them.

Some Americans wrote polemics of their own. Michael Crichton, a best-selling author whose previous book had been about dinosaurs and whose next book tackled sexual harassment, published *Rising Sun*. It featured murder and mayhem against the backdrop of Japanese contempt for Americans and continuing economic colonization of the United States. Crichton also included a bibliography of nonfiction books designed to hammer home his political and economic points.[67]

At the extreme end of Western paranoia stood Murray Sale, who wrote in the *Times Literary Supplement*:

> The Japanese are not, anymore than their island predecessors were, consciously plotting to take over the world, but they certainly have a neo-mercantilist system which could conceivably lead to that result, a system which can easily be taken for a conspiracy, especially by those on the receiving end.[68]

The Big Three automakers, suffering record losses, took their campaign against the Japanese "onslaught" to television. Pontiac dealers in New York City, for instance, ran commercials showing a picture of Rockefeller Center with a voice-over that ran: "It's December and the whole family's going to see the big Christmas Tree at Hirohito Center." If that was not sufficient, the advertisement ended with the barb, "Go on: keep buying Japanese cars."[69] Behind their bravado lay the uncomfortable realization that during the eighties Japanese car companies had successfully conquered the luxury car market, the last bastion of juicy corporate profits. Yet no media consensus on the Japanese threat coalesced. The 1990 U.S. trade deficit with Japan was $41 billion, or 16 percent lower than the 1989 figure of $49 billion. At the same time in 1989 the United States was importing $2.00 of Japanese goods for every $1.00 it exported to Japan.[70] American politicians still shied away from direct attacks on Japan, particularly since Richard Gephardt's 1988 attempt to make trade a major issue in presidential politics failed miserably. During the 1992 campaign, Bush continued to press Japan for more concessions while both he and Bill Clinton, the Democratic nominee, avoided trade questions.

Market economics, not diplomatic decisions, dampened trade disputes during the mid-nineties. The Japanese stateside buying spree of the late eighties in its own way proved as extravagant a folly as the American import orgy in the earlier part of the decade. Mitsubishi quietly unloaded MCA, Rockefeller Center went bankrupt, and Sony fired its movie moguls. The Japanese banking system teetered on the edge of collapse. Moreover, the Clinton administration's decision to allow the dollar to decline to an unrealistically low level against the yen was the equivalent of a whopping unilateral tariff on Japanese goods and accomplished the same result: it cut the Japanese trade surplus. To take one example, the Toyota Previa minivan cost $4,870 more to build than the Plymouth Grand Voyager when the yen was 80 to the dollar (its all-time low, reached in mid-1995) but $2,650 less if the dollar was worth 110.[71] (See Table 14–5.) Whether the improved U.S. balance of trade statistics were temporary remained to be seen. In the meantime the Clinton administration received a breather that put trade questions on the back burner.

Britain during its era of economic hegemony embraced free trade; during the Cold War the United States followed suit. As sixties-era Secretary of State Dean Rusk summed it up, "liberalization on a broader basis, while causing pain in some quarters, resulted in counter-vailing benefits to and support from others."[72] The United States did not need to trade—in the period 1945 to 1970, combined imports and exports averaged only 8 percent of gross national product.[73] Moreover, as long as American producers had the upper hand, it was easy to ignore specific complaints. But at the end of the 1960s the U.S. balance of trade turned from a surplus to a deficit. Domestic issues now increasingly clashed with foreign policy concerns. Diplomats sought to keep the Cold War security-financial nexus healthy while politicians oscillated between protecting producers and keeping consumers happy. Japanese relations with the United States matured against this backdrop. Each country had national goals that complemented each other: the United States sought to create the finest consumer society in history, while Japan built a mountain of trade surpluses. In fact the continuing need to provide U.S. consumers with the accoutrements of the good life, particularly when family income ceased its upward trajectory, partly explains the failure of serious protectionist measures to become American mainstream policy. (See Table 14–6.)

For the first half of the Cold War international economic questions and internal consumption priorities trumped the concerns of domestic producers. By 1971 pressure built on the White House and Congress to rescue deeply troubled American producers. Pressing Japan to change its trade practices always remained the favored option. It was consistent with free trade ideology and did not jeopardize consumers' interests. But differences in the two countries' economic and social cultures repeatedly stymied such attempts. American producers, with increasingly less justification, largely retained the arrogant approach that had alienated customers at home and abroad. Moreover, while American

TABLE 14–5
YEN/DOLLAR EXCHANGE RATE (AVERAGE JANUARY RATE)[a]

Year	Yen-to-dollar value
12/31/60	360
12/31/70	360
12/31/71	350.6775
12/31/72	303.1725
12/31/73	271.7017
12/31/74	292.0825
12/31/75	296.7875
12/31/76	296.5525
12/31/77	268.51
12/31/78	210.4417
12/31/79	219.14
12/31/80	226.7408
12/31/81	220.5358
12/31/82	249.0767
12/31/83	237.5117
12/31/84	237.5225
12/31/85	238.5358
12/31/86	168.52
12/31/87	144.6375
12/31/88	128.1517
12/31/89	137.9642
12/31/90	144.7925
12/31/91	134.7067
12/3192	126.6517
12/31/93	111.1975
12/31/94	102.2083
12/31/95	94.06
7/1/96	109.55[b]

[a]International Monetary Fund, *International Financial Statistics and International
Financial Statistics Yearbook* (Washington, various issues).
[b] Value on July 1, 1996. *New York Times*, July 2, 1996.

TABLE 14-6

UNITED STATES–JAPANESE MERCHANDISE TRADE BALANCE

(U.S. $ THOUSANDS UNTIL 1965; U.S. $ MILLIONS AFTER 1965)[a]

1945	501	1971	−3,204
1946	18,431	1972	−4,101
1947	24,672	1973	−1,333[i]
1948	260,702[b]	1974	−1,777
1949	385,529	1975	−1,862
1950	234,544	1976	−5,359
1951	392,773	1977	−8,021
1952	392,376	1978	−11,573
1953	409,014[c]	1979	−8,667
1954	400,865	1980	−9,911[j]
1955	211,141[d]	1981	−15,789
1956	343,943	1982	−16,778
1957	630,031[e]	1983	−19,289
1958	178,234	1984	−33,560
1959	−62,334	1985	−46,152
1960	181,734[f]	1986	−55,029
1961	684,647	1987	−56,326
1962	57,164	1988	−52,070
1963	199,400[g]	1989	−49,059
1964	144,559	1990	−41,105
1965	−356,628[h]	1991	−43,386
1966	−599	1992	−49,601
1967	−304	1993	−59,319
1968	−1,107/−1,100	1994	−67,320
1969	−1,398	1995	−60,600
1970	−1,223		

[a]U.S. Department of Commerce, *Statistical Abstract of the United States*, Volumes 70 (1949), 77 (1958), 79 (1958), 82 (1961), 85 (1964), 87 (1966), 90 (1969), 92 (1971), 95 (1974), 97 (1976), 102 (1981), 105 (1985), 107 (1987), 110 (1990), 114 (1994); Statistics-USA, 0496BOP.PDF
[b]Later revised to 262,009.
[c]Later revised to 403,153.
[d]Later revised to 218,988.
[e]Later revised to 637,796.
[f]Later revised to 182,074.
[g]Later revised to 216,146.
[h]Later revised to −334,000.
[i]Later revised to −1,363.
[j]Later revised to −9,924.

imports rose and fell in direct relation to economic fluctuations, Japanese imports did not.

Ironically, Nixon had sought changes in the original Bretton Woods system to enable the United States to compete more effectively in world markets. But the domestic economic deterioration he helped trigger made Americans dependent on Japanese products for their bit of the American dream. Politicians knew that their constituents had not signed on for a Cold War that required genuine sacrifice. Japan produced the items that filled the gap between high American expectations and declining reality. This nexus protected Japan from harsh American trade legislation as much as strict Cold War concerns.

But the bipolar confrontation provided the overarching reality in which the American-Japanese economic relationship thrived. Japan, whose Northern Territories remained in Soviet hands, was far nearer to Moscow than to Washington. Its looming neighbor, the People's Republic of China, possessed nuclear weapons and a huge standing army. Hampered by Article 9 of the Japanese constitution and its lack of nuclear weapons, Japan could not mount its own defense. This restriction proved fortuitous. Japanese politicians did not wish to divert their resources to military production. Its neighbors, most of which had been conquered and exploited by Japanese forces during World War II, did not want to see a large Japanese army either. The United States, which orchestrated the Western response to the Cold War challenge, willingly provided military protection as well as an economic umbrella beneath which the Japanese economic miracle occurred. In exchange Tokyo supported American external currency management, reluctantly acceding to drastic changes in the yen's valuation, and also purchased vast amounts of U.S. government securities. Japan showed no sign of coveting the burden of the world financial system. Throughout the Cold War then, Japan hid behind but also stood behind American economic leadership. Paradoxically, the Cold War had delivered the peace dividend, enabling us to have it all.

15

Conclusion

It's the economy, stupid.

Bill Clinton's 1992 campaign theme

The fall of the Berlin Wall on November 9, 1989, ushered in the greatest peaceful political cataclysm in history. The vaporizing of Eastern Europe's regimes proved that indigenous Communist parties had lost their internal backing. By 1992 the Soviet Union itself was relegated to the dustbin of history. For a brief period the United States, which had led the good fight, gloated in its position as the only superpower. President George Bush, who had successfully stage-managed the transition away from the bipolar system, repeatedly proclaimed a New World Order. Russia and the other former members of the Soviet bloc clamored to join the IMF and the European Union; Poland, the Czech Republic, and Hungary were equally insistent in their desire to become full members of NATO. For those who remembered only the Cold War, the world had turned upside down. But then came Yugoslavia: the new realities proved to be bloodier than the Cold War.

The Cold War had provided a rationale for a revolution in American foreign, economic, and social policy. Fighting the Communist threat became a total commitment. Militarily, economically, philosophically, Americans knew what to do. The beauty of the confrontation was that it gave a permeating rationale to a three-tiered set of changes in the United States that made the American half-century possible.

First, security. Before World War II most Americans believed that little abroad affected their security. The Cold War provided a weltanschauung connecting everything that happened abroad to American defense requirements: it all mattered. Cold War military requirements demanded a national security state with a standing army unprecedented in American history. The men and women would bear the best arms, devised by platoons of scientists from the best universities and legions of defense contractors. Americans did not begrudge the taxes raised to pay for this protection as they would have if presidents had suggested making social expenditures of such great magnitude. But the batteries of military bases spread out over the United States as well as the dollars disseminated through the economy via defense work provided long-term economic sustenance that in turn nurtured decades of prosperity. The prevailing ideology stamped the American dream as made in the private sector but in reality much of it was funded and focused by Washington. From the national highway system, to the expansion of universities, to aluminum foil, all had defense rationales and all were possible because the Cold War swept away ideological barriers to government spending as long as it was actually or ostensibly defense-related.

Second, domestic economics. Propagating the American dream became part of the Cold War arsenal as well. The United States promised an army second to none simultaneously with consumer heaven. Ultimately the ability of the West to beat the rest at having it all proved too much for Communist rulers. Their inability to provide guns and butter sentenced them to oblivion. Television and movies bested the forces of internal repression. The economic triumphs of one-party capitalism in Asian states such as Singapore, Taiwan, and Japan demonstrated the only viable alternative: using an expanding economy to buy off calls for genuine democracy. By contrast, the fate of European Communist regimes illustrated that bankrupt ideology combined with bankrupt economies generates a death sentence for regimes foolish enough to follow this path. China's aged leaders have apparently taken this lesson to heart. Their post–1989 strategy combined the continued suppression of human rights with a steady expansion of economic privileges for ordinary Chinese, turning that country into a gigantic version of Singapore with some copies of Marx in its bookshops.

Finally, foreign economics. For the first half of the Cold War–era the United States unquestionably dominated the Western economic order. U.S. officials embraced free trade as a means of strengthening the economies of their allies. Trade was cheaper and more ideologically acceptable than foreign aid. American imports also bolstered American consumer prosperity. Initially the price was small and the return—continuing international economic stability—well worth the cost. But as America's allies grew more prosperous, domestic support for free trade eroded. In 1971 Richard Nixon decided that the relative decline of the United States had made systemic leadership too difficult. The President was both wrong and lucky. His attempt to jettison international economic responsibility allowed Washington to retain its polar position at a reduced cost. No longer would the United States need to sacrifice to receive the benefits of a reliable international financial order as well as the particular privileges that accrue to the key currency nation: the ability to borrow from capital markets without IMF or other restrictions, the power to pile up huge deficits that could be funded internationally, the power to print money, and, most important, the ability to answer to no one.

American good fortune extended to the military sphere as well. With its allies agreed on the Communist threat but unable to provide their own defense, the United States became the unchallenged leader of the Western alliance. Its strident calls for burden sharing produced an increasing flow of funds from West Germany, Japan, and other nations. With all parties agreed on the goal, the tasks proved relatively easy to apportion. The theory of each according to his means provided the underpinnings for the division of labor within the Western alliance. While levels of Western defense commitments decreased over the course of the Cold War, the Reagan era brought a last upsurge in defense spending. The faltering Soviet Union could no longer afford to match Western defense expenditures. Every attempt at reform brought further disintegration until the nation itself disappeared.

Looking back at the Cold War, we can see clearly that all three factors—security, domestic economic policy, and foreign economic pol-

icy—were necessary for the West's triumph over the Communist challenge. Moreover, only the unique constellation of factors present
between the years 1945 and 1989 made possible America's enviable
position during the Cold War. Without the decision to fight the Cold
War, the United States could not have assembled allied financial support for American international and domestic economic decisions. The
Soviet decision to opt out, on its own and on behalf of its satellites, of
the American-constructed multilateral framework allowed Washington to dominate the Bretton Woods system and made the success of the
truncated international financial order possible. Had Stalin allowed
Communist participation, the fledgling international financial regime
would have been forced to deal with the problems of devastated
nations that would have been resistant to systemic controls and cooperation. The strain undoubtedly would have destroyed the nascent
Bretton Woods system. By making the Bretton Woods regime an American poodle, the Soviet decision also allowed the United States to guide
a unilateral wolf in multilateral sheep's clothing. Hence a triple paradox: the achievements of the American-run international financial
regime owed much to Stalin's decision to opt out from the Bretton
Woods regime. Moreover, the pressure exerted on the free world by the
existence and ongoing competition from Communist governments
tamed the excesses of capitalist economies, in the process magnifying
their attractiveness. Ultimately, the continued ability of the Bretton
Woods member nations to provide butter and guns produced the Western consumer miracle that rendered victory to the American side in
the Cold War.[1]

Without American domestic economic strength, the United States
could not have aided the West with the Marshall Plan or provided the
lure of material possessions to the East. Notwithstanding the decline in
relative U.S. economic strength, Washington presided over the birth of
the entitlement society during the second half of the Cold War. Even
better, the benefits of this win-win synergistic system were not confined
to the United States. OECD members posted the best economic results
in their histories. While the LDCs did not fare as well, the Cold War
confrontation for their hearts and minds generated more foreign aid
than will be on offer in the years to come. As the millennium
approaches U.S. leaders face the challenge of duplicating the domestic

economic results generated by the Cold War in an ideological and security vacuum while maintaining the foreign economic system that nurtured OECD domestic growth and attempted to bolster the condition
of LDCs. One conclusion: every system needs a foil—an enemy. Can
we have it all without one? Integrating the East bloc into the
post–Bretton Woods regime will only further remove the old foil. In
1946, George Kennan explained in his "long telegram" that for domestic reasons the Soviet Union needed a permanent enemy: "Soviet leaders are driven [by] necessities of their own past and present position to
put forth a dogma which [depicts] the outside world as evil, hostile and
menacing."[2] He was right—not only about the Soviet Union but about
the United States as well.

Of the three prongs of America's Cold War strategy, which was the
most important? A case can be made for economic diplomacy. It
formed the connection between military policy and OECD domestic
economic decisions. It bound together the participants in the Western
economic order and, equally important, tied them to the United States,
in the process multiplying American economic power. It allowed the
United States, alone and through its domination over ostensibly multilateral institutions, to have it all: an unprecedentedly affluent domestic
society as well as a state-of-the-art military-industrial complex.
Because the United States was the world's most important economy,
provided the world's largest market, and stood at the center of the
Bretton Woods system, its allies had to support its international economic decisions. The process worked in reverse as well—American
willingness to fill this leading position allowed other nations to enjoy
American-led prosperity, knowing that the United States had saved
them from the perils of anarchy or the risk of having to assume the burden of systemic leadership. Moreover, Washington turned the potential
burden of the NATO alliance into a benefit, using its commanding
position to offset the costs of Bretton Woods leadership and to increase
domestic prosperity. Only the United States possessed the combination
of economic and military might necessary to pull off this feat.

Economic diplomacy also played a crucial role in the institutional-
ization of the imperial presidency. Sanctions, which even if unsuccessful were widely accepted as the premier American tool of negative
economic diplomacy, were exclusively in the executive's hands until

degree of commitment and taken more painful measures to wage the conflict with the Soviet Union, the West's cause would have ultimately suffered. Sacrificing to win the Cold War would have lost the conflict because it was both the guns and the butter that won.

One lesson taught by the Cold War is clear: economic diplomacy is a superb interalliance tool but of limited immediate usefulness against the other side. It worked as the glue that held the free world together. The Bretton Woods and post–Bretton Woods orders, funded and run by the United States, provided an economic alliance that complemented and reinforced the NATO security relationship. Having two functioning reinforcing alliances gave each of them a safety net: fraying security ties received a boost from economic connections, while at other times military connections reinforced troubled economic ties. Moreover, negative economic diplomacy provided a useful method of disciplining straying allies. But economic diplomacy could never become a substitute for American military power against the Soviet Union—neither our economic carrots nor our economic sticks significantly affected the security challenge posed by the Communist bloc.

But economic diplomacy played a vital role in winning the Cold War. American economic might, the combination of butter and guns, gave us the wherewithal to win the Cold War. The American way delivered both—ultimately the Soviet system could not even match us militarily. The irony is that the Cold War itself made butter and guns possible: domestic economic prosperity basked in the light of post–World War II government spending and the economic support furnished by our allies. The national security state was not the most efficient way of injecting this continuing fiscal boost but it was the only way acceptable to the American public.

The end of the Cold War put having it all in doubt. A chain reaction set in: first came the apparent growing irrelevance of foreign policy to American politics. Next, the rapid decline in U.S. influence abroad. The lack of a consistent American response to the Yugoslavian wars of succession provided proof that no nation could or should rely on Washington. At the same time Western European nations demonstrated that they, too, were reprising their ignominious interwar-era performances, preferring appeasement to resistance. As a result the Western world lost its Cold War cohesion. The European Community (rechristened the European Union) could not produce a foreign policy and instead simply followed Germany's lead in its foreign economic decision making. At least as far as Europe was concerned, the deutsche mark began to assume the central role the dollar had hitherto occupied. The ever-strengthening yen made the same leap in the Pacific.

Incongruously, the new American insularity developed at a time of increasing U.S. overseas economic involvement. Imports and exports now exceeded 20 percent of GDP; whole product sectors could be obtained only abroad. American imports of oil stand at record levels. The globalization of foreign economic markets made traders in Singapore or Hong Kong as important to the course of the American economy as Wall Street. The choice of intervention vs. isolationism rang false in 1945; by 1995, at least economically, a decision to withdraw from the world economy was impossible. The world is connected as it has never been before. We have learned to our horror that developmental decisions made thousands of miles away can affect the air we breathe, the food we eat, the lives we lead. The destruction of the Brazilian rain forest is a timely example of the challenge developed nations face in trying to protect the environment. The legitimate aspirations of the Brazilian people to a better life can be met only in an environmentally positive fashion with the provision of foreign assistance. If this task is not accomplished, the health of American children and their children will suffer as much as that of Latin American families. It also illustrates the expansion in the scope of foreign relations—domestic developmental decisions have become the legitimate subject of international discussion.[3]

Demographic changes and immigration pose equally important challenges. Surging populations have placed growing pressure on fragile economies. Millions seek to immigrate into industrialized nations. The United States has seen its own demographics shift drastically—not since the turn of the century have so many Americans been foreign-born. During the Cold War, many who arrived in the United States sought political asylum; today's immigrants, by contrast, seek only what most Americans originally were after—a better life for themselves and their families. The challenge for the United States is to accommodate its new immigrants while helping developing nations accommodate their growing populations at home. As Soviet leaders learned to their horror, a failure to satisfy economic aspirations is fatal. Yet brittle nations such as Egypt, since 1978 a pillar of American Middle Eastern policy, are obviously unable to meet the challenge of growing urban populations and the consequent breakdown in government services. If they cannot manage to deliver the goods and services their people seek, the price will be steep—for both American economic and foreign policy.

The fall of the Soviet Union provided the comforting illusion that the United States as the only remaining superpower had no enemies and therefore was free to exempt itself from international relations. Americans would do well to heed the words of the nineteenth-century British Prime Minister Lord Palmerston: "We have no eternal allies and we have no perpetual enemies. Our interests are eternal and perpetual, and these interests it is our duty to follow." The American decision to fight the Cold War marked the recognition by U.S. leaders that the United States could no longer take an indifferent stance to the rest of the world. During the next half-century our affairs have grown steadily more intertwined with those of other nations. To protect our interests, our government has no choice but to maintain a steady degree of involvement abroad.

American chickens have been coming home to roost with a vengeance. The successful interrelationship of economic and foreign policy during the bipolar conflict masked a weakening American position. Bush thought that the successful Desert Shield and Desert Storm operations during the 1990–91 Persian Gulf War augured the era of American global leadership. He was mistaken. The United States had relied on vestigial Cold War impulses to garner financial support from Germany and Japan, as well as passivity from the People's Republic of China. Rather than being a vision of things to come, this following of the American leader was a hangover from the past. The United States would instead have to earn its leadership position by post–Cold War deeds—a challenge it has not yet successfully met.

The failure of the U.S. economy to keep up with new competitors became clear, as did the declining American investment in research and development. The chronically low American savings rate, which had dipped even lower during the 1980s, loomed as a larger problem when our allies lost their foreign policy imperatives for investing in the dollar. Concurrently the effects of the taxpayer revolt that began with California's Proposition 13 manifested themselves. With American voters unable to end their addiction to entitlements when they sliced the tax revenues available to pay for these goodies, local, state, and federal officials did the only thing guaranteed to bring short-term electoral success: they cut spending on infrastructure and unpopular programs, and borrowed or invested unwisely to keep the middle class happy. The default of California's wealthy Orange County illustrated that it had become acceptable among conservative Republicans to opt for financial shame rather than increased taxes.[4]

The results of these unsound policies became clear as the euphoria from the Cold War faded away. Great public institutions such as the University of California suffered at the same time as American bridges and roads literally crumbled. Relief was not in sight. As the 1994 midterm elections indicated, the ideological support for state-sponsored action had dwindled alarmingly. The death of communism turned the eighties predilection for free market ideology into unalloyed triumphalism, while the fall of the Communist economies removed any leftward pressure on capitalist impulses. As a result laissez-faire doctrine had the stage to itself. Formerly socialist parties such as the British Labour party jettisoned their long-standing ideological commitments and strove to prove that they were more free market than the opposition. In the United States, Democrats, having lost control of Congress for the first time in decades, scrambled to distance themselves from "big government" or indeed any government programs. Ronald Reagan promised not to remove the "safety net" under the poorest Americans; his ideological heirs gleefully cut it to shreds. Yet the free market cannot solve every ill.

The Cold War's abrupt end destroyed the synergy of the American postwar world. Domestic and foreign factors had combined to provide us with the best of all possible worlds: prosperity at home and peace abroad. The bipolar confrontation also papered over social and economic cracks in the United States. The Cold War provided an ideological web that bound Americans together at the same time as it produced a justification for concerted government domestic and foreign economic policies, and an active American strategic and military stance. We now face a vacuum similar to what we have seen twice before in this century. Both times it took a war to fill the void.

But Americans who joined the world in 1945 lacked a tradition of foreign involvement. Politically immature, we were never forced to grow up. Instead the Cold War provided easy answers to every dilemma: who was friend and who was enemy? what to do in every corner of the world? how to invest at home while avoiding the insurmountable objections that nonmilitary federal government spending generates? With the global struggle concluded, Americans confront issues they have always dodged. Finding the right answers won't be an easy task. But we bring to the search great strengths: self-sufficiency in food, abundant natural resources, enormous stocks of capital, and a strong democratic tradition. Although the United States is weaker relative to other nations than it was in 1945, it has sufficient reserves to solve the difficult problems facing it today. Josef Stalin rescued Americans fifty years ago. Can we rescue ourselves now?

Appendix

Provisions of the Declaration of the Americas

Title I of the charter set out the objectives of the program, most importantly, mandating that the rate of growth in each country in Latin America should exceed 2.5 percent per capita per year. Title II dealt with economic and social development while Title III discussed the goal of Latin American economic integration. Finally, Title IV focused on basic export commodities, most notably their trade and price. The charter's scheme included a council of "Nine Wise Men" to oversee the formulation of the economic and social programs of the alliance.[1]

Land reform, a basic need in Latin America, was not mandated but "encouraged." The declaration also included a pledge "to maintain monetary and fiscal policies that while avoiding the disastrous effects of inflation and deflation will protect the purchasing power of the many, guarantee the greatest possible price stability, and form an adequate basis for economic development." It would be impossible to meet these goals while simultaneously encouraging massive redevelopment and societal change of the sort contemplated by the rest of the declaration.

The charter noted that the United States would provide "a major part of the minimum of $20 billion, half of it in public funds, which Latin America will require over the next ten years from all external sources in order to supplement its own efforts." For their part, Latin American countries agreed to "devote a steadily increasing share of their own resources to economic and social development and to make the reforms necessary to assure that all share fully in the fruits of the Alliance for Progress." In imitation of the Marshall Plan's requirement for recipient blueprints as a precondition for American aid, each country also pledged to formulate a "comprehensive and well conceived" long-term national plan for its economic development. Unlike the Marshall Plan, these plans were to take the form of individual country efforts, not a joint Latin American submission. The group of experts known as the Committee of Nine would comment on the plans, which would then be sent to various inter-American lending institutions such as the Inter-American Development Bank, other international organizations, notably the IMF and the World Bank, and "other friendly governments," all of which would individually decided how to allocate their own assistance.[2] The catch to these fine promises was that since the charter was not a treaty, nothing contained in it was binding on any of the signatories. That so much of the funds would be in the form of loans meant that alliance recipients would be paying a heavy price for their good fortune.[3]

Notes

List of Abbreviations

B/E	Bank of England, London, England
CAB	Cabinet Papers (UK)
CEA	Council of Economic Advisors
CFR	Council on Foreign Relations
CIEP	Council on International Economic Policy
DD	Declassified Documents (Research Publications Inc., *The Declassified Documents Catalog* [Woodbridge, 1981 *et seq.*])
FO	Foreign Office
FRBNY	Federal Reserve Bank of New York
GFL	Gerald R. Ford Library, University of Michigan, Ann Arbor, Mich.
JFD	John Foster Dulles
JFKL	John F. Kennedy Library, Boston, Massachusetts
LC	Library of Congress
LBJL	Lyndon Baines Johnson Library, Austin, Texas
MRD	Mandatory Review Declassification
MRP	Mandatory Review Procedure
NA	National Archives, Washington, D.C.
N/N	National Security Files/National Security Histories
NP	Nixon Project, Alexandria, Virginia
NSF	National Security Files
NSF-Co	National Security Files–Countries
OV	Bank of England category denoting foreign affairs documents
POF	Private Office Files
PRO	Public Record Office, Kew, London, England
SD	State Department

SML   Seeley Mudd Library, Princeton University, Princeton,
                 New Jersey
TL   Harry S. Truman Library, Independence, Missouri
WHCF   White House Central Files
WHSF   White House Special Files

Chapter 1. Introduction

1. Stephen E. Ambrose, *Eisenhower: Volume II—The President* (New York, 1985), p. 612.
2. Karel Ann Marling, *As Seen on TV: The Visual Culture of Everyday Life in the 1950s* (Cambridge, 1994), pp. 244, 276.
3. David M. Potter, *People of Plenty: Economic Abundance and the American Character* (Chicago, 1954), p. 135. Potter quoted from an address to French Protestant businessmen in 1932 by André Siegfried.
4. See Alan Brinkley, *The End of Reform: New Deal Liberalism in Recession and War* (New York, 1995); Alfred E. Eckes Jr., *A Search for Solvency* (Austin, 1975); Richard N. Gardner, *Sterling-Dollar Diplomacy in Current Perspective: The Origins and Prospects of Our International Economic Order* (New York, 1980), pp. 1–23; Robert D. Schulzinger, *The Wise Men of Foreign Affairs: The History of the Council on Foreign Relations* (New York, 1984), pp. 81–112; Randall Bennett Woods, *A Changing of the Guard: Anglo-American Relations, 1941–1946* (Chapel Hill, 1990), pp. 189–91.
5. John Morton Blum, *V Was For Victory: Politics and American Culture During World War II* (New York, 1976), pp. 323–32; Brinkley, *The End of Reform*, pp. 227–64; and Woods, *A Changing of the Guard*, pp. 197–201.
6. In 1946 Congress eventually passed legislation proclaiming it to be American national policy "to attain and maintain a high level of employment, production and purchasing power." The means to these laudable goals did not include state intervention but rather featured private enterprise, business growth, and individual action. Woods, *A Changing of the Guard*, p. 206.
7. Gregory A. Fossedahl's book *Our Finest Hour: Will Clayton, the Marshall Plan and the Triumph of Democracy* (Stanford, 1993) contains an extensive account of Clayton's activities placed within the context of Washington's evolving foreign economic policy. See pp. 83–136. Also see Woods, *A Changing of the Guard*, pp. 207–9.
8. On the Anglo-American negotiations prior to the Bretton Woods agreements, see Harold James, *International Monetary Cooperation Since Bretton Woods* (Washington, 1996), pp. 27–53; D.E. Moggridge, *Maynard Keynes: An Economist's Biography* (London, 1992) pp. 670–94, 721–41; and L.S. Pressnell, *External Economic Policy Since the War: Volume I—the Post-War Financial Settlement* (London, 1988), pp. 116–57.
9. Article IV, Section 1(a) of the Articles of Agreement.
10. See Kenneth W. Dam, *The Rules of the Game: Reform and Evolution in the Inter-*

national Monetary System (Chicago, 1982), pp. 86–97. Also see James, *International Monetary Cooperation*, pp. 50–56.

11. Woods, *A Changing of the Guard*, pp. 138–43.

12. The governing structure of the IMF was complex. A country's quota determined its voting power just as a stockholder's shares determined his or her control over a corporation. Under this weighted system the United States received 31.46 percent and Britain 15.02 percent of the votes.

13. The Board of Governors of the IMF, in practice the treasury secretary or minister of finance from each nation, would normally meet only once a year. Power instead rested in the Executive Board. Only the five countries with the largest quotas would have their own executive director; smaller countries would share designated executive directors. The executive directors would then select a managing director who would be the IMF's chief executive officer. At the time of the IMF's founding, the five largest quotas belonged to the United States, Great Britain, the Soviet Union, France, and China—the nations that occupied the permanent seats of the United Nations Security Council. On the Soviet decision not to join the IMF see Harold James and Marzenna James, "The Origins of the Cold War: Some New Documents," *The Historical Journal*, 37:3 (1994):615–22.

14. The World Bank, owned by governments, would lend money for multimillion dollar capital projects. Its separate Articles of Agreement placed its authorized capital at $10 billion, only 20 percent of which would be subscribed immediately and only 2 percent of which had to be paid in gold or dollars. The World Bank was also permitted to guarantee private loans and to raise additional funds by issuing its own bonds or notes but could lend only 100 percent of its capital. While its purpose was to help ravaged nations, it would do so only on the basis of sound commercial principles and full financial disclosure. As designed, the World Bank would fulfill two needs. It would help in the process of reconstruction while making it safer for American banks to lend abroad. Dam, *The Rules of the Game*, p. 72; James, *International Monetary Cooperation*, p. 52.

15. Woods, *A Changing of the Guard*, pp. 229–30.

16. Gardner, *Sterling-Dollar Diplomacy*, pp. 129–43.

17. TL, Clayton-Thorp Papers, Box 1, Office of Information, British Supply Council, "Purpose of U.K. Reverse Lend-Lease Records," October 13, 1944.

18. PRO, FO 361/44555, Memorandum concerning meeting with Mr. Law and a Number of Congressmen, January 16, 1945.

19. Fossedahl, *Our Finest Hour*, pp. 137–49; Woods, *A Changing of the Guard*, pp. 236–38; *Time*, July 23, 1945.

20. TL, Frank McNaughton Papers, Box 7, McNaughton to Don Birmingham, June 8, 1945; Gardner, *Sterling-Dollar Diplomacy*, pp. 158–60.

21. Woods, *A Changing of the Guard*, p. 225. See also Lloyd C. Gardner, *Economic Aspects of New Deal Diplomacy* (Madison, Wisc., 1964), which covers the entire spectrum of New Deal economic diplomacy.

22. Dam, *The Rules of the Game*, p. 95.

23. Woods, *A Changing of the Guard*, pp. 144, 406.

24. The general subject of American economic diplomacy has received the most extensive treatment from members of the "Wisconsin school" of diplomatic historians. Its founder, William Appleman Williams, in *The Tragedy of Ameri-*

can Diplomacy (New York, 1959), expounded these historians' basic view: American foreign policy has been dominated by the need to make foreign markets safe for domestic producers. My own research indicates the subject is far more complicated.

Chapter 2. The Forties

1. TL, Frank McNaughton Papers, Box 7, McNaughton to Don Birmingham, April 14, 1945. On Truman's career generally, see Robert J. Donovan, *Conflict and Crisis: The Presidency of Harry S. Truman, 1945–1949* (New York, 1977) and *Tumultuous Years: The Presidency of Harry S. Truman, 1949–1953* (New York, 1982); Robert H. Ferrell, ed., *Off the Record: The Private Papers of Harry S. Truman* (New York, 1980), Roy Jenkins, *Truman* (London, 1986), David McCullough, *Truman* (New York, 1992), Harry S Truman, *Memoirs of Harry S. Truman, Volume II: 1945—Year of Decision* (New York, 1955) and *Volume II: 1946–52—Years of Trial and Hope* (New York, 1956).
2. *Life*, May 14, 1945. On American domestic conditions, see John Morton Blum, *V Was for Victory: Politics and American Culture During World War II* (New York, 1976), pp. 333–40; Joseph C. Goulden, *The Best Years 1945–1950* (New York, 1976); and John Patrick Diggins, *The Proud Decades: America in War and Peace, 1941–1960* (New York, 1988), pp. 98–102.
3. LC, Robert A. Taft Papers, Box 874, Taft to Francis Twinem, January 23, 1946.
4. *Time*, April 23, 1945, June 11, 1945; *Life*, July 23, 1945.
5. See Henry A. Wallace, *Sixty Million Jobs* (New York, 1945).
6. This analysis is drawn from Blum, *V Was for Victory*, pp. 329–32.
7. William L. O'Neill, *A Democracy at War: America's Fight at Home and Abroad in World War II* (New York, 1993), p. 94.
8. TL, President's Secretary's File, Box 160, Morgenthau to President, April 20, 1945; McNaughton Papers, Box 7, McNaughton to Birmingham, August 17, 1945.
9. Leonard Dinnerstein, *America and the Survivors of the Holocaust* (New York, 1982), p. 12; *Life*, September 3, 1945. While Congress gave State Department officials a hard time, the UNRRA deficiency proposal appropriation of $550 million, needed to complete the official commitment of $1.35 billion, won assent in October 1945.
10. Provisions for free elections had been set forth in the Declaration on Liberated Europe promulgated at Yalta. See John Lewis Gaddis, *The United States and the Origins of the Cold War 1941–1947* (New York, 1972), pp. 263–73. Concerning American policy toward the Soviet Union from 1945 to 1947 generally, see Dean Acheson, *Present at the Creation: My Years at the State Department* (New York, 1969, 1987); Gaddis, *Origins*; Melvyn P. Leffler, *A Preponderance of Power: National Security, the Truman Administration and the Cold War* (Stanford, 1992); Bradford Westerfield, *Foreign Policy and Party Politics* (New Haven, 1955).
11. Sidney Pollard, *The Development of the British Economy: 1914–1980*, 3rd ed. (London, 1983), p. 219.

12. On the Attlee government, see Kenneth O. Morgan, *Labour in Power 1945–1951* (Oxford, 1984).
13. See Gregory Fossedahl, *Our Finest Hour: Will Clayton, the Marshall Plan and the Triumph of Democracy* (Stanford, 1993); Charles L. Mee Jr., *The Marshall Plan* (New York, 1984), p. 79.
14. Author's interview with Lord Jay; D.E. Moggridge, *Maynard Keynes: An Economist's Biography* (London, 1992), p. 811.
15. See David Reynolds, *The Creation of the Anglo-American Alliance 1937–1941: A Study in Competitive Cooperation* (London, 1981), pp. 145–68, 269–80.
16. TL, Dean Acheson Papers, Box 27, Acheson discussion with Mr. Charles Bunn and Mr. Menafee, January 3, 1946.
17. *Life*, December 31, 1945, Morgan, *Labour in Power*, p. 149; Robin Edmonds, *Setting the Mould: The United States and Britain 1945–1950* (New York, 1986), p.102; PRO, FO 800/512, Churchill to Ernest Bevin, November 13, 1945.
18. These monies were allocated as follows:

IMF	$2.75 billion
IBRD	3.175 billion
Export-Import Bank	3.5 billion
Lend-Lease settlement:	
France	.575 billion
Soviet Union	.400 billion
UNRRA	2.70 billion

Source: PRO, FO 371/52950, Memorandum by Gustav Stolper, January 10, 1946.

19. *Life*, December 24, 1945.
20. LC, W. Averell Harriman Papers, Box 213, Fulbright to Harriman, April 30, 1946.
21. Ironically, the nation against which the British loan had been partially aimed, the Soviet Union, formerly had been the envisioned target of American largesse. Its devastated condition had convinced many in the United States that postwar economic aid to the Soviets would pay economic and political dividends; as *Life* magazine editorialized: "U.S. diplomacy has one strong card to play, and this is economic. . . . our economic power of persuasion can be used to generate its own propaganda." *Life*, July 30, 1945.

Giving economic aid with strings attached was standard American practice, as Britain had found out. During the war, however, many in Washington assumed that the prime benefit to the United States from any Soviet loan would be economic—dollars would pay for factory orders that would prevent U.S. unemployment from rising drastically, the specter haunting many Americans. By January 1945, as wartime optimism over the grand alliance faded, Soviet Foreign Minister Vyacheslav Molotov's request for a loan of $6 billion met with a frosty reception from the State Department, even though he linked it to a pledge of large orders of U.S. capital equipment for Soviet reconstruction. Roosevelt agreed with his advisers to table the request, hoping to use the loan as a bargaining chip at the upcoming Yalta conference. Treasury Secretary Morgenthau continued to push for a $6 billion loan without any conditions, but his position was a lonely one. Clayton expressed the general view that granting a large loan would be a mistake because the United States would "lose what appears to be the only concrete bargaining lever." By July 1945 any American loan to the Soviet Union was a dead letter. Indeed, incoming Secretary of State James F. Byrnes put Morgenthau's proposal in the State Department's "Forgotten File." See Gaddis, *Origins*, pp. 178–94. See also Robert A. Pollard, *Economic Security and the Origins of the Cold War, 1945–1950* (New York, 1985).

22. David Cannadine, ed., *Blood, Toil, Tears and Sweat: Winston Churchill's Famous Speeches* (London, 1989), p. 303. See also Martin Gilbert, *Never Despair: Winston S. Churchill 1945–1965* (London, 1988), pp. 180–220; Fraser J. Harbutt, *The Iron Curtain: Churchill, America and the Origins of the Cold War* (New York, 1986).

23. See Gaddis Smith, *American Diplomacy During the Second World War, 1941–1945* (New York, 1965).

24. Kenneth M. Jensen, ed. *Origins of the Cold War: The Novikov, Kennan and Roberts "Long Telegrams" of 1946* (Washington, 1991), pp. 30–31.

25. Hugh Thomas, *Armed Truce: The Beginnings of the Cold War 1945–1946* (New York, 1987), p.12.

26. An example of the permutation of interwar dissent into conventional wisdom is this comment from *Time* on March 10, 1947: "France's insistence upon security based on her insecure mistrust of all other nations had helped pave the way for the debacle of 1940."

27. See, e.g., PRO, CAB 128/6, Cabinet 102 (46), Conclusion of a Meeting of the Cabinet held on December 2, 1946, CAB 129/13, Germany, Memorandum by the Chancellor of the Exchequer, October 18, 1946; Alan Bullock, *Ernest Bevin: Foreign Secretary 1945–1951* (London, 1985), pp. 309–10; Jean Edward Smith, *Lucius D. Clay: An American Life* (New York, 1990), pp. 405–10. Also see Wolfram F. Hanreider, *Germany, America, Europe: Forty Years of German Foreign Policy* (New Haven, 1989), pp. 1–144 and Henry Ashby Turner, Jr., *The Two Germanies Since 1945* (New Haven, 1987), pp. 1–32.

28. Smith, *Lucius D. Clay*, pp. 388–89; Randall Woods and Howard Jones, *Dawning of the Cold War: The United States' Quest for Order* (Athens, Georgia, 1991), p. 126.

29. Goulden, *The Best Years*, p. 104.

30. See Kim McQuaid, *Big Business and Presidential Power, From FDR to Reagan* (New York, 1982), pp. 122–68; Samuel Eliot Morison and Henry Steele Commager, *The Growth of the American Republic: Volume II* (New York, 1960), p. 791.

31. TL, Clayton-Thorp Papers, Box 4, Francis Russell to Clayton, October 7, 1946, transmitting report "How Congress Voted on Foreign Policy Issues."
32. PRO, FO 371/61045, Washington to FO, No. 237, January 13, 1947; McCullogh, *Truman*, pp. 529–30.
33. Total American loans to France preceding the 1947 interim aid package equaled $1.962 million. In addition, the IBRD granted France a loan in May 1947; the United States supplied the capital for this loan. See William I. Hitchcock, "The Challenge of Recovery: The Politics and Diplomacy of Reconstruction in France, 1944–1952" (Yale University Ph.D, 1994); PRO, FO 371/61003, Roger Makins Memorandum, August 22, 1947.
34. PRO, CAB 129/17, C.P. (47) 100, March 21, 1947, "Exhaustion of Dollar Credit—Memorandum by the Chancellor of the Exchequer; TL, William L. Clayton Papers, Box 60, Clayton Memorandum, "The European Crisis," May 31, 1947.

Chapter 3. The Marshall Plan

1. *New York Times*, July 22, 1945; Jean-Pierre Rioux, *The Fourth Republic 1944–1958* (Cambridge, 1987), pp. 18–19.
2. Quote from a Policy Planning Staff report in Charles L. Mee Jr., *The Marshall Plan* (New York, 1984), p. 89.
3. Thomas G. Paterson, "The Economic Cold War: American Business and Economic Foreign Policy, 1945–1960" (Ph.d. diss., Berkeley, 1968), pp. 357–72.
4. See Clark Clifford with Richard Holbroke, *Counsel to the President* (New York, 1991), pp. 109–29.
5. Melvyn P. Leffler, *A Preponderance of Power: National Security, the Truman Administration and the Cold War* (Stanford, 1992), p. 144.
6. On Vandenberg's role, see Arthur H. Vandenberg, Jr., ed., *The Private Papers of Senator Vandenberg*, (Boston, 1952).
7. *Time*, March 10, 1947.
8. See, e.g., Dean Acheson, *Present at the Creation: My Years at the State Department* (New York, 1969, 1987), pp. 220–25; Clifford, *Counsel to the President* (New York, 1991); pp. 124–40; Joseph M. Jones, *The Fifteen Weeks (February 21–June 5, 1947)* (New York, 1955), pp. 1–198; Leffler, *A Preponderance of Power*, pp. 142–46.
9. SML, Arthur Krock Papers, Box 39, Krock memorandum, "c. March 1947."
10. SML, Allen W. Dulles Papers, Box 30, "Report on Moscow Meeting of Council of Foreign Ministers by John Foster Dulles broadcast over Columbia Network on April 29, 1947"; *New York Times*, April 29, 1947; PRO, FO 371/61054, Washington to FO, No. 2654, May 3, 1947; Forrest C. Pogue, *George C. Marshall: Statesman 1945–1959* (New York, 1987), generally and pp. 193–96.
11. Author's interview with Lord Sherfield; warnings from Europe had triggered a study by the joint State-War-Navy Coordinating Committee of possible American responses to requests for substantial military, financial, economic, or technical aid. Its interim report, delivered to Acheson on April 21, stressed

the importance of keeping areas containing strategic materials or major industrial installations in friendly hands, as well as continuing "military collaboration between the United States and foreign nations important to U.S. security." See Harriman Papers, Box 230, Minutes of General Council Meeting, March 12–13, 1947; CFR, Record of Meetings, Volume 11, Digest of a Meeting, The Honorable Herbert Hoover, April 7, 1947; B/E, OV34/14, Visit to Germany—March 1947; Robert J. Donovon, *Conflict and Crisis: The Presidency of Harry S. Truman, 1945–1948* (New York, 1977), p. 287; Pogue, *George C. Marshall*, pp. 201–10; Smith, *Lucius D. Clay*, pp. 428–30.

12. Harry S. Truman, *Memoirs: Years of Trial and Hope—Volume II* (New York, 1956), p. 112.
13. PRO, CAB 129/17, C.P. (47) 100, March 21, 1947, "Exhaustion of Dollar Credit—Memorandum by the Chancellor of the Exchequer; TL, William L. Clayton Papers, Box 60, Clayton Memorandum, "The European Crisis," May 31, 1947; Fossedahl, *Our Finest Hour*, pp. 220–34.
14. Acheson floated a trial balloon on May 8 before the Delta Council at Cleveland, Mississippi. In his address, entitled "The Requirements of Reconstruction," Acheson gave his listeners a preview of the Marshall Plan by wrapping basic economic facts in an internationalist package.
15. TL, Harry S Truman Papers, Post-Presidential Memoirs, Box 1, Acheson interview; Paul G. Hoffman Papers, Box 25, Remarks by George C. Marshall, June 5, 1947.
16. *New York Times*, May 18, 1947.
17. PRO, FO 371/62399, John Balfour to Nevile Butler, June 10, 1947. Quote is from Kennan.
18. Anna Kasten Nelson, ed., *The State Department Policy Planning Staff Papers 1947–1949, Volume 1—1947* (New York, 1983), PPS/1, May 23, 1947.
19. In this connection see, Nelson, *State Department Policy Planning Staff Papers*, PPS/13, "Resume of World Situation," November 6, 1947, "there is no reason to expect that we will be forced suddenly and violently into a major military clash with Soviet forces."
20. SML, George Kennan Papers, Box 23, Kennan Notes on the Marshall Plan, December 15, 1947.
21. Armin Rappaport, "The United States and European Integration: The First Phase," *Diplomatic History* 5:2 (Spring 1981): 123.
22. The disintegration of the Soviet Union and Yugoslavia have proved the falsity of this last assumption.
23. PRO, FO 371/62398, Washington to FO, No. 3398, June 12, 1947. See also, John Gimbel, *The Origins of the Marshall Plan* (Stanford, 1976) and Gard Hardash, "The Marshall Plan in Germany, 1948–1952," *Journal of European History* 16:3 (1987): 433–85, for accounts that focuses on the centrality of Germany.
24. TL, Bohlen Oral History. Kennan, in his TL oral history, recalled that Marshall asked for assurance that the Soviet Union would not participate. Kennan said he explained to the general that the demands of participation in a multilateral program ("the full horror of these alternatives") would prove too much for the Soviet system.
25. Scott Jackson, "Prologue to the Marshall Plan: The Origins of the American

Commitment for a European Recovery Program," *Journal of American History* 65 (March 1979): 1055; Jones, *The Fifteen Weeks*, pp. 210–14; Mee, *The Marshall Plan*, p. 79.

26. PRO, FO 371/62400, Paris to Moscow, No. 54, June 18, 1947, "European Reconstruction and the United States Offer: Report on the Secretary of State's Visit to Paris on the 17th to 19th June, 1947," June 23, 1947; Bullock, *Ernest Bevin*, pp. 405–9.

27. Marshall told Lord Inverchapel that he regretted the eponymous title because "this had stirred jealousies in certain influential quarters." PRO, FO 371/62403, Washington to FO, No. 3712, June 30, 1947. Clifford records a conversation with the president during which the latter rejected the suggestion that the plan be named the Truman Concept or Truman Plan because "the worst Republican on the Hill can vote for it if we name it after the General." Clifford, *Counsel to the President*, p. 144.

28. PRO, FO 371/62398, Washington to FO, No. 141 Remac, June 13, 1947, "Reconstruction in Europe; General Marshall's proposal," minutes dated June 16 and 17, 1947; FO 371/62402, "Aide Memoire for the Foreign Secretary," June 25, 1947; FO 371/62405, Summary Record of Meeting in the Prime Minister's Office at 10 a.m. on the 24th June."

29. PRO, FO 371/62401, Washington to FO, No. 3621, June 24, 1947; FO 371/62402, Moscow to FO, No. 1415, June 25, 1947.

30. PRO, FO 371/62403, Paris to FO, No. 583, June 28, 1947; No. 601, Paris to FO, June 30, 1947; FO 371/62404, Paris to FO, No. 627, June 3, 1947; Bullock, *Ernest Bevin*, pp. 427–32. The Russian historian M.M. Narinski attributes the Soviet walkout to Stalin's belief in the necessity of preventing the West from gaining any influence in Eastern Europe. See "*Le plan Marshall et l'Urss*" sent to the author on January 28, 1991.

31. Mee, *The Marshall Plan*, p. 136.

32. TL, Naval Aide Files, Box 21, State Department Summary of Telegrams, June 3, 1947; PRO, FO 371/62404, Paris to Brussels et al., No. 20, July 3, 1947.

33. TL, Official File, Box 1273, Truman to John D. Goodloe, Chairman, Reconstruction Finance Corporation, May 31, 1947; FO 371/61054, Washington to FO, No. 2802, May 10, 1947; No. 107 Saving, May 10, 1947; No. 118 Saving, May 26, 1947.

34. *New York Times*, May 22, 1947.

35. TL, Joseph Jones Papers, Box 2, Statement by the President, June 22, 1947; LC, Harriman Papers, Box 238, Thomas Blaisdell to Harriman, June 27, 1947.

36. Author's interview with Lord Franks; see Kim McQuaid, *Big Business and Presidential Power: From FDR to Reagan* (New York, 1982), pp. 152–55.

37. TL, WHCF, Confidential, Box 38, Memorandum for the President, June 19, 1947; FO 371/62398, Washington to FO, No. 3444, June 14, 1947; FO 371/62399, Washington to FO, No. 144 Remac and No. 3466, June 16, 1947.

38. See, e.g., TL, Jones Papers, Box 2, "Press and Radio Reaction to Secretary Marshall's Harvard Address, June 13, 1947"; Daily Summary of Opinion Developments, Department of State, June 16, 17, 18, 23, 25, 26, July 2, 1947; PRO, FO 371/61055, FO to Washington No. 130 Saving, June 22, 1947; *New York Times*, June 8, 1947.

348 NOTES

39. TL, Naval Aide Files, Box 21, State Department Summary of Telegrams, June 6, 12, 19, 30, 1947; PRO, FO 371/62402, Washington to FO, No. 3665, June 26, 1947.

40. *Life*, July 14, 1947.

41. TL, Jones Papers, Box 2, *Washington Post*, July 9, 1947, Joseph and Stewart Alsop column.

42. TL, McNaughton Papers, Box 12, McNaughton to Birmingham, July 11, 1947.

43. These last-minute decisions were clearly made under Moscow's pressure. On June 30 the Czech Commission of Ministers, appointed to consider the Marshall Plan, recommended full Czech participation, while on July 1 a Polish diplomat told his American counterpart that while the Soviet attitude would create difficulties, he believed Poland would possibly be able to cooperate, if on a limited basis. NA, SD, 840.50 Recovery/7-147, London to SD, No. 3602, July 1, 1947, Praha to SD, No. 820, July 3, 1947. Narinski, "*Le plan Marshall et l'Urss*," points out that TASS, the official Soviet news agency, transmitted a dispatch to Paris stating that Poland would not participate in the coming conference on July 7, two days before the Polish government announced this same conclusion. See also Sheldon Anderson, "Poland and the Marshall Plan," in *Diplomatic History* 15:4 (Fall 1991): 473–94.

44. *Foreign Affairs* 25 (July 1947): 566–82.

45. TL, McNaughton Papers, Box 12, McNaughton to Birmingham, July 14, 1947.

46. Herter had actually suggested the formation of a congressional committee to study European relief needs and the American ability to meet them at the beginning of the Eightieth Congress. The Truman Doctrine proposal and supplemental foreign aid bills gave impetus to his idea. Technically Herter was the vice-chairman and Charles Eaton, the chairman of the House Foreign Affairs Committee. But Eaton, "aged and ailing," never even went to Europe. In that way the power and the glory, such that it was, devolved upon Herter, a well-liked and respected congressman from Massachusetts who would end his career as Eisenhower's secretary of state. See, e.g., TL, McNaughton Papers, Box 12, McNaughton to Birmingham, October 10, 1947.

47. B/E, OV 46/3, Memorandum to Grafftey Smith and Sieppmann, August 21, 1947.

48. TL, Naval Aide Files, Box 21, SD, Summary of Telegrams, August 7, 1947.

49. LC, Harriman Papers, Box 247, Balfour to Marshall, August 5, 1947; TL, Naval Aide Files, Box 21, SD Summary of Telegrams, August 19, 1947. See also Alec Cairncross, *Years of Recovery: British Economic Policy 1945–51* (London, 1985), pp. 121–64, and Kenneth O. Morgan, *Labour in Power 1945–1951* (Oxford, 1984), pp. 330–58.

50. See, e.g., B/E, OV 45/30, Paris to FO, No. 157 Saving, July 1, 1947; Paris to FO, No. 214 Saving, August 31, 1947; Note of a Conversation with Monsieur Pierre Denis on 10th September 1947"; TL, Naval Aide Files, Box 21, SD Summary of Telegrams, September 5, 1947.

51. TL, Naval Aide Files, Box 21, SD Summary of Telegrams, August 15 and 25, 1947; NA, SD, 840.50 Recovery/8-2447, SD to Paris and Geneva, No. 3158, August 24, 1947.

52. Author's interview with Lord Franks; TL, President's Secretary's Files, Box 163, Committee of European Economic Co-Operation, Report of Financial Committee, September 8, 1947; Naval Aides Files, Box 21, SD Summary of Telegrams, September 8, 10, 1947; NA, SD, 840.50 Recovery/9-647, Paris to Secretary of State, No. 3627, September 6, 1947; PRO, FO 371/61056, Washington to FO, Nos. 4780 and 174 Saving, August 30, 1947, No. 178 Saving, September 6, 1947; FO 371/62576, Makins to Secretary of State, August 23, 1947.

53. TL, John W. Snyder Papers, Box 11, Frank Southard to Secretary, September 5, 1947; SML, Ferdinand Eberstadt Papers, Box 106, MP Chronology, p. 22.

54. See, e.g., a report from the Paris embassy that the French government had just transmitted to the United States an official communication predicting that French gold and dollar reserves would be exhausted between October 15 and October 30, and American Ambassador to Italy James Clement Dunn's account that Italy was on the verge of a financial crisis so grave that it would cause unheard of political turmoil: "Without assistance . . . the present government will fall, the end result of which could only mean the end of democracy in Italy." TL, Naval Aide Files, Box 21, SD Summary of Telegrams, September 15 and 18, 1947. Also see NA, SD, 840.50 Recovery 9/1047, Ness to Lovett giving Marshall gap estimates, September 10, 1947.

55. TL, Naval Aide Files, Box 21, SD Summary of Telegrams, October 2, 1947.

56. TL, Official File, Box 1273, Statement by the President, September 29, 1947, Box 1281, Statement by the President, September 25, 1947; Clayton-Thorp Papers, Box 4, Memorandum for the President: Special Session for Emergency Aid to Europe, September 20, 1947; SML, Eberstadt Papers, Box 106, MP Chronology, p. 26; Henry Pelling, *Britain and the Marshall Plan* (London, 1988), p. 20.

57. *Economist*, September 27, 1947.

58. See, e.g., NA, SD, 840.50/Recovery/[9-247], Carl Marcy Memorandum, September 2, 1947; TL, President's Secretary's Files, Box 87, Oscar Ewing to Truman, November 6, 1947.

59. PRO, FO 371/6105, Washington to Foreign Office, No. 199 Saving, September 29, 1947; B/E, OV 6/4, Foreign Office memorandum, "American reactions to the Paris Report" October 3, 1947; TL, McNaughton Papers, Box 12, McNaughton to Birmingham, October 3, 1947. Bevin hosted the Herter Committee on September 4 and the Senate Appropriations Committee on November 5. PRO, FO 800/514, Draft Record of Secretary of State's Meeting with Herter Committee of Congress on 4 September; Meeting between the Secretary of State and the Senate Appropriations and associated committees of the United States Congress on 5 November.

60. TL, Matthew Connelly Papers, Box 2, Cabinet Meeting, Friday, October 10, 1947; PRO, FO 371/61056, Washington to FO, No. 189 Saving, September 13, 1947; No, 5546, October 11, 1947.

61. These funds would have come from the Reconstruction Finance Corporation, Commodity Credit Corporation, and the Export-Import Bank. TL, Clifford Papers, Box 5, October 23, 1947; John W. Snyder Papers, Box 11, Southard to Snyder, September 11, 1947, Box 12, Southard to Snyder, October 22, 1947; PRO, FO 371/61056, Washington to FO, No. 5960, October 25, 1947. *New*

York Times columnist Arthur Krock lauded Truman on September 30 for adhering to the constitutional rule that Congress controlled the power of the purse, unlike his predecessor.

62. The guest list included the presidents of Harvard and Colgate Universities, the president of General Mills, the vice chairman of National City Bank, the president of the General Federation of Women's Clubs, and the secretary-treasurer of the Congress of Industrial Organizations. TL, Official File, Box 1269, "Original Guest List," October 11, 1947, Draft dated October 23, 1947, of Remarks by the President to the Group Meeting at the White House on October 27, 1947.

63. See, e.g., author's interview with Lord Franks; TL, Acheson Papers, Box 3, Patterson to Acheson, October 28, 1947, Minutes of Organizing Meeting of Committee for the Marshall Plan to Aid Europe, October 30, 1947; H.L. Oram to Acheson, November 4, 1947; Rauh to Acheson, November 21, 1947; Acheson interview, San Francisco News, November 28, 1947; Acheson Speech in Portland, Oregon, November 30, 1947; Acheson speech, Spokane, Washington, December 1, 1947; Acheson speech, Duluth, Minnesota, December 3, 1947; see also Immanuel Wexler, *The Marshall Plan Revisited: The European Recovery Program in Economic Perspective* (Westport, CT, 1983), pp. 31–34; and Michael Wala, "Selling the Marshall Plan at Home: The Committee for the Marshall Plan to Aid European Recovery," *Diplomatic History* 10:3 (Summer 1986): 247–65.

64. See, e.g., SML, Allen W. Dulles Papers, Box 221, A. Dulles speech before the Annual Congress of American Industry, December 3, 1947; A. Dulles speech before the Foreign Policy Association of Rochester, New York, December 6, 1947; JFD Papers, Box 31, J.F. Dulles speech before the British-American Parliamentary Group, (London) December 11, 1947; Box 32, Caffrey to Dulles, December 7, 1947; Box 34, Vandenberg to Dulles, July 19, 1947.

65. *New York Times*, September 25, 1947.

66. TL, Acheson Papers, Box 3, Rauh to Acheson, October 24, 1947.

67. See, e.g., NA, SD, 840.50 Recovery/12-947, Quincy Wright (University of Chicago) to the President, December 9, 1947.

68. *New York Times*, October 16, 1947.

69. Robin W. Winks, *The Marshall Plan and the American Economy* (New York, 1960), p. 29.

70. TL, Official File, Box 1273, Statements by the President, October 17 and 21, 1947; LC, Harriman Papers, Box 238, Natural Resources and Foreign Aid, Report of J.A. Krug and Committee, October 9, 1947; M.J. Meehan to Richard M. Bissell Jr., October 29, 1947, Meehan to Harriman, October 29, 1947; Box 257, Harriman to Truman submitting eponymous committee's report, November 6, 1947.

71. LC, Harriman Papers, Box 237, CEEC Aide Memoire, October 27, 1947.

72. TL, Truman Chronology, Part III, November 17, 1947; McNaughton Papers, Box 12, McNaughton to Birmingham, November 7, 1947; SML, Eberstadt Papers, Box 106, SD Press Release, No. 891, November 10, 1947.

73. TL, McNaughton Papers, McNaughton to Birmingham, November 14 and 21, 1947; PRO, FO 371/62750, Washington to FO, No. 6433, November 14, 1947.

74. NA, SD, 840.50 Recovery/12-947, SD to London, No. 2059, December 8, 1947.

75. PRO, FO 371/61057, Washington to FO, No. 7202, December 27, 1947.
76. LC, Taft Papers, Box 883, Taft to Mrs. William D. Leetch, December 31, 1947; Box 893, Taft to Frank Gannett, December 26, 1947; Taft to Atkinson, January 9, 1948; Box 900, Taft to Charles Hayes, January 13, 1948; SML, Allen Dulles Papers, Box 31, Dulles to Wisner, December 30, 1947; NA, SD, 840.50 Recovery/12-3147, Marcy to Bohlen, December 31, 1947; 840.50 Recovery/1-848, Dulles to Wisner, January 8, 1948.
77. NA, SD, 840.50 Recovery/1-748, Memorandum for the Secretary of State, January 7, 1958; SML, Eberstadt Papers, Box 106, Statement by John Foster Dulles before the Senate Foreign Relations Committee, January 20, 1948; TL, John Snyder Papers, Box 11, ERP Report No. 10, January 20, 1948; ERP Report No. 11, January 21, 1948; ERP Report No. 12, January 22, ERP Report No. 15, January 27, 1948; ERP Report No. 24, February 6, 1948; ERP Report No. 34, February 25, 1948; ERP Report No. 38, March 2, 1948; *New York Times*, February 25, 1948.
78. *Wall Street Journal*, February 9 and 12, 1948.
79. TL, Naval Aide Files Box 21, SD Summary of Telegrams, February 25, 1948; McNaughton Papers, Box 13, McNaughton to Birmingham, April 23, 1948; LC, Harriman Papers, Box 248, Memorandum for the President and the Cabinet by the Secretary of State, March 5, 1948.
80. The *Wall Street Journal* finally endorsed the Marshall Plan on March 3, 1948.
81. See, e.g., TL, McNaughton Papers, Box 12, Birmingham to McNaughton, January 17, 1948.
82. TL, WHCF-Confidential Files, Box 398, Memorandum, dated March 31, 1948, concerning press treatment of President Truman's March 17 Message to Congress; McNaughton Papers, Box 13, McNaughton to Birmingham, April 2, 1948; Records of the Democratic National Committee, Box 199, Clippings File, March 1947; *New York Times*, April 2, 1948.
83. TL, McNaughton Papers, Box 13, McNaughton to Hulburd, July 23, 1948.
84. Mee, *The Marshall Plan*, p. 249.
85. Hadley Arkes, *Bureaucracy, the Marshall Plan and the National Interest* (Princeton, 1972), pp. 141–42, 230, 279; Wexler, *The Marshall Plan Revisted*, pp. 100–101, 135.
86. Michael J. Hogan, *The Marshall Plan: American, Britain and the Reconstruction of Western Europe, 1947–1952* (Cambridge, 1987), pp. 85, 153–55; Alan S. Milward, *The Reconstruction of Western Europe: 1945–1951* (Berkeley, 1984), pp. 258–81; Gimbel, *The Origins of the Marshall Plan*. Robert A. Pollard's study, *Economic Security and the Origins of the Cold War, 1945–1950* (New York, 1985), also contains a chapter on the Marshall Plan. Biographical studies of Marshall, Acheson, and Truman contain significant information, as do memoirs by participants, most notably *Marshall Plan Days* by Charles Kindleberger, and Harry B. Price, *The Marshall Plan and its Meaning* (Ithaca, 1955). Hogan's exhaustive work contains extensive material, inter alia, on the connections between New Deal and Marshall Plan ideology and actions.
87. Paterson, "The Economic Cold War," p. 410.
88. Arkes, *Bureaucracy*, p. 245; Wexler, *The Marshall Plan Revisited*, p. 91; Winks, *The Marshall Plan*, pp. 42–43.

89. The United States and Britain agreed to French control over the Saarland and an international supervisory authority over the Ruhr, while France accepted the formation of the Federal Republic.
90. It is instructive that neither of the key 1947 Policy Planning Staff papers on the Marshall Plan delved into the question of political integration. See Nelson, PPS/1, Policy with Respect to American Aid to Europe, May 23, 1947, and PPS/4, "Certain Aspects of the European Recovery Problem from the U.S. Standpoint," July 23, 1947.
91. Franks, who became the British ambassador to the United States in 1948, articulated this sentiment in a letter to Hoffman: "Britain is a power with world-wide interests, responsibilities and commitments. Just as cooperation with the Western European Neighbors and the vigorous promotion of unity in Europe is a vital necessity for Britain, so her associations in the Commonwealth and in the Atlantic community are also vital. The foreign policy of Britain rests upon and draws strength from these vital relationships with Europe, the Commonwealth and the Atlantic community." TL, Hoffman Papers, Box 22, June 21, 1950.
92. Author's interview with Lord Franks, November 1991.
93. See, e.g., Acheson's warning of "the dangers of using terms such as 'unification' without being specific as to meaning." TL, Acheson Papers, Box 64, Memorandum of Conversation, November 3, 1949, concerning ECA Administrator Hoffman's forthcoming trip to Europe.
94. See, e.g., TL, Charles P. Kindleberger Papers, "Box 2, Criteria for Judging the OEEC/Four Year Plan," October 8, 1948; Kindleberger to Bissell and Arthur Smithies, November 8, 1948; LC, Harriman Papers, Box 271, draft cable No. 3312 to London, August 20, 1948; SD to London, No. 3312, August 20, 1948; Memorandum, August 25, 1948 (First Draft), concerning British leadership in ERP; SML, Arthur Krock Papers, Box 39, off the record press conference of Undersecretary of State Robert Lovett on October 25, 1948.
95. SML, JFD Papers, Memorandum dated April 27, 1948.
96. Rappaport, "The United States and European Integration," p. 121.
97. Hogan and Charles Kindleberger in *Marshall Plan Days* (Boston, 1987) take the view that the Marshall Plan was essential to Western European recovery, while Milward and, to a lesser extent, Charles Maier (see "American Visions and British Interests: Hogan's Marshall Plan," *Reviews in American History* 18:1 [1990]: 102–11) take the opposing stance. Hogan sums up his position by stating that "the Marshall Plan provided what Stephen A. Schucker calls a 'crucial margin' that made European self-help possible. It facilitated essential imports, eased production bottlenecks, encouraged higher rates of capital formation, and helped to suppress inflation, all of which led to gains in productivity, improvements in trade, and an era of social peace and prosperity more durable than any other in modern European history." (Hogan, *The Marshall Plan*, p. 432). Arkes also gives the Marshall Plan a sweeping endorsement: "On the strength of a remarkably wide consensus, then, the Marshall Plan stands out today as a signifi-

cant program, a successful policy, and a wise construction of the 'national interest.' It did not overpromise; the scale of expenditure was large, but the goals were modest, and the means were realistically measured. Altruism was tempered with a sober regard for self-interest, but the self ingredients were never so unreasonable as to obscure the enlightened and generous nature of what was done. Few policies, therefore, would seem to offer as many advantages for an inquiry into the theory of national interest in foreign policy" (Arkes, *Bureaucracy*, p. 4). Even Milward admits that neither France nor the Netherlands could have conjured up the same level of capital formation in the absence of American aid and that the Marshall Plan had a real effect in Austria and Germany (Milward, *The Reconstruction of Western Europe*, pp. 92, 470). Also see Gimbel, *Origins of the Marshall Plan*, and H. Price, *The Marshall Plan and its Meaning*.

98. Hogan, *The Marshall Plan*, p. 431; Herman Van Der Wee, *Prosperity and Upheaval: The World Economy 1945–1980* (London 1987), p. 44. (GNP statistics are in constant figures.)

99. PRO, CAB 129/25, Memorandum by the Secretary of State for Foreign Affairs and the Chancellor of the Exchequer, March 6, 1948; TL, Harry Price Interviews, Box 1, Interview with Robert L. Hall, November 12, 1952; Interview with Sir Leslie Rowan, November 10, 1952; Interview with Mr. Olivier Wormser, November 13, 1952.

100. TL, Price Interviews, Box 1, Interviews with Bohlen and Kennan; PRO, FO371/62405, Washington to FO, No. 3271, July 2, 1947; *New York Times*, October 13 and December 12, 1947.

101. TL, Price Interview with Robert Hall; SML, Allen W. Dulles Papers, Box 31, Jacobssen to Dulles, December 17, 1947.

102. See, *Life*, March 17, 1947, in which the editorial on the Truman Doctrine bemoans the "missing ingredient" of idealism.

103. From the fourth quarter of 1948 to the third quarter of 1949, the index of U.S. manufacturing production declined by 10 percent. See, Wexler, *The Marshall Plan Revisited*, p. 76.

104. SML, Krock Papers, Box 58, Interview between the President and the Publisher of the *New York Times*, May 8, 1948.

105. LC, Taft Papers, Box 900, Taft to Henry Hazlitt, March 5, 1949.

106. Vandenberg must have often prayed to be spared his friends. The degree of resistance to his ideas in the Republican party is summed up by the fact that Carroll Reece, the chairman of the Republican National Committee, denounced the 1947 special session of Congress because it represented a succumbing by the president to the "dictates of the radical fringe of the Democratic party." *New York Times*, November 4, 1947.

107. LC, Harriman Papers, Box 338, Harriman to Marny and Clark Clifford, June 19, 1953.

108. See Wexler, *The Marshall Plan Revisited*, p. 251. "The provision of such resources, at a relatively small real cost to the United States, may thus be regarded as the key contribution of the Marshall Plan to Eruope's industrial recovery." Also see Winks, *The Marshall Plan*, pp. 29–31.

Chapter 4. The Fifties

1. Stephen E. Ambrose, *Eisenhower: Volume I—Soldier, General of the Army, President-Elect, 1890–1952* (New York, 1985), p. 41.

2. Randall B. Wood and Howard Jones, *Dawning of the Cold War: The United States' Quest for Order* (Athens, 1991), pp. 251–54.

3. See John Lewis Gaddis, *Strategies of Containment: A Critical Appraisal of Postwar American National Security Policy* (New York, 1982); pp. 89–126, Melvyn P. Leffler, *A Preponderance of Power: National Security, the Truman Administration, and the Cold War* (Stanford, 1992), pp. 312–97, and Woods and Jones, *Dawning of the Cold War*, p. 154.

4. Vladimir Tchikov and Gary Kern, *Comment Staline a volé la bombe atomique aux américains: Dossiers KGB No. 13676* (Paris, 1996).

5. The collapse of the Soviet Union has led to the opening of the archives of the Communist Party of the United States (CPUSA). These documents have shed new light on the activities of American Communists in the years prior to 1945. See Harvey Klehr, John Earl Haynes, and Fridrikh Igorevich Firsov, *The Secret World of American Communism* (New Haven, 1995).

6. On McCarthyism, see, e.g., David Caute, *The Great Fear: The Anti-Communist Purge Under Truman and Eisenhower* (New York, 1978); John Patrick Diggins, *The Proud Decades: America in War and Peace, 1941–1960* (New York, 1988); Richard M. Fried, *Nightmare in Red: The McCarthy Era in Perspective* (New York, 1990); and David Oshinsky, *A Conspiracy So Immense: The World of Joe McCarthy* (New York, 1983).

7. Concerning the domestic debate occasioned by Truman's firing of MacArthur, see David Halberstam, *The Fifties* (New York, 1993), pp. 114–15.

8. Diggins, *The Proud Decades*, p. 179.

9. On Eisenhower's career see his own memoirs, *The White House Years: Mandate for Change, 1953–1956* (New York, 1963) and *The White House Years, Waging Peace, 1956–1961* (New York, 1965); Ambrose, *Eisenhower: Volume I* and *Eisenhower: Volume II—The President* (New York, 1985); Peter G. Boyle, ed., *The Churchill-Eisenhower Correspondence* (Chapel Hill, 1990); Piers Brendon, *Ike: His Life and Times* (New York, 1986); Robert A. Divine, *Eisenhower and the Cold War* (New York, 1981); Gaddis, *Strategies*, pp. 127–63; Fred I. Greenstein, *The Hidden-Hand Presidency: Eisenhower as Leader* (New York, 1982); and Herbert S. Parmet, *Eisenhower and the American Crusades* (New York, 1972).

10. On the career of John Foster Dulles, see Townsend Hoopes, *The Devil and John Foster Dulles* (New York, 1973); Richard H. Immerman, ed., *John Foster Dulles and the Diplomacy of the Cold War* (Princeton, 1990); Hans J. Morgenthau, "John Foster Dulles," in Norman A. Graebner, ed., *An Uncertain Tradition: American Secretaries of State in the Twentieth Century* (New York, 1961); and Ronald Prussen, *John Foster Dulles: The Road to Power, 1882–1952* (New York, 1982).

11. John Foster Dulles, quoted in Walter LeFeber, *The American Age: United States Foreign Policy at Home and Abroad Since 1750* (New York, 1989), p. 514.

12. For the effect of Cold War tensions on American popular culture, see Paul Boyer, *By the Bomb's Early Light: American Thought and Culture at the Dawn of*

the Atomic Age (New York, 1985); Douglas T. Miller and Marion Nowak, The Fifties: The Way We Really Were (Garden City, 1977), pp. 43–83.

13. Gaddis, Strategies, pp. 127–36.

14. Ambrose, Volume II, p. 612.

15. Ann Markusen and Joel Yudken, Dismantling the Cold War Economy (New York, 1992), pp. 52, 175.

16. As Galbraith continues, "No politician, regardless of formal party identification, could have it said that he or she was 'soft on Communism.' Given the need to avoid such a calumny and aware that military power was central to an effective resistance, he or she could not safely vote against appropriations for the military establishment or its weaponry. That in turn was to be 'soft on defense.'" John Kenneth Galbraith, The Culture of Contentment (Boston, 1992), p. 125.

17. On Americans' love affair with the car, see Karal Ann Marling, As Seen on TV: The Visual Culture of Everyday Life in the 1950s (Cambridge, 1994), pp. 128–62, and Miller and Nowak, The Fifties, pp. 139–43.

18. See Diggins, The Proud Decades, p. 183, and Kenneth T. Jackson, Crabgrass Frontier: The Suburbanization of the United States (New York, 1985).

19. Concerning American economic prosperity during the 1950s, see Diggins, The Proud Decades, pp. 177–88; Jeffrey Hart, When the Going Was Good! American Life in the Fifties (New York, 1982); Miller and Nowak, The Fifties, pp. 106–26; and William O'Neill, American High: The Years of Confidence 1945–1960 (New York, 1986).

20. John Kenneth Galbraith, The Affluent Society (Boston, 1958).

21. David Halberstam, The Reckoning (New York, 1986), p. 247.

22. Diggins, The Proud Decades, pp. 320–21.

23. Ibid., p. 321.

24. B/E, OV31/61, "The United States—1958", April 22, 1958.

25. Ambrose, Volume II, p. 313.

26. U.S. Department of Commerce, Bureau of the Census, Historical Abstracts of the United States, Colonial Times to 1970 (Washington, 1975), p. 1116.

27. Diggins, The Proud Decades, p. 336; Marc Trachtenberg, History and Strategy (Princeton, 1991), pp. 169–234.

Chapter 5. The Suez Crisis

1. Bernard Porter, The Lion's Share: A Short History of British Imperialism, 1850-1983, 2d ed. (London, 1984), generally and p. 320. On Britain's Middle-Eastern Empire in the postwar period, see Lawrence James, The Rise and Fall of the British Empire (London, 1994), pp. 525–629; Wm. Roger Louis, The British Empire in the Middle East 1945–1951: Arab Nationalism, the United States and Postwar Imperialism (Oxford, 1985); David Reynolds, Britannia Overruled: British Policy and World Power in the Twentieth Century (London, 1991), pp. 173–237.

2. Louis, The British Empire, p. 3. On Eden's career, see Anthony Eden, Full Circle: The Memoirs of Anthony Eden (London, 1960), David Carleton, Anthony

Eden (London, 1981), and Robert Rhodes James, *Anthony Eden* (London, 1986).

3. SML, JFD Papers, Personal Papers, Box 87, State Department Press Statement No. 594, October 19, 1954.

4. See, e.g., Keith Kyle, *Suez* (New York, 1991), pp. 70–72; Evelyn Schuckburgh, *Descent to Suez: Diaries 1951–1956* (London, 1986), pp. 242–315; Shimon Shamir, "The Collapse of Project Alpha", in Wm. Roger Louis and Roger Owen, eds., *Suez 1956: The Crisis and its Consequences* (Oxford, 1989).

5. Keith Kyle, *Suez* (New York, 1991), p. 52.

6. Jehan Sadat, *A Woman of Egypt* (New York, 1987), p. 153.

7. Ibid., p. 156.

8. Abba Eban, *An Autobiography* (New York, 1977), pp. 169–74.

9. B/E, OV 43/62, FO to Washington, Nos. 4813 and 4815, October 20, 1955. On Macmillan see, Alistair Horne, *Macmillan 1894–1956—Volume 1 of the Official Biography* (London, 1988) and *Macmillan 1957–1986—Volume II of the Official Biography* (London, 1989); Richard Lamb, *The Macmillan Years 1957–1963: The Emerging Truth* (London, 1995); and Harold Macmillan, *Tides of Fortune 1945–1955* (London, 1969) and *Riding the Storm 1956–1959* (London, 1971).

10. PRO, T 236/4270, Washington to FO, No. 2960, December 5, 1955.

11. *Foreign Relations of the United States, 1955–1957, Volume XIV, Arab-Israeli Dispute 1955* (Washington, 1989), No. 461, Telegram from the Department of State to the Embassy in Egypt, pp. 868–70, December 16, 1955. Keith Wheelock, *Nasser's New Egypt: A Critical Analysis* (Westport, 1960), pp. 173–86.

12. DD, 1981-581B, "Eden Talks," January 30, 1956, 2:15 p.m., DD, 1981-582A, State Department, "Eden Talks," January 30, 1956, 4:00 p.p., DD, 1981-585B, State Department, "Eden Talks," February 1, 1956.

13. Shamir, "The Collapse of Project Alpha," in Louis and Owen, *Suez 1956*, p. 80.

14. EL, Ann Whitman File, Box 13, Memorandum dated March 13, 1956, concerning conversation with Anderson, March 12, 1956.

15. NA, SD, 874.2614/3-1756, Mutual Security Appropriations Bill 1956, Senate Report to Accompany HR 1230.

16. PRO, FO 371/119056, Washington to Foreign Office, No.1545, July 19, 1956; NA, SD, 874.2614/7-1956, Memorandum of Meeting with Sir Roger Makins, July 19, 1956.

17. NA, SD, 874.2614/7-1956, Memorandum of Conversation, July 19, 1956.

18. PRO, FO 371/119056, Washington to FO, No. 1545, July 19, 1956; NA, SD, 874.2614/7-1956, Memorandum of Meeting with Sir Roger Makins, July 19, 1956.

19. NA, SD, 774.5 MSP/7-2256, William Rountree to Hoover, July 25, 1956; 874.2614/7-2556, Memorandum of Conversation concerning Aswan, July 25, 1956.

20. Author's interview with Sir David Dilks.

21. See, e.g., PRO, FO 371/119069, Wylie to Watson, February 29, 1956; FO 371/119073, Suez Company General Letter, January 26, 1956; FO 371/119045, "Suez Canal: Future Policy," draft, March 9, 1956.

22. Egyptian officials maintained that the revenues exceeded the larger number; not surprisingly Canal Company figures, used for calculating payments due to the Egyptian government, hovered below the lower figure. See John J. McCloy Papers, Amherst College, Amherst, Massachusetts, SC1/19, Spofford to Rosen, December 28, 1956.

23. *Foreign Relations of the United States, 1955–1957, Volume XV, Arab-Israeli Dispute, January 1–July 26, 1956* (Washington, D.C., 1989), No. 511; Cairo to SD, No. 146, pp. 906–8, July 26, 1956; Mohammed H. Heikal, *Cutting the Lion's Tail: Suez Through Egyptian Eyes* (London, 1986), pp.119–29; Mahmoud Fawzi, *Suez 1956: An Egyptian Perspective* (London, n.d.), pp. 33–46.

24. See, James, *The Rise and Fall of the British Empire*, pp. 578–79; PRO, CAB 128/30, CM, 54 (56), July 27, 1956; NA, SD, 974.7501/7-2756, London to SD, No. 481, July 27, 1956.

25. PRO, FO 371/119106, "Summary Record of the Tripartite Conference Held in London from July 29, 1956 to August 2, 1956."

26. *Foreign Relations of the United States, 1955–1957, Volume XVI, Suez Crisis, July 26–December 31, 1956,* (Washington, D.C., 1990), 34:62–68, Memorandum of a Conference with the President, July 31, 1956.

27. *FRUS, Volume XVI,* No. 35, Eisenhower to Eden, pp. 69–71, July 31, 1956.

28. Since "disgorge" is a standard legal term that means to force a malfeasor to return ill-gotten gains, Dulles's use of it did not necessarily imply a belligerent intent. But the secretary of state knew that his words gave solid grounds for British and French diplomats to infer a bellicose implication.

29. See *FRUS, Volume XVI,* 41:94–97, Memorandum of a Conversation, British Foreign Office, August 1, 1956.

30. The Treasury and Bank of England were able to move with alacrity because the groundwork for the Egyptian sanctions had been laid in the spring. See, PRO, T 231/715, Memorandum for Sir Leslie Rowan, July 27, 1956; B/E 3/356, Rickett to Hawker, April 11, 1956, "Use of Exchange Control Powers Against Egypt; "Blocking Powers," April 11, 1956; "Egypt," April 1956. For information on French sanctions see, B/E, OV 45/44, "Egypt," October 24, 1956.

31. FRBNY, C. 260.2, Federal Reserve Bank of New York, Fiscal Agent of the United States, Egyptian Assets Control Regulations, Circular No. 4354, July 31, 1956; NA, SD, 974.7301/82256, Arnold to Chief, International Financial Division, August 22, 1956; NA, SD, Lot File 62 D 11, Box 7, Arnold Memorandum of Files, August 13, 1956; SD, 974.7301/8-11576, SD to Oslo, No. 201, August 11, 1956; PRO, T 236/4635, Washington to FO, No. 1709, August 14, 1956; DD 1980-109A, Staff Notes No. 11, August 25, 1956; SD, 774.5-MSP/9-1956, SD to Cairo, No. 403, August 16, 1956; 774.5-MSP/9-1956, Rountree to Hoover, September 19, 1956; *FRUS, Volume XVI,* 34:62–68, Memorandum of a Conference with the President, pp. 62–68, July 31, 1956.

32. EL, White House Office, NSC, Office of National Security Advisor, Box 9, Intelligence Report No. 7312, "Possible Effects of Economic Sanctions on the Egyptian Economy," p. ii.

33. FRUS, Volume XVI, No. 151, "Memorandum of Conversation Between the President and the Secretary of State, pp. 334–35, August 30, 1956."

34. NA, SD, 974.7301/9-756, Memorandum of Conversation, September 7, 1956; 974.7301;9-8567, Memorandum of Conversation, September 8, 1956, 974.7301/9-956, Memorandum of Conversation, September 9, 1956.

35. See, e.g., FRUS, Volume XVI, No. 29, Memorandum of a Conversation, Department of State, pp. 50–53, July 30, 1956, No. 60; Memorandum from the Secretary of State's Special Assistant to the Secretary of State, August 4, 1956, No. 267. Memorandum of a Conversation, Department of State, pp. 582–83, September 26, 1956.

36. See Mordechai Bar-On, "David Ben-Gurion and the Sèvres Collusion," in Louis and Owen, Suez 1956, Selwyn Ilan Troen, "The Sinai Campaign as a 'War of No Alternative': Ben-Gurion's View of the Israel-Egyptian Conflict," pp. 297–99, in S.I. Troen and M. Shemesh, eds., The Suez-Sinai Crisis 1956: Retrospective and Reappraisal (London, 1990).

37. The best account of the Sèvres meeting is found in Mordechai Bar-On, The Gates of Gaza: Israel's Road to Suez and Back, 1955–1957 (London, 1994). Bar-On participated in the meetings. See also David Schoenbaum, The United States and the State of Israel (New York, 1993), pp. 107–13.

38. It was not that the U.S. government had not been clear about its views. After August 30, Eisenhower and Dulles repeatedly warned British and French officials that, in Dulles's words, "the use of force . . . would be a fatal mistake."

39. FRUS, Volume XVI, No. 419: Memorandum of a Conference with the President, White House, pp. 851–55, October 30, 1956.

40. SML, JFD Papers, Dulles Oral History Collection, Dwight D. Eisenhower interview.

41. SML, JFD Papers, JFD/DDE, Telephone Conversations Box 5, Telephone Conversation from the vice-president in Detroit, October 31, 1956.

42. International Financial Statistics, Volume 12, No. 5, May 1960, pp. 250–51.

43. B/E, G 1/124, "Sterling and the Suez Canal Situation," August 1, 1956.

44. Financial Times, October 3, 1956.

45. B/E, G 1/114, Rickett, "Emergency Action," November 2, 1956.

46. Alistair Horne, Macmillan, Volume 1, p. 440; Anthony Howard, RAB: The Life of R. A. Butler (London, 1987), p. 237, and Selwyn Lloyd, Suez: 1956 (London, 1986), pp. 210–11.

47. See Horne, Volume 1, pp. 440–45; Diane B. Kunz, The Economic Diplomacy of the Suez Crisis (Chapel Hill, N.C., 1991), pp. 131–33.

48. Kunz, The Economic Diplomacy of the Suez Crisis, p. 132.

49. NA, SD, 841.10/2-1857, Jordan-Moss to Lister, February 18, 1957, United Kingdom Treasury and Supply Delegation listing of sterling assets.

50. EL, Ann Whitman File, Eisenhower Diaries, Box 19, Memorandum of Conversation with the President, October 30, 1956.

51. By virtue of the invasion arrangements, once the British government decided to leave Egypt, French forces could only follow. Economic pressure played lit-

tle part in this decision. As the franc was not convertible, holders could not sell it for other currencies. The franc had indeed been overvalued and weak for years. The governor of the Bank of France, Wilfred Baumgartner, had solicited British interest in a joint devaluation of franc and pound during early 1956. If American pressure now forced this unhappy move, so much the better. Moreover, on October 17 the French government had borrowed $262.5 million (its maximum possible drawing) from the IMF. Thus fortified economically and psychologically, France could easily withstand economic pressure.

52. FRBNY, 798.3, "Memorandum to the Files: United Kingdom: Use of [IMF] Fund's Resources," December 11, 1956; B/E, OV 31/55, Washington to FO, No. 26 remac, December 20, 1956; OV 31/57, F.J. Portsmore, "Present Position on Exim Loan and Waiver," March 19, 1957.

53. SML, JFD Personal Papers, Box 104, W. Randolph Burgess to Dulles, December 7, 1956, enclosing draft speech to be delivered by Humphrey on December 8, 1956.

54. Ambrose, *Volume II*, p. 382.

55. SML, JFD Papers, JFD/DDE, Telephone Conversations, Box 6, Telephone call to Mr. Bowie, January 12, 1957.

56. John Hollister, head of the main American vehicle for foreign aid, the International Cooperation Administration, had immediately suspended all aid to Israel upon hearing of the invasion. The State Department rescinded this edict but in December the administration worked out this official position: there would be no formal suspension of aid but "every effort" would be made "to slow down the implementation" of fiscal 1956 aid while at the same time fiscal 1957 program approval would not be forthcoming. See NA, SD, Lot File 62 D ll, Hollister to Dulles, October 31, 1956; *FRUS, Volume XVI*, No. 632, Memorandum from the Regional Director of the Office of European Operations, International Cooperation Administration to the Deputy Director for Operations, pp. 1236–38, December 3, 1956.

57. *Time*, November 11, 1956.

58. Kyle, *Suez*, p. 538.

59. JFD Papers, JFD/DDE, Telephone Conversations Box 6, Telephone Calls to Dr. Roswell Barnes, February 19 and 22, 1957, Telephone Call to Dr. Edward Elson, February 22, 1957.

60. EL, AW, Eisenhower Diaries, Box 21, Bipartisan Legislative Meeting, February 20, 1957.

61. SML, JFD Papers, JFD/DDE, Telephone Conversations, Box 6, Telephone Call to Lodge, February 12, 1957.

62. On the Israeli-French relationship diuring the Suez crisis, see Michael Fry and Miles Hochstein, "The Forgotten Middle Eastern Crisis of 1957: Gaza and Sharm-el-Sheikh," *International History Review* 24 (February 1993): 46–83.

63. See Albert Hourani, A *History of the Arab Peoples* (Cambridge, 1991), pp. 401–15.

64. British forces simultaneously landed in Jordan.

65. This last action particularly galled the British government, but it could not stop the transfer without jeopardizing sterling's status as a reserve and trading currency.

66. SML, JFD Papers, JFD/DDE, Telephone Conversations, Box 6, Telephone Call to Lodge, February 24, 1957.

Chapter 6. The Sixties

1. John Patrick Diggins, *The Proud Decades: America in War and Peace, 1941–1960* (New York, 1989), p. 312–16; David Halberstam, *The Fifties* (New York, 1993), pp. 623–28.
2. Ibid., pp. 625–26.
3. Stephen E. Ambrose, *Eisenhower: The President, Volume II* (New York, 1985), pp. 541–42; Paul A. Krugman, "The Myths of Asia's Miracle," *Foreign Affairs* 73:5 (November/December 1994): 65.
4. William H. Chafe, *The Unfinished Journey: America Since World War II* (New York, 1986), p. 193.
5. The exception was 1957, when the Suez crisis sparked a flight into U.S. dollars. A multitude of factors caused the amount of dollars spent abroad by the U.S. government and people to exceed the amount that foreign governments and populations spent in the United States. Defense expenditures played a very important role in the outflow of American dollars, as did foreign aid. Foreign corporate borrowings in the United States further increased the U.S. balance of payments deficit. Every time an American company built a factory abroad or acquired a foreign subsidiary, the U.S. balance of payments deteriorated. Once the factory came onstream and generated income, its foreign currency earnings paid to its American corporate parent would reduce the American balance of payments. Unfortunately during the 1960s the start-up costs of overseas American plants exceeded their revenues. After the midpoint of the decade expenditures of U.S. citizens traveling abroad significantly contributed to the U.S. balance of payments deficit.
6. In December 1958 the European Monetary Agreement signed by various Western European nations came into effect, generally restoring convertibility. All settlements between members now had to be in convertible currencies or gold. The member nations also created a fund for the financing of temporary balance of payments difficulties. Various nations, however, still maintained exchange control restrictions. Most European currencies as well had the protection of the transitional clause of Article XIV of the IMF Articles of Agreement; in February 1961 they renounced this intermediate stage and accepted the full convertibility requirements of Article VIII. See Richard T. Griffiths, "'Two Souls, One Thought?': The EEC, the USA and the Management of the International Monetary System," in D. Brinkley, R.T. Griffiths, and S. Ward, eds., *Kennedy and Europe* (New Haven, 1995), p. 236.
7. See Robert Triffin, *Gold and the Dollar Crisis*, rev. ed. (New Haven, 1961).
8. See Table 6–1.
9. Griffiths, "'Two Souls, One Thought?'" in Brinkley, Griffiths, and Ward, *Kennedy and Europe*, p. 233.
10. Author's interview with Robert V. Roosa; Robert V. Roosa, *The Dollar and*

World Liquidity (New York, 1976), Appendix 2, "A Statement by Senator John F. Kennedy on the Balance of Payments," October 31, 1960, p. 268; author's interview with James Tobin.

11. On Kennedy's foreign policy generally, see John Morton Blum, *Years of Discord: American Politics and Society* (New York, 1991); Diane B. Kunz, ed., *The Diplomacy of the Crucial Decade: American Foreign Relations During the Nineteen Sixties* (New York, 1994); Thomas G. Paterson, ed., *Kennedy's Quest for Victory: American Foreign Policy, 1961–1963* (New York, 1989); Richard Reeves, *President Kennedy: Profile of Power* (New York, 1993); Theodore Sorenson, *Kennedy* (New York, 1965); Arthur Schlesinger, Jr., *A Thousand Days: John F. Kennedy in the White House* (New York, 1965).

12. Blum, *Years of Discord*, p. 55.

13. Private interview of the author.

14. Allen J. Matusow, *The Unraveling of America: A History of Liberalism in the 1960s* (New York, 1984), p. 40; Schlesinger, *A Thousand Days*, pp. 584–85.

15. Raburn McFetridge Williams, *The Politics of Boom and Bust in Twentieth Century America: A Macroeconomic History* (Minneapolis/St. Paul, 1994), pp. 325–26.

16. Schlesinger, *A Thousand Days*, pp. 583–90, 592–99; Matusow, *The Unraveling of America*, pp. 39-56.

17. U.S. Department of Commerce, Bureau of the Census, *Historical Statistics of the United States, Colonial Times to 1970* (Washington, D.C., 1975), p. 1116.

18. See, e.g., John F. Kennedy Library, Boston, Massachusetts, Council of Economic Advisors Oral History; author's interview with Raymond Bonham Carter.

19. The shares of the various European countries were calculated pursuant to agreed upon quotas.

20. Switzerland later joined but the group remained known as the G-10.

21. Kenneth W. Dam, *The Rules of the Game: Reform and Evolution in the International Monetary System* (Chicago, 1982), pp. 137–38; Paul Volcker and Toyoo Gyohten, *Changing Fortunes: The World's Money and the Threat to American Monetary Leadership* (New York, 1992), pp. 20–38.

22. See, e.g., JFKL, NSF, Box 325, Bator, "Draft Sketch of a U.S. Negotiating Position at DAG," March 14, 1961; Box 297A, Komer Memorandum for the President, March 2, 1963; *Foreign Relations of the United States, 1961–1963, Volume IX, Foreign Economic Policy* (Washington, 1995), No. 14, National Security Action Memorandum No. 171, pp. 25–26, July 16, 1962, No. 153, Memorandum of Conversation, pp. 329–34, September 26, 1962.

23. Charles A. Coombs, *The Arena of International Finance* (New York, 1976), pp. 174–75; Griffiths, "'Two Souls, One Thought?'" in Brinkley, Griffiths, and Ward, *Kennedy and Europe*, pp. 234–40.

24. GATT, the General Agreement on Tariffs and Trade, is a specialized agency of the United Nations that provides a mechanism for international tariff negotiations.

25. William S. Borden, "Defending Hegemony: American Foreign Economic Policy", in Paterson, *Kennedy's Quest for Victory*, p. 69. See also David P. Calleo, "Since 1961: American Power in a New World Economy," in William H. Becker and Samuel F. Wells Jr., *Economics and World Power: An Assessment of*

American Diplomacy Since 1789 (New York, 1984), pp. 406–407; Thomas W. Zeiler, *American Trade and Power in the 1960's* (New York, 1992).

26. For an exhaustive account of the TEA, see Zeiler, *American Trade and Power*.

27. For a full treatment of free and fair trade, see Chapter 14.

28. TL, Dean Acheson Papers, State Department and White House, Memorandum on Gold Agreement Proposal, July 24, 1962; Turpin to Ball with enclosures, August 17, 1962; JFKL, Gordon Papers, Box 32, Coppock to Gordon with enclosures, August 10, 1962. (Courtesy of Marc Trachtenberg.); *FRUS, Volume IX*, No. 57, Memorandum From the Chairman of the Council of Economic Advisors (Heller) to President Kennedy, pp. 138–41, August 9, 1962, No. 58, Memorandum from President Kennedy to Secretary of the Treasury Dillon and the Under Secretary of State (Ball), pp. 141–43, August 24, 1962; Griffiths, "'Two Souls, One Thought?'" in Brinkley, Griffiths, and Ward, *Kennedy and Europe*, pp. 247–49.

29. *FRUS, Volume IX*, No. 19, Memorandum from the President's Deputy Special Assistant for National Security Affairs (Kaysen) to the President's Special Assistant for National Security Affairs (Bundy), pp. 43–44, January 21, 1963; No. 20, Memorandum for the Record, pp. 45–47, February 26, 1963; No, 22, Memorandum from President Kennedy to the Cabinet Committee on Balance of Payments, pp. 49–50, March 2, 1963.

30. *FRUS, Volume IX*, No. 31, Letter from John Kenneth Galbraith to President Kennedy, pp. 77–78, August 28, 1963. JFKL, POF Box 90, Tobin to President, September 11, 1963.

31. *New York Times*, September 30, 1963.

32. *FRUS, Volume XI*, No. 76, Circular Telegram from the Department of State to Certain Diplomatic Missions, pp. 178–79, July 17, 1963.

33. Lyndon Baines Johnson, *The Vantage Point: Perspectives of the Presidency 1963–1969* (New York, 1971), generally and p. 71. Also see Blum, *Years of Discord*; Robert A. Caro, *The Years of Lyndon Johnson, Volume I: The Path to Power* (New York, 1981) and *Volume II: The Means of Ascent* (New York, 1990); Paul K. Conkin, *Big Daddy From the Pedernales* (Boston, 1986); Robert Dallek, *Lone Star Rising: Lyndon Johnson and his Times 1908–1960* (New York, 1991); Robert A. Divine, ed., *The Johnson Years: Three Volumes* (Lawrence, 1987); Kunz, *The Diplomacy of the Crucial Decade*.

34. Johnson failed to follow the Kennedy administration attempt to marry tax reduction with tax reform, which would reduce the many tax loopholes. See Blum, *Years of Discord*, pp. 61–63; Williams, *The Politics of Boom and Bust*, p. 329.

35. Blum, *Years of Discord*, p. 144; Chafe, *The Unfinished Journey*, p. 193.

36. Stuart Bruchey, *The Wealth of the Nation: An Economic History of the United States* (New York, 1988), p. 193.

37. Matusow, *The Unraveling of America*, pp. 57–60.

38. *Historical Statistics of the United States: Colonial Times to 1970*, p. 293; *New York Times*, January 7, 1996, review by Robert Kuttner.

39. Chafe, *The Unfinished Journey*, p. 235; Johnson, *The Vantage Point*, pp. 41, 69–87.

40. Chafe, *The Unfinished Journey*, p. 242.

41. *Historical Statistics of the United States*, 1975 ed., p. 1116; Geoffrey Hodgson,

America in Our Time: From World War II to Nixon—What Happened and Why (New York, 1976), pp. 244–53.

42. In fact, inflation became a problem throughout Western Europe during the 1960s. See Harold James, *International Monetary Cooperaton Since Bretton Woods*, pp. 178–79; David Calleo, *The Imperious Economy* (Cambridge, 1982), pp. 26–27; Matusow, *The Unraveling of America*, p. 155.

43. Matusow, *The Unraveling of America*, pp. 155–71.

44. Others concurred. Donald Cook, a possible successor to Dillon, and Robert Anderson, Eisenhower's secretary of the Treasury, both praised the balance of payments program. LBJL, NSF Memoranda for the President, Box 2, McGeorge Bundy to President, January 25, 1965; WHCF, Box FO 32, Ackley to President, December 10, 1964.

45. LBJL, WHCF-Fi Box 51, Memorandum for George Reedy, February 13, 1965.

46. JFKL, Walter Heller Papers, Box 47, EMB (LTD.), "Two Reports on International Liquidity," August 19, 1964.

47. JFKL, Abram Chayes Papers, Box 2, Roosa, "Agenda for Money and the Balance of Payments," September 23, 1964.

48. LBJL, Francis M. Bator Papers, Chronological Files, Box 1, Memorandum for the President, August 10, 1964.

49. Each member of the International Monetary Fund contributed to the organization its quota 25 percent in gold and the balance in the member's own currency. The IMF then made these amounts available to member nations facing financial problems. With the United States after 1964 among the borrowing nations, Washington had a real interest in increasing these assessments.

50. LBJL, Bator Papers, Chron Files Box 2, Bator to President, June 21, 1965, Johnson to Fowler, June 16, 1965.

51. LC, Harriman Papers, Box 454, President de Gaulle's Press Conference of February 4, 1965.

52. JFKL, Walter Heller Papers, Box 46, Statement by the Hon. Valéry Giscard D'Estaing, September 29, 1965.

53. Volcker and Gyohten, *Changing Fortunes*, p. 45. The statement was made by Volcker quoting an unnamed source.

54. One SDR was equivalent to 0.888671 gram of fine gold. The reason that the United States insisted on a gold value for the SDR was to make sure it was "a first class asset that would, like the dollar, be good as gold." When issued one SDR had the same gold value as did one dollar, but when the dollar was devalued in late 1971 one SDR then was worth $1.08571.

55. LBJL, Bator Papers, Chron Files Box 6, "U.S. Position on Reconstitution at Deputies' Meeting," July 27–28, 1967; Anthony Solomon Papers, Box 5, SD to Various Posts, No. 4968, July 11, 1967, WHCF-Co, Box 49, Memorandum for the President, July 28, 1967; Dam, *The Rules of the Game*, pp. 151–70; John S. Odell, *U.S. International Monetary Policy: Markets, Power and Ideas as Sources of Change* (Princeton, 1982), pp. 294–97, 330.

56. See Table 6-1.

57. LBJL, WHCF-Co, Box 58, Joseph Barr to President, July 23, 1965; NSF Memos to the President, Box 9, Bator to President, July 6, 1966.

Chapter 7. The Alliance for Progress

1. On the Good Neighbor Policy, see David Green, *The Containment of Latin America* (Chicago, 1971); Irwin F. Gellman, *United States Policies in Latin America 1933–1945* (Baltimore. 1979); Lester D. Langley, *America and the Americas: The United States in the Western Hemisphere* (Athens, Ga., 1989); Bryce Wood, *The Making of the Good Neighbor Policy* (New York, 1961).
2. Gaddis Smith, *The Last Years of the Monroe Doctrine 1945–1993)* (New York, 1994), p. 70.
3. Stephen G. Rabe, "Dulles, Latin America and Cold War Anticommunism," in Richard Immerman, ed., *John Foster Dulles and the Diplomacy of the Cold War* (Princeton, 1990), pp. 162–64.
4. Ibid., p. 165.
5. On the Guatemalan coup, see Richard Immerman, *The CIA in Guatemala: The Foreign Policy of Intervention* (Austin, 1982); Rabe, "Dulles, Latin America and Cold War Anticommunism," pp. 174–76; Stephen Schlesinger and Stephen Kinzer, *Bitter Fruit: The Untold Story of the American Coup in Guatemala* (Garden City, 1982); Bryce Wood, *The Dismantling of the Good Neighbor Policy* (Austin, 1985), pp. 152–90.
6. Stephen E. Ambrose, *Nixon: The Education of A Politician, 1913–1962* (New York, 1987), pp. 473–79.
7. The drastic deterioration in the terms of trade for Latin American countries provided a major impetus for these appeals. See Rosemary Thorp, "The Latin America Economies in the Nineteen Forties," in David Rock, ed., *Latin America in the Nineteen Forties: War and Postwar Transition* (Berkeley, 1994).
8. JFKL, Teodoro Moscoso Papers, Box 3, "How Much Progress," A Report to the Publisher of *Time,* the Weekly Newsmagazine by John Scott, 1963, p. 6.
9. On the Latin American roots of the Alliance for Progress, see Elenda Luisa Ortega Aranda, *La Carta de Punta del Este y la Alianza para el Progreso* (Santiago, 1967); J. Warren Nystrom and Nathan A. Haverstock, *The Alliance for Progress: Key to Latin America's Development* (New York, 1966); Sergio Gutiérrez Olivos, *Subdesarollo, Integración, y Alianza* (Buenos Aires, 1963); Jânio Quadros, *Os Dois Mundos Das Três Americas* (Sao Paulo, 1972).
10. JFKL, John Moors Cabot Oral History; Jerome Levinson and Juan de Onís, *The Alliance That Lost Its Way* (Chicago, 1970), pp. 39–40; Rabe, "Dulles, Latin America and Cold War Anticommunism," in Immerman, *John Foster Dulles,* pp. 184–86.
11. *Foreign Relations of the United States, 1958–1960, Volume V, American Republics* (Washington, 1991), No. 7, Special Report by the Operations Coordinating Board to the National Security Council, pp. 36–60, November 26, 1958.
12. Levinson and de Onís, *The Alliance That Lost Its Way,* p. 48; Rabe, "Dulles, Latin America and Cold War Anticommunism," in Immerman, *John Foster Dulles,* p. 184.
13. Thomas G. Paterson, *Contesting Castro: The United States and the Triumph of the Cuban Revolution* (New York, 1994), p. 257.
14. Gary Clyde Hufbauer and Jeffrey J. Schott, assisted by Kimberly Ann Elliott,

Economic Sanctions Reconsidered: History and Current Policy (Washington, 1985), p. 315; Paterson, *Contesting Castro*, p. 258.

15. Ambrose, *Nixon*, p. 590; Arthur M. Schlesinger Jr., *A Thousand Days: John F. Kennedy in the White House* (New York, 1965, 1971), pp. 183–84.

16. JFKL, Pre-Presidential Files, Report of the Task Force on Immediate Latin American Problems; Rabe, "Dulles, Latin America and Cold War Anticommunism," in Immerman, *John Foster Dulles*, p. 113; Walt W. Rostow, *The Stages of Economic Growth: A Non-Communist Manifesto* (Cambridge, 1960); Schlesinger, *A Thousand Days*, p. 183.

17. Schlesinger, *A Thousand Days*, p. 190; JFKL, Private Office Files, Box 65, Schlesinger to President, February 6, 1961.

18. Schlesinger, *A Thousand Days*, p. 191; JFKL, POF, Box 65, Schlesinger to Kennedy, May 6, 1961.

19. PRO, FO 371/159674, "Record of Anglo-United States Talks at the State Department, Thursday, February 9, 1961."

20. Richard N. Goodwin, *Remembering America: A Voice from the Sixties* (Boston, 1988), p. 162.

21. Levinson and de Onís, *The Alliance That Lost Its Way*, pp. 34–36; Goodwin, *Remembering America*, p. 157. On general policy toward Latin America, see Stephen G. Rabe, "Controlling Revolutions: Latin America, the Alliance for Progress, and Cold War Anti-Communism" in Thomas G. Paterson, ed., *Kennedy's Quest for Victory: American Foreign Policy, 1961–1963* (Oxford, 1989); William O. Walker III, "Mixing the Sweet with the Sour: Kennedy, Johnson and Latin America," in Diane B. Kunz, ed., *The Diplomacy of the Crucial Decade: American Foreign Relations During the Nineteen Sixties* (New York, 1994).

22. *New York Times*, March 15, 1961; April 14 and 20, 1961; PRO, FO 371/156446, Washington to FO, No. 206 Saving, March 17, 1961; JFKL, Alianza Para Progreso," An Address by Peter R. Nehemkis Jr., March 6, 1961; Eduardo Frei Montalva, "The Alliance That Lost Its Way," *Foreign Affairs* 45:3 (April 1967): 441.

23. JFKL, NSF Box 297, "Special Message on Foreign Aid," March 22, 1961; PRO, FO 371/156466, Washington to FO, No. 741, March 22, 1961.

24. See, e.g., the explanation given by Robert S. McNamara, Kennedy's secretary of defense, that the principal concern of the United States was "Cuba's military relationship with the Soviet Union. . . . Our second concern was Cuba's support for armed groups whose goal was to overthrow many, if not all, of the governments in Latin America and the Caribbean." Donald Kagan, *On the Origins of War and the Preservation of Peace* (New York, 1995), p. 457.

25. Salvador Allende, *Punta del Este: La Nueva Estrategia del Imperialismo* (Montevideo, 1976).

26. JFKL, NSF Box 12, Gordon to Goodwin, March 6, 1961.

27. Author's interview with Raymond Bonham Carter.

28. On problems with the private nexus of the Alliance, see Ariel Badano, *Autopsia del "Cabello Morte," Dos Anos de "Alianza para el Progreso"* (Montevideo, 1964); Hernando Agueldo Villa, *La Alianza para el Progreso: Esperanza y Frustración* (Bogata, 1966).

29. JFKL, POF Box 65, Schlesinger to President, March 10, 1961.
30. Private capital is also far more mobile than government aid; Kubitschek, recognizing the risks of reliance on private funds, observed that "Latin American states are in a rare situation. The doctor arrives to make a blood transfusion in one arm, while removing it from the other."
31. Levinson and de Onís, *The Alliance That Lost Its Way*, pp. 62–63.
32. Washington's subsequent treatment of Salvador Allende demonstrates a later application of this approach.
33. Author's interview with C. Douglas Dillon; Walt W. Rostow, *The Diffusion of Power: An Essay in Recent History* (New York, 1972), p. 216.
34. Ernesto Guevera, *La Profecía del Ché* (Buenos Aires, 1964).
35. Levinson and de Onís, *The Alliance That Lost Its Way*, pp. 64–67.
36. Schlesinger, *A Thousand Days*, p. 699.
37. Robert A. Pastor, *Congress and the Politics of U.S. Foreign Economic Policy, 1929–1976* (Berkeley, 1980), pp. 271–72.
38. JFKL, POF Box 88, Fourth Regional Operations Conference, Lima, Peru, October 9–11, 1961; Fifth Regional Operations Conference, San Jose, Costa Rica, October 16–18, 1961.
39. JFKL, NSF Box 339, National Security Action Memorandum No. 206, December 4, 1962.
40. See Joseph Comblin, *A Ideologia da Segurança Nacional*, trans. A. Viago Filho (Rio de Janerio, 1978), pp. 22, 64–69, 170; A.J. Langguth, *Hidden Terrors* (New York, 1978).
41. See Aranda, *La Carta de Punta del Este*, p. 88; Quadros, *Os Dois Mundos Das Tres Americas*; Carlos Sanz de Santamaria, *America Latiana: Progreso o Retroceso* (Bogatá, 1967).
42. See, e.g., JFKL, POF Box 112, "Brazil," revised October 1961, NSF Box 12, Memorandum to Mr. Bundy, "filed 1/26 or 1/27/61," "Establishing Relations with New Brazilian Administration," February 1, 1961," Memorandum for the President, March 21, 1961, Brazilian Finance Minister's Call on President Kennedy, May 16, 1961, Rio de Janeiro to Secretary of State, No. 1733, May 31, 1961; NSF Box 328, Rusk Memorandum for the President, February 1961; PRO, FO 371/156451, Rio de Janeiro to FO, No. 62, March 6, 1961, G.A. Wallinger to H.A.A. Hankey, April 5, 1961.
43. Quadros, *Os Dois Mundos Das Tres Americas*, pp. 241–48, 489.
44. Thomas E. Skidmore, *Politics in Brazil 1930–1964: An Experiment in Democracy* (Oxford, 1967), pp. 200–204.
45. JFKL, NSF Box 12, Memorandum of Conversation, August 26, 1961.
46. JFKL, NSF Box 12, Director, CIA to White House, August 25, 1961, Rio de Janeiro to Secretary of State, No. 478, August 26, 1961, No. 702, September 6, 1961 and No. 713, September 8, 1961; PRO, FO 371/155883, Fortnightly Summary, September 6 to September 20, 1961.
47. Levinson and de Onís, *The Alliance That Lost Its Way*, pp. 108–11.
48. JFKL, NSF Box 12, Hamilton to President, February 12, 1962.
49. See Allende, *Punta del Este*, pp. 26, 30; Aranda, *La Carta de Punta del Este*, pp. 32–33; Badano, *Autopsia del "Cabello Morte,"* pp. 63–65; Gregorio Selser, *Alianza para el Progreso: La Mal Nascida* (Buenos Aires, 1964), pp. 96–97.

50. PRO, FO 371/156448, United States/Latin American Relations, August 22, 1961; JFKL, NSF Box 290, Memorandum, Alliance for Progress, January 11, 1962.
51. JFKL, POF Box 88, Rusk to President, "Post Mortem on Punta del Este", April 6, 1962; *New York Times*, January 31, 1962; February 1, 1962; Schlesinger, *A Thousand Days*, pp. 713–17.
52. See, Agueldo Villa, *La Alianza para el Progreso*, p. 68; Badano, *Autopsia del "Cabello Morte,"* p. 25; Selser, *Alianza para el Progreso*, p. 65. Levinson and de Onis, *The Alliance That Lost Its Way*, p. 144; *New York Times*, June 19, 1962.
53. *New York Times*, September 21, 1962.
54. See, e.g., *New York Times*, June 10, 1962; November 4, 1962.
55. JFKL, POF Box 72 A, Memorandum dated February 16, 1962; NSF Box 12, SD to All Diplomatic Posts, April 4, 1962; *New York Times*, October 2, 1962.
56. Levinson and de Onis, *The Alliance That Lost Its Way*, pp. 71–74.
57. Barbara Ward Jackson, "Foreign Aid: Strategy or Stopgap?" *Foreign Affairs* 41:1 (October 1962): 100.
58. Alberto Lleras Camargo, "The Alliance for Progress: Aims, Distortions, Obstacles," 42:1 *Foreign Affairs* (October 1963) 25.
59. See Badano, *Autopsia del "Cabello Morte,"* pp. 30–52.
60. See Otto Morales Benitez, *Alianza para el Progreso y Reforma Agraria* (Bogatá, 1963); Mauricio Birabent, *Kennedy's Dream (Six Years Later: 1961–1967) [El Sueño de John F. Kennedy (Seis años después: 1961–1967)]* (Buenos Aires, 1967).
61. *New York Times*, March 6, 1962; Goodwin, *Remembering America*, p. 215.
62. Quadros understood the American resentment about the Latin American taxation system. See, Quadros, *Os Dois Mundos Das Tres Americas*, p. 241.
63. JFKL, POF Box 95, Haddad to President, March 9, 1962; NSF Box 12, "Notes on the Progress of the Alliance, April 6, 1962; Staff Report, Bureau of the Budget, on the Alliance for Progress Program in Brazil, Argentina, Chile, and Brazil, (for the period June 16–July 12, 1962); *New York Times*, August 11, 1962.
64. JFKL, NSF Box 7, "President Frondizi's Visit—Washington, September 26, 1961, Position Paper—Castro-Communism and OAS Action," September 26, 1961.
65. See, e.g., JFKL, NSF, Box 6, *Foreign Commerce Weekly*, August 7, 1961, "Argentina Offers Concessions for Expansion of Steelmaking Capacity."
66. Levinson and de Onís, *The Alliance That Lost Its Way*, pp. 79–80; *The Cambridge Encyclopedia of Latin America and the Caribbean* 2d ed. (Cambridge, 1992), p. 273; *New York Times*, September 21, 1962.
67. See, e.g., Nystrom and Haverstock (whose work was written in 1966), *The Alliance for Progress*: "In a sense the military juntas that have moved into power in half of the Latin American Republics since Castro converted Cuba into a Communist state are buying time needed to reorganize the political life of their nations before it is too late. Paradoxical though it may seem at the moment, when military juntas are fighting holding actions in so many countries, the Alliance is a supreme effort to end once and for all Latin American dependence on caudillos and to replace them with organs of democracy." (p. 38).

68. JFKL, NSF Box 335, National Security Action Memorandum No. 134, Report on Internal Security Situation of South America, March 12, 1962; Fowler Hamilton to Edwin Martin and Moscoso, March 20, 1962; NSF Box 8, Buenos Aires to SD, No. 1843, March 28, 1962; Meeting of President Kennedy and General Pedro Aramburu, November 6, 1962.

69. JFKL, NSF Box 250, Lima to SD, No. 245, June 17, 1961; Levinson and de Onís, *The Alliance That Lost Its Way*, p. 81.

70. *New York Times*, July 20, 1962.

71. Levinson and de Onís, *The Alliance That Lost Its Way*, pp. 81–82; JFKL, NSF Box 291, Summary Report of the Alliance for Progress, No. 21, October 12, 1962.

72. On the alliance in Brazil see Ruth Leacock, "JFK, Business and Brazil," *Hispanic American Historical Review* 59:4 (1979): 636–73.

73. JFKL, NSF Box 13, SD Director of Intelligence and Research, "Coup Possibilities in Brazil, August 8, 1962; Rio de Janeiro to SD, No. 608, September 13, 1962; SD Director of Intelligence and Research, "Showdown Near in Brazil," September 14, 1962; SD to Rio de Janeiro, No. 771, September 21, 1962; Memoranda of Conversations, October 16 and 17, 1962; call on President Kennedy by Governor Adhemar de Barros, November 29, 1962; Skidmore, *Politics in Brazil 1930–1964*, p. 236.

74. JFKL, NSF Box 13, Draper to President, November 3, 1962.

75. McGeorge Bundy, *Danger and Survival: Choices about the Bomb in the First Fifty Years* (New York, 1988); John Lewis Gaddis, *We Now Know: Rethinking Cold War History* (forthcoming); Kagan, *On the Origins of War*, pp. 493–546; Walter LaFeber, *America, Russia and the Cold War: 1945–1990* (New York, 1991), pp. 158–61; Arthur M. Schlesinger, *A Thousand Days*, pp. 726–69; Vladislav M. Zubok, "Unwrapping the Enigma: What Was Behind the Soviet Challenge in the Nineteen Sixties?" in Diane B. Kunz, ed., *The Diplomacy of the Crucial Decade: American Foreign Relations During the Nineteen Sixties* (New York, 1994), p. 159.

76. Hufbauer and Schott, *Economic Sanctions Reconsidered*, p. 316.

77. JFKL, NSF Box 13, Bureau of the Budget, Staff Report, "Survey of the Alliance for Progress Program," Introduction, dated August 7, 1962.

78. JFKL, NSF Box 13, "The Alliance for Progress," August 22, 1962, Memorandum of Conversation in the White House, December 13, 1962; POF Box 112, Talking Paper: Meeting of the President with Drs. Lleras and Kubitschek, December 12, 1962.

79. *New York Times*, February 13 and 28, 1963.

80. JFKL, Box 72A, COMAP Proposals, January 3, 1963.

81. *FRUS, 1961–63, Volume IX*, No. 166. Memorandum from the Administrator of the Agency for International Development (Bell) to President Kennedy, April 22, 1963, pp. 370–73; Pastor, *Congress and the Politics of U.S. Foreign Economic Policy*, p. 272; Richard Reeves, *President Kennedy: Profile of Power* (New York, 1993), p. 484; Schlesinger, *A Thousand Days*, pp. 547–49.

82. JFKL, POF Box 95, Conclusions of Dr. Juscelino Kubitschek, June 15, 1963, Conclusions of Dr. Alberto Lleras Camargo, June 15, 1963; POF Box 90, Dil-

lon to President, August 21, 1963; *New York Times*, June 24, 1963; Quadros, *Os Dois Mundos Das Tres Americas*, pp. 244–46.

83. *New York Times*, July 25, 1963, August 18 and 19, 1963.
84. Rabe in Paterson, *Kennedy's Quest for Victory*, p. 115.
85. *New York Times*, January 22, 1964.
86. Levinson and de Onís, *The Alliance That Lost Its Way*, pp. 87–88.
87. Agueldo Villa, *La Alianza para el Progreso*, p. 95; Selser, *Alianza para el Progreso*, p. 95.
88. Levinson and de Onís, *The Alliance That Lost Its Way*, pp. 132–40.
89. JFKL, Moscoso Papers Box 3, Time Report, p. 8.
90. Levinson and de Onís, *The Alliance That Lost Its Way*, pp. 309–10.
91. Allende, *Punta del Este*, pp. 17–18, 22–25, 43–44, 48, 51; Gutierrez Olivos, *Subdesarollo, Integración, y Alianza*, pp. 58, 63–64.
92. See Willliam L. Furlong, "Democratic Political Development and the Alliance for Progress," in Howard J. Wiarda, ed., *The Continuing Struggle for Democracy in Latin America* (Boulder, 1980), pp. 167–84.
93. Walt W. Rostow, *The Diffusion of Power*, p. 216.
94. Raul Prebisch, "Joint Responsibilities for Latin American Progress," *Foreign Affairs* 39:4 (July 1961).

Chapter 8. Fighting the Good Fights

1. JFKL, NSF Box 342, "National Security Action Memorandum" No. 270, October 29, 1963.
2. Sidney Pollard, *The Development of the British Economy*, 3d ed. (London, 1983), p. 364.
3. JFKL, NSF Box 72, "President de Gaulle in Discussion with H. Hopkins and Ambassador Caffery on January 27, 1945."
4. Jean Lacouture, *DeGaulle: The Ruler 1945–1970* (New York, 1992), p. 363. This analysis was told to the author by the journalist Joseph Kraft.
5. JFKL, POF Box 116a, "Memorandum for the President: Germany's Payments Position with the United States and the Rest of the World," March 1961.
6. LBJL, NSFCo Box 190, "German Offset Agreement," December 1963.
7. Gregory F. Treverton, *The Dollar Drain and American Forces in Germany* (Athens, Ga. 1978), p. 33.
8. LBJL, Henry W. Fowler Papers, Box 41, Richard E. Neustadt, November 15, 1963; "Skybolt and Nassau: American Policymaking and Anglo-American Relations"; David Reynolds, *Britannia Overruled: British Policy and World Power in the Twentieth Century* (London, 1991), pp. 210–16.
9. JFKL, NSF Box 124, "The Position of Sterling," May 13, 1963.
10. LBJL, WHCF-Co Box 305, Heller to President, February 13, 1964.
11. LBJL, NSF, Presidential Memoranda, Box 1, Dillon to Reginald Maudling, February 17, 1964, NSFCo Box 206, Paris to SD, No. 4508, February 26, 1964; NSFCo Box 208, CIA Directorate of Intelligence, "Britain's Economic Problems," July 12, 1965.

12. Philip M. Kaiser, *Journeying Far and Wide: A Political and Diplomatic Memoir* (New York, 1992), p. 210.

13. See author's interview with Sir Alec Cairncross and Sir Nicholas Henderson; LBJL, NSFCo Box 206, SD Action Circular, No. 739, October 26, 1964; London to Paris et al., No. 326, October 26, 1964; Administrative History-State Department, "B. Strengthening the International Monetary System." On Wilson's career, see Ben Pimlott, *Harold Wilson* (London, 1992) and Philip Ziegler, *Wilson: The Authorized Life* (London, 1993). Also see Clive Ponting, *Breach of Promise: Labour in Power* (London, 1989).

14. Indeed, the United States took the lead in arranging a $3 billion support credit for sterling on Thanksgiving eve. LBJL, Council of Economic Advisors Papers Box 2, Gardner Ackley to President, November 22, 1964; NSFCo Box 206, Ackley to President, November 23, 1964.

15. LBJL, NSFCo Box 213, "Waiver of British Loan Payment, December 3, 1964, Ball to President, "The Wilson Visit," December 5, 1964; NSFCo Box 214, Acheson to President, "The European 'Crisis' and the Wilson Visit," December 3, 1964, SD Memorandum of Conversation, December 7, 1964; Administrative History, SD, Vol. 1, "Great Britain, a. Our Tradionally Close Relations."

16. Pimlott, *Harold Wilson*, p. 366.

17. LBJL, NSFCo Box 207, Thomas L. Hughes to Secretary, March 5, 1965.

18. LBJL, WHCF Fi, Box 9, Heller to President, March 30, 1965; Henry Fowler Papers Box 72-3, Merlyn N. Trued to Kermit Gordon, April 1, 1965; NSFCo Box 207, Klein to Bundy, March 23, 1965; Martin to President, March 30, 1965; NSF Presidential Memos Box 3, Bundy to President, April 14, 1965; Rusk to President, April 14, 1965.

19. Federal Reserve Bank of New York, New York, N.Y., C261, Fousek Memorandum to the Files, July 7, 1965; LBJL, NSF Presidential Memos Box 4, Bundy to President, July 7, 1965.

20. Barbara Castle, *The Castle Diaries 1964–1976* (London, 1990), pp. 26–27.

21. LBJL, Francis M. Bator Papers, Chronological Files Box 2, "Preparation for Trend," July 28, 1965; George Ball Papers, Box 7, Telcon between Fowler and Ball, July 29, 1965; Telecon between Bundy and Ball, July 29, 1965; NSF Presidential Memos, Box 4, Bundy to the President, July 28, 1965; NSFCo Box 215, Bator to Bundy, July 29, 1965; CEA Papers, Box 2, Ackley to President, July 29, 1965.

22. LBJL, NSFCo Box 208, SD to London, No. 681, August 6, 1965.

23. LBJL, NSFCo Box 215, Ball Memorandum, August 6, 1965, Bundy to Trend, August 16, 1965; Bator Papers Chron Files Box 2, Fowler Memorandum, n.d., Bator Memorandum, August 25, 1965; Fowler Papers, Box 41, Notes of Telephone Conversation between Bator and Fowler, August 26, 1965, Telecon with Chancellor Callaghan, August 26, 1965.

24. LBJL, NSF Presidential Memos Box 4, Bundy to President, September 10, 1965.

25. Pimlott, *Harold Wilson*, pp. 304, 361.

26. LBJL, NSF Presidential Memos Box 4, Bundy to President, September 10,

1965; NSFCo Box 210-2, Joseph Barr to President, September 10, 1965; Fowler Papers Box 72-3, "The Operation-Press Guidance," September 10, 1965; WHCF Co Box 305, Ackley to President, September 15, 1965; Anthony M. Solomon Files, Chron Files Box 11, "The U.K. National Plan," September 25, 1965; James Callaghan, *Time and Chance* (London, 1988), p. 190.

27. LBJL, NSFCo Box 209, Bundy to Ball and McNaughton, November 3, 1965; NSFCo Box 215, Bundy to Wilson, December 16, 1965; Presidential Memos Box 5, Bundy to President, November 16, 1965, Bator to President, November 17, 1965; Bator Papers, Chron Files Box 2, Wilson Visit Talking Points, December 16, 1965.

28. LBJL, NSFCo Box 209, London to SD, No. 3936, February 22, 1966.

29. LBJL, NSF Presidential Memos Box 8, Bruce to Acting Secretary, June 2, 1966, Bruce to President, June 2, 1966, President to Prime Minister, June 14, 1966; Ziegler, *Wilson*, pp. 421–29; Pimlott, *Harold Wilson*, p. 459.

30. Pimlott, *Harold Wilson*, pp. 408–14; Ziegler, *Wilson*, pp. 250–63.

31. Confidential interview; interview with Lord Jenkins of Hillhead.

32. LBJL, NSFCo Box 209, Hughes to Secretary of State, July 27, 1966; "Economic Effects on the U.K. and the U.S. of the Proposed U.K. Actions," (n.d.), Ball to President, "Harold Wilson's Visit—The Opportunity for an Act of Statesmanship," July 22, 1966; NSFCo Box 209, Fowler to President, July 14, 1966.

33. LBJL, Bator Papers Chron Files Box 3, Bator to President, (two memoranda), July 28, 1966; NSF Presidential Memos Box 7, Bator to President, July 28, 1966; NSFCo Box 216, Rostow to President, July 29, 1966, "Visit of Prime Minister Wilson of the United Kingdom, to Washington," July 29, 1966.

34. JFKL, NSF Box 72, Ball to Bundy, January 23, 1963.

35. Jean Lacouture, *DeGaulle*, p. 379.

36. LBJL, NSFCo Box 169, SD to Paris, No. 2783, December 3, 1963.

37. The American willingness only to offer Polaris missiles to France after Macmillan had first been promised them further soured relations.

38. JFKL, NSF Box 71A, Ball to President, July 18, 1962; POF Box 90, Dillon to President, January 24, 1963.

39. As the French leader put it, "What they [the United States] owe those countries they pay, at least in part, in dollars that they themselves can issue as they wish, instead of paying them totally in gold, which has a real value, and which one can possess only if one has earned it." The idea of creating an alternative reserve asset was also seriously discussed in 1964–65 by a study commission labeled the Ossola group, which considered the French proposal. LBJL, Administration History—Treasury, Chapter 12, "International Monetary Negotiations and the SDR Plan; John S. Odell, *U.S. International Monetary Policy: Markets, Power, and Ideas as Sources of Change* (Princeton, 1982), pp. 119–20.

40. See, e.g., JFKL, NSF Box 72, Paris to SD, No. 3036, January 30, 1965; Memorandum of Conversation, "French Government Policy Toward American Investments in France," January 30, 1963.

41. LBJL, Administration History, SD, 2. Germany, a. The U.S. State; Vladislav

Zubok, "Unwrapping the Enigma: What was Behind the Soviet Challenge in the Nineteen Sixties," in Diane B. Kunz, ed., *The Diplomacy of the Crucial Decade: American Foreign Relations During the Nineteen Sixties* (New York, 1994).

42. LBJL, NSFCo Box 169, Hughes to Secretary, April 20, 1964; NSFCo Box 171, "Ambassador Bohlen's Conversation with General De Gaulle," May 5, 1965, Lacouture, *DeGaulle*, pp. 379–80, 384–85, 397–98.

43. Thomas Alan Schwartz, "Victory and Defeats in the Long Twilight Struggle: The United States and Western Europe in the Nineteen Sixties" in Kunz, *The Diplomacy of the Crucial Decade*, pp. 129–31, 134–37.

44. LBJL, Ball Papers, Box 3, Telecon between Ball and Kuchel, January 30, 1965; NSF Presidential Memos, Bundy to President, May 5, 1965; Administration History-SD, B. United States relations with NATO.

45. LBJL, NSFCo Box 172, Draft NSAM: France and NATO, September 25, 1965, Hughes to Secretary, September 30, 1965, SD to Paris, No. 1711, October 19, 1965, SD to Paris No. 658, November 12, 1965.

46. Lacouture, *DeGaulle*, p. 382.

47. LBJL, NSFCo Box 172, Paris to SD, No. 3135, December 6, 1965, Ball Papers, Box 3, Telecon between Ball and Leddy, March 7, 1966; McCloy Papers, Box NA 1/16, French Aide-Mémoire of March 11, 1966; Lacouture, *DeGaulle*, p. 384.

48. LBJL, Ball Papers Box 3, Telecon betwen Ball and Sevareid, March 15, 1966; Bator Papers, Chron Files Box 3, Bator to President, March 17, 1966; NSFCo Box 58, Johnson to de Gaulle, March 22, 1966; Author's interview with Walt W. Rostow.

49. LBJL, WHCF CF Box 8, Bundy to President, November 16, 1965, May 16, 1966; NSF Name File Box 2, Memorandum for the Record, April 25, 1966.

50. LBJL, NSF Presidential Memos Box 7, SD to Bohlen, May 23, 1966; Box 8, Bator to President, June 27, 1966; Ball Papers Box 3, Telecon between Ball and McNamara, May 24, 1966, Telecon between Ball and McNaughton, May 26, 1966; Bator Papers, Chron Files Box 3, Acheson Memorandum, "Broad Lines of Approach Toward Negotiations with France in NATO Crisis," April 1966; NSFCo Box 172, McNamara to President, May 25, 1966, CJCS to USCINCEUR, JCS No. 3057, May 27, 1966; Administration History, -SD, 3. France a. De Gaulle and U.S. French Relations and 5. French withdrawl and NATO countermeasures; Lacouture, *DeGaulle*, p. 384.

51. Lyndon Baines Johnson, *The Vantage Point: Perspectives of the Presidency 1963–1969* (New York, 1971), p. 306.

52. LBJL, Bator Papers, Chron Files Box 3, Bator to President, September 30, 1966.

53. Treverton, *The Dollar Drain*, p. 12.

54. LBJL, NSFCo Box 190, "Visit of Chancellor Erhard of Germany: Germany and the U.S. Balance of Payments, December 20, 1963," Dillon to President, December 20, 1963, Erhard Briefing Book [12/63], Basic Talking Points on Offset Arrangement.

55. Schwartz, "Victory and Defeat" in Kurtz, *The Diplomacy of the Crucial Decade.*p. 134.

56. Lacouture, *DeGaulle*, pp. 336–43.

57. LBJL, NSFCo Box 191, Box 191, Visit of Chancellor Erhard—U.S. Military Offset Agreement, May 28, 1965, Rusk to President, June 2, 1965.
58. LBJL, NSFCo Box 192, "Guidance on US/FRG Offset Arrangement, December 1965; The President's Appointment File, Diary Backup, Box 26, Ball to President, [December 1965].
59. LBJL, Fowler Papers, Box 69-70, Memorandum of Conversation, April 20, 1966; NSF Presidential Memos, Box 7, McGhee to Johnson, July 23, 1966.
60. See Walter LaFeber, *American, Russia and the Cold War: 1945–1990* (New York, 1991), pp. 206–58 and Zubok, "Unwrapping the Enigma," in Kunz, *The Diplomacy of the Crucial Decade*.
61. Treverton, *The Dollar Drain*, p. 34.
62. Ibid., pp. 61–66.
63. LBJL, N/N—Trilateral, Box 50, Leddy to Secretary, August 23, 1966, Bator to President, August 23, 1966, "Results of the Meeting with President on August 23, 1966"; President to Prime Minister, August 26, 1966; NSFCo, Box 210-2, "British Plans for Military Cutbacks in Europe," August 17, 1966.
64. LBJL, Fowler Box 193, Description of Erhard's remarks, September 19, 1966; NSF Presidential Memos Box 10, Rostow to President, September 19, 1966.
65. Author's interview with George C. McGhee; LBJL, Fowler Papers, Box 193, McGhee to SD, No. 3361, September 20, 1966; Box 69-70, Ball to President, September 23, 1966; Bator Papers, Chron Files Box 3, Bator to President, September 21, 1966, Bator to President, September 25, 1966; Administration History-SD, 2. Germany, a. The U.S. Stake; Treverton, *The Dollar Drain*, pp. 36, 73.
66. On the Trilateral Negotiations, see LBJL, N/N Box 50, Analysis of Major Decisions in Trilateral Talks; Chronology of Trilateral Talks; Trilateral Negotiations and NATO; Schwartz, "Victory and Defeats," generally, in Kunz, *The Diplomacy of the Crucial Decade*; Treverton, *The Dollar Drain*, generally.
67. See Table 6-1.
68. LBJL, Bator Papers Chron-Box 4, Bator to President, October 6, 1966; Fowler Papers, Box 69-70, "UK/German Military Offset Relationship, [n.d.]; N/N Box 50, Johnson to McCloy, October 6, 1966, "Issues for the Trilateral Talks," October 24, 1966; N/N Box 51, "Future Arrangements to Offset Military Expenditures in Germany," November 7, 1966.
69. Treverton, *The Dollar Drain*, p. 125.
70. Henry Ashby Turner, Jr., *The Two Germanies Since 1945* (New Haven, 1987), pp. 91–92; Treverton, *The Dollar Drain*, pp. 74–76.
71. See, e.g., LBJL, Bator Papers Chron Files Box 4, "Trouble with the UK–FRG Offset," January 25, 1967; Fowler Papers, Box 193, Rostow Memorandum for the Secretary, February 8, 1967.
72. LBJL, N/N Box 51, Rostow Memorandum of Conversation concerning Tripartite Talks on Troop Strength and Offset, December 9, 1966.
73. LBJL, N/N Box 50, "Results of the Meeting with the President on February 25, 1967; NSFCo Box 210-12, Rostow to President, February 26, 1967; Treverton, *The Dollar Drain*, pp. 106–9.
74. LBJL, Bator Papers, Box 13, Memorandum for the Record, March 2, 1967.
75. LBJL, Bator Papers, Chron-Box 4, Bator to President (two memoranda),

March 8, 1967; Chron-Box 5, McCloy to President, May 17, 1967, Johnson to McCloy, May 24, 1967; Fowler Papers, Box 69-70, Bator to President, March 8, 1967; Fowler Papers Box 39, Joint Release of the Treasury Department and Federal Reserve Board (with enclosures), May 2, 1967; SD Press Release, No. 104, May 2, 1967; N/N Box 50, McCloy to President, March 22, 1967; McCloy Papers, NA 1/27, Leddy to Secretary, March 8, 1967; FRBNY, C261-Germany, Crowley to Trieber, May 4, 1967; Treverton, *The Dollar Drain*, p. 151.

76. LBJL, NSFCo Box 216, "Visit of UK Foreign Secretary George Brown: UK Domestic Political Situation, October 13, 1966.

77. LBJL, N/N Box 50, President to Prime Minister, November 19, 1966, Memorandum of Conversation between McNamara and Healey, December 14, 1966.

78. See, e.g., LBJL, Bator Papers, Chron Files Box 4, Record of Meeting at Chequers on Saturday, 21st January, 1967; SD Circular Telegram, February 5, 1967.

79. Pimlott, *Harold Wilson*, pp. 414–15; Ziegler, *Wilson*, pp. 240–43.

80. LBJL, NSFCo Box 216, "UK Overseas Military Economies," [January 1967].

81. LBJL, NSFCo Box 210-12, London to SD, No. 7612, April 12, 1967.

82. LBJL, Diary Backup, Box 62, Meeting with Prime Minister Wilson, April 25, 1967; NSFCo Box 202, SD to London, No. 193089, April 12, 1967; Leddy to Secretary, April 15, 1967; Bator Papers, Chron Files Box 5, Leddy to Secretary, May 15, 1967.

83. LBJL, NSFCo Box 216, Bruce to SD, No. 9929, May 30, 1967; Bator Papers, Chron Files Box 5, Bator to President (two memoranda), May 31, 1967.

84. LBJL, NSFCo Box 216, Rostow to President, September 26, 1967.

85. LBJL, WHCF-Co, Box 44, Fowler to President, October 19, 1967; Fowler Papers Box 41, "The Economic Position of the United Kingdom, October 23, 1967; Callaghan, *Time and Chance*, pp. 211–12.

86. It increased the amount of guaranteed sterling it would hold from $250 million to $300 million. LBJL, Fowler Papers Box 41, Fowler to Callaghan, FLD Draft 2, October 23, 1967.

87. Callaghan, *Time and Chance*, pp. 213–25; Castle, *The Castle Diaries*, pp. 162–66; Pimlott, *Harold Wilson*, pp. 476–84; Ziegler, *Wilson*, pp. 262–86.

88. Pimlott, *Harold Wilson*, pp. 479–81.

89. According to Callaghan, the British government revived the idea of a long–term sterling support credit with the American Treasury Department and the Federal Reserve Board in the early summer of 1967, but the United States did not show sufficient interest in the proposal until it was too late.

90. John Brooks, *Business Adventures* (New York, 1969), p. 389.

91. LBJL, N/N Box 53, Rostow to President, November 13, 1967, Statement by the President, November 18, 1967; WHCF-Co, Box 49, Statement by the Chancellor of the Exchequer, November 18, 1967.

92. LBJL, N/N Box 50, John S. Brims to Mr. Spingsteen and Mr. Vest, March 29, 1967.

Chapter 9. The Seventies

1. On Richard Nixon's career see Jonathan Aitken, *Nixon: A Life* (London, 1993); Stephen E. Ambrose, *Nixon: The Education of a Politician 1913–1962* (New York, 1987), generally and p. 671, *Nixon: The Triumph of a Politician, 1962–1972* (New York, 1989) and *Nixon: Ruin and Recovery 1973–1990* (New York, 1991); Earl Mazo and Stephen Hess, *Nixon: A Political Portrait* (New York, 1968); Roger Morris, *Richard Milhous Nixon: The Rise of an American Politician* (New York, 1990); *RN: The Memoirs of Richard Nixon* (New York, 1978, 1990); Herbert S. Parmet, *Richard Nixon and His America* (New York, 1990); Tom Wicker, *One of Us: Richard Nixon and the American Dream* (New York, 1991); Garry Wills, *Nixon Agonistes* (New York, 1969).

2. Humphrey received 42.7 percent and Wallace 13.5 percent. In the electoral college Nixon had 302 votes while Humphrey garnered 191. John Morton Blum, *Years of Discord: American Politics and Society, 1961–1974* (New York, 1991), p. 316.

3. See George P. Shultz, *Triumph and Turmoil: My Years as Secretary of State* (New York, 1993), which is instructive on Shultz's personality and modus operandi; and Paul Volcker and Toyoo Gyohten, *Changing Fortunes: The World's Money and the Threat to American Leadership* (New York, 1992), pp. 59–162.

4. Theodore H. White, *America in Search of Itself: The Making of the President 1956–1980* (New York, 1982), pp. 130–31; 150–51.

5. On Kissinger's career see, Seyom Brown, *The Crisis of Power: An Interpretation of United States Foreign Policy During the Kissinger Years* (New York, 1979); Seymour Hersh, *The Price of Power: Kissinger in the White House* (New York, 1983); Walter Issacson, *Kissinger: A Biography* (New York, 1992); Henry Kissinger, *White House Years* (New York, 1979) and *Years of Upheaval* (New York, 1982); Robert D. Schulzinger, *Henry Kissinger: Doctor of Diplomacy* (New York, 1989).

6. On the Cambodian incursion see especially William Shawcross, *Sideshow: Kissinger, Nixon and the Destruction of Cambodia* (New York, 1979). On Moscow and Beijing's treatment of North Vietnam, see George C. Herring, *America's Longest War: The United States and Vietnam, 1950–1975*, 2d ed. (New York, 1986), p. 248.

7. See Raymond L. Garthoff, *Détente and Confrontation: American–Soviet Relations from Nixon to Reagan* (Washington, 1987); Franz Schuman, *The Foreign Politics of Richard Nixon: The Grand Design* (Berkeley, 1987); Richard C. Thornton, *The Nixon-Kissinger Years: Reshaping America's Foreign Policy* (New York, 1989); Vladislav M. Zubok, "Unwrapping the Enigma: What was Behind the Soviet Challenge in the Nineteen Sixties," Diane B. Kunz, ed., *The Diplomacy of the Crucial Decade: American Foreign Relations During the Nineteen Sixties* (New York, 1994).

8. See R.A. Doak Barnett, *China Policy: Old Problems and New Challenges* (Washington, 1977); Blum, *Years of Discord*, pp. 376–78; Warren I. Cohen, *America's Response to China* (New York, 1990); Herring, *America's Longest War*, pp. 248–49.

9. Blum, *Years of Discord*, pp. 351–56; Nixon, *RN: The Memoirs of Richard Nixon*, pp. 394–95; Walter LaFeber, *The American Age: United States Foreign Policy at Home and Abroad since 1750* (New York, 1989), p. 605.

10. Godfrey Hodgson, *America in Our Time: From World War II to Nixon—What Happened and Why* (New York, 1976), p. 378. On Nixon's relationship with the press, see James Keogh, *President Nixon and the Press* (New York, 1972); William E. Porter, *Assault on the Media: The Nixon Years* (Ann Arbor, 1976); Joseph C. Spear, *Presidents and the Press: The Nixon Legacy* (Cambridge, Mass., 1984). Concerning Nixon's later thoughts on the press, see Marvin L. Kalb, *The Nixon Memo: Political Respectability, Russia and the Press* (Chicago, 1994).

11. Nixon, *RN: The Memoirs of Richard Nixon*, pp. 620–21.

12. Gareth Porter, *A Peace Denied: The United States, Vietnam, and the Paris Agreement* (Bloomington, Ind., 1975).

13. See author's interview with Lord Bridges; Kissinger, *Years of Upheaval*, 128–94; Wolfram F. Hanrieder, *Germany, America, Europe: Forty Years of German Foreign Policy* (New Haven, 1989), pp. 85–105, 141–69, 171–94, 195–219; Henry Ashby Turner Jr., *The Two Germanies Since 1945* (New Haven, 1987), pp. 146–61.

14. On Watergate, see Ambrose, *Ruin and Recovery*, pp. 1–446; Theodore H. White, *Breach of Faith: The Fall of Richard Nixon* (New York, 1975); Carl Bernstein and Bob Woodward, *All the President's Men* (New York, 1974) and *The Final Days* (New York, 1976).

15. See Gerald L. Ford, *A Time to Heal: The Autobiography of Gerald R. Ford* (New York, 1979).

16. John Dumbrell, *The Carter Presidency: A Reevaluation* (New York, 1993), pp. 122–23; LaFeber, *The American Age*, pp. 637–38.

17. Stephen Ambrose, *Rise to Globalism: American Foreign Policy Since 1938*, 4th rev. ed. (New York, 1985,), p. 255.

18. Herring, *America's Longest War*, p. 257–69.

19. William Chafe, *The Unfinished Journey: America Since World War II*, 3d ed. (New York, 1995), p. 447.

20. The classic account of Carter's foreign policy is Gaddis Smith, *Morality, Reason and Power: American Diplomacy in the Carter Years* (New York, 1986). Also see Jimmy Carter, *Keeping Faith: Memoirs of a President* (New York, 1982); Dumbrell, *The Carter Presidency*; Burton I. Kaufman, *The Presidency of James Earl Carter, Jr.* (Lawrence, Kans. 1993); Richard C. Thornton, *The Carter Years: Toward a New Global Order* (New York, 1991). Also see author's interview with Lord Bridges.

21. See Henry S. Bradsher, *Afghanistan and the Soviet Union* (Durham, N.C., 1983).

22. Dumbrell, *The Carter Presidency*, p. 200. On SALT II see Strobe Talbott, *Endgame: The Inside Story of SALT II* (New York, 1982).

23. Dumbrell, *The Carter Presidency*, pp. 200–201; LaFeber, *The American Age*, pp. 665–66; Smith, *Morality, Reason and Power*, pp. 223–24.

24. On American–Iranian relations and the hostage crisis, see James A. Bill, *The Eagle and the Lion: The Tragedy of American–Iranian Relations* (New Haven, 1988); Hamilton Jordan, *Crisis: The Last Year of the Carter Presidency* (New

York, 1982); Gary Sick, *All Fall Down: America's Tragic Encounter with Iran* (New York, 1985).

25. Freezing Iran's deposits located in overseas branches of U.S. banks also represented a repudiation of long–standing American promises that such deposits were not subject to the long arm of American law.

26. The act mandated that the President consult with Congress "in every possible instance" prior to exercising any of the powers in the act and also required him to report to Congress periodically. (50 U.S. C. SEC. 1703 et sec.) However, the constitutionality of its provision permitting Congress by concurrent resolution to terminate a national emergency, was rendered dubious by *U.S. v. Chadha* (103 S. Ct. 2764, [1984]).

27. Harold James, *International Monetary Cooperation Since Bretton Woods* (Washington, 1996), p. 303.

28. Chafe, *The Unfinished Journey*, pp. 452–53.

Chapter 10. Bretton Woods Has a Great Fall

1. GFL, Arthur W. Burns Papers, Box B27, Remarks of the President, August 15, 1971; David P. Calleo, *The Imperious Economy* (Cambridge, 1982), generally and p. 25. Also see David P. Calleo, *Beyond American Hegemony: The Future of Western Alliance* (New York, 1987).

2. NP, WHCF-Fo, Box 46, Nixon to Kennedy, January 29, 1969.

3. NP, WHCF-Fi, Box 54, "Check List on International Monetary Issues For President's European Trip," February 20, 1969.

4. NP, POF Box 77, William Safire to H.R. Haldeman, March 7, 1969.

5. GFL, Arthur Burns Papers, Box A8, McCracken to President, November 11, 1969.

6. NP, WHCF-Fi, Box 54, McCracken to President, May 5, 1969, Burns to President, June 11, 1969.

7. Brown's memorandum listed three options: "fundamental but evolutionary change in the existing system," including the early activation of SDRs, realignment of exchange rates with special emphasis on an upward revaluation of the mark, and limited exchange rate flexibility; suspension of gold convertibility or an increase in the official price of gold. Foreshadowing Nixon's eventual approach, Brown apparently saw the third option as less painful than the second. While he pointed out that raising the price of gold would require formal congressional approval, which would undoubtedly meet stiff resistance, Brown did not mention that a unilateral suspension of gold convertibility would explode the cooperative principles of Bretton Woods. NP, WHCF-Fo, Box 43, Brown to Nixon, June 25, 1969.

8. NP, WHCF-Fi, Box 54, McCracken to President, August 8, 1969.

9. On Burns's career and ideas, see Wyatt C. Wells, *Economist in an Uncertain World: Arthur F. Burns and the Federal Reserve, 1970–1978* (New York, 1995).

10. NP, POF Box 31, News Summaries, February 2, 1970; POF Box 80, Patrick J. Buchanan to President, March 17, 1970.

11. NP, POF Box 82, Memorandum for the President's File, October 13, 1970.

12. John S. Odell, *U.S. International Monetary Policy: Markets, Power, and Ideas as a Source of Change* (Princeton, 1982), pp. 204–5.
13. NP, John D. Ehrlichman Papers, Box 4, Notes of Meetings, November 17 and 19, 1970.
14. NP, Ehrlichman Papers, Box 4, Notes of Meeting, December 15, 1970.
15. These loopholes faded away in stages, most importantly in the 1980s as American monetary authorities became alarmed by the potential implications of a market exceeding $1 trillion.
16. NP, Ehrlichman Papers, Box 4, Notes of Meeting, February 9, 1971.
17. NP, MRD, NLN 92/40/11, August 4, 1995, Memorandum for the President, January 22, 1971.
18. NP, Paul McCracken Papers, Box 7, Remarks by Paul McCracken, March 9, 1971; Herbert Stein Papers, Box 67, Memorandum for McCracken, April 1, 1971; GFL, Burns Papers, Box C15, Solomon to Burns, January 5 and March 22, 1971.
19. NP, POF, Box 84, Minutes of the First Meeting of the Council on International Economic Policy, April 8, 1971.
20. Calculated on an official settlements basis.
21. *New York Times*, May 23, 1971; GFL, Burns Papers, Box B4, Ilse Higgins to Solomon and Burns, March 30, 1971.
22. GFL, Burns Papers, Box B60, Klassen to Burns, May 4, 1971.
23. NP, Ehrlichman Papers, Box 5, Meeting with the President, May 6, 1971; McCracken Papers, Box 42, McCracken to President, May 7, 1971; GFL, Burns Papers, Box B65, IMF Press Release No. 839, May 9, 1971.
24. NP, POF Box 33, News Summary, May 8, 1971.
25. NP, WHCF-SF, Box 55, McCracken to President, May 17, 1971.
26. GFL, Burns Papers, Box B23, McCracken to President, June 2, 1971.
27. See, e.g., GFL, Burns Papers, Box B3, Higgins to Ghiardi, June 22, 1971, Kohn to Ghiardi, June 25, 1971.
28. NP, POF, Box 85, McCracken to Nixon, July 22, 1971; McCracken Papers, Box 42, McCracken to President, August 25, 1971.
29. NP, POF, Box 85, Peterson to President, July 27, 1951; POF Box 33, News Summaries, August 12, 1971; Herbert Stein Papers, Box 89, Notes for talk before World Affairs Council, Wilmington, Delaware, November 23, 1971; Ehrlichman Papers, Box 3, Meeting with the President, November 11, 1970.
30. GFL, Burns Papers, Box B24, Peter Peterson, "A Foreign Economic Perspective," December 27, 1971.
31. NP, POF, Box 85, Peterson Memorandum for the President's Files, July 27, 1971; Box 33, News Summaries, August 4, 1971, McCracken Papers, Box 42, McCracken to President, August 4, 1971; John Morton Blum, *Years of Discord: American Politics and Society, 1961–1974* (New York, 1991), pp. 401–9; H.R. Haldeman, *The Haldeman Diaries: Inside the Nixon White House* (New York, 1994) p. 335.
32. Haldeman, *The Haldeman Diaries*, p. 338; Odell, *U.S. International Monetary Policy*, p. 255.
33. NP, McCracken Papers, Box 42, McCracken Memoranda to the President, August 4 and 7, 1971.

34. NP, WHCF-SF, Box 55, McCracken to President, August 9, 1971; MRD, NLN 92-40/8, August 4, 1995, McCracken to President, August 9, 1971; Richard Nixon, *RN: The Memoirs of Richard Nixon*, (New York, 1978, 1990), p. 518; Paul A. Volcker and Toyoo Gyohten, *Changing Fortunes: The World's Money and the Threat to American Leadership* (New York, 1992), p. 76.

35. Haldeman, *The Haldeman Diaries*, p. 326.

36. Technically, the United States informed the IMF "that, with effect August 15, 1971, the United States no longer, for the settlement of international transactions, in fact, freely buys and sells gold under the second sentence of Article IV, Section 4(b) [of the Articles of Agreement]." GFL, Burns Papers, Box B65, Secretary, IMF to Members of the Executive Board, August 16, 1971.

37. Connally stated this demand as a fact. The sources disagree as to whether the British government actually made such a demand and if so, what its exact nature was. See. e.g., GFL, Burns Papers, Box KI, Safire Notes on Camp David Weekend, August 13–15, 1971; Nixon, *RN: The Memoirs of Richard Nixon*, p. 518; Odell, *U.S. International Monetary Policy*, p. 267; Volcker and Gyohten, *Changing Fortunes*, p. 77.

38. In Burns's absence Nixon told other participants that Burns would not be able to fight against closing the gold window: "After going so far because of people who think as he does, he can't run to the hill & [sic] piss on it." NP, Ehrlichman Papers Box 5, Notes of Meeting with the President, August 14, 1971.

39. NP, Ehrlichman Papers, Box 5, Notes of Meetings, August 13 and 14, 1971, Economic Stabilization Program, August 14, 1971; GFL, Burns Papers, Box B27, Remarks of the President on Nationwide Radio and Television, August 15, 1971; Box K1, Safire Notes on Camp David Weekend, August 13–15, 1971; Joanne Gowa, *Closing the Gold Window: Domestic Politics and the End of Bretton Woods* (Ithaca, N.Y., 1983) generally and pp. 150–70.

40. Author's interview with Sir Jeremy Morse; NP, MRD, NLN 92-40/23, August 4, 1994, "International Negotiations, Objectives, Issues and Conclusions, August 18, 1971; MRD, NLN 92-40/22, August 4, 1995, Carter Murphy to Paul McCracken and Ezra Solomon, August 20, 1971; GFL, Burns Papers, Box C6, R.F. Gemill to S. Pizer, August 16, 1971; *New York Times*, August 17, 1971.

41. GFL, Burns Papers, Box B27, Ralph Smith to Burns, August 17, 1971; Box B65, Reed Irvine to Pizer, August 18, 1971, Irvine to Robert Emery, August 18, 1971.

42. NP, McCracken Papers, Box 42, McCracken to Nixon, August 16 and 18, 1971, Stein to Nixon, Box 42, August 20, 1971 (two memoranda); Stein Papers, "A Forecast of the 1972 Economy Under the New Economic Policy," September 1, 1971;" *New York Times*, August 16, 1971.

43. For initial foreign reaction to the NEP see NP, MRD, NLN 92-40/6, August 4, 1995, Memorandum for the President, August 21, 1971, and NLN 92-40/5, August 4, 1995, Memorandum for the President, August 31, 1971.

44. GFL, Burns Papers, Box B65, Ralph C. Bryant et al., to Burns and J. Dewey Daane, August 19, 1971; NP, McCracken Papers, Box 109, E. Solomon, "The International Monetary System: Opportunities and Options; Whitman to McCracken, August 27, 1971.

45. GFL, Burns Papers, Box B54, Kathryn Morisse and Betty Barker to Solomon, August 30, 1971; Box C16, Robert M. Solomon, "Some Arithmetic Regarding Exchange Rate Realignment," September 12, 1971.
46. GFL, Burns Papers, Box B65, Foreign Exchange Board Briefing, August 23, 1971; Board Presentation, August 23, 1971.
47. The Japanese government took the Nixon administration's oft–repeated assertion that it wouldn't devalue the dollar at face value and assumed that the White House only wanted to sever the gold connection. It spent $4 billion to support the dollar, in the process doubling its dollar reserves, until it changed course. *New York Times*, August 29, 1971; Volcker and Gyohten, *Changing Fortunes*, p. 93.
48. The OECD was formed in 1960 and, in 1971, included the 16 Western European countries who had formerly belonged to the OEEC, together with the United States, Canada, Japan and Finland.
49. GFL, Burns Papers, Box B65, Wiley to Coombs, November 5, 1971.
50. NP, McCracken Papers, Box 8, U.S. Financial Developments Since the Mid–August Adoption of the President's New Economic Program; POF Box 86, Buchanan Memorandum for the President's File, November 16, 1971.
51. NP, McCracken Papers, Box 8, Volcker Remarks before the World Economy Study Group, Chicago, Illinois, November 11, 1971; Box 43, McCracken Memoranda to the President, November 23 and 24, 1971; December 1, 1971; *New York Times*, November 24, 1971.
52. NP, McCracken Papers, Box 84, McCracken to Connally, December 9, 1971; Volcker and Gyohten, *Changing Fortunes*, pp. 85–87; Author's interview with Sir Jeremy Morse.
53. Author's interview with Sir Jeremy Morse; NP, MRD, NLN 92-40/10, August 4, 1995, Memorandum for the President, December 8, 1971; Stein Papers, Box 43, Press Conference of John Connally, December 13, 1971; Henry Kissinger, *White House Years* (Boston, 1979), pp. 952–62; Leonard Silk, *Nixonomics* (New York, 1972), p. 138; Volcker and Gyohten, *Changing Fortunes*, pp. 87–88; *New York Times*, December 14 and 15, 1971.
54. The major currencies had new central rates against the dollar, which represented the following changes from their rates against the dollar from May 1, 1971, when the German mark began its float:

French franc	+8.57 percent
German mark	+13.57 percent
British pound	+8.57 percent
Japanese yen	+16.88 percent
Canadian dollar	+3.5 percent
Canadian dollar (from May 1970)	+10.5 percent

Source: GFL, Burns Papers, Box B34, Solomon to Board of Govenors, December 23, 1971.

55. Author's interview with Sir Jeremy Morse; NP, POF, Box 87, Bipartisan Leadership Meeting, December 15, 1971; POF Box 37, News Summaries, December 20, 1971; MRD, NLN 92-40/17, "Outline of Major Issues for Negotiation," December 17, 1971; GFL, Burns Papers, Box B34, Solomon to

Board of Governors, December 23, 1971; Harold James, *International Monetary Cooperation* (Washington, D.C., 1996), pp. 205–27; Volcker and Gyohten, *Changing Fortunes*, pp. 89–90.

56. NP, WHCF-Fi9, Box 55, Richard Erb to Flanigan, May 19, 1972; GFL, Burns Papers, Box B5, Solomon, "The U.S. Objectives in the International Monetary Reform Negotiations," March 6, 1972; Box C6, Daane to Burns, February 28, 1972; *New York Times*, February 23, 1972.

57. NP, POF News Summaries Box 38, February 2 and 3, 1972; WHCF-FO, Box 45, Memorandum for the President–Weekly Report on International Finance, February 11, 1972; *New York Times*, February 12, 1972.

58. NP, Ehrlichman Papers, Box 6, Presidential Meeting Notes, February 14, 1972.

59. The IMF Executive Board consisted of executive directors appointed by the five countries with the largest voting shares and by other groups of countries. The directors resided in Washington and selected the managing director of the IMF, who was the chief executive officer of the organization. The Executive Board agreed to the final resolution establishing the Committee of 20 on June 23, 1972. The Board of Governors of the IMF (the finance ministers of member nations) approved it a month later. NP, WHCF-FO, Box 45, Memorandum for the President, April 29, 1972; Kenneth W. Dam, *The Rules of the Game: Reform and Evolution in the International Monetary System* (Chicago, 1982), pp. 216–17; James, *International Monetary Cooperation Since Bretton Woods*, pp. 246–51; Margaret Garritsen de Vries, *The International Monetary Fund 1972–1978: Volume I: Narrative and Analysis* (Washington, 1985), p. 155.

60. NP, WHCF-FO, Box 45, Memoranda to the President–Weekly Report on International Finance: February 22 and 26; March 3, 13, 18; April 1, 8, 15, 22; May 6, 13, 27; June 3, and 9, 1972; *New York Times*, February 23, 1972; de Vries, *The International Monetary Fund* pp. 23–24.

61. *New York Times*, May 22, 1972.

62. NP, WHCF-FO, Box 45, Memoranda for the President, June 17 and 24, 1972; Stein Papers, Box 45, Stein to Nixon, June 22, 1972; GFL, Burns Papers, Box B3, Larry Promisel to Bryant, June 22, 1972; *New York Times*, June 24 and 25, 1972; John Campbell, *Edward Heath: A Biography* (London, 1993), pp. 454–55.

63. In fact, a comment of Denis Healey, shadow chancellor of the exchequer, that he did not "see devaluation being delayed beyond this July or August" made the devaluation practically inevitable. NP, WHCF-FO, Box 45, Memorandum for the President, June 24, 1972.

64. NP, WHCF-Fi9, Box 55, Stein to President, June 22, 1972; Flanigan to President, June 23, 1972; Stein Papers, Box 44, Stein to Shultz, Casper Weinberger, and Flanigan, July 5, 1972.

65. *New York Times*, May 17, 1972; Volcker and Gyohten, *Changing Fortunes*, pp. 119–20.

66. See, e.g., NP, WHCF-Fi9, Box 55, Erb to Volcker Alternates, June 15, 1972; Stein Papers, Box 44, Whitman to Shultz, September 11, 1972; GFL, Burns Papers, Box B73, Ralph Bryant to Burns, March 27, 1972, EMB (LTD.), Report No. 72/10, "Arthur F. Burns on International Monetary Reform, May

17, 1972, "International Monetary Reform: Possible List of Topics for Discussion," July 19, 1972, Burns to Leslie K. O'Brien, July 20, 1972, "Should the Two–Tier System for Gold be Modified?" August 2, 1973, Burns to Shultz, August 4, 1972; Volcker and Gyohten, *Changing Fortunes*, pp. 120–25.

67. The mechanism suggested by the United States provided that a country with a surplus unwilling or unable to adjust its exchange rate would lose the right to convert its currency reserves into gold or SDRs. Surplus countries could also fulfill their systemic obligations by lowering trade barriers or by donating more foreign aid. Deficit countries could devalue or take action to lower their inflation rates. *New York Times*, September 26 and 27, 1972; Volcker and Gyohten, *Changing Fortunes*, p. 119.

68. GFL, Burns Papers, Box B74, Willis to Members of Volcker Group, January 11, 1973; Comments on Treasury Draft on the Nature of Reserve Assets, January 12, 1973; Daane to Burns, January 12, 1973.

69. NP, Ehrlichman Papers, Box 7, Presidential Meeting Notes, February 7, 10, and 13, 1973; WHCF-FO, Box 45, Memorandum for the President–Weekly Report on International Finance, January 13 and 24, 1973, February 6, 10, and 17, 1973; MRD, NLN 92-39/52, September 14, 1994, "Statement on Foreign Economic Policy by Secretary of the Treasury George Shultz," February 12, 1973; Stein Papers, Box 45, February 6, 10 and 17, 1973; de Vries, *The International Monetary Fund*, pp. 66–67.

70. NP, POF Box 91, Flanigan Memorandum Concerning Meeting with Sir Christopher Soames, February 16, 1973; WHCF-BE, Box 2, Message to Congress, February 22, 1973.

71. NP, WHCF-FO, Box 45, Memorandum to the President–Weekly Report on International Finance, March 3, 1973.

72. NP, WHCF-FO, Box 45, Memorandum for the President–Weekly Report on International Finance, March 3, 1973; POF, Stein Memorandum for the President's File, March 3, 1973; Odell, *U.S. International Monetary Policy*, p. 320.

73. NP, MRD, NLN 92-39/15, August 4, 1994, CIA Intelligence Memorandum, 5 March 1973; Burns Papers, Box B55, Currency Summary, March 6, 1973; Press Communiqués of the Ministerial Meetings of the Group of Ten and the European Economic Community, March 9 and 16, 1973; de Vries, *The International Monetary Fund*, pp. 78–79; Volcker and Gyohten, *Changing Fortunes*, p. 113.

74. NP, POF Box 81, "Remarks of the President to Top Businessmen," March 6, 1973.

75. Walter LaFeber, *The American Age: United States Foreign Policy at Home and Abroad Since 1755* (New York, 1989), p. 605; Silk, *Nixonomics*, p. 141.

76. NP, MRD, NLN 92-39/17, August 4, 1995, CIA Intelligence Memorandum, "A Comparison of the US and Soviet Economies," September 1973.

77. On the Nixon approach to burden sharing see, NP, MRD, NLN 92-37/16, August 4, 1995, CIA Intelligence Memorandum, "The Nixon-Brandt Meetings: The Economic Background," April 1973; MRD, NLN 92-39/7, August 26, 1995, Ronald I. Spiers to C.E. McManaway, "Defense Burden Sharing Studies," November 29, 1971; Calleo, *Imperious Economy*, pp. 118–38.

78. NP, Ehrlichman Papers, Box 5, Notes of Meeting, June 28, 1971.

79. NP, McCracken Papers, Box 42, Memorandum for President's Files, June 8, 1971.
80. NP, McCracken Papers, Box 42, McCracken to Peterson, June 29, 1971; Walter LaFeber, *The American Age*, p. 612.
81. NP, POF Box 85, Memorandum for the President's File, July 22, 1971.
82. NP, POF Box 85, McCracken to President, July 22, 1971.
83. NP, WHCF–BE, Box 2, Nixon to Martin, June 28, 1973.
84. See, e.g., NP, Ehrlichman Papers, Box 4, Notes of a Meeting, November 17, 1970; GFL, Burns Papers, Box 34, Alfred Hayes to Burns, March 23, 1971; Box B5, Burns to Connally, Mary 19, 1971.
85. LBJL, Bator Papers, NSF Presidential Memos Box 9, Bator to President, July 6, 1966; Volcker and Gyohten, *Changing Fortunes*, p. 67
86. Calleo, *Imperious Economy*, pp. 123–24.
87. de Vries, *The International Monetary Fund*, p. 25.
88. NP, POF Box 81, "Remarks of the President to Top Businessmen," March 6, 1973.

Chapter 11. The Oil Shocks

1. Arab states blocked shipments to the West to bring OECD pressure on Israel and end support for the Jewish state. Within two days the flow of Arab oil had declined to 40 percent of its normal level. Fighting closed the Suez Canal. Saudi Arabia, Libya, and Iraq stopped exporting any oil, while Kuwait and Algeria embargoed oil to the United States and Britain. Iraq closed its own and the IPC pipelines. DD, 1978-569C, Anthony Solomon, "The Middle Eastern Oil Problem," June 9, 1967; DD, 1990-106, CIA, Directorate of Intelligence, Intelligence Memorandum, July 10, 1967; DD, 1981-602, London to SD, No. 6910, June 6, 1967.
2. For an account of the struggle between the oil industry and the federal government during World War II, see, Michael B. Stoff, *Oil, War, and American Security: The Search for a National Policy on Foreign Oil, 1941–1947* (New Haven, 1980). Also see Herbert Feis, *Seen From E.A.—Three International Episodes* (New York, 1947).
3. 93rd Congress, 2d Session, Multinational Oil Corporations and U.S. Foreign Policy, "Report by the Subcommittee on Multinational Corporations," January 2, 1975.
4. For example, while in 1949 Aramco paid the U.S. Treasury $43 million and Saudi Arabia $39 million, two years later Aramco paid Saudi Arabia $110 million and the U.S. Treasury $6 million. Daniel Yergin, *The Prize: The Epic Quest for Oil, Money and Power* (New York, 1991), p. 447.
5. Yergin, *The Prize*, p. 474.
6. Council on Foreign Relations, New York, N.Y., Digest of a Meeting: Mr. James Terry Duce, "The Operations of the Arabian-American Oil Company in Saudi Arabia," January 26, 1956.
7. H.W. Brands, *Inside the Cold War: Loy Henderson and the Rise of the American Empire—1918–1961* (New York, 1991), p. 177.

8. Ian Skeet, OPEC: *Twenty-Five Years of Prices and Politics* (Cambridge, 1988), p. 12. The prices given are for Arabian light from Ras Tanura (Saudi Arabia). Prices depended on the type of oil and differed according to the oil's point of origin.

9. On OPEC's rise and its internal politics, see Zuhayr Mikdashi, "Cooperation among Oil Exporting Countries with Special Reference to Arab Countries: A Political Economy Analysis," *International Organization* 28:1 (Winter 1978): 1–30; Paul Jabber, "Conflict and Cooperation in OPEC: Prospects for the Next Decade" *International Organization* 32:2 (Spring 1978): 377–99; see also Theodore H. Moran, "Modelling OPEC Behavior: Economic and Political Alterations," *International Organization* 38:4 (Autumn 1984): 597–624. On the fifteenth OPEC conference, see Skeet, *OPEC*, p. 47.

10. Skeet, *OPEC*, pp. 47–48. See also Chapter 8 above.

11. Ibid., 61.

12. Ibid., p. 67.

13. NP, WHCF, TA4/29, Kissinger and Flanigan to Nixon, January 18, 1973.

14. NP, WHCF-SF, Box 35, Flanigan to Henry F. Jackson, September 18, 1972; John G. Clark, *The Political Economy of World Energy: A Twentieth Century Perspective* (Chapel Hill, N.C., 1990), pp. 170–78; Skeet, *OPEC*, pp. 58–76; Yergin, *The Prize*, pp. 578–83.

15. GFL, CEA Papers, Box 73, Ben Massell to Gary Seevers, April 26, 1974.

16. NP, POF Box 77, Memorandum for the President's File, March 5, 1969; GFL, Burns Papers, Box A15, Dillon Anderson to Burns, December 8, 1969; Box A16, Tom Cole to Burns, February 9, 196[9]; Memorandum, dated March 12, 1969, for the President concerning oil import policy; Nixon to Shultz, March 25, 1969; Stans to Burns, December 15, 1969.

17. NP, WHCF, TA4/29, Kissinger and Flanigan to Nixon, January 18, 1973; MRD, NLN 92-39/11, August 4, 1995, CIA Office of National Estimates, "Possibilities of Disruption of World Oil Supplies Through 1975," August 17, 1972, p. 11; Skeet, *OPEC*, pp. 52, 74;, Yergin, *The Prize*, p. 644.

18. NP, Flanigan Papers, Box 3, Memorandum of Conversation, January 15, 1973.

19. NP, Flanigan Papers, Box 4, "Iranian Oil," January 29, 1954; WHCF-SF, Box 36, Nixon to Faisal, January 30, 1973; WHCF, TA4/29, Harold H. Saunders and James B. Loken to Flanigan and Nixon, November 10, 1972; Kissinger and Flanigan to Nixon, January 18, 1973.

20. NP, WHCF-SF, Box 36, Brent Scowcroft to Arleigh Burke, June 14, 1973.

21. Steven L. Spiegel, *The Other Arab-Israeli Conflict: Making America's Middle East Policy, from Truman to Reagan* (Chicago, 1985), pp. 240–43.

22. The report revealed that the United States in 1970 depended on imports of oil and gas for 12 percent of its total energy requirements and predicted that this figure would rise to between 20 and 25 percent by 1975. NP, Stein Papers, Box 133, "U.S. Energy Outlook," Full Report of the National Petroleum Council Committee on U.S. Energy Outlook, Preprint Copy, December 1972. See also NP, Flanigan Papers, Box 3, Flanigan to Nixon, September 18, 1972; Memoranda of Conversations, November 15, 1972; Memorandum concerning the Iranian problem, dated December 28, 1972.

23. As J.D. Darroch suggested to the Council of Economic Advisors on June 7,

perhaps the time had now come to think not only of increasing gasoline supplies but of serious conservation policies. After all, the United States with less than 6 percent of the world's population accounted for over 34 percent of annual energy consumption. Darroch suggested increased public mass transit, government subsidies for energy-related research and development, and revolutionary changes in urban planning to reduce commuting distances, minimize motor vehicle use for shopping, and encourage bicycle rights-of-way. This list demonstrates the revolution in the American way of life that any real effort toward energy conservation would require. GFL, CEA Papers, Box 66, Darroch to CEA, June 7, 1973; Darroch to Gary Seevers, June 11, 1973. See also NP, WHCF-BE, Box 2, Cole to Stein, May 31, 1973; WHCF-SF, Box 36, Memorandum of Conversation, February 6, 1973; Stein Papers, Box 44, Solomon to William Simon, March 8, 1973; GFL, Burns Papers, Box B24, Stein Memorandum for George P. Shultz, May 31, 1973; CEA Papers, Box 66, Statement by the President on the Energy Message, April 18, 1973; Lionel D. Edie & Company, "The President's Energy Message," May 7, 1973.

24. NP, MRP, NLN 92-39/11, August 4, 1995, CIA, Office of National Estimates, "Possibilities of Disruption of World Oil Supplies Through 1975," August 17, 1972.

25. David Schoenbaum, *The United States and the State of Israel* (New York, 1993), pp. 136–41.

26. Spiegel, *The Other Arab-Israeli Conflict*, p. 255.

27. Skeet, *OPEC*, pp. 87–91.

28. GFL, CEA Papers, Box 66, White House Fact Sheet—The President's Energy Emergency Address, November 7, 1973; Frank G. Zarb Papers, Box 1, "Memorandum for the President," March 26, 1975.

29. NP, Stein Papers, Box 53, Michael Raoul-Duval to Kenneth R. Cole Jr., October 29, 1973; Love to President, October 30, 1973; Flanigan to Kehrli, November 2, 1973; Box 183, Stein Memorandum, November 12, 1973; Darrell Trent to Sidney Jones, November 12, 1973; GFL, CEA Papers, Box 66, "Vulnerability of U.S. Oil Consumption to an Arab Boycott," October 7, 1973. Concerning long-term problems created by the oil shocks, see Walter J. Levy, "The Years That the Locust Has Eaten: Oil Policy and OPEC Development Prospects," *Foreign Affairs* 57:2 (Winter 1978–79): 287–305.

30. Author's interview with Walter Wriston; Western Europe and Japan faced greater problems. Persian Gulf and North African suppliers accounted for 84 percent of Western Europe's oil imports in 1973 and 76 percent of Japan's imported oil. The CIA reported in November that the EC commission was "in complete confusion, and some working-level officials believe that the lack of unity on oil might spread to other EC issues and policies." The oil weapon struck at Western Europe's economic viability; most OECD nations had begun climbing out of the slump that had plagued them for the past two years and during the first half of 1973 achieved higher than normal growth rates. The OPEC price increase announced on October 16, calculated the administration, would increase the oil annual import bill by $3 billion for the United States and Japan and $1.5 billion each for West Germany, the United Kingdom, Italy, and France. A renewed plunge in GNP was inevitable. NP, Stein

Papers, Box 164, Address by the President of Nationwide Radio and Television, November 25, 1973; GFL, CEA Papers, Box 66, The President's Energy Emergency Address, November 7, 1973; "The Impact on Oil Shortages of U.S. Emergency Usage," November 19, 1973; The White House Fact Sheet—New Energy Emergency Actions, November 25, 1973; Box 74, Stein to Shultz et al., November 1, 1973; Stein to Love et al., November 29, 1973.

31. Skeet, OPEC, pp. 100–102; Yergin, The Prize, pp. 625–26.

32. GFL, Burns Papers, Box B86, "Notes on Reserves and Flows of Funds of Arab Oil-Producing Countries," November 30, 1973.

33. GFL, Burns Papers, Box B86, Junz to Bryant, January 4, 1974; OASIA Research Memorandum, dated January 4, 1974.

34. NP, Stein Papers, Box 46, Memorandum for the President concerning crude oil price options, December 19, 1973; Memorandum for the President's File, December 20, 1973; Box 134, Remarks of the President, December 4, 1973; "Impact of One Dollar Increase on Domestic Crude Petroleum Prices," December 19, 1973; Box 135, Stein to Simon, December 27, 1973; GFL, CEA Box 66, Statement by the President, December 19, 1973.

35. NP, WHCF-SF Box 37, File Memorandum dated January 9, 1974.

36. NP, MRD, NLN 92-39/24, CIA Economic Intelligence Weekly, November 8, 1973; NLN 92-39/27, CIA, Economic Intelligence Weekly, November 22, 1973, p. 3; Clark, The Political Economy of World Energy, pp. 234–35.

37. Clark, The Political Economy of World Energy, pp. 233–34; Skeet, OPEC, pp. 106–7.

38. NP, NRD, NLN 92-39/40, August 7, 1995, CIA Briefing Book dated February 4, 1974, for the Washington Energy Conference, February 11, 1974; NLN 92-39/55, September 14, 1994, Herbert Stein to George Shultz, "Where We Are Going in the ECG," April 1, 1974; GFL, Burns Papers, Box B24, Flanigan to Shultz et al., January 24, 1974; Box B32, Washington Energy Conference, opening remarks of Henry Kissinger, February 11, 1974; Communiqué dated February 13, 1974; CEA Papers, Box 109, Washington Energy Conference, The World Energy and Economic Outlook; Yergin, The Prize, p. 630.

39. Economist, November 26, 1977.

40. Skeet, OPEC, p. 120; Spiegel, The Other Arab-Israeli Conflict, pp. 280–82; Yergin, The Prize, p. 632.

41. "National self-sufficiency" would be reached when American oil and natural gas imports constituted no more than a minor fraction (15 percent or less) of American energy supplies and no more than a small part of which (such as 5 percent) would come from a single source.

42. NP, Stein Papers, Box 135, "Project Independence Plan and Schedule," February 1974; GFL, Burns Papers, Box B32, "Project Independence," February 1974; "Project Independence—Summary," February 8, 1974.

43. GFL, Burns Papers, Box B103, "Oil Industry Profits: A Second Look," Treasury Survey of Nineteen Petroleum Companies, October 4, 1974.

44. NP, WHCF-SF, Box 37, Carlyle Maw to Scowcroft, May 19, 1974; GFL, CEA Papers, Box 73, B.F. Massell et al. to the Chairman, January 18, 1974.

45. 93rd Congress, 2d Session, Hearings before the Subcommittee on Multinational Corporations of the Committee on Foreign Relations, United States

Senate, Part 9, June 5 and 6, July 25, and August 12, 1974; 93rd Congress, 2d Session, Multinational Oil Corporations and U.S. Foreign Policy, Report dated January 2, 1975; Yergin, *The Prize*, pp. 656–60.

46. NP, Stein Papers, Box 44, Testimony by William Simon before the Senate Finance Committee, January 24, 1974; Box 54A, Roy L. Ash to Nixon, February 15, 1974; Stein to Noel Koch, February 28, 1974; David Gergen to Roy Ash et al., February 28, 1974.

47. NP, Stein Papers, Box 31, Flanigan to Kissinger et al., June 12, 1974.

48. GFL, CEA Papers, Box 24, Milton Russell Memorandum, November 18, 1974.

49. Clark, *The Political Economy of World Energy*, p. 237.

50. GFL, CEA Box 43, Memorandum for Alan Greenspan, November 14, 1974.

51. GFL, Frank Zarb Papers, Box 1, Zarb to Henry H. Jones, February 24, 1975.

52. GFL, Zarb Papers, Box 2, Zarb and Elliot Richardson to the President, October 6, 1976.

53. See, e.g., GFL, Burns Papers, Box B86, "Regulation of Domestic Crude Petroleum Prices," July 27, 1976; CEA Papers, Box 9, Zarb to the President (n.d.); CEA Papers Box 21, Testimony of Paul W. MacAvoy, January 22, 1976; "Gas Deregulation Strategy," Draft, February 20, 1976; Zarb Papers, Box 2, Zarb to the President, March 8, 1976.

54. GFL, Gerald R. Ford Papers, Presidential Handwriting File, Box 3, Ford letter, January 10, 1975; Box 46, Robert Goldwin to the President, January 31, 1975; O'Donnell and Jencks Files, Box 4, "Analysis of President Ford's Energy Tax and Import Fee Program," January 21, 1975; Burns Papers, Box B86, Talking Points on the Economy," January 27, 1975; CEA Papers, Box 1, William J. Fellner to the President, February 7, 1975; Box 9, "The Energy Situation and Status Report on Energy Legislation," September 17, 1975; Milton Russell Papers, Box 3, Russell to CEA, February 4, 1975; Zarb Papers, Box 1, Meeting with Republican leadership on energy and related issues, June 5, 1975; Yergin, *The Prize* pp. 660–61.

55. Yergin, *The Prize*, pp. 661–64.

56. *New York Times*, January 20, 1978.

57. GFL, Russell Papers, Box 3, "Prospective Petroleum Production," February 14, 1975; Yergin, *The Prize*, pp. 664–70.

58. GFL, Zarb Papers, Box 2, Zarb to the President, August 12, 1976.

59. GFL, CEA Papers, Box 25, "Walter Levy on Oil Prices," August 26, 1976.

60. James A. Bill, *The Eagle and the Lion: The Tragedy of American-Iranian Relations* (New Haven, 1988), p. 202.

61. Yergin, *The Prize*, p. 672.

62. Clark, *The Political Economy of World Energy*, p. 237.

63. Yergin, *The Prize*, p. 713.

64. See Bill, *The Eagle and the Lion*; Gaddis Smith, *Morality, Reason and Power: American Diplomacy in the Carter Years* (New York, 1986), pp. 180–207; Gary Sick, *All Fall Down: America's Tragic Encounter with Iran* (New York, 1985); Skeet, *OPEC*, pp. 158, 162–63; Yergin, *The Prize*, pp. 680–98.

65. The CEA had estimated that "each 5 percent oil price rise would reduce real GNP by 0.3 percent and add a similar amount to consumer prices in the major

developed nations as a group." For the United States the figure was .2 percent loss for each 5 percent rise. GFL, CEA Papers, Box 15, "Impact of Another Oil Price Rise," November 1976.

66. Clark, *The Political Economy of World Energy*, p. 237. *Economist*, July 27, 1996.
67. Ibid., pp. 246, 251.
68. Lawrence Freedman and Efraim Karsh, *The Gulf Conflict 1990–1991: Diplomacy and War in the New World Order* (Princeton, 1992), pp. 180–88.
69. Yergin, *The Prize*, p. 718.
70. DD, 1988-3176, National Intelligence Estimate: Middle East Oil, December 13, 1960.
71. American oil companies ultimately found their best source of Middle Eastern oil in Saudi Arabia, a country whose king, Abdul Aziz bin Abdul Rahman bin Faisal al Saud (better known as Ibn Saud), was hostile to Great Britain. Beginning in 1933 Socal, not a party and therefore not bound by the Red Line Agreement, began exploring oil deposits in the sands off Riyadh and Jidda. Eventually Socal, joined by Jersey, Texaco, and Mobil, formed the Arabian-American Oil Company (Aramco), which won the bulk of the Saudi concessions. However, most U.S. oil came from American fields, the largest of which, the East Texas field, had come on stream during the Depression. During World War II Roosevelt arranged for Saudi Arabia to receive lend-lease aid although the nation was immune from the ravages of World War II, and met with King Ibn Saud when Roosevelt was on his way home from the Yalta conference. In 1957 King Ibn Abd-al-Aziz Saud (one of the four sons of Ibn Saud who ultimately succeeded their father) became the first ruler of any Middle Eastern state (including Israel) to make an official visit to Washington. Throughout the next decade the United States augmented its pro-Saudi policy. American officials solidified relations with the monarchy while American military men established ties with their Saudi counterparts. To avoid offending Saudi sensibilities, the Defense Department adopted the policy followed by MNOCs of not sending American Jews to Saudi Arabia.
72. Clark, *The Political Economy of World Energy*, p. 303.
73. Ibid., pp. 207–13. Also see McCloy Papers, "oil."
74. Ibid., p. 305.
75. During the Ford administration, at the highwater mark of détente, U.S. and Soviet officials discussed purchases of Soviet energy supplies. Administration officials remained ambivalent until negotiations finally broke down. See, e.g., GFL, MR 93-24, #6, "Agreement between the Government of the United States of America and the Government of the Union of Soviet Socialist Republics," Draft of February 12, 1976; CEA Papers, Box 141, Russell to Greenspan, October 29 and 31 and November 4, 1975.
76. Clark, *The Political Economy of World Energy*, p. 306.

Chapter 12. Public Becomes Private

1. Personal knowledge of the author.
2. GFL, Burns Papers, Box B 86, "Sterling Reserves of Oil-Exporting Countries,"

November 22, 1974; Irvine to Wonnacot, November 22, 1974; Box B87, Ditchley Foundation, Anglo-American Conference on the Problems Arising from the Oil Surpluses, January 31–February 3, 1975, Background Paper 4; CEA Papers, Box 17, OASIA Research, December 17, 1974, "OPEC Revenues and Current Balances in 1980"; NP, MRD, NLN 92-39/35, August 4, 1995, CIA, "International Economic Impact of Increased Oil Prices in 1974," January 1974.

3. NP, MRD, NLN 92-39/37, August 7, 1995, CIA, "International Oil Developments," January 4, 1974; GFL, Burns Papers, Box B87 Ditchley Foundation Conference, Background Paper 4; Box B86, Gonzalez to Burns, May 28, 1974; Box B87, R.H. Mills Jr. to Burns, September 25, 1975; Box B102, U.S. Treasury Department, International Economic Reports, The Absorptive Capacity of the OPEC countries, September 5, 1975; Karin Lissakers, *Banks, Borrowers and the Establishment: A Revisionist Account of the International Debt Crisis* (New York, 1991), p. 23; John Maynard Keynes, *The Economic Consequences of the Peace* (New York, 1920).

4. *Economist*, March 8, 1980.

5. GFL, Burns Papers, B86, S. Pizer et al. to Burns, January 9, 1975.

6. NP, MRD, NLN 92-39/44, August 7, 1995, CIA, "Arab Investment Institutions and Policies," April 1974, p. 4; MRD, NLN 92-39/45, August 7, 1995, CIA, Economic Intelligence Weekly, April 24, 1974, p. 1.

7. NP, WHCF-SF, Box 49, "Talking Points on Foreign Investment and Arab Oil Money for the July 25, 1974, Meeting with Senator William E. Brock; GFL, Box B101, Volcker to Burns, January 8, 1974.

8. NP, MRD, NLN 92-39/41, August 7, 1995, CIA, International Oil Developments, February 15, 1974; on arms sales see Andrew J. Pierre, *The Global Politics of Arms Sales* (Princeton, 1982).

9. GFL, Presidential Handwriting File, Box 46, Zarb and Greenspan to Ford, August 7, 1975; DD, 1988-463, Kissinger to Ford, August 6, 1975; *Economist*, August 28, 1976.

10. GFL, WHCF-SF, FO Box 28, John Niehuss to W.D. Eberle, December 5, 1974; Scowcroft and Seidman to the President, February 14, 1975; Malcolm Butler to Scowcroft, May 6, 1975, Box 29, Memorandum on Proposed Iran/Occidental Investment, July 26, 1976; Presidential Handwriting, Box 21, Seidman to the President, March 3, 1975; L. William Seidman Papers, Box 40, Shepard to Rumsfeld, February 4, 1975; "Survey of Laws and Regulations on Foreign Investment and Safeguards Against Undesirable Behavior by Foreign Investors," February 6, 1975; CEA Papers, Box 16, Memorandum on Proposed Iran/Occidental Investment, August 3, 1976; Box 162, "Foreign Investment in the United States," Treasury Department, April 25, 1975.

11. GFL, WHCF-SF, FO Box 28, Ford to Secretary of State et al., March 4, 1975, Oakley to Scowcroft, July 7, 1975, Box 29, Oakley to Scowcroft, October 30, 1975; CEA Papers, Box 161, "Foreign Investment in the United States, Treasury Department, April 25, 1975; Burns Papers, Box B2, Legal Division to Board of Governors, August 4, 1975, Burns to Benjamin S. Rosenthal, June 3, 1976; *Economist*, February 15, 1975.

12. 50 U.S.C. 2407. One of the most celebrated prosecutions, that of Baxter International, was not settled until 1993.

13. Columbia University, Oral History Collection, Eugene Black Oral History; D.E. Moggridge, *Maynard Keynes: An Economist's Biography* (London, 1992), p. 735.

14. Columbia University, George D. Woods Papers, Box 18, Address by George Woods, President, World Bank, IFC and IDA, before the Business Council Meeting, May 7, 1965; Henry Owen, "The World Bank: Is 50 Years Enough?" *Foreign Affairs* 73:5 (September-October 1994): 97–108.

15. See Burton I. Kaufman, *Trade and Aid: Eisenhower's Foreign Economic Policy* (Baltimore, 1982).

16. As Secretary of State Dean Rusk advised the President, "in three underdeveloped continents we have reached a watershed where the holding operations of the past are clearly inadequate and where new initiative[s] of a dramatic and positive kind are essential." *Foreign Relations of the United States, 1961–1963, Volume IX, Foreign Economic Policy* (Washington, 1995), No. 95, Memorandum from Secretary of State Rusk to President Kennedy, March 10, 1961, p. 210.

17. Philip M. Kaiser, *Journeying Far and Wide: A Political and Diplomatic Memoir* (New York, 1992), pp. 188–93.

18. Columbia University, George Woods Papers, George Woods, The Development Decade in the Balance," *Foreign Affairs.*

19. *Economist*, November 3, 1979.

20. GFL, Burns Papers, Box B67, "Staff Comment on the Special Interests of the Developing Countries," June 6, 1974.

21. NP, Stein Papers, Box 54, Flanigan to Shultz et al., October 25, 1973; Margaret de Vries, *The International Monetary Fund 1972–1978: Volume I: Narrative and Analysis* (Washington, 1985), p. 307.

22. GFL, CEA Papers, Box 109, "The Energy Crisis: A Review of the Additional Resource Needs of the Hardest Hit LDC's [sic]," April 16, 1974; Kvasnicka to Seevers, April 23, 1974; Burns Papers, Box B86, IBRD, "Some Implications of Rising Trend in Petroleum Prices for Developing Countries," December 20, 1973.

23. NP, CIEP Papers, Flanigan to Simon et al., July 2, 1974; GFL, Burns Papers, Box B24, Randy Jayne to Secretary of State et al., April 11, 1974; Harold James, *International Monetary Cooperation Since Bretton Woods* (Washington, 1996), pp. 320–21. For an examination of how OECD governments shaped private lending, see Philip Wellons, "International Debt: The Behavior of Banks in a Politicized Environment," *International Organization* 39:3 (Summer 1985): 441–71.

24. The IMF ultimately raised SDR 3,046.9 million for the 1974 facility of which SDR 464.077 million was made available for the 1975 facility. de Vries, *The International Monetary Fund*, p. 346; James, *International Monetary Cooperation Since Bretton Woods*, p. 316–22.

25. GFL, Burns Papers, Box B66, IMF Secretary to Members of the Executive Board, February 19, 1974; IMF Secretary to Members and Associates of the Interim Committee, December 26, 1974; Box B86, Solomon to Wallich, Sep-

tember 24, 1974; Box B87, Communiqué of the Ministerial Meetings of the Group of Ten, January 16, 1975; IMF Press Release No. 75/2, January 16, 1975; de Vries, *The International Monetary Fund*, pp. 305–60; *Economist*, March 1, 1975.

26. This trend continued into the Reagan and Bush years. Of the foreign aid packages, hovering in the $7–10 billion per annum range, increasingly significant portions went to military assistance. The U.S. government required huge chunks of aid to be tied to the purchase of American products; in 1982, for example, 70 percent of bilateral aid was so designated. *Economist*, December 15, 1979; June 26, 1980; April 17, 1982; July 3, 1982; December 3, 1983.

27. GFL, Seidman Papers, Box 53, International Economic Policy Issues, Summary Status Report, December 15, 1975; CEA Papers, Box 20, Helen Junz to Paul MacAvoy, December 10, 1975; Box 105, State Department, "Linkage and Reverse Linkage Among Commissions," December 1975; Box 130, MacAvoy to Charles W. Robinson, December 12, 1975, SD to All Diplomatic Posts, No. 9398, December 19, 1975; DD, "Robinson to Secretary of State, December 19, 1975; DD, 1989-2776, "General Orientation Paper for CIEC," December 5, 1975.

28. GFL, CEA Papers, Box 105, Background Statement on Secretary's UNCTAD Speech," May 5, 1976; Burns Papers, Box B62, Briefing Book, June 1976, "Relations Between Developed and Developing Countries; *Economist*, May 8, 1976.

29. *Economist*, February 15, 1975; August 9, 1975; January 31, 1976.

30. Lissakers, *Banks, Borrowers and the Establishment*, pp. 53–62.

31. The Euromarkets began in the 1950s as Soviet officials, afraid of possible U.S. sanctions, deposited their dollar holdings in foreign banks abroad. American bankers, beginning their expansion abroad, quickly grasped the advantages of this innovation: overseas deposits were apparently immune from the dictates of American regulators and were not subject to the reserve requirements applied to bank loans in the United States. For just these reasons the exponential growth of the Eurodollar market posed a looming threat to the safety of the international financial system as a whole.

32. On the debt crisis generally, see Chris C. Carvounis, *The Foreign Debt/National Development Conflict: External Adjustment and Internal Disorder in the Developing Nations* (New York, 1987); Benjamin J. Cohen, *In Whose Interest? International Banking and American Foreign Policy* (New York, 1986); Rudiger Dornbusch, John H. Makin, and David Zlowe, *Alternative Sources to Developing Country Debt Problems* (Washington, 1989); Richard E. Feinberg and Ricardo Ffrench-Davis, *Development and External Debt in Latin America: Basis for a New Consensus* (Notre Dame, Ind., 1988); Jeffry A. Frieden, *Debt, Development and Democracy: Modern Political Economy and Latin America* (Princeton, 1991); Lissakers, *Banks, Borrowers and the Establishment*; Seamus O'Cleiracain, *Third World Debt and International Public Policy* (New York, 1990); Stephen A. Schucker, *American "Reparations" to Germany, 1919–1933: Implications for the Third-World Debt Crisis* (Princeton, 1988); John Weeks, ed., *Debt Diasaster? Banks, Governments and Multilaterals Confront the Crisis* (New York, 1989).

33. That this steadily growing pool of funds was lightly regulated accelerated the pace of LDC lending further, as did the decision of the Nixon administration to abandon the various controls over foreign investment that the Johnson administration had erected to protect the Bretton Woods system. See NP, MRD, NLN 92-39/47, CIA, Economic Intelligence Weekly, May 22, 1974, pp. 2–3.

34. Cohen, *In Whose Interest?* pp. 46–47.

35. *Economist*, June 26, 1976; November 20, 1976.

36. GFL, Burns Papers, Box B61, Fred Ruckdeschel to Mr. Henry, November 4, 1976.

37. Eurodollar loan agreements typically contained clauses placing the risk of a market collapse on the borrower. But if a crisis proved general, banks would be caught in the resulting disaster.

38. Interest rates were calculated at LIBOR (London Interbank Offerred Rate), a floating rate then usually computed at three- or six-month intervals.

39. GFL, Burns Papers, Box B64, Henry S. Terrell, "U.S. Bank Lending to Less Developed Countries," November 9, 1976; Ralph W. Smith to Burns, November 22, 1976, Ted Truman to Burns, November 29, 1976; Box B60, Telex from President Zijlstra to A.F. Burns and H.C. Wallich, January 5, 1978; Wyatt C. Wells, *Economist in an Uncertain World: Arthur F. Burns and the Federal Reserve, 1970–1978* (New York, 1995), p. 195.

40. GFL, Burns Papers, Box B64, Terrell to Truman, September 22, 1977.

41. GFL, Box B61, Rene Larre to Henry C. Wallich, July 1, 1977; R.H. Mills Jr. to Governor Wallich, December 6, 1977; Wells, *Economist in an Uncertain World*, p. 196.

42. Lissakers, *Banks, Borrowers and the Establishment*, p. 91.

43. *Economist*, March 18, 1978; August 5, 1978.

44. GFL, Burns Papers, Box B64, Terrell, "U.S. Bank Lending to Less Developed Countries," November 9, 1976; Gustav H. Peterson, "Latin America: Benign Neglect Is Not Enough," *Foreign Affairs* 51:2 (April 1973): 598–607; *Economist*, October 21, 1978; July 5, 1980.

45. *Economist*, May 19, 1979; November 3, 1979; Lissakers, *Banks, Borrowers and the Establishment*, pp. 234–35; Joan Edelman Spero, *The Politics of International Economic Relations*, 2d ed. (New York, 1981), p. 175.

46. David Halloran Lumsdaine, *Moral Vision in International Politics: The Foreign Aid Regime, 1949–1989* (Princeton, 1993), pp. 162, 165; Spero, *The Politics of International Economic Relations*, p. 176.

47. Lissakers, *Banks, Borrowers and the Establishment*, pp. 84, 114–36.

48. Personal knowledge of the author.

49. *Economist*, August 16, 1980.

50. Walter Wriston interview with the author.

51. *Economist*, April 23, 1982; June 23, 1984; Lissakers, *Banks, Borrowers and the Establishment*, p. 138.

52. *Economist*, May 1, 1982; September 25, 1982; April 14, 1984.

53. *Economist*, April 30, 1983; James, *International Monetary Cooperation Since Bretton Woods*, p. 482; O'Cleiracain, *Third World Debt and International Public Policy*, p. 227; Paul Volcker and Toyoo Gyohten, *Changing Fortunes: The*

World's Money and the Threat to American Monetary Leadership (New York, 1992), pp. 200–207.

54. *Economist*, March 20, 1977; September 11, 1982.
55. *Economist*, March 5, 1983; April 30, 1983. On the development and course of the debt crisis, see also Jahangir Amuzegar, "Dealing with Debt," *Foreign Policy* 68 (Fall 1987): 140–58; Pedro-Pablo Kuczynski, "Latin American Debt, " *Foreign Affairs* 61:1 (Winter 1982–83): 344–64; Lars Schoultz, "Politics, Economics, and U.S. Participation in Multi-National Development Banks," *International Organization* 36:3 (Summer 1982): 537–74.
56. James, *International Monetary Cooperation Since Bretton Woods*, pp. 322–35.
57. GFL, Burns Papers, Box B62, Address by H. Johannes Witteveen, May 8, 1978.
58. Carvounis, *The Foreign Debt/National Development Conflict*, p. 31.
59. On the connection between IMF programs and political stability, see Henry S. Bienen and Mark Gerovitz, "Economic Stabilization, Conditionality and Political Stability," *International Organization* 39:4 (Autumn 1985): 729–54; on Washington's neglect of the effect of the debt crisis on political stability, see Riordan Roett, "Democracy and Debt in South America: A Continent's Dilemma," *Foreign Affairs* 62:3 (Winter 1983): 695–720; concerning Latin American fears of the debt crisis on their nations, see Stephen B. Webb, "Comparing Latin American Debt Today with German Reparations after World War One," U.S. Department of State: Bureau of Commerce and Business Affairs, Planning and Economic Analysis Staff, PAS Working Paper #5, Washington, U.S. State Department (February 1988). On the comparison between Latin American defaults in the 1930s and the 1980s, see Marilyn E. Skiles, "Latin American International Loan Defaults in the 1930s: Lessons for the 1980s (unpublished paper, 1989).
60. Lissakers, *Banks, Borrowers and the Establishment*, pp. 190–91.
61. Personal knowledge of the author.
62. *Economist*, August 20, 1983; May 5, 1984; February 6, 1988.
63. *Economist*, June 2, 1984.
64. *New York Times*, April 16, 1984.
65. For the conflicting interests of North and South governments in the debt crisis, see Miles Kahler, "Politics and International Debt: Explaining the Crisis," *International Organization* 39:3 (Summer 1985): 357–82; for various proposals to resolve the debt crisis, see Pedro-Pablo Kuczynski, "Latin American Debt: Act Two," *Foreign Affairs* 62:1 (Fall 1983): 17–38.
66. *Economist*, October 12, 1985; James, *International Monetary Cooperation Since Bretton Woods*, pp. 396–99; Lissakers, *Banks, Borrowers and the Establishment*, pp. 228–29, 234.
67. *Economist*, January 31, 1987; May 23, 1987; February 6, 1988; March 12, 1987; April 2, 1988; Lissakers, *Banks, Borrowers and the Establishment*, p. 238.
68. *New York Times*, April 16, 1984; Jeffrey Sachs, "Making the Brady Plan Work," *Foreign Affairs* 68:3 (Summer 1989): 87–104; James, *International Monetary Cooperation Since Bretton Woods*, pp. 399–408.
69. Personal knowledge of the author.
70. Concerning the position that international lending required fundamental

reforms, see Charles F. Meissner, "Debt: Reform Without Governments," *Foreign Policy* 68 (Fall 1987): 140–58.

71. *Economist*, April 30, 1983.

Chapter 13. The Eighties

1. Ronald Reagan, *An American Life: The Autobiography* (New York, 1990), p. 219.
2. Lou Cannon, *President Reagan: The Role of a Lifetime* (New York, 1990), pp. 108–9; Walter LaFeber, *The American Age: United States Foreign Policy at Home and Abroad Since 1750* (New York, 1989), p. 677.
3. Cannon, *President Reagan* p. 305.
4. See Paul Volcker and Toyoo Gyohten, *Changing Fortunes: The World's Money and the Threat to American Leadership* (New York, 1992), pp. 163–86.
5. *Economic Report of the President* (Washington, 1995); Cannon, *President Reagan*, pp. 235, 270; LaFeber, *The American Age: United States Foreign Policy at Home and Abroad since 1970* (New York, 1989), p. 667; Donald T. Regan, *For the Record: From Wall Street to Washington* (New York, 1988), p. 175.
6. Cannon, *President Reagan*, p. 282.
7. LaFeber, *The American Age*, p. 671.
8. Martin Malia, *The Soviet Tragedy: A History of Socialism in Russia, 1917–1991* (New York, 1994), p. 413.
9. Cannon, *President Reagan*, p. 739; Malia, *The Soviet Tragedy*, p. 415.
10. Malia, *The Soviet Tragedy*, p. 415; Cannon, *President Reagan*, p. 280.
11. Malia, *The Soviet Tragedy*, pp. 454–55.

Chapter 14. Free Trade Forever?

1. On American free trade ideology, see Barry Buzan, "Economic Structure and International Security: The Limits of the Liberal Case," *International Organization* 38:4 (Autumn 1984): 597–624; Alfred E. Eckes Jr., *Opening America's Market: U.S. Foreign Trade Policy Since 1776* (Chapel Hill, N.C., 1995); Stephen D. Krasner, "U.S. Commercial and Monetary Policy: Unraveling the Paradox of External Strength and Internal Weakness," *International Organization* 31:4 (Autumn 1977): 635–71.
2. *Life*, May 19, 1947.
3. *Life*, November 4, 1946.
4. The RTAA was first passed in 1934 and renewed periodically thereafter. *Time*, April 2, 1945.
5. See, e.g., SML, Princeton University, Allen W. Dulles Papers, Box 27, Preliminary Outline of Remarks to National Foreign Trade Council Convention, November 11, 1946; Truman Library, McNaughton papers, Box 13, McNaughton to Birmingham, June 18, 1948.
6. Richard N. Gardner, *Sterling-Dollar Diplomacy in Current Perspective: The Origins and the Prospects of Our International Economic Order* (New York, 1980), p. 159.

7. TL, Clayton-Thorp Papers, Box 2, "Current Popular Opinion on Foreign Trade Issues," October 21, 1946.
8. Gregory A. Fossedahl, *Our Finest Hour: Will Clayton, the Marshall Plan and the Triumph of Democracy* (Stanford, 1993), pp. 237–38; Thomas W. Zeiler, *American Trade and Power in the 1960s* (New York, 1992), pp. 23–24.
9. Will Clayton, fresh from working on the Marshall Plan and leading the GATT talks, devoted his efforts next to the abortive United Nations Conference on Trade and Employment, which was held in Havana, Cuba, in December 1947. Clayton wrote the *New York Times* columnist Arthur Krock explaining his support of the Havana charter: "Heretofore each Nation [sic] acted unilaterally when considering measures relating to international trade. Usually a neighbor was hurt, promptly retaliated, and in the end all were hurt and mad. This is not the way to preserve world peace or world prosperity." But the charter and its creation, the International Trade Organization, represented an unsuccessful compromise, neither sufficiently free trade for some countries but too protectionist for others. That it died in a congressional committee pleased not only many American legislators but other nations as well. GATT instead became a permanent organization with headquarters in Geneva, Switzerland, taking over many of the duties that the ITO had been intended to fulfill. Congress may have blocked the ITO, but its previous delegation of authority to the President allowed the executive branch to enter into the GATT, the most important trade agreement ever signed by an American president, without further consultation. SML, Arthur Krock Papers, Princeton University, Box R1, Clayton to Krock, February 26, 1949.
10. SML, JFD Papers, Box 128, Press Release No. 335, Statement by the Honorable John Foster Dulles, June 20, 1958.
11. Zeiler, *American Trade and Power in the 1960s*, p. 36.
12. Ibid., p. 27.
13. DD (courtesy of Andrea Ashworth), No. 2912, Bator to Johnson, May 11, 1967; John M. Blum, *Years of Discord: American Politics and Society, 1961–1974* (New York, 1991), p. 64. Also see Zeiler, *American Trade and Power in the 1960s*, generally.
14. I.M. Destler, *Making Foreign Economic Policy* (Washington, 1980), pp. 144–47.
15. DD (Ashworth), No. 3370, Rusk to President, February 11, 1967.
16. LBJL, NSF Co Box 253, Memorandum of Conversation between Secretary of State Dean Rusk and Foreign Minister Ohira, January 28, 1964; Tokyo to SD, No. 2016, December 23, 1964; "Recommended Policy Actions on Japan," December 1964; "Summary of Current Problems in U.S.–Japan Relations," December 1964; DD (Ashworth), No. 2078, Memorandum dated July 7, 1965, concerning the fourth meeting of the Joint United States–Japan Committee on Trade and Economic Affairs, to be held on July 7, 1965.
17. William Horsley and Roger Buckley, *Nippon—New Superpower: Japan Since 1945* (London, 1990), p. 37.
18. DD (Ashworth), No. 657J, Tokyo to SD, No. 349, July 11, 1969; DD (Ashworth), No. 54E, CIA Directorate of Intelligence, Intelligence Memorandum, "Japan: Impact of the Import Quota Liberalization Program," May 1972.

19. NP, WHSF, POF Box 77, Paul McCracken to Cabinet Committee on Economic Policy, March 5, 1969; POF Box 78, Stans to President, April 28, 1969, POF Box 80, C. Fred Bergsten to President's Files, April 6, 1970; GFL, Wesley G. McCain to Arthur Burns, "Brief Summary of U.S. Foreign Trade," February 27, 1969. On the institutional bases of Nixon's position, see Judith Goldstein, "The Political Economy of Trade: Institutions of Protection," *American Political Science Review* 80:1 (March 1986): 161–84.

20. Henry Kissinger, *White House Years* (New York, 1979), p. 1053; Richard M. Nixon, *RN, The Memoirs of Richard Nixon* (New York, 1978, 1990), pp. 560–67; Tad Szulc, *The Illusion of Peace: Foreign Policy in the Nixon-Kissinger Years* (New York, 1978), pp. 521–24. (Courtesy of Michael Schaller)

21. NP, WHSF, POF Box 85, Nixon to Chung Hee Park, July 16, 1971, Nixon to Eisaku Sato, July 16, 1971; CIEP, 1971, Ernest Shrenzel to R. Galvin, June 29, 1971; Flanigan Papers, Box 11, Kissinger to President, May 9, 1970; McCracken Papers, Box 11, "Japanese Import Restrictions," August 27, 1971, Basic Developments in U.S.–Japan Trade Relationships, 1966–1971," November 1, 1971, "Japanese Exports to the U.S." August, 1971; DD (Ashworth), No. 41, "CIA, Intelligence Memorandum, "Japan: The Effectiveness of Informal Import and Investment Controls," May 1969; Destler, *Making Foreign Economic Policy*, pp. 1–2.

22. Indeed, the President told aide John Ehrlichman that potential economic adviser Pete Peterson could not be appointed to an administration job if his views fit that category. NP, Ehrlichman Papers, Box 3, Notes of a meeting with the President, April 2, 1970; Notes of a Meeting with the President and George Shultz, November 17, 1970; Notes of a Meeting with the President, January 11, 1971.

23. LBJL, NSFCo Box 253, Memorandum for the President concerning visit of Prime Minister Sato, January 11–14, 1965.

24. On the role of MITI, see Chalmers Johnson, *MITI and the Japanese Miracle: The Growth of Industrial Policy* (Stanford, 1982).

25. American negotiators were also hampered by their lack of command of Japanese; when the embassy in Tokyo sought to explicate Japan's trade policy it found that its work suffered immensely because few texts were available in English. See DD (Ashworth), No. 660I, Tokyo to SD, March 1, 1971.

26. Horsley and Buckley, *Nippon—New Superpower*, pp. 103–4.

27. Nixon, *RN*, p. 555.

28. NP, Flanigan Papers, Box 11, Peterson to the President, August 6, 1971, Flanigan to the President, August 7, 1971; Paul Volcker and Toyoo Gyohten, *Changing Fortunes: The World's Money and the Threat to American Leadership* (New York, 1992), p. 93.

29. NP, POF Box 34, News Summary, October 15, 1971; McCracken Papers, Box 11, Summary of Meeting of Joint Executive Committees of Japan–U.S. Economic Council, August 21, 1971; Box 12, Paul Wonnacott to McCracken, November 2, 1971; CIEP, 1971–74, Harold B. Scott report dated December 14, 1971 on trade negotiations with the Japanese delegation, December 11–12, 1971.

30. On Japanese political economy after 1971, see Taskashi Inoguchi and Daniel

I. Okimoto, *The Political Economy of Japan: Volume 2, The Changing International Context* (Stanford, 1988); Johnson, *MITI and the Japanese Miracle*; Edward J. Lincoln, *Japan: Facing Economic Maturity* (Washington, 1988); Karel van Wolferen, *The Enigma of Japanese Power* (New York, 1989); Kozo Yamamura and Yasukichi Yasuba, *The Political Economy of Japan: Volume 1, The Domestic Transformation* (Stanford, 1987).

31. FRBNY, C261-Japan, P. Kuwayama to Mr. Hayes, September 21, 1972, P. Kuwayama to Mrs. Ehrlich, September 29, 1972, and October 10, 1972.
32. David Halberstram, *The Reckoning* (New York, 1986), p. 505.
33. DD (Ashworth), No. 242C, CIA Directorate of Intelligence, "The Japanese Electronic Industry: Out of Adolescence," February 1972.
34. DD (Ashworth), No. 16G, CIA Intelligence Memorandum, "The Nature of Japanese Export Controls: Some Implications for the United States," January 1972.
35. NP, Mandatory Review Declassification, NLN, 92-39/28, August 4, 1995, CIA, Economic Intelligence Weekly, November 28, 1973; NLN 92-39/31, August 5, 1995, CIA, "International Oil Developments," December 14, 1973; John G. Clark, *The Political Economy of World Energy: A Twentieth Century Perspective* (London, 1990), p. 204.
36. Ian Skeet, *OPEC: Twenty-Five Years of Prices and Politics* (Cambridge, 1988, 1991), p. 106.
37. NP, MRD, NLN 92-39/33, August 5, 1995, CIA, "International Oil Developments," p. 9; NLN 92-39/39, August 7, 1995, CIA, "International Oil Developments," January 11, 1974, pp. 4–5.
38. Clark, *The Political Economy of World Energy*, pp. 262–63.
39. FRBNY, C261-Japan, D. Christelow to A.R. Holmes, April 16, 1975; Tadayuki Koizuma to FRBNY, September 20, 1976; Robert Z. Aliber to Volcker, January 14, 1977. Also see U.S. Congress, "New Realities and New Directions in United States Foreign Policy" (1972, H382-4), A Report by the Subcommittee on Foreign Economic Policy of the Committee on Foreign Affairs, U.S. House of Representatives, February 28, 1972 (Washington, 1972), pp. 9–13; U.S. Congress, "United States/Japanese Trade Relations and the Status of Multilateral Trade Negotiations," (1978, S361-20) Hearing Before the Subcommittee on International Trade of the Committee on Finance, United States Senate, Ninety-Fifth Congress, Second Session (Washington, 1978); U.S. Congress, Session on an Overview of the State of the United States/Japan Bilateral Relationship," (1978, S382-30) Hearing Before the Subcommittee on East Asian and Pacific Affairs of the Committee on Foreign Relations, United States Senate, Ninety-Fifth Congress, Second Session, April 27, 1978 (Washington, 1978).
40. NP, POF Box 34, News Summary October 14, 1971; Box 86, Memorandum concerning the President's meeting with the Commission on International Trade and Investment Policy, September 13, 1971.
41. NP, WHCF-BE, Presidential Message to Congress, Feb. 4, 1974.
42. Destler, *Making Foreign Economic Policy*, pp. 148–90.
43. *New York Times*, December 11, 1980; Halberstram, *The Reckoning*, p. 613.

44. GFL, Burns Papers, Box B64, E.M. Truman, "Notes on What Might Be Done about the U.S. Trade Deficit," September 23, 1977; CEA Papers, Box 161, "Strategy for Multilateral Trade Negotiations," April 1975; U.S. Congress, "Export Promotion, Export Disincentives, and U.S. Competitiveness: Reports by the President Pursuant to Section 1110(a) and (b) of the Trade Agreement Act of 1979," (1980, S242-12) printed for use of the Committee on Banking, Housing and Urban Affairs, United States Senate, September 1980 (Washington, 1980); Destler, *Making Foreign Economic Policy*, pp. 200–206.

45. Destler, *Making Foreign Economic Policy*, pp. 196–200.

46. *Wall Street Journal*, August 2, 1977.

47. See U.S. Congress, "U.S.–Japanese Trade Relations," (1980, J841-12), Hearings Before the Joint Economics Committee, Ninety-Sixth Congress, First Session, October 10, 1979 (Washington, 1979); U.S. Congress, "Export Trading Companies and Trade Associations," (1980, S241-70), Hearings Before the Subcommittee on International Finance of the Committee on Banking, Housing and Urban Affairs, United States Senate, Ninety-Sixth Congress, First Session on S. 864, S. 1499, S. 1663, and S. 1744, September 17 and 18, 1979 (Washington, 1979); U.S. Congress, "Trade and Technology in the Electronics Industry," (1980, S241-25), Hearings Before the Subcommittee on International Finance of the Committee on Banking, Housing and Urban Affairs, United States Senate, Ninety-Sixth Congress, Second Session, Part II, January 15, 1980 (Washington, 1980); U.S. Congress, "U.S. Trade," (1981, H781-18.1), Hearings before the Subcommittee on Trade of the Committee on Ways and Means, House of Representatives, Ninety-Sixth Congress, Second Session, Serial 96-119, June 26 and July 21, 1980 (Washington, 1980).

48. Concerning Japanese tariff and nontariff barriers to trade, see "Tax Incentives for Exports," (1979), S361-48), Hearing Before the Committee on Taxation and Debt Management Generally of the Committee on Finance, United States Senate, Ninety-Sixth Congress, First Session on S. 231, S 700, S. 935, S. 1003, S. 1065, June 18, 1979 (Washington, 1979), pp. 269–300; "United States–Japan Trade Report," (1980), (H782-48), Subcommittee on Trade of the Committee on Ways and Means, U.S. House of Representatives, September 5, 1980 (Washington, 1980).

49. NP, CIEP 1971, Summary of Discussion, Government-Business Debriefing Session, Eighth Japan–U.S. Businessmen's Conference, June 18, 1971; McCracken Papers, Box 16, "Japan's Restrictions on Foreign Direct Investment in Japan" (ca. autumn 1971); GFL, Burns Papers, Box B66, IMF-C20 Discussions, July 1973, "A Report on Japan's International Monetary and Trade Strategy," Box B75, Truman to Burns, "Proposals for Increasing Japanese Imports," October 11, 1977; CEA Papers, Box 40, Puerto Rico Summit, June 1976—Briefing Book, "Talking Points on Japan"; DD (Ashworth), No. 231C, "Japan: Informal Barriers to Foreign Competition," September 8, 1977; DD (Ashworth), No. 242B, CIA Intelligence Memorandum, "Japan's Eight Point Economic Program: Progress and Prospects," September 1971.

50. *Wall Street Journal*, November 6, 1984.

51. *Economist*, January 5, 1985; Clyde V. Prestowitz Jr., *Trading Places: How We Allowed Japan to Take the Lead* (New York, 1988), pp. 26–70.

52. Harold James, *International Monetary Cooperation Since Bretton Woods* (Washington, 1996), p. 435.

53. *Economist*, January 16, 1982.

54. James, *International Monetary Cooperation Since Bretton Woods*, pp. 433–66; Volcker and Gyohten, *Changing Fortunes*, pp. 229–30, 245, 260.

55. U.S. Library of Congress, Congressional Research Service, "Foreign Direct Investment in the United States," April 29, 1991, CRS, Order Code IB 87226 by James K. Jackson, (Washington, 1991), p. 2; U.S. Library of Congress, Congressional Research Service, "Japanese Investment in the United States," CRS Report 90-13E by James K. Jackson, Washington, 1990). For an alternative view lamenting the effect of the decline in Japanese investment on the real estate, see the *Journal of Commerce*, January 3, 1991; *Wall Street Journal*, January 3, 1991; *Economist*, December 8, 1990.

56. Books written on this subject include Robert L. Kearns, *Zaibatsu America: How Japanese Firms Are Colonizing Vital U.S. Industries* (New York, 1992); Martin Tolchin and Susan Tolchin, *Buying into America: How Foreign Money Is Changing the Face of Our Nation* (New York, 1988) and *Selling Our Security: The Erosion of America's Assets* (New York, 1992).

57. See Dick K. Nanto, "United States–Japanese Trade Relations," (1982, J842-9) in U.S. International Economic Policy in the 1980s: Selected Essays Prepared for the Use of the Joint Economic Committee, Congress of the United States, February 11, 1982 (Washington, 1982), pp. 92–112.

58. See, e.g., Clyde V. Prestowitz, *Trading Places*, pp. 272–302.

59. Destler, *Making Foreign Economic Policy*, pp. 36–49.

60. DD (Ashworth), No. 2914, Economic Summit, Fourth Session, Monday, November 17, 1975.

61. *Economist*, January 16, 1982; Gary B. Born and David Westin, *International Civil Litigation in United States Courts, Commentary and Materials* (Devanter, the Netherlands, 1988), p. 482.

62. U.S. Congress, "Free Trade—Myth or Reality: The Auto Industry, A Case Study," (S381-28) Hearing Before the Subcommittee on International Economic Policy of the Committee on Foreign Relations, United States Senate, Ninety-Eighth Congress, Second Session, June 27, 1984 (Washington, 1984); U.S. Congress, "Competitiveness of the U.S. Automobile Industry," (H241-27), Hearing of the Subcommittee on Economic Stabilization of the Committee on Banking, Finance and Urban Affairs, House of Representatives, Ninety-Ninth Congress, First Session, February 19, 1985, Serial No. 99-2 (Washington, 1985); U.S. Congress, "United States–Japanese Trade in Auto Parts (1990, J841-14). Hearing Before the Subcommittee on Trade, Productivity, Economic Growth of the Joint Economic Committee, Congress, Second Session, 24 April 1986 (Washington, 1987); Doron P. Levin, *Behind the Wheel at Chrysler: The Iacocca Legacy* (New York, 1995).

63. On the market share cap on Japanese automobile sales, see *Washington Post*, March 26, 1991; on Japanese voluntary quotas, see *Journal of Commerce*, January 14, 1991.

64. See Library of Congress, Congressional Research Service, "Foreign Direct Investment: The Economics of National Security Issues," Order Code IB

90143 by James K. Jackson, Washington, 1991, p. 1; U.S. Congress, "Threat of Certain Imports to National Security," (1987, S361-15-3), Hearing Before the Committee on Finance, United States Senate, Ninety-Ninth Congress, Second Session on S. 1871, August 13, 1986 (Washington, 1987). Concerning U.S.–Japanese competition in high-technology manufactures see, "International Competition in Advanced Industrial Sectors: Trade and Development in the Semiconductor Industry," (1982, J842-7), A Study Prepared for the Use of the Joint Economic Committee of the United States, February 18, 1982 (Washington, 1982). For efforts to make the United States more competitive in international markets see, *New York Times*, January 21, 1991.

65. Lawrence Freedman and Efraim Karsh, *The Gulf Conflict 1990–1991: Diplomacy and War in the New World Order* (Princeton, 1993), pp. 120–25, 187, 215–16, 358–61.

66. Shintaro Ishihara, *The Japan That Can Say NO: Why Japan Will Be First Among Equals* (New York, 1989).

67. This list included Clyde Prestowitz's account of Reagan-era trade policies, *Trading Places: How We Are Giving Our Future to Japan and How to Reclaim It*; Karel van Wolferen's history of the development of Japanese postwar society, *The Enigma of Japanese Power*; and Pat Choate's *Agents of Influence* (New York, 1990), which focused on Japanese lobbying in the United States. James Fallows also made Crichton's reading list. Both in the *Atlantic* and in his book *More Like Us*, Fallows provided a mirror image of Ishihara, stressing the theme that Japanese and American cultures were irreconcilably different. See James Fallows, *More Like Us: Putting America's Native Strengths and Traditional Values to Work to Overcome the Asian Challenge* (Boston, 1989). Richard J. Elkus Jr. presented the argument that Japanese competition posed a grave threat to the United States in "The Strategy of Leverage," *International Economy* (August-September 1990): 78.

68. Murray Sale, "Bowing to the Inevitable," *Times Literary Supplement*, April 28–May 4, 1989, p. 445.

69. Horsley and Buckley, *Nippon—New Superpower*, p. 240.

70. Library of Congress, Congressional Research Service, "Japanese–U.S. Trade Relations," Order Code IB87158 by William Cooper, June 6, 1991 (Washington, 1991), p. 6; *Business America*, April 9, 1990; *Wall Street Journal*, December 10, 1990; *Chicago Tribune*, January 20, 1991.

71. *New York Times*, February 2, 1996.

72. LBJL, NSF Co, Box 250, Memorandum of Conversation concerning visit of Prime Minister Sato and other topics, December 23, 1964.

73. Zeiler, *American Trade and Power in the 1960s*, p. 22.

Chapter 15. Conclusion

1. For an analysis of the relationship between United States and the Soviet Union during the Cold War using newly declassified documents, see John Lewis Gaddis, *We Now Know: Rethinking Cold War History* (forthcoming).

2. George Kennan, "Long Telegram," 1946, quoted in Thomas G. Paterson, ed., *Major Problems in American Foreign Policy—Volume II: Since 1914,* 3d ed. (Lexington, 1989), p. 285.
3. See Paul M. Kennedy, *Preparing for the Twenty-First Century* (New York, 1993).
4. See, e.g., Benjamin M. Friedman, *Day of Reckoning: The Consequences of American Economic Policy Under Reagan and After* (New York, 1988); Peter G. Peterson, *Facing Up: How to Rescue the Economy From Crushing Debt and Restore the American Dream* (New York, 1993); Lester Thurow, *Head to Head: The Coming Economic Battle Among Japan, Europe, and America* (New York, 1992).

Appendix

1. Jerome Levinson and Juan de Onís, *The Alliance That Lost Its Way* (New York, 1970), Appendix B.
2. JFKL, POF, Box 89, Charter of Punta del Este, August 1961; Levinson and de Onís, *The Alliance That Lost Its Way,* pp. 68, 69, 108.
3. See, e.g., Gregorio Selser, *Alianza para el Progreso: La Mal Nascida* (Buenos Aires, 1964), pp. 56–57.

Index